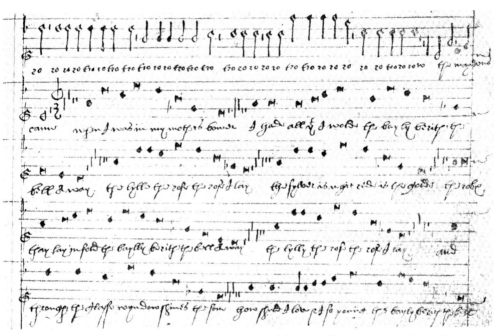

A photograph of MS Harley 7578, first side of folio 110, reproduced by kind permission of the Director of The British Museum. See Chapter 6.

To:
Beryl,
Michael, Rachel, Ruth, William
and the Grandtribe – with thanks

PREFACE

In 1970 Peter de Ridder, Director of the famous Dutch linguistics publishing house, Mouton, visited my wife, Beryl, and me at our home in Kent. I had suggested to him that he might consider the possibility of establishing a new international *Journal of Literary Semantics*, with me as the first editor. He had already published a short monograph of mine, *The Semantics of Literature,* and accepted a second longer one, *Theoretical Semics*. We pursued our negotiations surrounded by our four children, then aged 4, 6, 8 and 10. This domestic scene provided an arresting example of **reciprocal perspective**, one of the prime theoretical devices employed in this book. The self-important preoccupations of the adult world are rudely shattered by the mysterious thought processes of a child. At one point in our discourse, there was a pregnant hush as the youngest, William, made it clear *he*, four years old, wished to make a pronouncement. 'I *hope...*' he began aloud and with studied intent, '...that Mr. de Ridder' – we all waited in silence for verb and closure – '...has brought his pyjamas.' Indeed he had. And he had also brought an agreement which shaped my life.

Peter de Ridder left the next day, happy with my assurance that, as editor of *Journal of Literary Semantics*, I had little to offer but a very strong sense of direction; yet he, nevertheless, had entrusted me with the task of assembling material for the first issue. This duly appeared in 1972. I edited the journal for thirty years, handing over gratefully in 2002 to the safe and steady judgment of Professor Michael Toolan of the English Department at the University of Birmingham. He has established an Editorial Board comprising a dozen distinguished scholars from across the globe and has confidently steered *JLS* into its 38th volume and beyond.

Meanwhile there was held in the summer of 1992 the Inaugural Conference of the International Association of Literary Semantics (IALS) at the University of Kent at Canterbury, presided over by Professor Günther Kress. Since then, conferences have been convened at the Universities of Freiburg in Germany (1997), Birmingham (2002), the Jagiellonian University of Krakow (2006) and the fifth is scheduled for July, 2010 at the University of Genoa. Professor

Monika Fludernik became the first President of IALS in 1997 and with energetic leadership led the Association for ten years before handing over the Presidency during the Krakow Conference to Michael Toolan. Such has been the inception and development of literary semantics.

Against this academic background, the present book was written step by step. Part I, Chapters 1 to 3, based on *The Semantics of Literature*, presents the trichotomy theory of knowledge. It is, so far as I am aware, a completely original analysis. The net is cast wide to include everything that could ever be considered to be knowledge. Instead of a knowledge/belief bipartite scheme the analysis begins with a threefold modal *totality*. Diagrams, some newly designed, will help to illustrate just how the trichotomy works. The theories of affidence and value are also introduced at this stage and it will become clear to the reader by the third chapter that the chosen approach to literary semantics has its foundation in philosophy. What is here being put forward is an epistemology which seamlessly coalesces with both ethics and aesthetics.

Having limned out the philosophical structures implicit in the trichotomy theory, the argument, in Part II, Chapters 4 to 11, moves on to a theory of science. Just as, at the philosophical level, a modal analysis of knowledge was put forward, so, using the device of reciprocal perspective, science itself, and specifically psychology and linguistics, is described modally, in terms of the analeptic-kinetic theory. Analepsis may be seen as the received structures of scientific theory; kinesis is the raw 'reality' of worldliness, as it impinges upon the human brain. Scientific health is enjoyed in the balance of the two. Chapters 4 to 6 set out to judge a number of examples of literary criticism – and one of linguistic analysis – against the analeptic-kinetic criterion. The modal focus elucidates what I consider to be the flaws in each. But, contrariwise, in Chapters 7 and 8, I have tried to show that it is possible for this text to bend back modally *upon itself*, by supplying, at the level of theoretical semics, an extravagant model of the working of the brain, such as took place – if we are to believe him – just before Coleridge was harshly interrupted by the visitor from Porlock. Speculation, *carefully labelled as such by the use of the term 'theoretical semics'*, is the begetter of possible scientific progress. Chapter 9 begins with a robust defence of technical terms and goes on to define further the concept of modality. Chapter 10 provides a dual definition of style which, at one modal level, takes in what style has always been considered to be and, at another, presents style as a phenomenon which can be empirically investigated. Chapter 11, a close examination of Segers' seminal book *The Evaluation of Literary Texts*, insists that there is a qualitative distinction between *style* and *(intrinsic) value*.

Part III is concerned with theory and practice. Chapter 12 re-formulates

Rescher's definition of propositional modality to produce a definition of textual modality, which in turn in Chapter 13 is combined with the Ogden-Richards' notion of external and psychological contexts to produce a new version of frame theory. This leads to a theory of fictionality and an analysis of Geoffrey Chaucer's *Miller's Tale* in the light of simultaneous and sequential frame theory. The complexity of modality in the *Miller's Tale* (and the *Merchant's Tale*, whose fictional strata are depicted in Appendix Three,) challenges the adequacy of the traditional categories of modal auxiliary verbs. Chapter 14 is the shortest in length, but in my view the most important of all in that it ties together all the loose ends of the preceding theories. The Document, reprinted in Chapter 15, originally offered for critical comment to readers of *Journal of Literary Semantics*, encapsulates what I see as the main features of literary semantics. I discuss the questions raised by two scholars who kindly responded. A final mention should be made of Appendix Four, which briefly applies theoretical semics to the problems inherent in discourse about education: from the educationalist's standpoint, the discussion takes place within a pentadic, not a triadic, relationship.

Literary Semantics is the accumulated result of this forty years' journey. In 1966, I described my earliest published effort as 'little more than a sketch'. And, in retracing my steps through these Chapters, I have seen them as fifteen carefully interlocking sketches, covering, though not in close detail, the entire expanse of the study and enjoyment of literature. It is an unusual book, but a book which I believe to be both tidy and sane. I hope others wiser than I will be incited to confront, or even inspired to expand, the views which I have expressed. The accompanying Glossary has been compiled to assist the reader.

In the past, I have acknowledged the debt I had to various scholars, friends and institutions. This is my opportunity to make special tribute to those to whom I am particularly grateful. Merton College, Oxford and Corpus Christi College, Cambridge each granted me a sabbatical term; and at the Institute of Languages and Linguistics within the University of Kent at Canterbury, for a long time the Headquarters of *Journal of Literary Semantics*, I spent a blissful year just reading and discussing linguistics in the company of Rob Veltman, Tony Bex, Francis Cornish and John Partridge. Without their help this book would still remain unfinished.

My tutor at Oxford, Christopher Tolkien, by a chance remark set off the questionings that led to this book. But, as will be manifest, the most power-ful determining force was I. A. Richards. I became acquainted with him first through his writings which I read with alternating joy and frustration. How could the man who was, with Charles Ogden, brilliantly responsible for *The Meaning of Meaning*, possibly, in his later writings, sanction literary criticism as the foundation for university courses in English? When he returned from the

United States to Magdalene College, Cambridge, in 1974, I came to know him personally and actually edited a volume of his essays, *Poetries: Their Media and Ends*. I remember his powerful intellect and generous spirit. The other people who figure large in my roll of thanks are friends. Günther Kress of the Institute of Education in London and Mike Thickett, former Head of English at the Norton Knatchbull School in Ashford spent time and effort in reading various drafts of the work and making valuable criticisms. Graham Thomas, of the French Department at the Norton Knatchbull School, must be one of the most accurate readers in the country. With effortless speed he proofread all thirty volumes of *Journal of Literary Semantics* and virtually my entire academic output with breathtaking perception. I am convinced that no needle in any haystack could ever escape him. This would be distinction enough, yet I cannot help adding that not only is he a consummate Jazz Practitioner but also that he has represented Great Britain at athletics.

Finally, I thank my lovely wife Beryl, who, after a 16-month illness, died in 2005 – and to whom I was married for 46 years. I thank my four children, Michael, Rachel, Ruth and William; and my Grandtribe, too many to name, for they number twelve.

Trevor Eaton
Hythe, Kent

TYPOGRAPHICAL NOTE

In linguistic works, it is a common practice to place technical terms in bold type when they are first introduced. In this volume, nearly 200 such usages are employed, some coinages like **affidence** and **dynaxial**; some, such as **universe of discourse** and **centre**, already widely occurring in philosophical and mathematical works – but here used in a different sense. An *apologia* for their use is made at the beginning of Chapter 9.

Here, bold type draws the attention to, or reminds the reader of, the inclusion of the term in the Glossary. It is also employed to emphasize some central principles of literary semantics. The practice of typographic emboldening is not as consistent as the author would have wished, but its purpose has been to assist the reader. In this book the ideas have driven the technical terms and not the jargon the ideas.

Cross references are placed in square brackets, marked LS and followed by page numbers, thus [LS: 56-8].

ACKNOWLEDGEMENT

The author is grateful to Mouton de Gruyter Publishers of Berlin for their friendly support over many years and their transference to him of entire copyright. He also thanks Taylor and Francis Group (www.informaworld.com) for permission to publish the re-shaped version of Appendix Four, which originally appeared in *Educational Studies*.

I thank the Melrose Books team – specifically Kathy Wagner-Kimbrough, Matt Stephens and Marion Cundall – for their very friendly co-operation and their tenacity in putting this book together.

by which mediators are evoked, and the distance from the origin determined by the intensity of the evocation.

MISTRESS

	Extremely	Quite	Slightly	Neither/Nor	Slightly	Quite	Extremely	
Happy		X		Neither Happy Nor Sad				Sad
Hard				Neither Hard Nor Soft		X		Soft
Pleasant	X			Neither Pleasant Nor Unpleasant				Unpleasant

So, the subject is asked to locate the concept MISTRESS, say, in relation to the bipolar adjectives happy/sad, hard/soft, pleasant/unpleasant, by crossing one of seven boxes in each case. A rough illustration of their measurement would be to imagine these choices as located within a large cube, whose centre represents Neither/Nor (neutrality) and whose outermost divisions represent Extremely (highest intensity of evocation). The authors derive their notion of a semantic space from this basically simple notion. The subject's linear choices above are mapped into the 'cubic' semantic space and a profile, resembling the molecular models used in chemistry, can be assembled. The authors actually construct such fascinating, three-dimensional profiles and it is possible to view solid clusters of 'concepts' arranged in collocations for an individual subject. If only psychology were so simple. Of course the authors realise that their measurement of meaning is 'crude and very provisional' (1957:329), but amply demonstrate its uses in personality research.

The device cannot be worked backwards, and whole clusters of concepts may occupy the same region of the semantic space. It might be argued that the discovery of new factors will make it possible to identify a concept precisely, from its position in space. The authors, however, incline to the view that their measurement is connotational, and that the denotation of a concept is determined by context: 'Although lexical items a, b, c and d may be associated by the same representational process, x, indiscriminately, context 1 plus x selects a, 2 plus x selects b and so forth'. [9]

The Principle of Congruity[10] expounded in the same book is a step in the direction of the semantics of literature. Where two concepts located in different regions of the semantic space are presented simultaneously the 'mediating reaction of each shifts towards congruence with that characteristic of the other, the magnitude of the shift being inversely proportional to the intensities of the interacting reactions'. To explain what they mean by this, we may consider metaphors or, for instance, similes:

1.   My mistress's lips are like cherries.
2.   My mistress's lips are like freshly-cut dog's meat.

The choice of comparison affects the rhetorical impact of, and attitude towards, the juxtaposed entities: LIPS v CHERRIES; LIPS v FRESHLY-CUT DOG'S MEAT, the profiles for which would be differentiated, one presumes, on any scale semantically related to pleasant/unpleasant. The authors seem here to be initiating a study of the semantics of more complex linguistic units and textually-sensitive judgments.

The Semantic Differential, its possible application in therapeutic psychology and other fields, is impressive. The work of these authors is not without its philosophical importance: for example, one of their aims is to ascertain the psychological components of judgment itself. The difficulty seems to be, as always, that they have found no way into the black box. Language is the behaviour which is observed but it is only a part of the psychic activities into which enquiry is made. The assumption must be made that the linguistic behaviour is in some way a reflection of the total semantic behaviour. Thus the concept which is given to the subject is usually a linguistic one, and the subject's judgment is expressed in language. The relation between linguistic and non-linguistic behaviour is obscure, so that although the concept of a multi-dimensional semantic space has demonstrated its usefulness there is still no answer as to how it is representative of the state of affairs within the mind itself. Even where a greater range of behaviour than the linguistic is observed there is always the possibility that other behaviour remains unobserved. Nowhere can the impasse be seen more clearly than in the attempt by the authors to establish the important factors in human judgment. Any selection of possible factors with which research must commence, is itself bound in some measure to be influenced by the very factors that are the object of investigation.

Max Black, *Language and Philosophy*,[11] considers the theory of interpretation put forward by Ogden and Richards', *The Meaning of Meaning*, to be behaviouristic. This opinion would seem at variance with the views expressed by Osgood, Suci and Tannenbaum, for Ogden and Richards' theory of interpretation is hardly to be held separate from their exposition of meaning. Ogden and Richards constantly refer to thoughts, and the **Basic Triangle** [LS:10] itself seems to be the product of a mentalistic conception of meaning. However, if Ogden and Richards are not as behaviouristic as the later authors would like, the scientific investigations at Illinois are, in a degree, the outcome of the publication of *The Meaning of Meaning*. Indeed, it is a tribute to Ogden and Richards that at a conference on semantics held at Nice in 1951 there was almost unanimous agreement upon a definition of meaning,[12] a state of affairs which would have seemed impossible before the First World War.

There is not innate in us any immutable certainty as to the purpose of exist-ence. It does not follow that because no such awareness is in us that there is no ultimate knowledge (such as, to use the terms of religion, the Omniscience of God might be considered). Since we are obliged to admit as a result of experience that there are probably things beyond the grasp of our minds,[44] and since many still believe in an ultimate knowledge, it is intellectually prudent that some place be given to it in the classification. This we shall call **knowledge one**. If knowledge one does not exist we have included in the classification a symbol without a refer-ent – to use the terminology of Ogden-Richards. The use of the symbol does not imply existence of the referent, for, by definition, knowledge one is beyond our awareness. If knowledge one exists most of us would consider it of the greatest importance and the other knowledges defined below would be thought to have either no importance or importance only in so far as they are related to or are identical with knowledge one.

If we take a naturalistic view of the universe,[45] that is, if we believe that nothing exists outside 'nature', then the possibility of occurrences having a supernatural significance is ruled out. If this universe is all that there is, and if the attempts of science to probe it are successful, or in a state of becoming successful, then we might say that science is in the process of discovering knowledge one.

An alternative view might be that there are other universes which exist outside this universe, quite independent, not connected by space and time with us, and without any possibility of contact with this system. Such systems would be irrel-evant in any theory of knowledge.

A supernaturalistic view that there are other systems not connected in spatio-temporal relation with this universe, which, nevertheless, do or might influence events in this universe has to be reckoned with. An event in this universe might then have a dual significance, natural and supernatural, or even, further, its natural significance might, in the light of the supernatural significance, turn out to be illusory. Knowledge one would in this case be the supernatural significance and whatever of the natural significance proved not to be illusory. One of the difficul-ties of the human situation is that man seems to have some knowledge yet has not access to knowledge which he knows to be unalterable. There is always a possibility that what he learns will radically alter what he believed he knew. This problem has already been briefly discussed [LS:9–10]. If we have found in some cases that we did not know what we thought we knew, how can we be certain that our present knowledge is not illusory in the light of the supernatural or of what may later be discovered about the natural?

If we can never know that what we believe we know is knowledge one what then is the reason for including this category of knowledge in our theory? Again, why include in a theory of knowledge something which might never be known? The **trichotomy of knowledge** was devised to render discourse easier. Man has no certain knowledge of knowledge one, but it is not infrequent that claims are made that amount to claims to knowledge one. The Logical Positivists were concerned to defend their **principle of verifiability** which was itself not subject to verification.[46] Value judgments cannot be arrived at solely through observation and logic, and yet these are the very judgments which men tend to make with greatest assurance. The language we inherit has a tone of dogmatism which it is hard to avoid in making statements of any sort, and the frequent resort to 'perhaps', 'possibly', 'might' and 'almost' is sometimes regarded as a stylistic weakness.

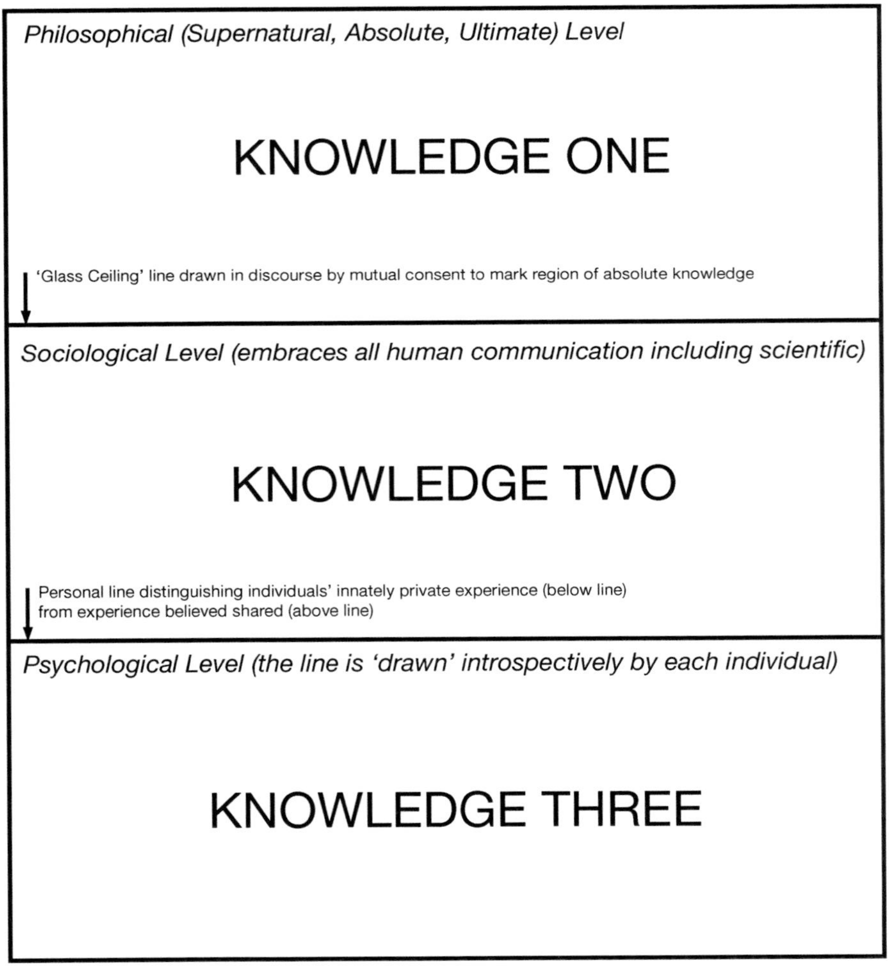

Philosophical (Supernatural, Absolute, Ultimate) Level

KNOWLEDGE ONE

'Glass Ceiling' line drawn in discourse by mutual consent to mark region of absolute knowledge

Sociological Level (embraces all human communication including scientific)

KNOWLEDGE TWO

Personal line distinguishing individuals' innately private experience (below line)
from experience believed shared (above line)

Psychological Level (the line is 'drawn' introspectively by each individual)

KNOWLEDGE THREE

The above diagram indicates how the universality of human knowledge/ experience can be encompassed by a set of propositions (referents, entities or whatever) divided by two lines into three subsets.

Figure 2. The Trichotomy of Knowledge

Knowledge one accommodates man's natural dogmatism; knowledge one seems to be what he is looking for, and, in many cases, it is what he appears to claim that he has found. The difficulties arise when conflicting claims to knowledge one are made. If, for the purposes of discussion, the knowledge one protagonists will agree to call the knowledge about which they are not agreed knowledge three (as defined below), then the barrier to discourse is removed.

Knowledge two is any psychic experience which a person has and is satisfied is similar in all or at least certain respects to the psychic experience, where *psychic* is defined as 'cognitive in the broadest sense', of any other person. **Knowledge three** is a psychic experience which a person has and is not satisfied is similar in all or at least certain respects to the psychic experience of any other person. All psychic experiences, both within knowledge two and knowledge three, will be designated by the Ogden-Richards' term 'reference'.

One of the difficulties here is that there are many factors at work in our assessment of similarity. If I assert that I can see Mephistopheles, I can expect that those who are present when I make my assertion will, according to their varying beliefs, have varying references. One hearer may be convinced that he can also see Mephistopheles; another may, however, though he understands what I mean by Mephistopheles, believe that I am imagining Mephistopheles, and may claim that this is a reference with no immediate referent; it might be thought by someone else that I am lying and have not seen Mephistopheles at all; or that Mephistopheles is present but visible only to me; another may believe that there is such a person as Mephistopheles but that what is present now is not Mephistopheles, and so forth. Any satisfactory theory of knowledge must be capable of organizing all these degrees of difference within similarity. We return to the realisation that what we call knowledge is a relation between an event, or 'non-event', in the external world and a resulting series of psychic experiences, the precise nature of these experiences being still obscure.

Philosophy and psychology have here a reciprocal relation. Philosophy gives present 'knowledge' an organization and suggests what direction psychology should take. Psychology undertakes research into the psychic experiences constituting a part of knowledge and is able to bring to philosophy fresh material for organization. If the important factors in human judgment are still undetermined [LS:6], then the best we can hope for is a theory designed to accommodate the discoveries of psychology when and if they come.

Knowledge two and knowledge three may in some cases be a part of knowledge one but it seems to be man's lot never to know exactly where the correspondence lies.

It may be objected that this view does not solve the epistemological problem; that like Ullmann we are limiting ourselves to the left side of the Basic Triangle. If the referential world has a place in the theory it can only be within knowledge one, and we can never be certain that we know knowledge one [LS:11–12]. But on the other hand whatever exists in the referential world that is of importance in the theory of knowledge will be reflected in knowledge two or knowledge three. Who can assert that such and such an occurrence should be included in the theory of knowledge without, *ipso facto*, admitting that it has found a place, at least in knowledge three?

Nor are we lapsing into subjectivism.[47] We take as our starting point the combined and compared experience of a given **universe of discourse** (any discrete system of communication, but see Glossary). We assume that the observations of a group are more likely to be sound than the observations of one man. If the concept of a semantic space is found in time to have any established stable correspondence with the state of affairs in the mind of an individual, then the **affidence tests** suggested [LS:16] may be made more complex, and it will be possible to speak, in terms of averages, of the semantic space of a given universe of discourse. A crude version of this has of course long been practised in opinion polling. Our feeling of objectivity springs in some measure from the fact that we expect a reference to an object to be understood.[48] It might be argued that brainwashing technique is the removal of an individual from his accustomed universe of discourse into another where he is relentlessly confronted with a different standard of **affidence**, a concept which I shall explore. The 'objectivity' of the Middle Ages is vastly different from ours in this century.[49] It is true that knowledge two and knowledge three omit the right side of the Basic Triangle, but what we are doing is to take a large number of left hand sides, comparing them, eliminating disagreement, and building up a conception of the right hand through this, through the medium of **reciprocal perspective**. The traditional approach is to disregard other triangles altogether and to put forward an 'objective' theory which is really a distorted projection of the Basic Triangle of one person. The modal structures in this book − philosophical, linguistic, psychological and sociological − are designed to eliminate such distortion.

The trichotomy theory can be applied to other vexed questions, for instance: What is truth? **Truth one**, we may say, is identical with knowledge one. **Truth three** is what any individual believes to be true. **Truth two** is affidence [LS:15–21].

CHAPTER 2

THE THEORY OF AFFIDENCE

Knowledge and Communication

It follows from what has been said that discussion takes place at the level of knowledge two. As soon as discussion on the basis of knowledge three becomes possible, the level of knowledge two is reached. Discussion on the basis of knowledge one is similarly ruled out. It might be worth remarking at this point that most reasoning in the **highest universes of discourse**[1] seems to proceed on the assumption that knowledge two is, or is related to, knowledge one. Also, it frequently happens that the thoughts/**references** or parts of references to which we personally attach greatest importance belong, at least in the first instance, to knowledge three.

The range of **knowledge two** is wide. At all levels of discourse people attempt to communicate their references. The intentions which give rise to these attempts and the criteria whereby an attempt is considered successful vary according to the particular universe of discourse.

The Theory of Affidence

A reference which is successfully communicated in the highest universe of discourse may be said to have **affidence**. The affidence of a **reference** might be measured thus: the reference, suitably **symbolized**, is presented to one hundred subjects from the particular **universe of discourse** considered apposite to the reference symbolized. The subjects are selected in such a way as to ensure that all shades of group opinion are included.[2] The semantic differential is then operated on the lines established by Osgood, Suci and Tannenbaum, in *The*

Measurement of Meaning. In this case there is only one dimension, the symbolized reference being judged against the polar adjectives *true-untrue*. Where the reference as symbolized is judged true by all subjects it is said to be **affident**, or to have 100% **affidence** rating. This form of measurement is a suggested one. The actual method used would be changed to accord with the defined context and purposes of the research. The measurement of **affidence** would also keep pace with the latest findings in experimental psychology.

A symbolized reference which had a low affidence rating in the highest **universe of discourse** might find a high rating in a lower universe of discourse. This reference would be said to have **local affidence**. It goes almost without saying that all the participants in an **affidence test** should be satisfied they understand the symbols in which the reference is expressed and that they understand the reference as a whole. Where the participants are agreed that an isolated symbol is understood we may say that this symbol is **secure**. No statement can be affident unless the terms which constitute it are secure.

Most attempts at the communication of a reference contain a fluctuation between varying degrees of affidence or local affidence. The affidence of evidence is as a general rule, high, of interpretation, low. Affidence is open to investigation as described above; it is not a peculiar quality with which a reference is endowed but simply its measure of regard as 'discussion currency' in the highest universe of discourse. Any person communicating will usually have his own assessment of the affidence of any one reference he symbolizes. This we shall call his **affidence assessment**. It is desirable that a serious work directed at the highest universes of discourse should be well presented. A satisfactory presentation is one which makes clear at all points the writer's affidence assessment. Where no indication is given that affidence assessment has changed the reader may be misled [LS:38–40]. This entire book is written at the level of **theoretical semics** (see chapter 4 and glossary).

At this point it is well to consider the **trichotomy theory** in the light of the more familiar knowledge/belief analysis.

Let us suppose that on my way to work I see a car which is overturned. When I reach my place of work I tell my colleagues that I saw an overturned car. I have no reason to doubt that they will believe that what I say is true; they will believe that, had they been accompanying me, they would also have seen the car. But if I say that I actually saw a leprechaun driving the car and that it was through his negligent driving that the car turned over we have a different situation. Not only will most of my colleagues disbelieve me when I say I saw the leprechaun, but their belief in the car itself will be impaired. It is a species of Osgood's Principle of Congruity at work [LS:5]; the juxtaposition of the credible and the incredible decreases the authority of what would not normally be doubted.

In what sense would it be true to say that the leprechaun was knowledge? Suppose, even further, that I were not prepared to say that I *knew* I had seen a leprechaun but only *thought* I had seen one. If we were to insist upon the principle of verification then it would be impossible to verify that my reference had a referent and that that referent was a leprechaun. I agree with Armour[3] that knowledge is best used as a term inclusive of more than the outcome of scientific investigations. In the trichotomy theory the realm of knowledge is extended to include *all* thought and experience.

In any act of knowledge there are two possibilities: either the knower and the known are different or they are the same thing, as in Descartes' '*Cogito ergo sum*': **reciprocal perspective** observed in the coalescence of self with self. Thus, when I thought I saw a leprechaun, either there was some sort of external causation or it was a spontaneous psychic event without cause if indeed it be possible for any event to be without cause, or with causes which could not be directly attributed to a source outside my brain. If there were external causes, that is, an actual leprechaun – this theory at the highest philosophical level rules nothing out – or an **external context** which acted upon me in such a way that I formed my belief, then the leprechaun or the external context were what was known and my seeing the leprechaun or belief that I saw it were in epistemo-logical relation with them and according to the present theory would be called knowledge. If the belief, on the other hand, was a spontaneous psychic event the epistemological problem is still present. For when I remember the experi-ence of thinking that I saw the leprechaun, I may say I know that I thought I saw it. My thought then thus becomes an object of my knowledge now. Even though the thought arose spontaneously it nevertheless happened, and whatever happens should find some place in a theory of knowledge.

In the philosophical journals there appear frequent articles discussing the respective territories of knowledge and belief.[4] The point I am concerned to make here is that the traditional knowledge/belief dichotomy prejudges the state of things in the psyche. Woozley says that the traditional division of cogni-tion into two essentially different kinds, knowledge and belief, is false and rests upon a confusion.[5] But his definition of knowledge, 'Being sure and being right, on evidence which is conclusive',[6] helps to perpetuate the knowledge/belief dichotomy, and is not satisfactory because it rests upon factors which cannot be ascertained. If being right and having conclusive evidence are precondi-tions of knowledge we can never know that we know anything. Before we can know that we know *x* we must know that we are right and know that we have conclusive evidence; but being right and having conclusive evidence are preconditions of knowledge.

And A. J. Ayer's analysis enters the same regress, even introducing an ethical clause[7]: '... the necessary and sufficient conditions for knowing that something is the case are first that what one is said to know be true, secondly that one be sure of it, and thirdly, *that one should have the right to be sure*' (my italics). The italicized clause glaringly begs the question of how 'the right to be sure' could be corroborated, even in terms of his own stated conditions. How can we be sure that we have the right to be sure? This assertion is delivered with **knowledge one** assurance of philosophical rectitude, whereas it is just one of a host of rival conditions which are best guesses. Unlike the **trichotomy theory** (see next page), it offers no modal escape.

With Woozley's and Ayer's conditions, as with all definitions which attempt to define what the present theory calls **knowledge one**, we must either reach the conclusion that we do not know whether we know anything or we have to make assumptions. We must presuppose in Woozley's case, that we are right and that we have conclusive evidence; in Ayer's case, that we, before claiming x to be knowledge, must, in our ignorance, posit the truth of x in order to establish our claim; and further assume that we know we have 'the right to be sure'. And this is just where we begin to encounter difficulties in discussion. For if the assumptions of others are different from my own, and if they are unwilling to set their assumptions aside, then an immovable barrier is erected.[8]

Figure 3 illustrates the process of **modal reduction** which the trichotomy of knowledge allows. The monolithic view of knowledge put forward by Woozley, which places knowledge in opposition to belief without providing an all-inclusive region for everything that could ever be considered knowledge, is modally reduced in just such a region to the level of knowledge two. The **trichotomy of knowledge** can itself be modally reduced to stand 'within knowledge two', as also shown, just beneath Woozley's knowledge/ belief box – which, prior to its inclusion at knowledge two level seemed to be dangling in an epistemological vacuum. The trichotomy of knowledge, which includes *all* knowledge, may be seen by the process of modal reduction to include itself; **the trichotomy of knowledge itself contains the trichotomy of knowledge**. The reader will decide whether this is a strength or weakness of the trichotomy.

But it is worth pointing out, since this is a book about literary semantics, that Geoffrey Chaucer brought off a precisely analogous feat in the *The Canterbury Tales*. The *pilgrim-persona Chaucer,* within one of the most ingenious and monumental narratives ever devised by man, is called upon by the Host to tell a story. The only story he can come up with is a piece of doggerel so tedious that the Host silences him with a scatalogical riposte: 'Thy drasty rymyng is nat worth a toord' – 'Your dreadful rhymes don't rate a turd'. By a self-effacing **modal reduction**, Chaucer the *virtuoso* poet is simultaneously projected, and

MODAL REDUCTION

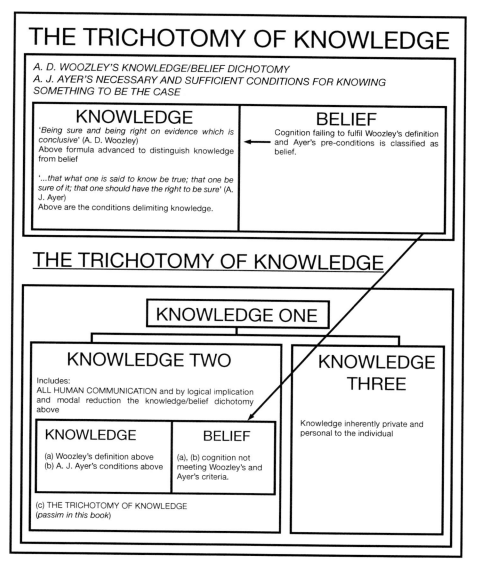

THE TRICHOTOMY OF KNOWLEDGE

A. D. WOOZLEY'S KNOWLEDGE/BELIEF DICHOTOMY
A. J. AYER'S NECESSARY AND SUFFICIENT CONDITIONS FOR KNOWING
SOMETHING TO BE THE CASE

KNOWLEDGE

'Being sure and being right on evidence which is conclusive' (A. D. Woozley)
Above formula advanced to distinguish knowledge from belief

'...that what one is said to know be true; that one be sure of it; that one should have the right to be sure' (A. J. Ayer)
Above are the conditions delimiting knowledge.

BELIEF

Cognition failing to fulfil Woozley's definition and Ayer's pre-conditions is classified as belief.

THE TRICHOTOMY OF KNOWLEDGE

KNOWLEDGE ONE

KNOWLEDGE TWO

Includes:
ALL HUMAN COMMUNICATION and by logical implication and modal reduction the knowledge/belief dichotomy above

KNOWLEDGE

(a) Woozley's definition above
(b) A. J. Ayer's conditions above

BELIEF

(a), (b) cognition not meeting Woozley's and Ayer's criteria.

(c) THE TRICHOTOMY OF KNOWLEDGE
(passim in this book)

KNOWLEDGE THREE

Knowledge inherently private and personal to the individual

THE ABOVE DIAGRAM PRESENTS A MODAL ANALYSIS OF KNOWLEDGE

The trichotomy of knowledge, which includes everything that could ever be considered to be knowledge, is thus 'self-reduced', to the level of Woozley's and Ayer's analyses and other theories of knowledge, so that - paradoxically, unlike Builder Jarvis's Bucket [see LS:181] - it modally contains these other theories and simultaneously contains itself with them, at a different level, cf the discussion of Russell's Paradox and Geoffrey Chaucer's Tale of Sir Topas [LS:181, 201]. See also the Principle of Subsumption in the Glossary.

Figure 3. Modal Reduction

rejected, as a bumbling incompetent. In this brief interlude: Chaucer the poet contains Chaucer the not-poet. There is further discussion of this episode on [LS:201].

The logician whose belief in the principle of verifiability is strengthened by fresh examples of successful scientific investigation is not, when he undertakes discussion with someone who does not accept the principle, in an essentially different position from the Venerable Bede who took comfort from the ubiquitous reports of miracles and would doubtless have regarded a logical positivist as the Devil's messenger. Hagiography and the principle of verifiability may, within certain universes of discourse, be accepted as knowledge one but to those outside they will appear to be, in the certainty with which they are held, initiated at the level of knowledge three.[9] Even the scientific method may be belittled as a convention which has gained popularity because an increasing number of people rely upon its principles.[10] The limitations of logic have been argued at length by Urban.[11] To these limitations I shall return in chapter 12.

This theory applied to philosophical speculation and debate will in some cases reorganize the references in such a way as to make the issues clearer. The trichotomy of knowledge expounded above includes and organizes all which has ever been, or, at least within our terrestrial region, could ever be, considered knowledge and it is so basic to the classification of knowledge that I find it hard to believe that any theory of knowledge which does not recognize this trichotomy can be thought to be satisfactory.

Four brief examples of the application of this theory to philosophical questions follow. Firstly, when Ayer in *Language, Truth and Logic*[12] says that metaphysics is nonsense, he is not saying – according to the trichotomy theory – that metaphysics does not belong to knowledge one but that what was **affident** in the Middle Ages has now only **local affidence** [LS:16]. The affidence of metaphysics has waned because the number of people in the **highest universe of discourse** who would give it a plus-three rating in the appropriate semantic differential test has decreased. We must beware of claiming that knowledge two is knowledge one. The trichotomy of knowledge substitutes for the traditional bipolar absolutes of dogmatic discourse a more civilised set of **modal** categories.

Moving to my second example, I refer to Max Black, *Language and Philosophy*.[13] In the first chapter of this book Black considers a sceptical doctrine as formulated in C. I. Lewis in *Mind and the World Order*. In a lively study Black illustrates the absurdity of the sceptic's position. In terms of the theory of knowledge outlined above, this particular sort of sceptic is a person who avails himself of knowledge two in order to claim that there is no such thing as knowledge two.

Thirdly, Wittgenstein, at the end of his *Tractatus Logico-Philosophicus*, says: 'My propositions are elucidatory in this way: he who understands me finally recognizes them as senseless, when he has climbed out through them, on them, over them. (He must so to speak throw away the ladder, after he has climbed up on it).'[14] The truth of Wittgenstein's argument, at the level of knowledge two, is the degree of **affidence** at each individual stage in its development. It does not follow that, because an argument has had at all points a high degree of affidence, the conclusion has also. Either the Wittgenstein ladder has a high degree of affidence, in which case its removal is not entirely in his hands, or Wittgenstein has been climbing an **inaffident** ladder, in which case its removal is likely to occasion small inconvenience other than to Wittgenstein himself.

Finally, some Christians or Buddhists, some men who have experienced the Aesthetic State, even some men who believe that metaphysics is nonsense may be said to believe that they have access to knowledge one. But in the highest universe of discourse any such claim may be viewed from the standpoint of knowledge two. Thus the successfully communicated parts of their reference will be considered of low affidence, and the experience underlying the communication (that is frequently the very part of the reference which the individual is unable to communicate and which he himself identifies with, or relates to, knowledge one) will be **modalised** as knowledge three.

Emotive Truth

In Ogden and Richards,[15] a distinction is made between symbolic and emotive truth. The test, they say, for symbolic truth is to ask whether a statement is true in the ordinary scientific sense. If such a question is relevant, the statement is to be considered **symbolic**; if it is irrelevant the utterance is **emotive**. In *The Principles of Literary Criticism*, I. A. Richards further explains the distinction.[16] In emotively used language, it is here stated, the truth or falsehood of the references symbolized is of no consequence. Emotive truth is concerned with artistic acceptability. The truth, in this sense, of the ending of *King Lear* rests upon its internal necessity. Its truth or falsehood is ultimately decided by the character of the attitude it evokes in a reader. If the ending of King Lear co-operates with the rest of the play to arouse our ordered response (the response, I would understand, is to be judged according to Richards' theory of value expounded in chapter 3), it is true emotively. Despite Richards's care to be scientific, a reader could not be blamed for believing that Richards considered emotive truth to be of a different kind from symbolic truth. This symbolic/emotive dichotomy seems, as I have earlier indicated, inelegant: 'emotive' becomes a filter for philosophical waste.

My **principle of subsumption** (and here I am anticipating [LS:161–163] and chapter 14 which describes the chain of modality) ascribes to aesthetics and ethics an integral rôle in the cognitive processes: having moved clockwise (logically and empirically) along the chain, we may intuitively, or by conscious decision, track anti-clockwise at any point. Given the concept of a multi-dimensional semantic space, then the two apparently contraflow movements can and usually do take place simultaneously. What Richards regards as separate processes, are subsumed within cognition as of equal status in the quest for knowledge one. What seemed therefore to be two horses confronting each other in a tug of war becomes just one free horse capable of moving in either direction or even both at once. This freedom arises as a corollary from the trichotomy theory and it is a part of our humanity.

The theory of knowledge outlined above, and the theory of the meaning of literature defined [LS:8–9], will, I think, throw light on the relation between symbolic and emotive truth.

Taking Geoffrey Chaucer's *Pardoner's Tale* by way of illustration, I shall consider three statements: 'This table is made of wood'; 'The Pardoner is quite sober';[17] 'The Pardoner's sobriety is in accordance with artistic necessity.' This last statement Richards would presumably classify as an utterance to be judged according to the criterion of emotive truth.

It is unlikely that the **affidence assessment** of a suitable person in respect of a particular and present table would differ from the **affidence** as assessed by means of the semantic differential. The terms used are **secure** and the **references** are appropriate to **referents** which are widely agreed upon. This table exists in space and time and is not an abstraction.

In what sense can the Pardoner's sobriety be said to have existed in time and space? We may see, by applying the theory of the meaning of literature, that we might define the Pardoner's physical state as either the total references in Chaucer's mind relevant to the Pardoner and all referents appropriate to these references (e.g. the physical state of pardoners encountered by Chaucer in real life; or Chaucer's own conception of whether it would be artistically appropriate for his Pardoner to be drunk – this conception, of course, in turn determined partly by artistic referents which Chaucer had come across, partly by other non-artistic referents, and so forth); *or*, the references, and referents appropriate to these references, evoked in the mind of the modern reader (to the modern reader any conception of a pardoner of any sort is bound to be an **assign**: that is a sign reconstructed by a subject from indirect evidence, in this case from written descriptions of pardoners). The Pardoner's supposed physical state is either a part of Chaucer's psychological activity or of the modern reader's. In this respect the Pardoner's physical state can be said to exist in time and space in Chaucer's mind then, or in the modern reader's now.

The symbols of the second statement, by Kittredge, are **insecure**. 'The Pardoner is quite sober' is ambiguous; it may refer to Chaucer's reference or to the modern reader's. We shall assume that in the semantic differential test the subjects are told in exactly which sense the symbols are to be interpreted (an advantage they would have over the readers of Kittredge).

If we are to take the first sense, i.e. Chaucer's reference, and assess the statement 'The Pardoner is quite sober', according to whether the subjects participating in the semantic differential test believe it to have been true for Chaucer at the time he wrote the *Pardoner's Prologue and Epilogue*, we shall find that the statement is rated somewhere near the origin in most cases; the statement is thus of low **affidence** (this at least is my own **affidence assessment**). The statement has a **referent** (i.e. Chaucer's **reference**) and if we had access to it we could make a judgment. But the referent is buried with Chaucer and an honest man is obliged to admit he does not know the answer.[18]

If we are to take the second sense, i.e. the reader's own reference, then we should probably discover a wide range of difference. The Pardoner's Prologue and Epilogue contain several *non sequiturs*. These could be explained by various interpretations one of which might be the Pardoner's drunkenness.

The remembrance of the **semic accompaniments** of various readings, together with diverse other considerations of greater and less logical relevance to the **reference**, would play their part in the judgment of each individual. The semantic differential on this occasion would probably show the individuals' judgments scattered at intervals along this semantic line, not clustered about the origin. Again there would be low affidence.

The reasons for the low affidence would be different in the two cases. In the first, the reason would be the inaccessibility of the referent. In the second, the referent is more accessible, but in fact there are now as many referents as there are subjects (the referents being the subjects' own references) and knowledge three will in each individual case play a part in the judgment.

As for the woodenness of the table, the judgment depends largely upon visual criteria, which are, in degree, constant from one individual to another and lead to a high degree of affidence, in the highest universe of discourse. If the reference tested is symbolized: 'The Pardoner's sobriety is in accordance with artistic necessity', the criteria are less constant. Our concept of artistic necessity, if we have one, has been built up complexly from diverse experiences and over a long period of time. In so far as our experiences are different, so our criteria will differ, and we shall find variation from the judgment of one individual to another. I would expect the reference 'The Pardoner's sobriety is in accordance with artistic necessity' to be less affident than 'This table is made of wood'.

If my argument is sound, far from vitiating I. A. Richards' concept of two types of truth, one of which, emotive truth, seems to be an anomalous misfit, the above analysis allows emotive truth to emerge, as it were, an equal cognitive and humane partner. I believe he might even have approved of this view. Where Richards fell short, in my judgment, was in lending credence to the contention that examination systems, which are measuring devices to which young brains are subjected, could be fairly operated on the basis of what he called 'emotive truth'. Chapters 3 to 6 are directed to those who still adhere to this doctrine.

Consent

We have now discussed the application of this theory of knowledge to some philosophical and literary problems. It is claimed that the theory accommodates everything which has ever been or could ever be called knowledge.

I would like to return briefly to the earlier discussion [LS:18–20] of theoretical self-containment. How far, in the light of its own definitions, may the theory of knowledge here expounded itself be considered knowledge? Does the **trichotomy of knowledge** actually include the **trichotomy of knowledge**? Because it lacks the *concrete* properties of Builder Jarvis's Bucket and the *rigorous, abstract, mathematical* pretensions of set theory, which I shall discuss later [LS:181], there is a sense in which my trichotomy of knowledge may sensibly be said to contain itself. The book you are at present reading belongs, solipsism apart, to knowledge two, because something of what is in my brain is being communicated to you. The necessarily private regions of my **references** belong to knowledge three. But I would not have written this book if I had not believed that at least something of what I am transmitting is knowledge one. At times I look at this book from the standpoint of knowledge one. At other times I see it from the standpoint of knowledge two or knowledge three. These three standpoints are in **reciprocal perspective**. From one bridge, I espy through my binoculars some person eyeing me from another bridge upstream. Reciprocal perspective is a frequently employed device in the **theory of modality** central to the thesis of this book.

There can be no doubt that some of the parts of this argument are weaker than others. Also the variation in affidence which I have chosen to blame in others is doubtless to be found in this theory. If we select one sentence as an example, 'If knowledge one exists most of us would consider it of the great-est importance and the other knowledges defined below would have either no importance or importance only in so far as they are related to or are identical with knowledge one' [LS:11]; this looks, on the face of things, like a truth claim, and it might well be asked what evidence I have to support it. In defence I would like to suggest a different approach. Perhaps the truth of a theory resides not, as is commonly believed, in the theory itself (for that is **truth one**), nor in the mind of the author (unless it be **truth three**), but in the recognition by each particular reader that here is something that organizes and explains (**truth two**). Nor is it to be hoped that any theory will be completely **affident** throughout. Richards in *Speculative Instruments* puts the matter in this way 'We may seem to make assertions, to lay out statements in arguments as though they were ironfast links in a chain and to unfold conclusions from what will formally appear to be premises. But our "may…may" brackets may remind us that any meaning any word may have floats upon a primitive raft of consents. It can mean what it may only for those who will let it'.[19]

If I were asked for an affidence assessment of the trichotomy of knowl-edge, I should be obliged to admit that I think the trichotomy of knowledge is potentially more affident than the theory of affidence. It seems to me that much discourse would be facilitated if the scope of knowledge were widened and if it were divided into three categories by two lines. I feel fairly confident that I have drawn both lines appropriately. But this book is not written within the mode of dogmatic assertion. It is to be regarded as a theoretical exploration, capable of being refuted at every turn.

Some Problems of the Semantics of Literature

Let us revert to Richards' symbolic-emotive dichotomy and examine the theory of emotive truth as it works out in practice. If truth and meaning are of two kinds it follows that language too must be dual. If the division is going to fulfil a need in method we must have a means of determining which is emotive and which symbolic language. If there is no agreed means of deciding this, then the division will be of little use in practical purpose. It is generally agreed by writers on symbolic and emotive meaning that there is a cognitive element in emotive statements; that is, they contain information. The extremely emotive word 'Hurrah!' contains the symbolic meaning 'I am enthusiastic'. We are not then dealing with two different types of language but two different aspects which are responded to simultaneously. In addition, the degree of emotive power in language is rarely the same from one sentence to the next in any piece of 'emotive' writing. Morris's solution to this, the admixture of functions of language in any given sentence, is to speak of the 'dominant sign'.[20]

Morris's approach to the problem is behaviouristic and biological.[21] Such treatment is most successful when it is directed to those very customs which humans have in common with rats and mice.[22] The simplicity of his biological method contrasts with his elaborate table of the major types of discourse.[23] There are three major factors in sign behaviour: the designative, the appraisive and the prescriptive components of signifying. These correspond to the relation of an organism to its environment: it may locate a region of the environment (designative); it may determine that this location is important for the satisfaction of its needs (appraisive); it must discover ways of acting upon the environment in order to satisfy its needs (prescriptive).[24] Human discourse, with a fourth type added (formative) is then classified into these categories. Further classification is added according to the use which is made of a mode of signifying. There are sixteen categories in all. The categories are proposed only as an approximation. A classification which separates fictive (designative-valuative) from poetic (appraisive-valuative); and mythical (appraisive-informative) from moral (appraisive-incitive) and from religious (prescriptive-incitive); such a classification seems to be something less than an approximation.[25] Also, since the author claimed that the behaviourist approach would make the material of semiotic more accessible to scientific investigation, it may be asked how we would go about to verify that political discourse or any political utterance is prescriptive in mode and valuative in use. It is typical of this sort of construct that it tends to obscure the central problems.

These more fundamental problems relating to emotive language, emotive meaning and emotive truth I take to be as follows: What are we to include in our definition of 'understanding': is it to be limited to the narrow scientific sense, or are we to include in it all means by which we become aware of the world about us? How are thinking and feeling related? What is the relation between a symbolic and an emotive utterance? What is the part played by cognition in aesthetic appreciation? If we accept the term 'emotive meaning', is it meaning in the same sense as in 'symbolic meaning'? What is the part played by metaphor in the process of thinking? What is the place of emotion in ethical judgment? What is the nature of ethical disagreement (is it parallel to scientific disagreement or is it entirely different)? Is it necessary that we should divide language into the categories symbolic and emotive; if so, how is this to be achieved? What sort of 'clarification' of these problems is necessary? Will observation of what takes place in discussion help us? [26]

I am going to deal specifically now with the last two questions; my sugges-tions here, and in other parts of this book, may perhaps indicate methods of approaching some of the other problems enumerated above. I believe that the findings of experimental psychology may sooner or later yield information which will provide a firmer foundation for discussion of these problems. In the meantime it has been suggested that we need a 'speculative instrument'. What sort of instrument? Is it to be a prose instrument?[27]

Most of us would agree that we are in a different psychological state (whether ontologically different or not) when we are enjoying a symphony from when we are engaged in the processes of serious and systematic thought. In the former state we might be said to be less 'aware' of the 'cognitive' aspects of the experience. If, in this state of enjoyment, we utter this sentence: 'What an enthralling performance!' then our utterance assumes something of the behaviourist expressions of emotion such as laughter. It seems certain that if feeling and cognition are ultimately to be separated, 'What an enthralling performance!' uttered under these circumstances is a statement of feelings.

But when we come in our more ratiocinative moments to reflect upon the meaning or the truth of this statement we are obliged to bring in the whole paraphernalia of cognition. We try to 'demonstrate', 'prove', 'justify' our statement. But the only symbols which we know will be readily acceptable in 'proof', 'demonstration' and 'justification' are the very ones which would have seemed less adequate at the moment of enjoying the concert than the ones we in fact used.

The reason for this difficulty is not far to be sought. In the collective and traditional experience of mankind, those symbols which refer to regular and stable human experiences – *This table is made of wood* – make more reliable linguistic currency than the symbols which are typically used during experiences of a more transient sort.

In cognitive statements we discipline ourselves to employ **symbols** or rather, symbol combinations, which have earned the reputation of reliability in cognitive circles. As a result, emotive truth and meaning is at a severe disadvantage, for it will inevitably be at least one stage removed from the state of mind in which we typically contemplate it.

For this reason the term 'emotive' has undergone a deleterious change and has become a wastepaper basket for aspects of language regarded as non-scientific. One alternative to a prose instrument to assist in the solution of the problems of emotive meaning might be an emotive treatment in emotive language. But the venerable terms of cognition would still 'refute' it; 'reject it as unsound'. Richards gives the following mandate: 'The instrument must be able to mediate, it must have a foot in each boat and yet be run away with by neither. And yet again, it must leave both functions free, in the sense that it is their creature and has no support or authority which does not derive in the end from them.'

I believe that the theory of affidence may provide the beginnings of a solution. The theories of Osgood, Suci and Tannenbaum have been strongly criticized in some circles. However, it is not their theories so much as their method which would be employed in research into affidence. One of the charges which is levelled against their method is that it measures only connotational meaning. But there seems no reason why denotational meaning should not be measured. If the methods were developed and their use extended there seems further no reason why the semantic differential should not become a most powerful instrument of inquiry into academic thought. If we are unable to answer at the moment what, in psychological terms, is the difference between thought and feeling, we can at least investigate the attitudes to these problems within given universes of discourse. We can learn what are taken to be the principles underlying judgment and evaluation. The semantic differential thus opens up a vast new field for empirical study. It is possible that the semantics of literature would profit greatly from such an investigation.

Also the division of language into affident and inaffident would be preferable to the symbolic/emotive dichotomy. As we have seen it is impossible to classify language satisfactorily on this basis, and by studying the ways in which people actually believe themselves to be employing language we would stand to learn more than from an arbitrary classification when the *differentiae* were unclear.

With regard to the thought/emotion binary, I would make these brief remarks. If it be true that knowledge one may exist, and if it be true that we cannot know that we know knowledge one, then there is no reason to assume that the cognitive function has priority over our efforts to attain to knowledge one. But it seems that the 'consistent and coherent theory' has such a strong hold over the higher universes of discourse that a speculative instrument which relies upon symbolic language (whatever we may mean by this) will be more widely acceptable than a 'theory' in emotive language.

It might be asserted that the theory of affidence sets the individual entirely at the mercy of the universe of discourse in which he finds himself. A consequence, however, of defining truth two as affidence is we must allow that truth, in this sense, constantly changes.

The extent to which an individual can influence truth two/affidence depends on many factors. Academics' views can be influenced either by the offering of new material which cannot be assimilated into present philosophical orientation or by the suggesting of a new organization of material which is already possessed. The Copernican Revolution came about, it has been argued, not so much because the Ptolemaic system was wrong, but because the new theory offered a simpler organization of the known facts of the universe.[28]

I have approached the problems of the semantics of literature throughout with the tacit assumption that 'strict symbolism' is the only possible treatment. This, of course, is not the case. The highest universe of discourse relevant to the consideration of the study of literature is, presumably, literary criticism. What literary criticism says about literature is therefore, by definition, truth two. What then can be said in contradiction to bring about an affidence change?

CHAPTER 3

A THEORY OF VALUE

I. A. Richards' Theory of Value

In *The Principles of Literary Criticism* Richards expounds a theory of value. Richards has been repeatedly criticized for trying to establish a science of criticism. Nowhere are his scientific preoccupations more clearly to be seen than in his theory of value. Although few would now accept Richards' theory of value and its application to poetry, I believe that Richards expressed with perception and vigour the problems of criticism. I intend therefore to restate his views and to comment upon them. I do not believe that the conclusions he drew followed from the premises he so clearly set out.

The critic is a judge of values and he is concerned with the health of the mind.[1] The mind is a part of the activity of the nervous system and mental events may be regarded as identical with certain neural events.[2] The scientific method is the only technique of satisfactory investigation.[3] Before successful inquiry into art can be made it is necessary to eliminate the assumption that aesthetic experiences are *sui generis*; even in ethics the theory that 'good' is an unanalysable quality intuitively recognized[4] is cryptic and a theory is to be sought which is in accordance with the verifiable facts.[5]

Scientific research into aesthetics is limited in scope, for only the simplest of human activities is at present amenable to laboratory methods.[6] Useful though these investigations are, the theory of criticism shows no great dependence upon experimental aesthetics.[7]

A statement by a critic may often be divided into two parts: technical and critical. The critical part is concerned with the value of the critic's experience; the technical, with the relation between the critic's experience and objective features in the work of art.[8] The tendency to regard the technique of the artist as more important than the value of the work of art is one of the snares which waylay the critic.[9] No special ethical or metaphysical ideas need to be introduced to explain value; critical remarks are a branch of psychological remarks.

The nervous system is the means whereby stimuli result in appropriate behaviour. Mental events occur in the course of adaptation between the stimulus and a response. Mental events are both conscious and unconscious.[10] The process, occurring between the stimulus and the resulting act, in the course of which a mental event may take place, is called an impulse.[11] The reception or rejection of a stimulus by an organism depends on the state of the organism rather than the stimulus itself.[12] Impulses may be divided into appetencies and aversions.[13] Most appetencies are unconscious. Anything is valuable which will satisfy an appetency without involving the frustration of some equal or more important appetency.[14] The importance of an impulse is the extent of the disturbance of other impulses in the individual's activities which the thwarting of the impulse involves.[15] Richards admits that this definition of importance is vague but it is, he claims, suitable to our at present incomplete and hazy knowledge of how impulses are related.

The successful co-ordination of impulses is happiness. Every systematization of impulses involves a degree of sacrifice, but that organization is best which is least wasteful of human possibilities.[16]

The organization of impulses within any individual varies from hour to hour.[17] However the community within which he lives requires uniformity and the individual is obliged to modify his organization in conformity.[18] All past societies have imposed obligations involving appalling waste and misery.[19] The obligations take the form of religious, legal and superstitious impositions; obsolete moral principles are among the worst offending of these impositions. A more adaptable morality is needed if we are to survive the turmoil of change. The organization of impulses is not primarily an affair of conscious planning. Literature and the arts are the chief means by which organizing influences are diffused. Free, varied and unwasteful life relies upon the arts to a great degree in a numerous society.[20]

The problem of morality is how to obtain the greatest possible value from life.[21] The most valuable states of mind are those which involve the widest and most comprehensive co-ordination of activities and the least curtailment, conflict, starvation and restriction.[22] No one systematization of impulses can claim a supreme position, for men are naturally different. Art and criticism are often thought to be redundant. This is not so. A critic is a judge of values and he is concerned with the health of the mind;[23] the joy which the experience of supreme art brings is a sign that the nervous system is in a state of health.[24] *A*

critic is obliged to say 'I am better than you'; he should be ready with reasons
of a clear and convincing kind [my italics].[25]

There are three qualifications for a good critic: the ability to experience, without eccentricities, the state of mind relevant to the work of art he is judging; the ability to distinguish experiences from one another as regards their less superficial features; the ability to give sound judgment of values.[26] He will be better qualified to carry out these tasks if he has some knowledge of the psychological form of the experiences.

When a poem is read the printed words are stimuli which initiate a complex stream of reactions in the mind.[27] All experiences evoke attitudes and these are the important part of the experience. A work of art can, through the attitude which results, permanently modify the structure of the mind.[28] An attitude is a group of incipient activities.[29] Familiar activities set in different conditions compel the habitual impulses to readjust themselves and the activities evoke fresh attitudes.[30] This is what happens in art experience.[31]

The purpose of art is neither instruction nor amusement.[32] Pleasure – which is not a sensation but would appear to be the fate of an impulse – has an important place in the account of values, [33] but it should not be made the goal of activity.[34] The approach of the reader to any poem should be adapted to the character of the poem itself;[35] poetry is of more than one kind and different kinds are to be judged by different principles. The poem is not to be judged independently of its 'place in the great structure of human life'. The numerous 'ulterior worths' of a poem are to be taken into account.[36] Permanence in itself is no criterion of value; other factors than merit determine the survival of literary pieces.[37] Also, poetry is not to be made subordinate to beliefs and assertions. Poetry sets forth a hypothetical state of affairs and develops from this point. The amplitude and fineness of the response depend upon the freedom from assertion, particularly where the belief is questionable. This is particularly true of religious belief.[38] It is in terms of attitudes, the resolution, interinanimation, and balancing of impulses that the most valuable effects of poetry must be described.

It is impossible for a state of mind to be transferred by communication from one person to another in such a way that the experience can be said to be identical for both people.[39] Communication takes place when one mind so acts upon its environment that another mind is influenced, and in that other mind an experience occurs which is like the experience in the first mind and is caused in part by that experience.[40] The arts are the supreme form of the communicative activity.[41]

The artist himself, like the critic, is to be pre-eminently accessible to external influences and discriminating with regard to them. He can connect different elements of his experience with great range, delicacy and freedom.

It is the availability to him of past experience which is important.[42] Also, in a state of vigilance, or high neural potency, the nervous system reacts to stimuli with highly adapted, discriminating and ordered responses. The artist is a man of high vigilance; he is able to admit far more than the ordinary man of the impulses which a situation arouses, without confusion. The artist's organization is such that he can lead a fuller life than the average, but it is nevertheless essential that he should be a normal man.[43] The artist is the man who is most likely to have experiences of value to record.[44]

However, the artist is not as a rule consciously concerned with communication, but with making his work 'right', that is, representing the precise experience upon which its value depends.[45] But although communication is consciously neglected, when the work is 'right' it will have greater communicative power. The degree to which it accords with the relevant experience of the artist is a measure of the degree to which it will arouse similar experiences in others.[46] The efficacy for communication seems to be a part of the 'rightness', though the artist may not be aware of this.[47]

We come now to the application of the principles of criticism. Richards gives in illustration a sonnet by Ella Wheeler Wilcox which he considers bad. There is no lack of success in communication, for many readers find pleasure in it. The strongest objection to it is that the very organization of responses which enables a person to enjoy it debars him from appreciating many things which, if he could appreciate them, he would prefer.[48]

A Theory of Value

In Richards' view of criticism the theory of value is of great importance. Value, in its normal ethical usage, denotes that which is worthy of esteem for its own sake. Richards' theory of value goes contrary to the usage of the word value, yet his case is so cogently argued that it might be easy to fall into the error of believing that a problem which still remains with us has been solved.

In my synopsis of Richards' argument the theory of value may be seen to rely on the terminology of psychology. An appetency is a psychological phenomenon and if we knew enough about the nature of an appetency and the incidence of appetencies in any individual we should know all about the individual's values.

The problem which still remains is: Why is value, in this sense, valuable? Richards would presumably reply that when the body is functioning satisfactorily it is said to be in a state of health; likewise, the nervous system with all its important appetencies satisfied is in a state of neural health. By value we mean that which promotes neural health, nothing more. What Richards does not tell us is: By what criterion should neural health be looked upon as the highest good? He may have given an interesting theoretical account of what takes place in the psyche when a man has what he believes to be a valuable experience, but, to call that which promotes neural health, value, seems to be entering a realm in which science can have no jurisdiction and to be using the word *value* in a way not in keeping with usage.

Value seems to me a concept which has survived the onset of the enemies of metaphysics. Leslie Armour derives the emotivist view of value from the belief of the logical positivists who made an onslaught against ethical statements because they were not amenable to verification by scientific method. There is much evidence, he says, to show that people are acquainted with values even though we cannot prove the presence of value in a particular case.[49]

Our valuing faculty is innate in us and endowed as a corollary of our sense that we have choices. Each of three men – one of whom decides he will eat soon, one who decides he will not and one who simply has not made a decision – has an attitude, positive, negative or indifferent, underlain by a scale of values, his choice. Appetencies and aversions are doubtless a part of the biological machinery, but we need a definition of value which will include everything that could ever be considered valuable. Individuals may then whittle this down, by **modal reduction**, to their preferences at the levels of knowledge two and knowledge three.

Value can, I believe, be more satisfactorily defined in terms of the trichotomy of knowledge. The human situation is such that man seems to know some things but does not know everything. It is impossible to say what his position would be if he *did* know everything but one imagines there would be no need for a theory of knowledge. A theory is needed not so much as to organize material which is already complete as to give direction to the inchoate. Probably the widespread awareness of value springs from this same knowledge deficiency. Man feels the need for complete certainty but does not have it; value is his *intuitive* substitute. Or, to express this in terms of the trichotomy theory: **value is a man's conviction (knowledge three) that he has access in some degree to knowledge one**. This conviction may be (a) unconsciously accreted; (b) consciously induced; or (c) a combination of these two processes.

Although Richards' theory of value is no longer widely accepted, his statement that the literary critic is concerned with values seems to be little challenged. My concern here is not with literary criticism but with serious study and courses in English at university level. If value is to be the basis of literary criticism in English, it follows that, with Wellek and Warren, we must reject the idea that literary criticism should be bound to the scientific ideals of objectivity, impersonality and certainty.[50] If, further, the teaching of English at university level is to be primarily a training in literary criticism, the same rejection must be made. This brings us to the question of communication in literature.

Returning to the definition of the meaning of literature [LS:8–9], it seems as if Richards regards the second (**semics**) as of paramount importance in the principles of criticism. Comparatively small space is given to the experience of the artist (**semantics of literature/transmission semantics**). Richards comprehends the complexity of the art experience. What is surprising is that after enquiring minutely into all aspects of artistic experience he can emerge with such confidence in his own views. If we admit, as he does, that the simplest of human activities is not amenable to laboratory methods; that the scientific method is the only technique of satisfactory investigation; that we must take account of the complexity and obscurity of the nervous system; that when a poem is read the printed words are stimuli which initiate a complex stream of reaction in the mind; that it is impossible for a state of mind to be transferred by communication from one person to another in such a way that the experience can be said to be identical for both people; have we not now passed beyond the point where any satisfactory normative statement about general artistic experience can be made? If artistic experience is so complex and diverse, and, if Richards' analysis of artistic experience is sound, then the conclusions which follow seem to be the reverse of the ones he draws. Would we not expect to find in literary criticism a series of value disagreements, of contrary emphasis, of entirely different critical principles? And is this not precisely what we do find?

The best illustration I have seen of this point is the documentation in Richards' own book, *Practical Criticism*. Yet, if I have read *The Principles of Literary Criticism* correctly there is an underlying assumption that, despite his *caveat* about the impossibility of identical transmission of art experience, the literary experiences of the writer and the good reader are the same; that is, the two definitions of the meaning of literature might just as well be one. That is to say, his general conclusions about the unique 'rightness' of true artistic communication are in flat contradiction of his own analysis of artistic transactions.

A Theory of Literature

In *Practical Criticism* Richards considers criticisms made by students, whose average age was about twenty, of thirteen short poems.[51] He sets out to give guidance in criticism and the book is an application of the principles of criticism expounded in the author's previous book. *Practical Criticism* contains a detailed examination of many concepts of literary criticism and a discussion of the tools of criticism as used by the students.

When we read a poem, Richards argues, we must set aside all preconceptions and critical dogmas, firstly, because these cause us to read into the poem things which are not there, and secondly, because through these preconceptions our judgment is disabled.[52] The most delicate instrument we possess in judging experiences is the choice of our whole personality.[53] The poem must be read with great thoroughness and our acceptance or rejection of it must be *direct*.[54] Arguments and principles have useful functions: for instance, they can protect us from irrelevancies. But the critical act is very important because it is a moment of sheer decision. At this point in our experience the mind selects the direction of its future development.[55] At these moments inadequate critical theories often obstruct us, withholding what we need and imposing upon us what we do not need. Richards places great emphasis upon this critical act: 'Only by penetrating far more whole-mindedly into poetry than we usually attempt, and by collecting all our energies in our choice can we overcome these treacheries within us. That is why good reading, in the end, is the whole secret of good judgment'.[56] The lesson of all criticism is that we have nothing to rely upon in making our choices but ourselves.'[57]

Richards considers that the majority of the students who underwent the critical tests were bad readers.[58] The inference, the critical principle, which might be thought to emerge from the documentation of these students' critical observations is *'quot homines tot sententiae'* – 'there are as many opinions as there are men'.[59] The guidance Richards gives in the ensuing pages is meant to allay any suspicions the reader might entertain of the soundness of the critical approach.

I do not believe that Richards has succeeded in his aim. *Practical Criticism* would seem an indictment of the very methods and principles it sets out to defend. Richards states that an overtone of despairing hopelessness haunts his protocols in a degree which his selections do not sufficiently display.[60] Yet *Practical Criticism* is presented as a positive approach to the problems and it can be said to have succeeded only if it offers satisfactory alternatives to a state of affairs agreed to be bad.

The critical act, the act of judgment, is of great importance in Richards' view. Acceptance or rejection of the poem, he says, must be direct. Acceptance or rejection of the poem are taken as the only possible alternatives and the word 'must' implies obligation. Richards could, however, bring nothing forward, save his self-invested authority, to support this statement; there seems, in fact, to be no way of substantiating such an assertion. Richards is making a knowledge one claim. Richards' reputation as a thinker and his massive treatment of critical problems might predispose his reader in favour of belief. But, before such a statement is taken on trust, it might be remarked that this ill accords with Richards' other affirmation that in criticism we have nothing to rely on but ourselves.[61] Richards has argued himself into a dilemma. If we are to rely only on ourselves why should we read *Practical Criticism*? And if we accept his advice and try to rely only on ourselves are we not, in doing so, relying on Richards' advice? To put the point differently: if the experience of reading makes a permanent modification of the structure of our minds, then this moment of sheer choice is an illusion; for we are bound to be influenced in such moments by previous readings of literary critics, including Richards, which have permanently modified the structure of our minds. This is true whether the modifications include preconceptions and dogmas or, equally, the determination not to be influenced by such notions. In a sense, then, the future development of our minds at this moment of sheer choice is, if Richards were consistent, largely determined for us by our previous experience.

My own impression is that most of the students who took part in this test were confused. I do not think that Richards offers a satisfactory alternative to this state of affairs. His theory of value without which his whole argument would be considerably weakened is not satisfactory. As Max Black has observed, even if it be theoretically sound Richards offers us no way of putting its principles into practice – we have no means of measuring the satisfaction or thwarting of our impulses.[62] Richards sets out to give reasons why the critic may say 'I am better than you'. We have noticed that a critical principle on which he lays great stress, the infallibility of the personal critical choice, would, if accepted, render the literary critic superfluous.

It was earlier suggested that Richards treats as one the two possible meanings of the literary work [LS:8–9]. I believe that this assumption is widespread in literary criticism, see for instance Iser's concept of concretization (Eaton 1980:179-182), and I believe it is an assumption detrimental to the organization of literary studies.

The findings of Osgood, Suci and Tannenbaum concerning meaning are highly speculative. Their concept of a semantic space is metaphorical. However I am going to assume that their theories are sufficiently well based to enable us to give an account of the literary experience which is not a gross distortion of the truth.

If, on reading a word, a person experiences a mediating reaction, and if this reaction can be located in a semantic space, then, when many words are read, it may be inferred that the resulting experience consists of a series of mediating reactions in different parts of the semantic space. Each one of these mediating reactions will represent and refer to a diversity of past experience in the life of the individual concerned. Simplifying, for the sake of illustration, we might say, using the terms of C. C. Fries, that 'function' words such as 'the', 'from' and 'until', will perhaps cause no separate mediating reaction but will merely contribute to the mediating reaction of neighbouring 'form' words, nouns, verbs, adjectives and adverbs.[63]

But this experience is cumulative. We are not dealing with a series of compartments but with a growing composite experience whereby mediating reaction 'b' is influenced by mediating reaction 'a' which precedes it, and in turn influences mediating reaction 'c' that follows. Mediating reactions which take place when a work of literature is read are thus determined, firstly, by past experiences (which would often include the influence of the critical opinions of others), and, secondly, by linguistic contiguity. The series of mediating reactions which a person experiences when he reads continuously at his normal speed a passage which contains for him no linguistic difficulties I shall call his **semic accompaniment**. The semic accompaniment is a continuum of mediating reactions. The study of semic accompaniment I shall call **semics**. Semics can be either **empirical** or **introspective**.

Let us call the first alternative definition of the meaning of literature [LS:8], the **semantics of literature** (and its experimental counterpart, where authors are still alive and available, **transmission semantics**). As was admitted [LS:23], such a definition presents insuperable difficulties to the investigator. Also, research into the semantics of literature is bound to be influenced by the investigator's own personality,[64] and this might be said to move his researches towards the second definition. However the distinction is one of degree: biographical, linguistic, textual and historical work may be said to be orientated towards the first definition, interpretation towards the second.

This is not a mere theoretical refinement of the critical approach. Many critical works can be seen to alternate between the semantics of literature and semic accompaniment without any indication that such a switch has taken place and without any apparent awareness on the part of the author that this is what he is doing. The first two chapters of J. L. Lowes' *Geoffrey Chaucer*[65] are concerned with the semantics of literature; the final chapter is devoted to semic accompaniment.

G. C. Coulton's *Chaucer and his England*[66] is a good example of a book devoted almost entirely to the semantics of literature. The unfortunate paradox is that the approach to the semantics of literature is bound to be oblique. To arrive at the semantics of literature, in so far as this is possible, the scholar must immerse himself in the historical background which influenced the writer. As far as this process of immersion continues the scholar may be said to be orientated towards the first definition; in most cases, however, when he tries to draw conclusions he reverts to the second. The usefulness of the definition is that it draws attention to a fact which has often gone unregarded: that in language, both referential and non-referential, what is transmitted is frequently not what is received.

Kittredge's book *Chaucer and his Poetry* is chiefly concerned with Kittredge's semic accompaniment. The last paragraph of the book, where he states, without offering evidence,[67] that Chaucer 'Found no answer to the puzzle of life but in truth and courage and beauty and belief in God', is the product of a lively semic accompaniment, as is his interpretation of the Pardoner's character (my readers may recall the 'very paroxysm of agonized sincerity' to explain the Pardoner's three self-contradictory lines in the Epilogue to his Tale).[68]

Kittredge's approach may be contrasted with W. C. Curry's in *Chaucer and the Medieval Sciences*. Curry's book, it is true, illustrates how silent this transition from the semantics of literature to semic accompaniment can be. Curry, as he explains in his introduction, has investigated natural and celestial physiognomy, geomancy, alchemy, medieval medicine and so forth.

The first chapter concerns the Doctor of Physic and medieval medicine and is divided into two parts: the first dealing mainly with medieval medical theology and practice and the Doctor's own learning; the second with the Doctor's character. There is in the second part of this chapter a sudden reversal from the semantics of literature to Curry's semic accompaniment. Putting this more explicitly: the first part is an examination of the authorities a medieval physician might be expected to have read and an explanation of astrological beliefs and practices. Authorities are cited frequently, and at length, and diagrams of the zodiac are given. In part two there is an abrupt change and we plunge into conjecture and possibilities; 'For the good Doctor I suspect talks too much'[69] ... ' if anybody is interested, he doubtless lectures with a show of wisdom upon diets, illustrating his points by reference to his own personal habits in that matter; everybody, of course, waits breathlessly to learn what so eminent a medical man has for breakfast in January, for dinner in March, or for supper in April.'[70] But this flight of fancy belies the patient scholarship which underlies this book and contrasts with his analysis of the Pardoner.

Curry's interpretation of the Pardoner, his discovery of the Pardoner's 'secret', for instance, is the result of a different approach from Kittredge's. Curry's method seems to be to investigate the semantics of literature and then to let this investigation influence his semic accompaniment. His exposition of 'The Pardoner's Secret' illustrates this: he claims that the portrayal of the Pardoner's physiognomy betrays a typical *eunuchus ex nativitate* – 'a eunuch from birth'. The argument is as close to the semantics of literature as a scholar of medieval texts can get: careful research into contemporary medieval lore combined with a credible, non-trivial hypothesis which coheres with and explains the textual facts. In Kittredge's book, on the other hand, semic accompaniment plays a much greater part.[71]

It will be useful at this point to consider questions of relevance in the light of the trichotomy theory. A consideration may be relevant at the three levels of knowledge. **Relevance one** need not concern us. At the level of knowledge three, anything may be relevant. At the level of knowledge two that is relevant which accords with agreed principles. At the level of knowledge three, then, the scientist may have many experiences which he does not record (i.e. translate into knowledge two terms) since these would not be in accord with scientific principles of relevance.

In literary experience also, there are two levels of relevance. It would be impossible to formulate any principles of relevance at the level of knowledge three. An individual may have his own, possibly subliminal, principles of **relevance three**, or not. But when he decides that he will participate in a universe of discourse he is obliged to consider **relevance two**. In literary criticism there are no universally accepted criteria of relevance two, see ([LS:87–88] the discussion of Bateson's **Principle of the Semantic Gap**, for instance). The criteria of relevance which are successful in science are rejected and it is seen as inevitable and desirable that in criticism there should be different approaches and different frames of reference.[72]

Objectivity of approach to literature is impossible as long as there is no attempt to separate semics from semantics. Similarly, that value is taken as the basis for study is bound to preclude impersonality. It is not that value, in some senses of the word – see chapter 11 – cannot be studied, but that there is often in talk concerning values a confusion between knowledge one and knowledge three. A statement that a literary work is valuable may mean that in the speaker the reading of the work produced what he believed to be a valuable experience. In this case the speaker will be a subject for investigation rather than an investigator. Any statement which he makes about his experience is to be treated with the care experimental psychology would accord to introspective statements. The study of value, *in this sense*, is related to the study of other psychological processes. Perhaps because the results of such an approach to value would be slow and possibly unrewarding it is the custom in literary criticism to make intuitive statements about a supposedly objective scheme of value – see chapter 5. Instead of a vast co-operative effort there is, as a result, a fragmentation of endeavour, prolonged disagreement, and the direction of studies by a hierarchy of taste, which may seem to be self-appointed and self-perpetuating. [73]

Before serious study can take place there must be an isolation of the subject material and objectivity of approach. I regard the university as a depository of knowledge on any given subject and I would expect to find a progression of knowledge in the study of literature in the same sense in which this can be seen in scientific subjects. R. S. Crane has drawn attention to contemporary claims that there is progress in criticism and that progress has been rapid in recent years. The case that I am presenting is in conflict with this view.

The Contradiction Underlying
I. A. Richards' Theories

A large proportion of this book so far has been devoted to a discussion of the theories of I. A. Richards, to whose intellect I have already paid tribute. I believe, however, that his pioneering work in semantics might have led *naturally* to the establishment of a discipline of literary semantics. That it did not is due to a contradiction by which his later theories are underlain. In the course of this book I shall offer an alternative analysis.

It might be concurred that there is no field of study in which philosophy is not relevant; there is no study of human thought, and literature is part of the history of human thought, in which psychology is not relevant. That linguistics is central to the study, as opposed to the enjoyment, of literature, I see as self-evident. Other writers do not – as I shall show in Part II of this book.

It frequently occurs that an individual's philosophy contains inconsistencies which remain simply because certain mutually incompatible assumptions have never been brought to logical adjacency. An individual believing that beliefs should be logical and that his own beliefs are logical who is nevertheless shown and convinced that a given belief of his is illogical will normally make some adjustment either to his belief that his beliefs are logical or to the given offending belief.

The position into which Richards manoeuvred himself I would analyse as follows:

(1)   He regarded scientific inquiry as the 'only technique with which anything has ever been successfully investigated'.[74]

(2)   He held that the principles of literary criticism should be central to the study of literature.[75]
        He defended the hierarchy of taste within literary criticism and, by implication, **academic criticism**.[76]

My argument is that the tenets 1 and 2 above are in mutual contradiction. Any attempt to conjoin them was bound to fail. Richards 'solved' the problem by abandoning 1 and retaining 2. It is my contention that he should have persevered with 1. My trichotomy of knowledge and its epistemological theory of value, which takes account of *intrinsic* values, provide the foundation in turn for a theory of science, which will be described in chapter 4.

Literature and Education

Another universe of discourse which is relevant to literary semantics is education. This section briefly describes two examples of lack of rigour in literary criticism. The theme will be taken up in more detail in the next three chapters leading to the Sections entitled 'Academic Criticism' and 'The Supposed Intersubjectivity of Literary Criticism'.

From the theory of affidence, there arise two points which require further discussion: the difficulty of determining the highest universe of discourse, and the consequence of equating truth two with affidence. It is admitted [LS: chapter 2, note 1], that the distinction between high and low universes must be arbitrary. A universe of discourse which claims infallibility or superiority (e.g. the logicians, or critics who say 'I am better than you'), and excludes other universes of discourse isolates itself. Nothing can be done extramurally to break down this isolation; change can only be worked from the inside.

I feel that the need for a synthesis of knowledge is so pressing that we can ill afford to consider irrelevant the views of intelligent and educated men and women whose notions are different from our own. This is perhaps consonant with recent developments. Just as, for instance, theologians are becoming more tolerant towards science, one conclusion that might be drawn from Passmore's book[77] is that the holders of the principle of verifiability have been unable to show that there is any difference in kind between their own assumptions and those of the metaphysicians: 'throw metaphyics into the fire, and science goes with it, preserve science from the flames and metaphysics comes creeping back.'

There is a danger that non-empirical factors even in scientific procedure may pass unobserved and there is a possibility that what is considered to be confirmed will be regarded as knowledge one. A theory which assumes that man has access to knowledge one, the human situation being what it is, can become unstable. We are unable to predict how what we may later come to 'know' will affect what we 'know' now. L. J. Cohen in *The Diversity of Meaning* discusses at some length the theories of Popper and others concerning the problems of confirmation in science. It is clear from such discussion that even though the *caveat* [LS:10] may sometimes be ignored, confirmation and acceptance are in science fairly coextensive. Predictions made as a result of observations lead to further observations which either confute or refine previous observations.[78]

If even scientific discourse needs steady vigilance to ensure that laxity does not destroy results (see [LS:225–226] for an arresting example), the problems with literary criticism are endemic. Here, confirmation and acceptance are not coextensive, largely because it is difficult to establish what has been confirmed

– see the discussion of Bateson's arguments in chapter 5. Also it would be difficult to find any measure of agreement on critical method. As far as the enjoyment of a work of literature is concerned this might be all to the good. For the reading of literature is not a communal effort like science and its end product, silently humane, may emerge even though the reader never speaks of his experience. The cerebral activity of reading a work of literature would seem therefore to be more in accord with **knowledge three** than is the experiment of a scientist. The reading may be subject to misconceptions historical and linguistic, but providing that the reader is satisfied his experience has been worthwhile then these misconceptions need not be relevant: see Bateson's discussion of Blake's poem 'Jerusalem' at the end of chapter 4.

Misconceptions only become relevant when the reader commits himself to a **universe of discourse** and is obliged to record his experience. Now if a universe of discourse is to impose criteria of relevance upon the reading of a work of literature it should be clear about what purpose these criteria are to serve. The lack of agreement concerning criteria of relevance and critical method in literary criticism would seem to place the student in a false position. He hears lectures and reads books which propagate conflicting views; no clear distinction is drawn between **semics** and **semantics**; study and enjoyment are not precisely differentiated; and the student is finally expected to answer examination questions couched in emotive language. The result is, I believe, in some cases, the worst of both worlds. The student is deprived of what has been called the 'finest flower and test of a liberal civilization', a thorough grounding in scientific method,[79] whilst the result of being in a community where not to enjoy one's books is regarded as something to have guilty feelings about is a permanent detrimental effect upon the capacity for enjoyment of literature.

The examiner's final judgment on a candidate will be **affident**. That is to say it will be accepted as an assessment of the candidate's ability in the circles in which he will move. Great importance is therefore attached to the examiner's decision. An examination is a measuring instrument. ' "Milton was of the Devil's own party without knowing it." Discuss with reference to *Paradise Lost*'. This would be a fairly typical question in an examination in literature. Indeed, it was a practice question that was laid before me at Oxford. It seems to be aimed at testing the attitude rather than the belief or knowledge of the candidate (Stevenson's distinction, see *Ethics and Language*, chapter One in his book). In marking the answer to such a question the examiner is assessing one of two things: the affidence of the candidate's answer or the correspondence between the candidate's answer and knowledge one (i.e. the examiner's knowledge three). The latter is, by definition, impossible, or raises questions about the wisdom of accepting the examiner's knowledge three as a criterion.

To make an **affidence assessment** of such a question is impossible. The terms of the question, 'Devil', 'Milton', 'party', are **insecure**. 'Devil' means very different things for the Christian and non-Christian. Secondly, what was the 'Devil' referred to in this case? The actual Devil of Christian theology, if such there be, or a Devil one stage removed from this, a literary Devil? If we are referring to a literary Devil, in what way does he differ from the Christian Devil? Are we to draw our conception of the literary Devil from Milton's portrait of Satan in *Paradise Lost*? If we assume that Milton is of the Devil's own party without knowing it does this not therefore mean that his portrait of the Devil is likely to be distorted? But we are using his portrait as a yardstick whereby to judge Milton's own position. If the actual Christian Devil is referred to, are there not implicit in the question assumptions which would place the agnostic candidate in a perplexing position? The concept of emotive truth may have its uses in some universes of discourse but its use in examination questions is, I think, unsatisfactory.

It is unsatisfactory not only because it is impossible to operate the examination as a measuring device, but also because it creates confusion, I think, in a certain type of intelligent candidate. If we compare this question with the more factual type set in English examinations at German universities I believe we may fairly conclude that the German type is far better suited to employment as a measuring device.

The difficulties which we have encountered in examinations are present also in books of criticism which students are expected to read. Examples of what I refer to are frequent and accepted, but in order to illustrate what I mean by terminological **insecurity** I choose a book by R. W. Chambers, *Man's Unconquerable Mind*. Most students reading *Piers Plowman* would find chapters 4 and 5 of this book on their reading list. Chambers' view is that *Piers Plowman* is not merely the 'last dying spasm', in the words of Quiller Couch, of Anglo-Saxon literature, 'It is our first great modern poem'.[80] A little further on he says: 'Now Fuller, of course, was wrong in making the poet a proleptic Protestant'.[81] The first statement comes over as an almost *ex cathedra* pronouncement made with all the authority of someone with access to **knowledge one**. But Chambers in the second assertion accuses Fuller of perpetrating the same looseness of expression that he himself has just indulged in.

There is inconsistency here arising from vagueness in definition. Chambers seems to be saying that Quiller Couch, because he failed to recognize *Piers Plowman* as a modern poem, was not entirely right; that Fuller was wrong because he called Langland a Protestant by prolepsis. *The Shorter Oxford Dictionary* will here help in clarification: *Protestant A12*, a member or adherent of any Christian church or body severed from the Roman communion in the Reformation of the 16th c.; hence, gen. any member of a Western church outside the Roman communion. *A11c*, one who makes a protest *against* any decision, proceeding, practice, custom, or the like; a protester. Secondly, *Modern, A2*, of or pertaining to the present and recent times; originating in the current age or period. *A3*, characteristic of the present and recent times; not antiquated or obsolete.

If we consider *Piers Plowman* in the light of these definitions of *modern* we shall find that definition *A2* is inapposite. *Piers Plowman* was written in the 14th Century and is a Middle English poem. Chambers must be using the word in sense *A3*. He sees in the poem something which he considers characteristic of the 20th Century.

Chambers goes on to say that Fuller was wrong in calling Langland a proleptic Protestant. Here again there is a variance in definition. If Fuller was using *Protestant* in sense *A12*, then he was clearly wrong. Langland could not have been severed from the Roman communion in the Reformation of the 16th Century. But Fuller may have been using the word in the sense *A11c*. Chambers is not allowing to Fuller the same laxity of definition which he himself uses. This is the discourse of the Sunday newspaper reviews.

My literal approach to these passages is, I believe, justified. A large number of students read this book and their most powerful motive is to pass the examination. In the present state of our culture, where the possession or lack of academic qualifications can further or blight a career, this is unavoidable. For the student who knows there is a possibility that his future may depend on his ability to discuss successfully whether Langland was a proleptic Protestant the issue has more than casual interest. He might reasonably expect some guidance in the matter. Is he to be allowed in his paper the same laxity of definition which seems to be the custom of many literary critics? Will he get more marks for saying that Langland *is* a proleptic Protestant, or that Langland *is not* a proleptic Protestant, or should he seek some entirely different term of his own? Would not any careful inquiry show that it is impossible to operate the examination as a measuring device successfully under these circumstances?

I am not here being hostile to the type of statement which is made by literary critics. The nature of an individual's semic accompaniment depends upon the chance links between words and chance associations. A person's semic accompaniment can be modified as a result of reading literary criticism of a given work and the result can be increased enjoyment. This sort of criticism seems to be intended for the knowledge three level. The criticism reflects the semic accompaniment of the critic and he may help the reader to a similar semic accompaniment. Communication at this level − though frequently important in the sense of one human '*talking to another*' − is fortuitous and often intermittent. To set examination questions in this type of language is to pretend that such statements are **secure**.

Reading Tillyard's *The Muse Unchained*, I sympathized with the feelings which motivated the Cambridge English Faculty in the years following the First World War. The revulsion against the German phonological school, on the one hand, and the type of criticism which treated poetry as pure gold, on the other, is easy to understand. The issue is one of emphasis. One could sense the enthusiasm with which these students, trained in clause analysis and the classics, set themselves to the study of English Literature. But, as Tillyard admits, the enthusiasm declined, and practical criticism has often degenerated into a dreary game.[82] For the purposes of genuine scholarship – as opposed to recreation – I do not regard the work of art as having a 'special ontological status'.[83] This view of Wellek and Warren seems to be a widespread attitude underpinning that degeneration. It is an attempt to build knowledge three into knowledge two/affidence, or even into knowledge one.

Where there were discovered no common accepted principles it could hardly have been otherwise. Students who were taught no rules could not reasonably be expected to observe them. An application of the scientific method would have led to the sharp distinction in theory and an attempted distinction in practice between the semantics of literature and semics, and all that this entailed, but no one, not even Richards, was prepared to face the consequences of this. His commitment to scientific principles enabled him to produce the most intelligent analysis of 'literary' problems that I have ever set eyes on. Unfortunately, he stopped short of what I believe to be the derived consequences of his reasoning: the abandonment of literary-critical theory as the basis for English teaching in universities. The I-am-better-than-you dictum not only dresses the academic critic in a sacerdotal robe but baulks the professed aims of literary studies by encouraging the student to believe that, as his enjoyment of literature increases, so will his chances of succeeding in the examination.

In these opening chapters, I have described knowledge as being tripartite. The usual approach to knowledge is: 'This is true and therefore it is to be accepted'. An alternative way of considering knowledge is to say: 'This is accepted and therefore it is true'. I have attempted to follow through the implications of the second possibility. The problems of traditional approaches, which begin by delimiting the domain of knowledge, were discussed [LS:17–18]. I am aware that the concept of affidence also presents difficulties, not least in the entailment that: *truth two changes*. But we construct our speculative instruments and then see to what use they may be put. The curious attribute of the trichotomy theory, as opposed to affidence theory, is its capacity – through reciprocal perspective – to modalise itself. This is, I emphasize, an introspective verdict at the level of theoretical semics.

In succeeding chapters I shall describe a number of conceptual devices within a modal structure, which the trichotomy of knowledge makes available in establishing literary semantics as a science.

LITERARY SEMANTICS

PART II
THE THEORIES DEVELOPED

Insistence on keeping poetics apart from linguistics is warranted
only when the field of linguistics appears to be illicitly restricted.

Roman Jakobson

A. ANALEPTIC THEORY

CHAPTER 4

LITERARY SEMANTICS

The Linguistic Basis of Literary Semantics

The title of the present chapter might seem to suggest that an attempt is here being made to erect a formal linguistic category: *literature*. This, however, is not the aim. My underlying supposition in this book is that no extra-linguistic principles should be employed to describe a literary work, which, self-evidently, comprises just language.

Terms such as 'literature' and 'poetry' have obvious uses, for they succinctly include whole regions of human activity; but unfortunately the connotations of value and enjoyment, taste and appreciation, attendant upon them, are apt to render an objective approach to the problems impossible. Also, preoccupation with individual texts, while intellectually defensible, has led – an avenue I shall explore in chapters 7 and 8 – to a neglect of the rôle played by the semantic machine, the brain itself.

The critics who have tried to solve the problem of just what constitutes poetic language have generally ended by postulating a supreme poetic quality – irony, wit, paradox, texture, ambiguity, gesture or iconicity – and then proceeded to reinterpret literary works in the light of this insight. Brooks actually suggests a scale for determining the value of poetry: 'Higher in the scale, one would find poems in which the variety and clash among the elements to be comprehended under a total attitude are sharper. In tragedy... one would probably find the highest point in the scale.'[1] Further discussion of the poetic object may be found in Ransom,[2] Empson,[3] Blackmur,[4] Wimsatt[5] and Wheelwright;[6] there is a full account of the various treatments of poetic language in Hester.[7]

I find these approaches unsatisfying, and there has been no lack of critics' critics who have systematically exposed the weakness of these philosophical procedures – Righter[8] and Foster,[9] for instance. Foster argues that the so-called New Critics are distinguished by romantic sensibility and rhetoric. He even goes so far as to say that the New Critics have turned poetry into a religion.[10] The contrary view, that poetic discourse does not consist in some single and simple aesthetic function or purpose, has been expressed philosophically by Hungerland,[11] and critically by Nowottny.[12]

In order to demonstrate the type of critical statement to which I am objecting, I will cite two passages from Blackmur, *Language as Gesture*, which show lack of rigour. In chapter 1 of that book, a fundamental statement of his critical philosophy, occur:

(1)   'Past reason hunted: and no sooner had,
           Past reason hated.'[13]

           'Reading these lines, the play of meaning between *hunted* and *hated*
           so grows upon me that I cannot help thinking somewhere between the
           two, as a kind of backward consequence, of the poet as past reason
           haunted as well, for that is what the whole sonnet gives as gesture out
           of the focus of the phrases quoted. Surely one is haunted by what one
           both hunts and hates.'[14]

(2)   'The clearest and most familiar example of gesture in architecture is
           the spire on a church, for we have all seen church spires whether we
           go to church or not. Bad spires weigh a church down and are an affair
           of carpentry rather than architecture, an example of formula stifling
           form. A good spire is weightless, springing, an arrow aimed at the
           Almighty, carrying, in its gesture, the whole church with it.'[15]

Whilst there would be no difficulty in formulating objections to Blackmur's approach to the problems of literary theory, it is the purpose of the present chapter to be constructive rather than destructive. Before we proceed further, it might perhaps be helpful if some attempt were made to indicate the difference in objective between literary semantics, as I conceive of it, and literary criticism. The following passage is from Aristotle's *Poetics*:

(3)   'A tragedy, then, is the imitation of an action that is serious and also,
           as having magnitude, complete in itself; in language with pleasurable
           accessories, each kind brought in separately in the parts of the work;
           in a dramatic, not in a narrative form; with incidents arousing pity
           and fear, wherewith to accomplish its catharsis of such emotions.'[16]

As a definition of tragedy, this leaves much to be desired; the meaning of *catharsis* has been a source of endless discussion, but when we consider that this statement was made in the fourth century BC, its insight and objectivity are notable. Aristotle had many other interests besides poetics. Although in nearly all cases a slavish medieval reliance upon his authority impeded progress, scientific theory has gradually gained its autonomy, and many of Aristotle's pronouncements seem quaint when measured by the standards of scientific thought.

But let us compare with the passage from the *Poetics* a statement from a book, published in 1966, by an eminent critic at an English university:

(4)   Radiance – the requirement that literature (as distinct from other forms of verbal communication) shall satisfy and illuminate by its verbal surface, by what John Crowe Ransom calls its texture. Here we find ourselves speaking in metaphor; but in criticism we cannot get on without metaphor. By radiance we mean (it is best to get this over) all that those who deal in 'pure poetry' call 'magic'.[17]

Whilst I am not asserting that passage (4) is typical of modern critical statement, or even that it is representative of Hough's philosophy as a whole, the passage gives no evidence of marked scientific advance in poetic theory since Aristotle propounded his theory of tragedy. Nor would I wish to be hostile towards either Hough, or to literary critics in general. Literary criticism is an important human activity, always provided that it does not usurp its position. The place of literary criticism is in that vast and indefinable region of human contacts and relationships which exists in informality, wherever men and women discuss literature. No attempt should be made to legislate for it; criticism will take place within an institution, but it is not to be institutionalized; in this respect Robson's remarks might be noticed.[18]

Literary critics at universities, however, seem to me to be in an indefensible position. If the purpose of reading literature is enjoyment, or appreciation, or improvement – whatever is meant by these terms – then what purpose can university examinations in literature serve? What does an examiner aim at assessing? Does he want to know what the student's capacities for appreciation are; or how humane a person the student is? How can he be sure that the candidate would have been less appreciative, less humane, had (s)he not sat the examination? And if the purpose of reading literature is the furtherance of knowledge, then why do not the academic critics sensibly adjust, try to relate their subject to other disciplines, define their terms and attempt a classification of their subject matter?

Literary problems have been unduly complicated by a confusion of the two functions, recreative and cognitive; and by a lack of self-discipline on the part of the academic critics themselves. Blackmur's statement (1), that he cannot help thinking somewhere between 'hunted' and 'hated' to 'haunted' is an observation concerning his own mental processes. This is introspective statement, and introspective evidence deserves a place in literary theory just as much as evidence of a more objective kind. When he proceeds, however, from what he observes to have taken place in his own head to the assertion that this is what the whole sonnet gives as gesture out of the focus of the phrases quoted, he makes an illicit transposition of introspective evidence. This is the sort of shift which is constantly taking place in literary criticism. Nor am I objecting to it on the critical level. If a critic finds a reading more worthwhile as a result of an experience of this sort, and if, as a result of reading Blackmur, my own experience of reading the poem is enhanced, then this is a justification of this method at the critical level.

But literary semantics deals with such statements in a different way [LS:59–62].

A Theory of Science

The analeptic diagram [LS:52] is an attempt to show the relation between the theory of knowledge and the theory of literature expounded in Chapters 1 to 3. 'Analeptic' (derived from Greek ἀναλαμβάνω = 'I take up') is a term I use to indicate the upward movement which would appear to take place in models of this sort. I distinguish two functions of a science: the **kinetic** (Greek κῑνέω = I stir up) and the **analeptic**. This is a **modal** device – where **modality** is provisionally defined as **reciprocal perspective**: two or more components, each with different functions within the science, each in a process of co-operative but critical tension with the others. What I am about to describe, and in the remaining chapters to illustrate, is a many-layered modal theory.

The **kinetic function** is defined as that component of a science which mediates between the material from fresh observations and the received structure of the concepts of the science. The **analeptic function** is that process whereby the received structure of the science accommodates the fresh notions generated by the theorist at the level of the kinetic component. There is a fundamental opposition between these two functions; the kinetic function, being autonomous, works dynamically to organize the scientific data into new constructs, which are very often recalcitrant to the analeptic function; the analeptic function acts as a shock absorber, so that the kinetic impact, as it moves upwards analeptically, is progressively decreased.

We may say that that **science** is in a healthy state *in which the analeptic and kinetic components are functioning in equilibrium*. The analeptic function may be compared to a mobile, a hierarchy of suspended rods attached to a

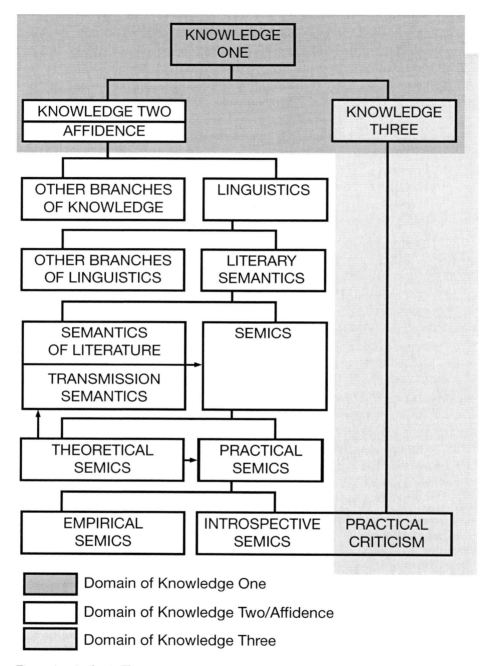

Figure 4.   Analeptic Theory

central string. The lowest sections of the hierarchy are unstable, responding to the slightest breath of air by violent rotation. A chain reaction moves up the hierarchy becoming weaker at each successive transmission upwards until, at the central string, the agitation is scarcely registered at all.

A brief illustration would be: Galileo beholds the swinging chandelier (observation); he formulates his theory of the isochronism of the pendulum (**kinetic function**); the scientific establishment assimilates his theory (**analeptic function**). In this example the analeptic function is tractable; against some of Galileo's later theories, it is unduly resistant.

More notorious is the case of Ignaz Semmelweis, the Hungarian obstetrician, who became convinced that puerperal fever was transmitted to mothers in a Viennese hospital by the student doctors themselves. He ordered the doctors to wash their hands: the mortality rate in the division concerned then rapidly decreased. His superior, Klein, remained unconvinced and, although Semmelweis was afterwards appointed obstetric physician at Budapest, he never during his lifetime received the recognition which his discovery deserved. In this case the **analepsis** worked slowly. Semmelweis' treatment illustrates the paradox of scientific progress.[19] Generalizations made on the basis of previous experiments, or perhaps in Klein's case more ignoble motives, sometimes predispose a scientific body to reject new findings. There are no infallible principles which will demonstrate whether, in any individual case, the analepsis or the kinesis is 'correct'.

This analeptic-kinetic theory of science is developed and refined more generally in the later chapters of this book. The present chapter will focus upon literary semantics.

The Organization of Literary Semantics

The **trichotomy of knowledge – knowledge one, knowledge two** and **knowledge three**, the darkly shaded frame in the diagram [LS:52], is a classification which includes everything that could ever be considered knowledge. The aim is to avoid demarcation disputes, to extend the boundaries of the term 'knowledge' and then to make clarification possible within the extended sphere of knowledge. The theory of knowledge has been expounded in chapter 1, but a synopsis and brief commentary may help at this point. **Knowledge one** has been described as 'metaphysical' by a reviewer, T. A. van Dijk, in *Neophilologus*;[20] I would prefer the term 'ultimate' where ultimate indicates a knowledge which, whether physical (in the sense of natural) or metaphysical (in the sense of supernatural, the theory being neutral to such philosophical speculation) is unalterably fixed. Man's access to knowledge one, if any he has, is through **knowledge three** and, where he believes this knowledge to be communicable, through **knowledge two**. All systems of human communication therefore belong to knowledge two. The theory postulates a hierarchy of **universes of discourse**, that is, discrete systems of communication. In reality, such systems are never discrete; nor is there any way of grading them from lowest to highest which does not lay the theorist open to a charge of arbitrariness. Finally, given that the concept of a universe of discourse, notwithstanding the above objections, is a useful one, we can, at least in theory, carry out a test to decide whether there is a high statistical acceptance of a given statement (proposition) within a given universe of discourse. Where a proposition is universally considered to be true within the highest universe of discourse proper to the branch of learning concerned, it is said to be **affident.**

The analeptic function described in the previous section is fulfilled in the **literary semantics** diagram [LS:52] by the **semantics of literature (transmission semantics), semics, theoretical semics** – in some respects the most important constituent, being the node where **kinesis** and **analepsis** meet (see the diagram [LS:101]): the controlling theoretical device for **literary semantics**, analysing, 'stirring' analeptic theory to make better sense of the raw material of kinesis. Then moving across the diagram to **practical semics**, which subsumes **empirical semics** and **introspective semics**, the latter shading off into practical criticism and **knowledge three**, the 'seat' of **value.**

In the remainder of this chapter, I shall deal briefly with each of these in turn.

Literary Semantics

Since communicable knowledge is knowledge two, we may, for theoretical purposes, equate the various university disciplines with knowledge two – though clearly they comprise only a minute subset of human communication. This is represented by the chain of boxes in the diagram subsumed beneath the knowledge two/affidence box. For the sake of clarity the darkly shaded frame [LS:52] has been confined to the three knowledge boxes, though of course theoretically it includes the boxes shown outside. The relation between a higher and a lower level in the chain is 'comprises'. Thus, trivially, knowledge two comprises linguistics and 'other branches of knowledge'.

Moving downwards, literary semantics is seen to be a branch of the linguistic sciences.[21] The definition of a literary work does constitute a difficulty – even harder than defining, as grammatical categories, a word or a sentence. At the moment, the claim for special treatment is a pragmatic one: vast numbers of writings are recognized as literary, and many scholars are struggling with the problems they present. Let these writings be the material of literary semantics; and let 'literary' remain undefined. The margins of the study, which lies completely within linguistics, will be blurred, but I hope to show that obscurity in one region of enquiry can lead to lucidity in the discipline as a whole. The linguist may thereby tackle the material of the literary critic, but with linguistic rather than 'literary' assumptions.

I choose the term 'literary semantics' rather than 'poetics' because the latter term seems to imply a rather restricted view of the literary work; and rather than 'stylistics', which would perhaps invite an oblique approach and neglect the deeper philosophical problems.[22] The definition of the term *style* is just one small problem within the massive scope of literary semantics, see chapter 10, Section, 'A Modal Theory of Style'.

The literary semanticist is concerned to draw conclusions concerning the nature of literature itself and its relation to other relevant disciplines, notably philosophy, psychology and neurophysiology; he commences with linguistic assumptions, but without linguistic dogma. In my view this ordering of literary semantics within other directions of inquiry is the central task. Textual activities I regard as important but subordinate: he tries to describe a work in linguistic terms – this would include the phonetic, lexical, syntactic and metrical elements of a work of literature – but is ready to accept the possibility he will find that parts of his text defy linguistic description, certainly in any narrow grammatical sense. In this case it is the task of the literary semanticist to extend the scope of linguistic theory to accommodate the problems posed by the text, which is, after all, by definition, a sample of language. Two books which, taken as a whole, would be classified as literary semantics are *Style in Language*,[23] and *Essays on Style and Language*.[24]

The difficulty which one faces in attempting to classify such an amorphous body of material as constitutes the description of works of literature is that the categories are bound to be a compromise between the shapelessness of what *is* and the neat classes one feels *ought* to exist – a familiar problem in science, seen for instance in the instability of flowering plant taxonomy which lingers into the 21st Century. What the two books mentioned above have in common is an apparently serious desire on the part of the various contributors to map out the problems and domain of literary studies, and to relate these to other disciplines. Sections of these books deal with specific problems within literary semantics, and would therefore be classified at a lower level within my diagram, see, for instance, Carroll, 'Vectors of Prose Style'.[25]

The Semantics of Literature
(with Transmission Semantics)

Transmission semantics is at present more of an idea than a reality. J. L. Lowes's book, mentioned below, pioneered this field of inquiry into the processes of creative composition and I have added speculation to his speculation – his fanciful reconstruction of Coleridge's alleged dream which led to

the creation of *Kubla Khan* [LS:102–104; 131–134]. With the development
of electronic technology, it may advance research into the important creative
activities of the brain.

The approach to the **semantics of literature** is always oblique. The
assumption is made that the work of literature is an event in history, and as
such is subject to historical investigation. Works such as Dorothy Whitelock's
The Audience of Beowulf,[26] G. C. Coulton's *Chaucer and his England*,[27] E.
M. W. Tillyard's *The Elizabethan World Picture*[28] and J. L. Lowes' *The Road
to Xanadu*[29] are attempts to reconstruct the semantics of literature; as also are
linguistic studies of literary works – with the reservations which are formulated
in chapter 6 – and many editions of texts in which a careful presentation is made
of historical (including biographical, textual and linguistic) material relevant to
the semantics of the text (cf. the Klaeber edition of *Beowulf*). The emphasis is
upon objectivity, upon descriptive adequacy rather than explanatory adequacy,
which latter naturally tends to belong, at least initially, to theoretical semics.
Roger Fowler's essay in Malcolm Bradbury, ed., *Contemporary Criticism* 'The
Structure of Criticism and the Languages of Poetry',[30] advocates an approach
to literature which would be classed as the study of the semantics of literature.
Fowler calls for a theory of linguistic performance sufficiently rich to accommodate the stylistic selections of the writer of those texts commonly regarded as
literary. Anthropology, he hopes, may supply a 'powerfully explanatory model
of the culture (or relevant parts of it) which makes the texts the way they are'.

Semics

Semics, the second component of literary semantics, is the study of **semic
accompaniment** – that series of **mediating reactions** which a person experiences when he reads continuously at his normal speed a passage which contains
for him no linguistic difficulties.[31] At the theoretical level, this is a purely neutral
term, objective, scientific, without any built-in ethical or aesthetic assumptions.
It is concerned with how people in reality *do* read, not how they *ought* to read.
Where such assumptions are found to underlie subjects' reading, then, by **modal
reduction**, they become a part of what is studied. As was stated [LS:48], this
avenue leads to the brain itself.

Just as in linguistics it may be assumed that no two idiolects are the
same, so the assumption is here made that no two semic accompaniments
are identical; not only do they vary from person to person, but also with the
same person from one reading of the same literary work to the next. Literary
critics normally assume uniformity, that is to say that there is one given literary
object which exists independently of their experience; the diversity of view
expressed by other beholders of the object is held to result from their imperfect

comprehension of the object. The semic approach is to assume diversity (which, given the complexity of the human brain on the one hand, and the diversity of 'literature' on the other, seems to be a commonsense working assumption) and, where there is a large measure of agreement, to allow inferences concerning referential properties of the art object.

The advantages of this method are twofold. Firstly, much of the vehement dispute which takes place at the moment is curtailed, the protagonists accepting at the outset that they are referring to two or more different entities: the **modal** approach places disparate semic accompaniments in **reciprocal perspective**. Secondly, objective investigation of semic accompaniment is rendered more practicable when a descriptive method replaces a prescriptive one. At present, students are expected to persuade their mentors that they have had a particular kind of semic accompaniment: one which shows 'sensitivity', appreciation, originality or even political bias, irrespective of disciplined judgment. They are rewarded or punished according as their professions concerning their semic accompaniments please or displease the academic critics within the department.

Theoretical Semics

Semics comprises **theoretical semics** and **practical semics**. The function of **theoretical semics** is explanatory whilst the function of practical semics is experimental and descriptive. Scientific progress depends upon the co-ordination of the functions within a discipline, and it is one rôle of the **theoretical semicist** to generate possible explanations of the problems of literary semantics. In reality, the theoretical function cannot be divorced from the other functions, though it is a fact that scientists tend to be primarily either theorists or practitioners (see, however, the distinction between the individual scientist and the science [LS:105]); in astronomy, for instance, it is one function to use the telescope and another function to build the telescopic observations into a cosmology. An example of a work in theoretical semics is *Recurrence and a Three-Modal Approach to Poetry*, by W. Koch,[32] in which the author experiments with the possibility of applying a transformational approach to poetry. My own **dynamic-axial theory**, expounded in chapters 7 and 8 – and version of frame theory, from which a new **theory of fictionality** is derived – are also classified as exercises in theoretical semics.

There is a reciprocal arrow from theoretical semics to the semantics of literature. This is illustrated in Fowler,[33] for, although the approach is one which advocates the study of the semantics of literature, his actual essay would belong to theoretical semics. Expressing this differently, he is not so much concerned to make an historical description of a particular piece of literature, as to show through examples how this would be theoretically possible.

Practical Semics

The function of practical semics is the description and classification of the data furnished by empirical and introspective semics. For an understanding of how this works, please see [LS:60–62; 116–126; chapter 13 *passim*].

Empirical Semics

The empirical semicist tries to be objective. His material is the description by subjects of their semic accompaniments, and any other behaviourist evidence, psychological or neurophysiological, relevant to the semic accompaniment of a subject. An example of the rigour demanded of an empirical semicist may be seen in J. B. Carroll's paper, 'Vectors of Prose Style'.[34] Carroll selected 150 short prose passages in various styles and carried out a detailed analysis of the objective 'measures' (sentence length, clause structure etc.) and, aided by eight expert judges, 'all with interest and training in English literature', obtained subjective judgments against twenty-nine bipolar scales. His aim was to find out how reliable the measures, both objective and subjective, were, and to assess the 'dimensions of prose style'. Carroll's method is an adaptation of Osgood's semantic differential. More recently, David Crystal and Derek Davy in *Investigating English Style* have undertaken a similar enquiry, but on Firthian lines, finding their 'dimensions' in the situation of the speaker/writer rather than in the subjective response of the reader. Having attempted to refine the Hallidayan concept of 'register', which they find inadequate, they carry out with some sophistication textual analyses. None of the texts chosen is literary. The analysis of situation belongs normally to the semantics of literature (or **transmission semantics**), and the emphasis in their theoretical discussion is upon the speaker/writer in his original situation.[35] This is not the place for a detailed consideration of the respective merits of the semantic differential and the Firthian techniques in stylistic analysis but see the further comment [LS: 183].

Applying the theory of affidence to Blackmur's statement (1), we may formulate the two following propositions:

(5)   At a given reading of the quoted lines, Blackmur's semic accompaniment – stimulated by the similarity, partly phonetic, partly semantic, of 'hunted' and 'hated' – supplied by association a third term 'haunted'.

(6)   'Haunted' is what the whole sonnet gives as gesture out of the focus of the phrases quoted.

Taking any linguistics association as the appropriate universe of discourse, I would predict that (5) is affident. We have no reason to believe that Blackmur was not telling the truth, and our best access to the **semic accompaniment** of others is, short of electronic investigation, their own description. Proposition (6), however, judged according to my own **affidence-assessment**, is **inaffident**. Blackmur's use of the term 'gesture' is notoriously **insecure**; see for instance the discussion in Righter[36] and Foster[37]. A **secure** term is one which all participants in an **affidence test** are satisfied they understand within the context of the given proposition. By this theoretical device we can separate Blackmur's assertion into two parts. We do not say that (5), because it describes a subjective experience, is unimportant. As a statement of the sort of verbal coalescence which takes place under some circumstances during the reading of a work of literature, it is of potential interest. As long as the passage is seen as the description of one man's semic accompaniment, it will have been afforded a location at the correct theoretical level. But Blackmur will not be permitted to transmute his description into something objective to which he, by poetic perceptivity, has acceded.

This is an example of **modal reduction**: the theorist at the level of **theoretical semics** rewrites the statement at two levels – (5) for **empirical semics**, and (6) for **introspective semics**. Within the organization of **literary semantics**, there are many functions; the assumption is that an attempt to separate and classify these functions in a hierarchy of modes will clarify problems and lead to progress. This cognitive analysis has nothing directly to do with the enjoyment of literature. I am certain that many millions of enjoyable semic accompaniments are occurring at this very moment and such valued recreative activities are independent of literary semantic inquiry.

Introspective Semics

We come finally to the box labelled 'introspective semics'. It will immediately be observed that this adjoins the 'practical criticism' box located within the knowledge three lightly-shaded frame [LS:52]. As with most diagrams, this representation simplifies the reality. Blackmur's statement (1), concerning the coalescence of 'hunted' and 'hated', would, according to the present theory, be introspective semics. Blackmur would doubtless have regarded it as practical criticism. My own analysis of the statement, if correct, showed, above, that it was of limited communicability. Blackmur has conveyed to me that he had a semic accompaniment in which 'hunted' and 'hated' in some way for him stimulated the association 'haunted', but he has failed to convince me that this is what the whole sonnet 'gives as gesture'; and, what is more, he has not succeeded in persuading me that he has said anything of importance. This is not to deny the possibility that some of Blackmur's readers may have been led by his statement to experiences which they considered valuable. What transpires is that where value judgments and interpretations are concerned, communication is limited, intermittent and fortuitous. It is limited because, although a critic may persuade us that an experience was valuable for him, or that an interpretation was the correct one for him, he may or may not cause it to become valuable for us; may or may not convince us of the rightness of the interpretation. The communication is intermittent in that only parts of his value-judgment may be accepted with ethical or aesthetic commitment by any reader. Finally, it is fortuitous in that ethical and aesthetic exhortations, unlike many intellectual propositions which are **affident**, are blatantly unpredictable in the reception they meet with: educated and intelligent men are prone to give widely differing value judgments concerning the same object and, what is more, investigators themselves vary from day to day in their judgments.

Introspective Semics, Practical Criticism and Value

It follows from what we have just said that the scientific structure of literary semantics shades off into a new domain at that point where value statements begin to be made. In Hough,[38] there occurs the following assertion:

(7)   'Literary works like other works of art are constructed to be objects of value; so value judgements cannot be peripheral and accidental things; they must be of central importance.'

To this, we may firstly object, in the absence of a definition of value, that a scientific treatise is also constructed to be an object of value; nor is value-judgment absent in the decision of a reader who accepts or rejects a given scientific treatise. But a scientist who allows value language to pervade his criticism of a treatise abandons the principles of his science.

Secondly, the form of this statement is deceptive. It bears a superficial resemblance to:

(8)   This creature is an insect, so it ought to have three pairs of legs.

Hough is using his argument to vindicate the fundamental rôle which value judgment plays in literary criticism. To support his claim he invokes the intentions of those who created the art object. But does it necessarily follow that the student of any entity must adopt as germane to his own purpose the attitudes of those human agents responsible for the entity? If this were the case, then by the same token we might claim that the most satisfactory mental state for investigation of spiritualism is a *trance*, or alcoholism, a *stupor*. Plainly, Hough's assumption could, if pressed to its logical termination, oblige him to defend absurdities. Although, in fact, (7) resembles the analytical statement (8), it is not really analytical at all: Hough has conjoined two separate assumptions, but in such a way syntactically as to imply that the second is necessitated by the first. If I may therefore, without disrespect, rewrite (7) in the form that I believe it should have assumed, it would read as follows:

(9)   'Literary works, like other works of art, are constructed to be objects of value. *I would further assert* that value judgments must be of central importance in literary criticism.'

Hough's argument contains a secreted assumption which, in my view, has impeded the study of literature: that such study can be satisfactorily performed only when the investigator allows his attitudes to change the 'ontological shape' of the entity described. This is what is happening in the case of (1) and (2).[39] Should this not be self-evident, a decision as to whether the 'ontological shape' of a text has in fact been distorted by a subjective view could be made on the basis of the **criterion of principles** for empirical semics [LS:87–88]. If the second part of Hough's statement (7) presents us not with a corollary of the first, but rather with a second questionable assumption, it could be the case that this second assumption has diverted students from fields of enquiry that might with profit be explored. Of course, this argument does not affect Hough's position: he is a literary critic and not a literary semanticist.

One final illustration in this chapter will serve to show the location of value judgments within the diagrams [LS:52; 174]. F. W. Bateson makes a brief critical exposition of Blake's poem 'And did those feet in ancient time'.[40] The title of the chapter in which this occurs is 'The Primacy of Meaning', and Bateson is attempting to show that, far from being the simple straightforward affair it is sometimes supposed to be, poetry is often very obscure, and impossible to understand without detailed notes. He is in effect arguing in favour of the semantics of literature: that is to say, by historical research we can recover references in the text which are missed by the modern reader.

Turning to Blake's poem, which now has a popular hymn setting, Bateson says, 'How many of the millions of men and women who chant these lines every year could really say what they are all about?' He draws attention to several respects in which the putative semic accompaniments of modern churchgoers fail to correspond with the semantics of literature. The 'dark Satanic mills' have, he says, nothing to do with the Industrial Revolution. Further, he argues that in the following stanza,

(10)   I will not cease from mental fight,
         Nor shall my sword sleep in my hand,
         Till we have built Jerusalem
         In England's green and pleasant land.

'Jerusalem' does not refer to a 'Utopia of garden cities and national parks', but
to 'sexual liberty'. The semantics of literature therefore shows this to be an
'anti-clerical paean of free love', and Bateson finds it amusing that so many
devout people should be unaware of what they are singing.

It is not my purpose to examine the evidence upon which Bateson bases
his reconstruction of the semantics of literature. What is at issue here is that,
on Bateson's own admission, this hymn is sung by millions of people who
believe the sentiments to be wholly acceptable to the Almighty. For many of
them, no doubt, the singing of the hymn is an experience of **value**, where value
is a man's conviction (knowledge three) that he has access in some degree to
knowledge one. We have here the odd spectacle of a literary critic employing
the principles of the semantics of literature in order to legislate the value out of
a religious experience. For it is surely implicit in Bateson's argument that, if the
people really knew what they were singing, that is, the semantics of literature
of Blake's poem, then the experience of singing the hymn would lose its value
for them.[41] What could have been a clear rational enquiry into the semantics
of literature, supplemented perhaps by investigation into the semic accompaniment of the singers, has, as a result of the introduction of value-discourse,
been turned into a convolved and perplexing skein of intellectual, ethical and
aesthetic considerations. The discourse, we may say, is gradually moving out of
the realms of literary semantics into the domain of knowledge three. Chapter 5
will deal with Bateson's views in more detail.

CHAPTER 5

LITERARY SEMANTICS AND LITERARY CRITICISM

The Bateson-Fowler Controversy

A dispute referred to between F. W. Bateson and Roger Fowler was initiated in a review by Helen Vendler in *Essays in Criticism*, October 1966, of the book edited by Fowler, *Essays on Style and Language*. I will summarize the general points made in the review and the subsequent arguments of Bateson and Fowler, as these provide a useful synopsis of the language-literature controversy. There then follows a discussion of the points raised by Vendler and Bateson, during the course of which it will be demonstrated how literary semantics treats the material traditionally the subject-matter of literary criticism.

Vendler: Ineptitude of Linguists

Mrs. Vendler concentrates her attack upon the literary ineptitude of the linguists. The best linguists can barely manage to cope scientifically with even simple sentences[1] and they are undereducated in the reading of poetry, whose primary sense and value they are not equipped to absorb.[2] Linguistic critics are continually guilty of missing 'the indispensable point of grief or pleasure' in the poems they read,[3] and she cites examples of what she calls 'crudities' of literary perception.[4] Referring to the essays in Fowler's book, she accuses most of the contributing linguists of being over-general or trivial[5] and she compares the book unfavourably with David Lodge's *Language of Fiction*.[6] The latter work shows how far ahead of the linguists the literary people are in the ability 'to respond rightly to a piece of literary language'. What she awaits is proof that the linguist can help the critics with a given text.[7]

The superiority of the critical approach is to be seen in the type of questions its exponents attempt to answer.[8] She cites Roger Fowler's essay on Bacon; Fowler's principles, she thinks, are sensible, but his description of Bacon's 'tripartite scheme in his grammatical constructions' is nothing more than useful pre-critical material. The critical act goes beyond description and asks, 'What is the effect here of threes in preference to fours? Are there more threes elsewhere in Bacon? Who else, like Bacon, has a liking for threes? Why?'

Thirdly, she complains about the linguists' use of technical terms. The linguist triumphantly 'discovers' the old figures of rhetoric, affixing to them scientific labels.[9] Her attack upon their jargon reaches its peak in her review of Mr. Sinclair's essay in Fowler's book. Sinclair's analysis, she says, is an example of cumbersome and unpalatable exposition of a particularly inept Larkin poem, and she finds irony in the fact that Sinclair claims he has carried out his exercise without evaluation.[10]

Her view of the potential contribution of the linguists to literary studies is more optimistic. Freudian theory has proved useful to the critics and we may expect that the linguists will, in the end, be extremely helpful.[11] They cannot be expected to turn overnight into exquisite readers of poetry, and the literary critics have in the meantime the obligation to study the output of the linguists in the hope that it will provide new, critical approaches.[12]

Bateson's Model

In a brief Editorial Postscript to Vendler's review, Bateson argues that her optimism for the future contribution of linguistics to literary criticism is ill-founded.[13] Her point about Freudian criticism betrays the linguistic case: only the amateur psychoanalysts have succeeded as literary critics – the experts do not seem to know 'what criticism is all about'. The study of literature is primarily one of *parole*; what is needed is a *stylistics* which will concentrate upon that specialized form of *langue* which may be extrapolated from the *parole*, the individual works of literature; this specialized form Bateson calls *style*. This stylistics will limit itself to whatever aspires to literary value in manuscript or print, and the student of style should go 'forwards' from his text into its *context of situation* rather than 'backwards' into the language he already knows.

Fowler's Three Approaches

Fowler's reply to the review and to Bateson's Editorial Postscript is an attempt to clarify the linguistic position. He distinguishes three approaches, which, for the sake of present reference, I shall here label (a), (b) and (c): (a) a wholly linguistic analysis; (b) an exercise with critical motives, which nevertheless employs a selection of linguistic apparatus; (c) an entirely critical treatment by a critic who happens also to be a linguist. Nothing is to be gained from representing the differing orientations of the two disciplines as a confrontation between two diametrically opposed camps. Fowler argues that it is just as important for critics to realise that there are many forms and functions of linguistics as for linguists to comprehend the various activities of critics.

The simplification of the issues is to be seen in the widely held view that science and poetry are polar opposites. This is a distortion of the true state of affairs: the problem of objectivity is the same for the critic as for the linguist,[14] and their positions are closer than is realised. Linguistic analysis is a subsequent process; it is undertaken to confirm a prior 'hunch'. In other words, far from being 'dedicated to an ideal of objective description, that is unsullied by the values of ordinary human experience' as Bateson claims,[15] the 'hunch' builds in values at the outset.[16] Fowler takes pains to moderate his claims for the scientific revelations of linguistics; he even alleges that, overall, linguistics merely *affects scientism*;[17] this drastic assertion he later qualifies.[18] Conversely, an indictment which can be made of literary criticism, even of the New Criticism, is that there has been a failure to achieve objectivity, a failure to come to grips with 'the poem itself'.[19]

Fowler then proceeds to consider the relation between linguistic description of and critical comment upon a given text. I assume that the approach is the second, (b), of the three listed by Fowler at the beginning of his argument: a critically motivated exposition employing a selection of linguistic techniques. Fowler will not accept Mrs. Vendler's allegations that the linguist merely provides useful pre-critical material, if that means that this is all he can ever do.[20] There is no reason why a linguist should not be a critic as well as a linguist, his linguistic techniques constituting a useful function within his critical approach.[21] There is a reciprocal relation between linguistic analysis and critical comment: the critical faculty guides the linguistic analysis and the analysis in turn confirms the critical intuitions.

Fowler admits finally that some linguists have made over-confident claims for their discipline. The rôle of linguistics should not be exaggerated: in time, its jargon will settle down and become a useful medium in the communication of critical ideas. Linguistics is an essential part of literary education[22] and Fowler appeals to the literary people 'who hold the reins of power almost everywhere in the humanities nowadays' to try and understand the case for the linguists, who want neither rivalry nor subordination but a chance 'to help educate the next generation of critics in an approach indisputably relevant to their labours and to their greater pleasure'.[23]

Bateson's Reply to Fowler:
Criticism is Independent of Linguistics

Bateson's reply to Fowler's argument amounts to an acceptance of Fowler's approach (a), a wholly linguistic analysis. Bateson defends Sinclair's essay, which Vendler had reviled;[24] he sceptically agrees to differ concerning (c), an entirely critical treatment by a critic who happens to be a linguist;[25] and he absolutely rejects any suggestion that the linguistic-critical twain shall meet – point (b). The latter rejection constitutes the core of his argument, and I will attempt a summary.

Bateson admits that, in any discourse, evaluation and description are inextricably linked: evaluative phrases, he says, creep into Sinclair's 'objective' analysis.[26] Literary criticism, on the other hand, cannot get by without some descriptive material. Nevertheless when we have allowed that linguists may in unguarded moments find themselves talking like literary critics, and that literary criticism needs some information content, it must be accepted that most discourse takes unmistakably either an evaluative or a descriptive *direction*.[27]

Bateson, being more ready than Fowler to allow linguistics the rank of science, defends Sinclair's use of jargon against Mrs. Vendler.[28] Descriptive linguistics is a science 'headed towards total description – a detached, objective, universally available discipline'.[29] Literature, on the other hand, has its 'ineradicable subjective core'.[30]

In practice, this means that the science of linguistics is committed to division of the verbal material, whereas literary criticism, through style, attempts a *synthesis* of literature's disparate linguistic parts.[31] Bateson thus reasserts the polarity of the linguistic and critical activities, which Fowler strove to avoid; grammar is analytic, style is synthetic.[32]

Bateson then quotes Professor Sol Saporta's essay in *Style in Language*.[33] Saporta suggests that the language of poetry is characterized by the density of its 'sequences of lower-order grammaticalness' rising at times to an 'optimum ungrammaticalness'. Bateson approves of this and cites an example from Pound, 'Papyrus',[34] to illustrate that the principles underlying poetic word-order are not those of grammar:

(1)   Spring …
               Too long …
               Gongula …

is a sequence of words which 'undoubtedly functions as a poem'. Grammatically, the poem is incomplete, but Bateson sees the dots as 'a kind of visual rhyme, which is reinforced both by the actual half-rhymes (-ing, -ong, Gong-) and by the 'syllabic crescendo' (one-syllable line followed by two-syllable line followed by three-syllable line)'.[35] Literary comment confines itself to stylistic points and avoids the grammatical as irrelevant. This is why the impression left by such analyses as Sinclair's is one of futility.

Bateson then goes on to attack the type of question set in the Oxford Modern English paper, part of the Final Examinations. The candidates are asked to comment on and explain major points of historical interest in the language of a passage, in this case from *Troilus and Criseyde*.[36] Bateson suggests one or two points which the examiners might be expecting, the survival of the inflected infinitive 'to doone', for example. But the examiners avoid the stylistic consequences of the question, 'Why was not Chaucer embarrassed or distressed by such linguistic inconsistencies and oddities?' Bateson's answer is that Chaucer employed stylistic peculiarities in order to avoid sounding pretentious when *Troilus and Criseyde* was delivered orally at the court of Richard II. Bateson seems to be in no doubt concerning the satisfactoriness of his 'esemplastic' approach. His exposition of the passage is confident and he prefers indicative to subjunctive statement: 'Social presumption was thus cancelled out by bourgeois clumsiness or vulgarity'. 'But Chaucer is careful not to show off his learning too blatantly before the King and his court'. [37]

Bateson sees in the *Troilus* passage further illustration of Saporta's 'optimum ungrammaticalness', and hopes he has made his point that the student would be more usefully employed in such esemplastic exercises than in memorising the finer points of Middle English linguistics or modern neo-grammatics. 'Stylistic discrimination is the one indispensable prerequisite for the aesthetic appreciation of great literature'.[38] Bateson allows linguistics certain minor uses in literary studies, but the central point of his argument is that Fowler is presenting the study of language as a necessary concomitant to the study of literature: 'For the native speaker, except occasionally and superficially, this is simply not true'.

Fowler: A Definition of Style

Fowler, in his second reply, moves from a defence of the linguistic critic to an attack upon Bateson's own position.

Bateson's own aesthetic, says Fowler, is a complicated set of criteria, drawn from Coleridge, Richards and de Saussure. By equating non-grammatical structures with literary structures, Bateson is giving sanction to the belief, of which Mrs. Vendler complained in her review,[39] that Dylan Thomas is the normative model of literary language.[40] Bateson is further importing magical concepts from Coleridge to account for phenomena which it would be within the scope of a more sophisticated linguistic analysis to explain. Bateson perpetuates the emotive-descriptive dichotomy of Richards, although it has long been acknowledged that it is an undue simplification of the thousands of varieties of specialized usages adapted to the needs of topic, function and situation.[41] Bateson, finally, in his reference to *langue* and *parole* has misunderstood de Saussure.

Fowler leads on from this to the second main strand of his argument: because Bateson has misunderstood the nature of linguistics his attempt to disqualify this discipline from literary studies fails. Fowler makes the distinction, now a commonplace in linguistic circles, between 'Bloomfieldian, *alias* structural, *alias* descriptive' linguistics, which proceeded mechanically, and Chomskyan linguistics, which aims at explanatory adequacy. Just as the Chomskyan approach has proved fruitful with non-deviant language, so it may well be applicable to literary studies. 'The "linguistic analysis" of literature is an attempt to make explicit part of the process of reading by the use of terms and concepts which have psychological reality (are humane even if they are scientific) through being appropriate to the reader's individually internalized yet culturally shared grammar of the language.'[42] Fowler does not see why such a linguistics should be intrinsically alien to certain parts of literary study.

Fowler now attempts a definition of style which is not exclusively literary: 'a formal, but non-grammatical, level of language at which interesting, if syntactically insignificant, patterns occur'. He goes on to outline the Chomskyan explanation of how language provides an infinite number of possible sentences out of a finite number of syntactic patterns, and he indicates the capabilities and limitations of a grammar. But where *langue* (or competence) ceases *parole* begins. *Langue* is the undisputed province of the linguist; *parole* is subject to extra-linguistic factors. But even *parole* is within the scope of *applied linguistics*.[43]

Reverting to his essay on Bacon's 'tripartite structures', Fowler suggests that these structures might be said to conform, not to a syntactic, but to a 'stylistic rule'. 'They have an indispensable linguistic basis, however, and this makes grammatical description both valuable and necessary'.[44] Fowler's reconstruction of the situation would appear to be as follows: the grammatical rules of linguistic competence, supplemented by rhetorical (in a very broad sense) rules appropriate to the social context, produce a stylistic text. These rhetorical rules are based upon, but are superordinate to, the rules of grammar. The process, whether purely grammatical or stylistic, depends upon the same performance mechanisms, phonetic, neurophysiological, genetic etc. – and the end product, whether rhetorical rules operate or not, is a linguistic text.[45]

Fowler concludes: 'The false norm of non-literary language is being invoked to provide background for a spurious category "literary language". But in reality the sense in which there is a gap between the "normal language" and any distinctive text is the same for all texts: there is the grammar (*langue*, competence) and what you do with the grammar (*parole*, performance, e.g. texts identified stylistically). In the light of this fundamental tenet of linguistic theory there is no formal category literature'.[46]

Bateson's Second Reply:
An Aesthetic View of Style

Bateson is disturbed by Fowler's wooing of the literary critics, when he is unable to provide examples of the usefulness of the linguistic approach in literary studies. Fowler's silence on the subject would imply that Sinclair's essay is critically indefensible; nor has Fowler explained Bacon's predilection for threes.[47] Mr. Bateson now offers his own explanation: five of the ten 'tripartite structures' may be explained away without recourse to grammar; the remaining five may be accounted for by saying that Bacon 'occasionally used a triad to add variety to the predominant antithesis'.[48]

Nor has Fowler accepted the challenge which Bateson laid down, in his earlier argument, to the historical and descriptive linguists to apply their tools to the literary interpretation of the passage from *Troilus and Criseyde*. Bateson suggests that this is a necessary incompetence; a native speaker takes grammar and vocabulary in his stride, but the complexities of style are almost infinite, and have to be taught.

Reverting to the Saussurean *langue-parole* dichotomy, Bateson accuses Fowler of not fully realising that '*parole* (actual conversation between a real A and a real B) is always logically prior to *langue*'. The sequence of events is: extra-linguistic events bring about a new human context for *parole*; *parole* takes on new characteristics; a new or modified *langue* emerges. There is an exact parallel in literary usage: a writer inherits a particular *langue* and certain literary conventions; these are modified by extra-linguistic and extra-literary conventions; *parole* then reconstructs *langue* and a new fashionable usage is born.[49]

Bateson then gives an account of a literary transaction. The author knows what he wants to say and how he wishes to say it. This knowledge constitutes his 'style' and it precedes the act of writing. For the reader, the process is reversed: confronted by the written formulation, he works his way through to the style. 'And it is only via the style that he becomes capable of a proper literary response to what he is reading'.[50] Bateson suggests that Fowler cannot get beyond the linguistic phase to the stylistic phase and that, as a result, the full aesthetic response is denied to him. This verbal immobility of the linguists explains why the critic finds so little nourishment in modern linguistics in any of its forms. Bateson concludes, 'Not here, O Apollo, are haunts meet for thee'.[51]

Roger Fowler, then, contends that the study of language, by the methods of linguistics, is a necessary condition of literary studies, and that there is a reciprocal relation between linguistics and literary criticism.[52] He argues, in effect, for a reasonable compromise. The contrary view, as argued jointly, or in some cases separately, by Mrs. Vendler and F. W. Bateson, may be recapitulated under four headings:

(i)   that the critical approach is superior;
(ii)   that linguistics is not necessary for the study of literature;
(iii)   that linguists are unable to respond rightly to a piece of literature;
(iv)   that linguists, instead of going forward into the style, go backwards into the language they already know;

Bateson thus bluntly spurns compromise.

Literary Criticism

In the above argument, Mr. Bateson rejects any suggestion that linguistics might not after all be a science. His motives are not altruistic: he fears that a concession here may lead to the de-polarization of disciplines which Mr. Fowler would bring about. Bateson, in other words, is contending that there are two discrete **universes of discourse**: the linguistic and the critical. We begin by accepting Bateson's argument that the two are, for all practical purposes, mutually exclusive. My ultimate purpose in this book will be to demonstrate that literary semantics, as a sub-division of linguistics and the philosophy of language, provides a theoretical structure which is both tidy and sane.

Firstly, I will demonstrate that the critical approach as evinced in the Bateson/Vendler argument in support of literary criticism is *unnecessarily* lacking in rigour; that because it falls short of the standards we have the right to demand of an academic discipline, literary criticism is scantly provided for the task it professes to undertake. *Secondly*, I will contest Bateson's statement that linguistics is not necessary to the study of literature. *Thirdly*, I shall show that Bateson fails to draw obvious inferences from authors whom he cites in support of his own arguments – inferences which refute the very conclusions he is claiming to draw. *Fourthly*, I shall show that his analysis of style raises serious educational questions. These four contentions seem to constitute the core of the Bateson/Vendler argument.

(i) *that the critical approach is superior*

Mrs. Vendler observes that, whilst Mr. Fowler's principles are sensible, he stops short of asking questions which a good critic would ask. His material is therefore 'pre-critical'. The questions a critic asks, continues Mrs. Vendler, after observing the tripartite structures in Bacon, are: (a) What is the effect here of threes in preference to fours? (b) Are there more threes elsewhere in Bacon? (c) Who else, like Bacon, has a liking for threes? (d) Why?

The precise meaning of (a), 'What is the effect here of threes in preference to fours?', is not clear. Does the question mean 'What effect does this have on a particular reader?' (**introspective semics**), or 'What effect ought it to have upon an ideal reader?' Alternatively, has it something to do with Bacon's conscious or unconscious intentions (**semantics of literature**; **transmission semantics**)? Questions (b) and (c) are within the scope of the **semantics of literature** and are not 'critical' questions; Fowler's method is not being impugned – he might simply have covered more ground, searching further in, and beyond, Bacon's writings. Question (d) is in the field of psychology (**empirical semics**) and could perhaps be answered if psychology were further advanced and we had more evidence of the working of Bacon's psyche (**semantics of literature**). There emerges from these four questions only one which could be considered the exclusive territory of the literary critic, and that is the question in (a) which Mrs. Vendler does not make explicit, but which, bearing in mind the literary critical obsession for avoiding the 'intentional' and 'affective' 'fallacies',[53] I think she means, 'What ought the effect here to be, upon an ideal reader, of threes in preference to fours?'

The concept of the ideal reader is one to be regarded with misgiving; it is paralleled in linguistics, but not exactly, by the concept of the ideal speaker-listener. The latter is a useful procedural device which enables linguists to render their material more tractable (but see also the discussion in chapter 15). The notion of the 'ideal reader' in literary criticism does not serve solely the purpose of convenience: there exists a deal of difference between 'This is grammatical, is it not?' and 'A sensitive and perceptive reader would rightly respond in the following manner'. Aesthetic and ethical considerations are here exposing themselves, and we are moving towards a hierarchy of taste.

But let us take a generous view of the domain of literary criticism, and allow that these questions are the sort which only literary critics are qualified to answer. Boundaries between disciplines can be justified only as long as they are useful; if a scholar, in order to make an important discovery, must trespass upon the territory of other disciplines, so much the worse for the boundaries which tend to discourage him. Are these questions so momentous that answering them will add considerably to our understanding of the problems of literature? We can scarcely give judgment upon this until we know the answers, and Mrs. Vendler and F. W. Bateson are no more encouraging in their failure to answer the questions than Fowler is in his failure to ask them. Bateson's answer to the question 'Why did Bacon prefer threes?' that 'Bacon occasionally used a triad to add variety to the predominant antithesis' comes very close to asserting that Bacon preferred threes sometimes because he sometimes preferred threes. Bateson admits that this observation is not 'earthshaking'.

Bateson further argues that whereas the linguists divide, the critics synthesize the verbal material.[54] The linguist is here receiving less than justice at Bateson's hands. Certainly, linguists tend to be analytical in their approach, but this does not entail that analysis is the frontier of their ambitions. Analysis is frequently the first step towards synthesis, and some of the most analytical discoveries in the natural sciences have proved to be synthetic, or 'esemplastic'; a microscopic discovery is not necessarily a trivial one. Of course, if it can be demonstrated that the linguists are groping analytically whilst the critics are providing the sought answers synthetically, then this would be a forceful indictment of the linguists. It may be that the critics are answering important questions, but I see no evidence of this in the critical arguments offered in the discussion. Certainly, Bateson's attempt to show that grammar is not essential to poetry does nothing to reinforce his position.

(ii) _that linguistics is not necessary for the study of literature_

At the point in his argument where he wishes to illustrate that poetry and grammar are independent of each other, Bateson quotes a text from Ezra Pound's collected poems 'Papyrus':

(1)   Spring ...
           Too long ...
           Gongula ...

This is, says Bateson, 'generally recognized today to be a good English poem in its own right'.[55]

In order to prove his contention, Bateson argues that (-ing, -ong, Gong-) are actual 'half rhymes'; that the succession of one, two and three syllables constitutes a syllabic crescendo; and that even the dots act as a kind of visual rhyme.

Let any linguistic element which occurs twice or more be called a **recurrence**.[56] Let us further assume that what Bateson says about the unmistakable direction of a particular stretch of discourse is true [LS:66]; let 'recurrence' be a descriptive, not an evaluative word. There are forty or so phonemes in English, and the text we are considering contains about sixteen – the uncertainty as to the exact number depends upon the pronunciation of 'Gongula'. Given any random succession of English morphemes of comparable length, it is highly probable that certain phonemes, and even sequences of phonemes will recur. The sentence 'This is the news', for example, – [ðis iz ðə njuːz] in Jones/ Gimson transcription – contains phonemic recurrence of [ð], [i], [z]; also [i] + sibilants [s]...[z]; and graphemic recurrence of – is...is. Pound's text gives no more evidence of recurrence than might many groups of four words drawn randomly from a text, or even an alphabetical list of names. Bateson uses this text to comment adversely on Sinclair's work, and he belittles the grammatical content of poetry as a relic of the primitive linguistic basis in common speech.

By 'grammar', Bateson seems to imply what most grammarians, speaking strictly, would call 'syntax'. He thus imposes an initial restriction upon the grammarians, which they would not accept: that the text is beyond their competence because it contains no syntactic structures, though it might be mentioned that 'Too long' is in fact so structured. Lexical, phonological and semantic items are just as much within the scope of a grammatical theory as syntactic items.[57]

Bateson's informal syllogism seems to run: this is a poem; this is not grammatical; therefore some poetry is not grammatical. The second premise has already been called in question. The first premise begs the important question 'What is poetry?' The answer to this objection might be that there is no need to define poetry; poetry is intuitively recognized by literary critics. Mr. Bateson himself in a footnote cites, in support of his statement, a book by G. S. Fraser, *Ezra Pound*. The passage to which Bateson alludes is a reply to Robert Graves, the poet and literary critic, who, in his book *The Common Asphodel*,[58] expressed surprise that 'Papyrus' could be considered a poem. Fraser considers Graves's attack a splendid piece of invective, but he also believes that he is 'making heavy weather of what is a simple but rather good little joke'.[59] Fraser goes on to explain that the poem is an imaginary translation of a papyrus fragment, the dots indicating parts of the work which have been lost. Gongula, he infers from the context, is a girl's name. Fraser rewrites the work, filling in the gaps:

(2)   Spring (has come again).
        Too long (have I been away from thee),
        Gongula (my dearest).

'The little joke is that simple love lyrics are monotonously the same in any civilization', concludes Fraser.

Although Fraser's judgment would seem to be that 'Papyrus' is a little joke, and he does not seem to be suggesting that the work functions as a poem, Bateson has cited him apparently in support of his claim that there is a consensus of opinion in literary circles which regards this as a good English poem. We have arrived at the following position: we know that this is a poem because Bateson and the literary critics assure us that it is; and they know it is a poem because, according to Bateson's analysis, it contains typographic recurrence (the repetition of the dots), phonological recurrence (the repetition of vowel + ng) and because the number of syllables in successive lines is one: two: three.

A simple exercise would be to remove the lines one by one. We know that if we remove all three lines, the 'poetry' will have disappeared, for Bateson implies that he would not accept a blank page as possessing literary merit.[60] If we progressively shorten the text, there should be a point at which we eliminate the 'poetry'.

(3)   Spring ...
            Too long ...

In (3), the (vowel + (ng)) recurrence, and the typographical recurrence have been decreased by one in each case; the number of syllables, which was before one: two: three, is now one: two. Has the 'poetry' decreased proportionately?

(4)   Spring ...

In (4), the recurrence has disappeared altogether, as has the syllabic increase. Has the 'poetry' also disappeared? I must confess that I do not know the answer to this, but I am forced to the conclusion that either poetry is co-extensive with certain textual signals, or the critic will have, at this point, to invoke mysticism. For this insight, I am grateful not to the literary-critical training I received at Oxford, but to logic and to elementary linguistics.

(iii) *that linguists are unable to respond rightly to a piece of literature*

Literary critics are entitled to build mysticism into their basic assumptions, though any show of rational argument on these lines can be little more than a masquerade. The linguist, on the other hand, is generally suspicious of mysticism, and if he is going to pay the price of surrendering his rational procedures, he will want to see the possibility of real gain. Capitulation at this point will entail his being manoeuvred into a position where he is obliged to recognize 'Papyrus' as a poem. This, I would predict, is too high a cost.

Bateson, in his attempt to treat grammar in poetry as a mere relic of the primitive linguistic basis in common speech, cites, with apparent approval,

Fraser's reconstruction, which he obviously believes supports his contention that 'Papyrus' is a poem. This would appear to be a further betrayal of his own case. The argument is: this is a poem; this is not grammatical. Bateson alludes to Fraser's remarks in support of his contention that literary critics regard 'Papyrus' as a poem. But in order to illustrate its poetic function, Fraser fills in the gaps. This he does by supplying complementary phrases, in other words, by giving the poem a syntax, which, to Bateson, is a grammar. The position we have now reached is: Bateson assumes that this fragment is a poem, uses the fragment to prove that a poem need have no grammar, and then cites in support another literary critic who, in order to prove that it is a poem, supplies his own grammatical constructions. Responding rightly *as a linguist*, to a poem, if I do my best to follow Bateson's contention, entails committing myself to the task – thought by philosophers to be inadvisable if not impossible – of seriously maintaining two contradictory propositions at one and the same time.

An inference which might be drawn from this preposterous position is that it would be much simpler to 'neutralize' our terms at the outset, and to operate the principle of objectivity: *empirical semics recognizes only entities which are textually signalled.* The linguist working at the level of empirical semics recognizes the recurrence and the syllabic increases.

As 'Papyrus' stands in Pound's collected poems, it is a succession of words which have no more sense than any random sequence. G. N. Leech formulates the following principle: 'the human mind in poetry seeks *as much sense as it reasonably can*'[61] (his italics). Fraser's answer to this problem is to rewrite the poem so that it makes sense, (2). But, in order to do this, he adds eleven words to a text which originally comprised only four, and deletes the dots, which Bateson sees as one of the poetic merits. Let us suppose that the reader who was incapable of responding to the text as Pound wrote it, now responds to Fraser's version. Would this not raise the question of authorship? Is the reader responding to Pound, who wrote four words, or to Fraser, who trebled the length and removed the typographical recurrence?

The conceptual structures of literary criticism are inadequate in the face of the problems that have been raised. Can literary semantics handle the situation more satisfactorily? According to the structure I have outlined, Fraser's commentary upon the text belongs to **introspective semics**. Bateson also cites two other references in his treatment of 'Papyrus'. C. M. Dawson, in *The Explicator*,[62] refers to a fragment by Sappho. It was discovered on a sixth century parchment and published in 1907, several years before Pound's poem was written; 'the coincidence can hardly be accidental' says Dawson. The same point is taken up by N. E. Collinge.[63] Collinge argues that despite Pound's doctrine of the dance of 'the intellect among words',[64] we should be prepared for the 'occasional possibility of his faithfulness to an original'. Collinge provides a transliteration of Sappho's original, and demonstrates that, allowance made for textual cruces, Pound's 'Papyrus' is a straightforward attempt at translation. Pound is therefore 'guilty, under the heading of academic faults, only of a conscious exploitation of an accidentally marred original poem and perhaps of confusing parchment with papyrus'.

Given the facts upon which Collinge and Dawson base their argument, their case seems wholly convincing. That Pound should independently have created a 'fragment' which bears so striking a resemblance to an actual fragment is inconceivable. The approach of Messrs. Collinge and Dawson may be said to belong to the **semantics of literature**.

Are we therefore to say that Fraser's account is inadequate? And where do values belong? It is unreasonable to insist upon a scholarly reconstruction of the semantics of literature before value judgments are made. If the poem seems valuable to a reader, at any point, then this is *his* gain. This is **knowledge three**. Research into the semantics of literature is an historical quest, and, at any point in the investigation, the historian may have value experiences; but there is no determinate point at which we may pronounce, 'Now a value judgment is possible'. Fraser's account is perfectly adequate as **introspective semics**: it is, so truth transpires, inadequate as a reconstruction of the **semantics of literature**. **Value** is a **kinetic variable**, and only through delusion can it be transformed into an **analeptic constant**.

(iv) *that linguists, instead of going forward into the style, go backwards into the language they already know*

I have constructed the following diagram to represent Bateson's allegation that linguists simply cannot respond to *style*.

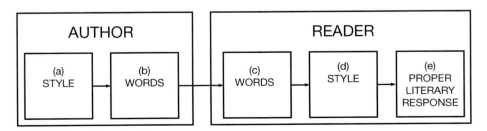

Bateson's Concept of a Proper Literary Response.

I hope it does not distort his argument. The linguist, says Bateson, remains verbally immobile at point (c), and never attains to point (d), still less to point (e), the proper literary response. This explains why the critic finds so little nourishment in modern linguistics in any of its forms.

In chapters 1 to 3, I contended[65] that I. A. Richards failed to follow through, in his later work on literary theory, the semantic insights of *The Meaning of Meaning*.[66] I argued there [LS:35], that the underlying assumption in *The Principles of Literary Criticism*[67] is that the literary experiences of the writer and the good reader are the same, and that this assumption is widespread in literary criticism; literary criticism makes no clear distinction between the **semantics of literature** and **semics**. This seems to be exactly what Bateson is doing: he assumes that his own (d) is a reconstruction of the author's (a). In fact, he is confronted by the same (c) as the linguists, and is blaming them for not contributing the (d) and the (e). But where, it is apposite to ask, do the (d) and the (e) come from? Not directly from (a); for the author, typically, is not in a position to help us; nor from (c), the text, for 'verbal immobility' will lead us to the linguists' position. The invited answer is that (d) and (e) are supplied by those readers capable of a proper literary response. Now how do we decide what is a proper literary response? We have to ask the critics presumably. In other words, we have come back to the point where the critic, like Richards, proclaims to the linguist, 'I am better than you'.[68]

Such defence strategies might be thought to place the literary critic in an impregnable position: he may pursue the discourse of cognition until such time that his arguments are made to seem cognitively indefensible, and then finally seek insulation in an aesthetic cocoon. That is perfectly acceptable for a literary critic as such; but Bateson is also an academic employed by a university. Education is central to this argument.

Academic Criticism

The second main section of this consideration of the Bateson/Vendler Argument will be concerned with the educational implications of the literary critical approach. We need a theory of the **syllabus**.

Let the term 'syllabus' designate all the obligations placed upon the teacher by his employer, and further, let these obligations be subdivided into **jussive** and **hortative**. A **jussive obligation** is a rule, the infringement of which will lead to disciplinary action against the offending teacher. A **hortative obligation** is a view, philosophical, methodological or otherwise, held prescriptively by the employer, which he may try to persuade the teacher to accept, but which the teacher can, if (s)he so chooses, disregard, without detriment to his or her own professional position. The accepted custom, teaching being a profession, is to reduce jussive obligations to a minimum.

The syllabus is that system of obligations, both jussive and hortative, which will best enable the teacher to reconcile with the ethical drive of his/ her own personality the needs of the community on the one side, and the 'politics' (in the neutral sense of dynamics) of the classroom situation on the other, whether it be a university or a school classroom.

I make an important distinction clear at this point: the difference between a **literary critic** and an **academic critic**. An academic critic participates in two **universes of discourse**: literary criticism and education. An **academic critic**, therefore, is a literary critic who commits himself to a **syllabus**. Whilst the position of the literary critic is unassailable, because when standpoints become logically untenable he can make appeal to aesthetic immunity, the academic critic is more vulnerable. It will become clear as I proceed that the case here argued is not primarily against literary criticism as such, but against academic criticism. Literary criticism, and this is of course not ultimately to be held separate from cultural criticism,[69] is an essential, *but informal*, function of university life. To overlook that *caveat* would be to misunderstand the direction of this book.

If the definition of the syllabus offered above is accepted and followed through to its logical termination, we shall arrive at a point where a paradox in the position of the academic critics will be revealed.

My definition of the syllabus is an extension of the established concept but it includes most of what would traditionally be regarded as syllabus. It would seem self-evident that Bateson regards his argument not merely as a defence of literary criticism but also of academic criticism. A passage which illustrates Bateson's commitment to academic criticism, if such illustration is needed, occurs in the course of his argument;[70] he claims that the student is more usefully employed in 'esemplastic', stylistic exercises than in memorizing the finer points of Middle English linguistics or modern neo-grammatics: 'Stylistic discrimination is the one indispensable prerequisite for the aesthetic appreciation of great literature'. Bateson is here committing himself to examinations. In other words, a degree course in English literature constitutes a 'training' in a 'discipline'. At the end of the course, the student may be 'examined' and the degree he receives will be a public token of his successful completion of the period of training.

From the Bateson/Vendler Argument, I will attempt to reconstruct the underlying purposes of this training in literary criticism. The case might be abstracted as follows: the student should be educated in the reading of poetry; he should be brought to the point where he is capable of absorbing its sense and value; he should be less likely at the end of the course to miss the indispensable point of grief or pleasure in the poems he reads than he was at the beginning; he should attain to literary perception; he should respond rightly to a piece of literary language; he should try to answer 'critical' questions ; the student should go 'forwards' from his text into its context of situation, rather than 'backwards' into the language he already knows; the student should accept the ineradicably subjective core of criticism; he should adopt a synthetic rather than an analytic approach; he should be taught that grammar is irrelevant; that linguistic analysis is futile; he should be verbally mobile.

The justification therefore, if I may summarize and interpret these hints given by Helen Vendler and F. W. Bateson, is that academic criticism is concerned to educate the 'full man', to make the student capable of mature response to literature, and to enrich his life by developing in him that human perceptiveness and sensibility so that he is, in some moral or aesthetic sense, 'the better' for his training. Let us call this the **principle of humanism**.[71]

Most academic disciplines at university level seem to work on a different principle. John Holt[72] attacked this alternative principle, but nevertheless summed it up very neatly: '(i) Of the vast body of human knowledge, there are certain bits and pieces that can be called essential...(ii) the extent to which a person can be considered educated, qualified to live intelligently in today's world and be a useful member of society, depends on the amount of this essential knowledge which he carries about with him; (iii) it is the duty of schools, therefore, to get as much of this essential knowledge as possible into the minds of children'. In (iii) read 'universities' and 'students' for 'schools' and 'children' respectively, and we have a summary of the rival principle operated by most other departments at universities: let us call this the **principle of information**.[73]

In my argument at this point, Bateson's acceptance of a 'literary' examination is vital. His commitment may be seen in his approach to the question on *Troilus and Criseyde*. Bateson accuses the philologists of not explaining why Chaucer was not embarrassed by the linguistic inconsistencies in his text. His answer to this problem is that, as *Troilus and Criseyde* was written for oral delivery at the Court of Richard II in the presence of Chaucer's social superiors, Chaucer needed to avoid social pretentiousness; 'Chaucer's literary genius transformed a social necessity into an individual poetic style by a continuous juxtaposition of verbal units that say more than he ought to have said with those saying less than he ought to have said'.[74] Bateson presents his argument at this point as though he has unquestionably established the semantics of literature; as though he has reached a stylistic terminus beyond contradiction. Can it be that Bateson's reconstruction is the *sine qua non* of a proper literary response to Chaucer's style? What Bateson does not admit is that his exegesis of the semantics of literature is relative, itself an interpretation likely to be confronted by alternative interpretations, and, theoretically, subject to contradiction in the light of new evidence.[75] *Literary criticism distinguishes itself in the above assertion as the art of appearing certain, where, by other academic standards, one has no right to be.* The semantics of literature is generally to be approached in the subjunctive, not the indicative, mood.

Let us consider the following examination question:[76] ' "In *Troilus and Criseyde* an admixture of sentimentalism adulterates the pure wine of tragedy". Discuss.' If I have understood Bateson correctly, I believe that he would consider this a more stylistic, or esemplastic, question than the other questions on *Troilus and Criseyde* which he mentions. Now Bateson himself has supplied us with an answer to the philological questions which occurred in the A4 (Oxford University English) paper. But what is the answer to this stylistic question? Let us call the statement for discussion P (a propositional variable: here = "The cited assertion is 'true'"), and the negative of this statement ~P. Logically, it is not the case that (P&~P), where the ampersand conjoins two propositional variables, the first conjunct, P, being affirmative and the second the negative of the first; (P&~P) is, in other words, a contradiction. An examiner who awards high marks to a candidate's answer is asserting that the answer is, in some sense, 'true'. It follows that an examiner who awards high marks both to candidate A, who argues P, and to candidate B, who argues ~P, is accepting a logical impossibility, or he must be testing the candidates' original assumptions and attitudes, or he is assessing their ability to argue from those assumptions and attitudes. If it is the assumptions and attitudes that matter, why is it necessary to ask a fatuous question in order to elicit them? What are the assumptions and attitudes that are acceptable to the academic critics? Does the candidate not have the right to know what these are, at least in principle, when the examiners' judgment will be accepted by society as an assessment of his ability? And if his ability to argue from assumptions is being tested, would it not be more satisfactory to give him a training in logic, and set questions which tested his attainment in that discipline?

The answer to this might be that this is a bad question, and that all examiners occasionally set a bad question. But a glance at many literary examination papers will show that English departments are adept at producing this type of question.

Although he usually does not realise it at the time, the situation which confronts a candidate at school is that he is committing himself to an entirely different kind of examination if he chooses to read English literature at university. If he selects English, he will be judged according to the principle of humanism; if he selects a subject other than English, he will be assessed according to the principle of information. As Robson puts it, 'English is different'.[77]

It is patently impossible satisfactorily to operate an examination on the basis of the principle of humanism. Such a system presupposes that humanity is a measurable quality, like intelligence, and that the academic critics are capable of measuring it; that they are qualified to sit in judgment over the humanistic achievements and failures of their students.

Consider the position of a student who sees a degree as a means to achieving a professional position. Having chosen English, he finds himself obliged to give evidence of his progressive humanization. As a pragmatist, he will want to give the examiners what they ask for, and his assignments will be prepared to that purpose. I think the direction of the argument is clear. Far from exerting a humanizing influence, the operation of examinations according to the principle of humanism can produce an even less 'human' graduate than would have been the case given the humbler aims of the principle of information. Against this it might well be argued that examinations should, on humanistic grounds, be abolished altogether. But, short of this extreme, the philosophy, implicit in the arguments of the academic critics, that the success or failure of humanist education can be tested by examinations, seems to me misconceived. The academic critics are once more attempting to translate kinetic variables into analeptic constants [LS:76].

The principle of humanism is of paramount importance, and the problem is how to make it possible for the principle to operate without legislating for it. I do not think there is an answer to this. The insensitive teacher ignores all but jussive obligations anyway. Teachers cannot be coerced into the principle of humanism, any more than students. It may be that there are some lecturers in English departments whose responses to literature have become weak and jaded,[78] and who would welcome a system where human response, **knowledge three**, was the private property of the individual and the institution demanded only the principle of information. At all events, I am sure that we cannot rest content with a university organization which builds in the principle of humanism vertically by one discipline standing on its head. Bateson ends his argument with the quotation: 'Not here, O Apollo, are haunts meet for thee'. The right of the literary critics to keep haunt with Apollo is not here being questioned; what is at stake here is whether Apollo's right to sit in judgment, with perverse psychometry, over the thousands of students who take examinations in English every year should pass unchallenged.

The Supposed Intersubjectivity of Literary Criticism

Further to the public controversy between Bateson and Fowler, *Essays in Criticism* published a short article by Cay Dollerup, of the University of Copenhagen, which calls in question the degree to which critical activities are intersubjective, and derides the epistemological pretensions of the New Critics.[79] In his reply, Bateson argues that critical judgments *are* intersubjective. I shall summarize the respective arguments of Dollerup and Bateson, and then analyse Bateson's submissions, according to the standards of literary semantics.

Dollerup and Intersubjectivity

Taking Wellek's definition[80] as his starting point, Dollerup challenges the established views: firstly, that a work of art is a system of norms of ideal concepts which are intersubjective; secondly, that the experiences and interpretations of some people, by reason of their specialized education, cultivated taste, maturity or super-sensitivity, are more correct and valuable than those of others.

Claims that the art experience is of something 'objective', he argues, are based ultimately upon the fact that it is *subjectively* felt to be objective. How do we know that the reaction and evaluation of even the best critics are not determined by idiosyncratic features?

Dollerup contrasts literary usage with ordinary language communication. In ordinary language, the message is usually short and simple; its reference is familiar to both speaker and listener, and errors are eliminated by intersubjective control. The work of literature, on the other hand, is a 'complex and many-faceted linguistic entity, though it admittedly conforms to certain more-or-less well-defined rules and laws'. Our experience of aesthetic reality is related to, but not the same as, the world of everyday life.

Because of the complexity of the literary work, and the lack of intersubjective control, may it not be that individual responses are just as varied as the styles of the authors? Even the technique of 'close reading', much vaunted by the New Critics, relies upon a selection of passages and is therefore not as scientifically detached as might at first appear. 'At best the reader of a work of criticism will feel that the critic has made some good points and that there are others where he disagrees with him.'[81]

Criticism is an affair between a critic whose response can only be his own and a reader who has already made up his mind about the work in question. Dollerup concludes that the work of art we speak about in criticism is the one we experience individually, and that it is criticism's function to record an individual opinion of a work of art. This is sufficient to justify criticism as a pursuit without the epistemological pretensions of the New Critics, and the appeal to intersubjective norms.

Bateson and Intersubjectivity

I turn now to a summary of Bateson's reply.[82] If Bateson accepts Dollerup's arguments and retires to read the masterpieces, how shall he know which are the masterpieces for him? He will rather attempt to defend the position which Dollerup is attacking, and argue that there *is* intersubjectivity in critical judgments.

In order to defend this position, Bateson takes three illustrations which he believes strikingly attest to consensus of judgment: (a) The Newdigate Prize poetry of the Nineteenth Century has for the most part been consigned to oblivion, and only one line of one poem is remembered, 'A rose-red city – "half as old as Time" !', from Burgon's *Petra*. This line has appeared in all the standard dictionaries of quotations from 1923 onwards, but it is remembered in isolation from the rest of the works. 'Some such degree of critical consensus is surely a *fact*…'.[83] (b) Some years ago, Bateson was himself examiner for the Newdigate Prize, with Mrs. Ing and W. H. Auden. Bateson and Mrs. Ing persuaded Auden that Jon Stallworthy should have the prize. Stallworthy has since become a Yeats' expert and a competent minor poet. 'His six or seven rivals for the Prize, as far as I know, have never been heard of again'.[84] (c) As a young man Bateson read Branston's *The Art of Politics*, and transcribed what he thought was the best passage. A few years later, David Nichol Smith included the exact passage in the *Oxford Book of Eighteenth Century Verse*. 'The young man and the old man had thought as one!'[85]

Returning to Dollerup's argument, Bateson, whilst admitting that Wellek's definition is not entirely satisfactory, wishes to inquire in what respects literature appeals to norms different from those of everyday speech. He disagrees with Dollerup's claims that ordinary speech is rarely misunderstood. Both ordinary language and literature presuppose an intersubjective relationship; equally, literary context controls meaning, eliminating misunderstanding, just as linguistic context does in everyday language. Rather than follow Wellek, and take aesthetic normality to be correct literary behaviour, Bateson prefers to rely on his principles of the Semantic Gap, and the Human Context.

The Principle of the Semantic Gap,[86] explained in *English Poetry: A Critical Introduction* is further illustrated here. I shall attempt a reconstruction.

The poetic function is to synthesize discordant units of meaning. The more discordant the units, the greater the poetic triumph if a synthesis is achieved. There is thus a cline between the point where the discord is so trivial as to present no challenge and where the division is so great as to render synthesis impossible. The Principle of the Semantic Gap is the aesthetic limitation which this avoidance of triviality on the one hand and cleavage on the other imposes. The critic regards as most poetic that synthesis of units which are most discordant. This Principle is the one which Johnson was operating when he criticized Donne's famous 'compasses' image. 'It is in the reconciliation of the two ideals that criticism finds its most useful function'.[87] At this point in his discussion, Bateson observes that a measure of disagreement can be tolerated in the application of these ideals; further, the degree of toleration allowed changes over the centuries.

Bateson then offers Dollerup a challenge. He quotes A. E. Housman's 'Epitaph on an Army of Mercenaries':

(5)   These, in the day when heaven was falling,
                 The hour when earth's foundations fled,
              Followed their mercenary calling,
                 And took their wages and are dead.

              Their shoulders held the sky suspended;
                 They stood, and earth's foundations stay;
              What God abandoned, these defended,
                 And saved the sum of things for pay.

This poem, says Bateson, was offered to him when an undergraduate as a 'touchstone', which might enable him to distinguish between good and bad poetry. Bateson has never been impressed by this poem, and the crux of his reply in this essay is that it is possible to communicate his distaste, which springs from valid intersubjective defects, to Dollerup. If he can do so, Dollerup's case, Bateson believes, will be destroyed.

He then operates his Principle of the Semantic Gap. In this case, the Semantic Gap is between the actual British Expeditionary Force, dismissed as it was by Kaiser Wilhelm II, and the tawdry literary portrayal. Indeed, 'Followed their mercenary calling' is the one good line in the poem. Further, the Human Context is particularly distressing. Bateson compares the battle unfavourably with the stand of the Spartans at Thermopylae commemorated by Simonides. The B.E.F. stand was less glorious, for many of the force survived, and Housman is unduly patriotic, neglecting the heroic qualities of the French and Germans.

Dollerup will, Bateson anticipates, object that it is easier to demonstrate that a work of literature is defective, than argue its virtues. But this fact is the result of a general defect in human nature 'which does nothing to discredit the critical act *per se*:'... 'And the defect is to be cured by more criticism, not by less'.[88]

What *is* Intersubjectivity?

Before a reply to Bateson is undertaken, it may be useful to repeat several theoretical fundamentals of literary semantics.

In what sense can a work of art be said to exist as an object? We may here reaffirm the usefulness of the **trichotomy of knowledge** for dealing with aesthetic discourse.[89] If A claims he perceives an aesthetic reality in work of art X, then, assuming he is 'correct', the reality he perceives is **knowledge one**. If B does not accept that what A has seen constitutes an aesthetic reality, whatever B may mean by that, then B will regard what A regards as knowledge one as A's **knowledge three**. But in this very disagreement there has been some communicated content, that is to say **knowledge two**. A may not have convinced B that X constitutes an aesthetic reality, but he has communicated to B that he *thinks* it is.

Empirical semics is not immediately concerned with questions of aesthetic reality, at the knowledge one level, save by implication (see discussion in chapter 11). 'All men value X' may suggest that X is valuable, but I believe the **empirical semicist** will be most profitably employed in trying to establish or refute the universal, leaving, in the meantime, its possible corollary to those of metaphysical bent. The empirical semicist will seek to establish principles, in accordance with the **criterion of principles**, whereby **affident**, or potentially affident, statements can be made concerning **semic accompaniment**. In accordance with the **principle of objectivity**, we may conclude that those features of a work of art are objective to the extent that they are intersubjectively recognized.

Let us begin with Bateson's statement concerning what he calls the literary commonplaces in Housman's 'Epitaph on an Army of Mercenaries'; 'Their function in fact turns out to be merely to set off the one good line in the poem':

(6)   'Followed their mercenary calling.'[90]

Bateson is concerned to argue that there is intersubjectivity in literary criticism. The above quotation constitutes a critical judgment, and he might well have made this his point of departure. No elaborate preparations would be necessary to carry out an **affidence test** to put this point to the proof. Given, perhaps, one hundred students of literature wholly unacquainted with

Bateson's views upon this passage, how many, reading individually, would concur that there is one good line, and that this is it?

Instead of conducting such an experiment within a closed universe of discourse, Bateson selects three open universes of discourse which have to be considered diachronously.

In his first example, concerning *Petra*, he has traced a patronizing contemporary review in the *Athenaeum* which quotes a passage including the line 'A rose-red city – "half as old as time"! '. Burgon himself showed little confidence in his own poetic merits when he published his collected *Poems (1840 to 1878.)*. Finally, his name has appeared in all the standard dictionaries since 1923, and this has been the sole quotation in each case. Bateson does not say whether the critical consensus consists in the general neglect of Burgon as a poet, or the particular preservation of this one line. Now the neglect of a poet need not be the result of intersubjective rejection; nor need the reappearance of the same line in successive dictionaries of quotations be a guarantee that the editors had in each case read Burgon's *Petra* and decided, like Bateson, that this was the best line. Is it not possible that compilers of dictionaries rely upon previous compilations? The only positive consensus here with regard to this line is of three people: the writer of the *Athenaeum* review, the compiler of the first dictionary to include the line, and Bateson himself.

The second example concerns Jon Stallworthy. Bateson and Mrs. Ing persuaded Auden that Stallworthy merited the Newdigate Prize, and he received the award. Stallworthy has subsequently proved himself, says Bateson, to be a competent minor poet. Stallworthy's merits as a poet will not be discussed here; we are concerned rather with the conclusiveness of Bateson's example. Firstly, the consensus itself was not unanimous – Auden was a redoubtable dissenter, and we are not informed whether he acquiesced because he was persuaded that his co-examiners were right, or because he bowed to the majority verdict.

Secondly, the important step of awarding Stallworthy Oxford's major poetic accolade is hardly to be held separate from his subsequent fame; similarly, with the obscurity of his rivals for the prize. We may not reasonably argue that the ten-yard start a runner received was later vindicated by his winning the race. Nor may we retrospectively justify the award of a third-class rather than a first-class degree to a candidate by observing that he afterwards failed to secure a post of responsibility. In other words, it would be impossible to prove that Stallworthy's career was not influenced by the fame and encouragement he derived from winning the Newdigate, and that his rivals did not suffer commensurately. It may be that Bateson is referring not to the present reputation of Stallworthy when he speaks of his being a competent minor poet, but simply relying upon his own critical judgment of Stallworthy's more recent output. In this event, all that Bateson is saying is: he and Mrs. Ing thought, at the time of the award, that Stallworthy was a competent poet, and that Bateson, at least, thinks that events have proved their decision correct. This argument will not prove critical intersubjectivity.

Bateson's third example is more satisfactory. The odds against two people selecting by chance an identical passage from a long poem are very high, and it would therefore seem possible that, without prejudice to the question of aesthetic absolutes, Bateson and David Nichol Smith were operating similar aesthetic criteria. Even so, an anecdotal demonstration of a consensus of two is no substitute for carefully conducted research.

We move now to a consideration of the second part of Bateson's argument: the challenge which he offers to Dollerup. He claims that if Dollerup will set aside his theoretical prejudices, he will accept that some knowledge of the defects of the poem has been communicated to him.[91]

Bateson formulates his **Principle of the Semantic Gap**. Would this satisfy the **criterion of principles** for **empirical semics**? An adequate principle is one which, having been defined and demonstrated, can be operated independently by other linguists.

Bateson nowhere clearly specifies just what the entities are between which this semantic gap is supposed to occur, but he does give two examples of its operation which enable us to make the necessary inferences. Johnson, Bateson says, was applying the principle when he objected to the comparison of the lovers to a pair of compasses. He then operates the principle himself in order to communicate to Dollerup a defect in Housman's poem. Semantic criteria are notoriously difficult to operate in any linguistic analysis. Bateson operates his principle upon Donne's image of the pair of compasses. The criterion of principles is satisfied if, after considering this example, we can successfully predict how Bateson will apply his principle to the Housman poem. I would submit that such prediction is impossible, for the entities between which the gap occurs are quite different. In the Donne poem, the two items (a) 'two soules' (line 21) and (b) 'stiffe twin compasses' (line 26) are both textually signalled. But in the case of the Housman poem, the gap seems to be between the British Expeditionary Force as represented by Housman, and the same Force as Bateson knows, or thinks he knows, it, in reality, to have been. In the one case the semantic gap is between two textual entities; in the other, it is between the text and the critic's interpretation of the historical events upon which the poem is based. The Principle of the Semantic Gap is thus shown to be blatantly *ad hoc*.

What then has Bateson communicated to me? Not, that the poem is defective, but that *he thinks* it is defective [LS:85]. He has further communicated to me that his reasons for thinking it defective are based upon a principle which as it stands is inoperable at the level of empirical semics.

Bateson undertakes to demonstrate critical intersubjectivity; he avoids the obvious course of an **affidence test** on the lines suggested, choosing instead three illustrations, only one of which is convincing; and he then invokes an ill-defined principle to persuade Dollerup that critical communication is possible. The real problems of critical intersubjectivity – just how much? and under what circumstances? – remain unbroached. Any critic who decides to argue that critical decisions are intersubjective must infer and accept the consequence: **intersubjectivity entails reference to other subjects.**

CHAPTER 6

LITERARY SEMANTICS AND LINGUISTIC ANALYSIS

An Example of Linguistic Analysis

The article I have chosen to illustrate the relation between literary semantics and linguistic analysis is by Alex Rodger, 'Linguistic Form and Literary Meaning'.[1] First, I shall summarize as fairly as I can, and as fully as space allows, the argument; then I shall explore its theoretical implications.

(1)   MS Harley 7578 (Folio 110)

          The maydens came
          When I was in my mothers bower
          I hade all yt I wolde
          the bayly berith the bell away
    5   the lylle the rose the rose I lay
          the sylver is whit red is the golde
          the robes thay lay in fold
          the baylly berith the bell away
          the lily the rose the rose I lay
    10   and through the glasse wyndow
          shines the sone
          How shuld I love & I so young
          the bayly berith the bell away
          (the lily etc.)[2]

Rodger's Linguistic Analysis of Harley 7578

Rodger's argument runs as follows. The poem is a very late fifteenth or very early sixteenth century lyric; as it is anonymous, any extrinsic approach to its meaning is impossible. Rodger, believing Archibald MacLeish's judgment 'senselessness in sense' to be astray[3], will enquire firstly *how* and *what* the poem means, and secondly, will seek an explanation for the self-contradictory effect of 'obscure simplicity'.[4]

He then formulates three categories of question to which he would like an answer:

(i)   Questions concerning the 'inner situation': Who are the participants? Who addresses whom? What are the subject matter, purpose and situation of the discourse?

(ii)   Linguistic questions: What is the tense of *lay* in the refrain and in line 7, present or past? And if present, does it refer to habitual or unique happenings?

(iii)   Questions of a mixed sort. Whose are the robes in line 7? Is the bower in line 2 an arbour or a boudoir? What is the significance of the refrain, of *sylver* and *gold* in line 6, and of the sun's shining through the glass window in lines 10 and 11? Rodger observes that, since we have nothing but the language of the text from which to infer the answers, all the questions are really linguistic ones.[5]

We may be fairly certain that the whole text is spoken by one person – 'P', who is young and involved in some love situation, whether erotic, marital, filial or religious.[6] After raising various situational conjectures, Rodger commences his analysis.

He seeks to 'establish a number of contextual footholds' in the text;[7] and he begins with a discussion of *lay* in the refrain and in line 7. If *lay* is intransitive and in the simple past tense, then *lylle* and *rose* in the refrain, and *thay* in line 7 must be in apposition to *I* and *the robes* respectively. If, on the other hand, *lay* is transitive and simple present, then *lylle*, *rose* and *robes* must be complements (direct objects) ; *I* and *thay* will accordingly be subjects. Because there is no comma after the second occurrence of *rose* in the refrain 'in the text as it has been punctuated by the modern editors', Rodger concludes that *the rose*, at its second occurrence, operates as an extensive complement. He then assumes, on the grounds of homogeneity of time reference, that *lay* in line 7 is also present transitive, and that *thay*, which is therefore the subject, must refer to *The maydens* and perhaps *my mother* in lines 1 and 2.[8]

Rodger's subsequent analysis deals with cohesion,[9] firstly at clause structure level. The poem is notable for its lack of 'bondage': there is only one subordinate clause in the text, and most of the lines could be punctuated with full stops at clause boundaries.[10] This lack of cohesion is evident also at group structure level; twenty of the thirty-five nominal groups are 'definite article plus noun', and only one of these is self-determining, *the sun*, the rest being unrelated to other items in the poem.[11] Likewise, four of the eight verbal items are lexically weak, and three of the remaining four collocate with prepositions or adverbial groups that give us little additional information.[12] *Lay* in the refrain takes no adjunct at all 'which is rather unusual for this transitive verb'.[13] In this simplicity of structures, in this lack of cohesion, 'we have at least a partial explanation of the poem's self-contradictory effect of "obscure simplicity" '. Rodger now asks what it is that gives the poem its mysterious unity and significance.

In order to answer this question, he proceeds to an analysis of the sentence and stanza structure.[14] The total amount of text, discounting repetitions, is five sentences (this figure based on the 'modern printed version'). Whilst the proportion of lines per new sentence diminishes, the number of newly introduced topics increases, 'Rapid progressive shortening of sentence is accompanied by the rapid introduction of new matter'. In two sentences are introduced four new topics: 'window', 'sunshine', 'love' and 'youth'.[15]

Rodger then analyses the 'foregrounded features'.[16] The normal affirmative clause order is SP(C)(A).[17] But a number of clauses in the text depart from this pattern: lines 10/11, AAPS; line 5, CSP; line 6 (second clause), CPS; line 7, CSPA. Such deviations might be due to the exigencies of the rhyme scheme, but certainly in the case of the refrain the poet could have written,

(2)   'I lay the lily, the rose, the rose;
         Away with the bell the bailey goes'

(i.e. the couplet, lines 4-5, could have been written SPC/AASP instead of the original SPCA/CSP − Rodger omits to point out that he has transposed the lines of the couplet and supplanted the original rhyme).

Rodger argues that these departures are the result of 'foregrounding'.[18] The items upon which particular emphasis is placed are *the rose* (second occurrence in the refrain), *red* in line 6, and *the robes* in line 7. Rodger further contends that these foregrounded elements may be semantically equated. Two such semantic equations are 'the rose = red = the gold = the robes' and 'maidens = I = lily = silver = white'[19]

From this point, Rodger moves to interpretation of the text as a whole.

(i)   The lily represents maidenhood: the rose is emblematic of womanly fulfilment.
(ii)   P is a young girl about to be married.
(iii)   Attended by the maidens she is probably strewing her boudoir, shortly to be the scene of semi-public consummation of her marriage, with symbolic flowers.[20]
(iv)   The girl is wealthy – she uses silver and gold as her measures of value and, as only the feudal aristocracy and the richer of the bourgeoisie could afford glazed windows, she is 'clearly no peasant wench'.[21]
(v)   The sun is 'clearly established as an emblem of masculinity', its light penetrating into the bower, the feminine sanctum; 'the whole notion is emotionally ambivalent'.[22]
(vi)   The text expresses the speaker's fears at the thought of the impending marriage.[23]
(vii)   It is a 'running commentary' upon her stream-of-consciousness.
(viii)   The marriage has probably been arranged by the girl's parents without her consent, and the bayly is an official called in to ensure that the ceremony takes place, 'Finality and inevitability are phonetically hammered home in the first refrain-line'.[24]

Rodger admits that other interpretations may be possible 'for we have not examined all the data with equal care', but this interpretation is consistent with the linguistic data taken as a whole.[25] 'All our critical decisions have been based upon the known facts of usage and the given facts of the text.' 'What matters most is not some particular technique in itself, nor the terminology used, but the value of the basic attitudes and central concepts of linguistics as aids to the proper reading, understanding and enjoyment of poetry.'[26]

His final paragraph is concerned with the teaching of literature. He recommends that a course be steered between 'Literary Humpty Dumpty and Linguistic Alice'.[27] 'To discover literary meaning for oneself is to discover language and its modes of operation; and to discover those is to enter the world of literature by its front door, the texts, with a firm sense of possession, not sidelong, with the suspicion, or fear that one is peering into the incomprehensible.'[28]

The Semantics of Literature and Linguistic Analysis

From the diagram [LS:52], it may be seen that literary semantics has four sub-divisions: **semantics of literature** (**transmission semantics**, where the investigator has experimental access to the creative processes of the author), **theoretical semics**, **empirical semics** and **introspective semics**. Whilst none of these sub-divisions is exclusive, the structure provides, as was demonstrated in chapter 5, a means of analysing the material of critical discourse: it can likewise be used in meta-analysis of linguistic treatment of a text. In this chapter, I shall treat the sub-divisions, with the exception of introspective semics, in turn. The reader will infer from this book that one consequence of adopting literary semantics is the modal reduction of a vast body of literary criticism to the level of introspective semics. Transmission semantics is ruled out in this case as there is no clue as to the author of MS Harley 7578.

Principles of the semantics of literature may be formulated as follows: '*Ceteris paribus*, primary sources are preferable to secondary sources'; '*Ceteris paribus* a contemporary manuscript is a more reliable guide to the author's text than a later copy'; 'An interpretation informed by a knowledge of the historical background of the author is preferable to one written in ignorance of the historical facts'; 'In the case of early English, an interpretation of the textual facts which is in accordance with the known dialect and date of the author is superior to one which is not'; and so forth, as dictated by agreed common sense. We may now measure Rodger's article by these standards.

There seems to be no doubt that Rodger believes himself to be establishing the meaning of the lyric (**semantics of literature**): 'Many have come nearer the mark without being able to say how or why…',[29] 'the real keys to its significance lie, I suggest, in the relations between its metrical and its linguistic form…';[30] 'Mr MacLeish's impressionistic description of the poem…';[31] 'The moment we stop guessing intuitively…';[32] 'All these are linguistic questions demanding linguistic answers…';[33] 'Clearly, mere situational conjecture of this kind might lead us anywhere'.[34]… 'until we can confirm that subjective response by more evidence drawn from objective text, our guess is still only as good as the next reader's.'[35] Rodger's conception of his own approach seems to be: the text exists as a linguistic object; other commentators have neglected the linguistic data and their judgments have been impressionistic; if we analyse the language of the poem, we shall obtain 'footholds' which will enable us to proceed to a sound interpretation; this will be demonstrably superior to the superficial analyses of those who have gone before. Rodger's article includes five tables which analyse the clause, sentence and stanza structure and the nominal, verbal and adverbial groups of the lyric. These constitute the linguistic analyses upon which the article rests.

How far does the interpretation of the text, the establishing of the semantics of literature, arise as a corollary from the linguistic analysis? Mr Rodger's argument shows a very clear logical thread: if there is no comma after *lay, lay* must be simple present, and if it is present, it is transitive, and if it is transitive, *lylle* and *rose* must be complements: $P \rightarrow Q$, $Q \rightarrow R$, $R \rightarrow S$, where P,Q and R are propositional variables and the arrows read as 'materially implies'.

Enquiry into the semantics of literature is often an unrewarding task. Such facts as are available tend to be trivial or irrelevant, and attempts to form coherent semantic reconstructions are frequently speculative. Providing a treatment is avowedly tentative, and makes use of the best materials available, then we may judge it to be in accordance with the principles of the semantics of literature.

Mr Rodger's argument depends upon an original assumption that *lay* is transitive and present. The overriding consideration in his selection was that in the modern printed versions, there occurs no comma after the second instance of *rose* in the refrain. His discussion implies that there is a certain linguistic inevitability in his logical progression: the tables entail the conclusions. But the earlier modern editors who punctuated the text according to recent conventions were not able to operate the principles of stylistic analysis upon which Rodger leans. In punctuating the text, they presumably relied upon their linguistic intuition.[36] The initial assumption therefore embodies a subjective judgment of the sort that Rodger's analysis is aimed at superseding. Further, at a later point in the logical process, Rodger assserts that *lay* in the refrain takes no adjunct at all 'which is rather unusual for this transitive verb.'[37] Now if this is true we have here a consideration which should have been raised at the time Rodger adopted the original assumption. If a construction is unusual for a transitive verb, and the form is neutral, perhaps we have here, after all, an intransitive verb? And if it is an intransitive verb, then, by implication, this usage is normal, and the point he is making about simplicity is weakened. Rodger is ingeniously employing a possible weakness in his original assumption to reinforce his argument at a later point.

When we come to inspect the reasons for Rodger's statement that it is unusual for *lay* to be used transitively without an adjunct, we come to a further rather disturbing aspect of the article. This is the way he treats late Middle English as though it were a sub-species of modern English.[38] Whilst we *lay*, without adjunct, a number of items, including, he says, linoleum and charges of explosive, we usually lay roses and lilies on, or in, something.[39] But the point here, as far as the semantics of literature is concerned, is not what *we* say, but what they, the late medieval people, said. They did not speak of *laying linoleum*: linoleum was in fact not patented until the late nineteenth century. If the principles of the semantics of literature are to be followed, we need a scholarly search for medieval contexts in which *lay* is used transitively with flower complements with or without adjunct. The findings will then be inconclusive, but they will be relevant, in the sense of **relevance two**.

Similarly, and more important, Rodger uses the modern printed version of the text for his analysis of sentence structure.[40] As intimated in footnote 36, and may be seen in the photograph at the front of this book, there is an absence of punctuation in MS Harley 7578. Rodger consequently bases his sentence analysis upon the modern printed version. But at the point where he comes closest to discussing the possible punctuation, he observes that the majority of the lines in the lyric could be punctuated 'with full stops at the ends of all clauses'.[41] If this is the case, why does he base his analysis upon the modern printed version, which punctuates in an entirely different fashion? And how can his assertion that 'rapid progressive shortening of sentence is accompanied by the rapid introduction of new matter' have any validity?

The third observation that should be made, in assessing this exercise in the light of the semantics of literature, concerns the function of the tables, which are the foundation of Rodger's analysis. Have they any use? In order to answer this question, we shall consider the crucial word *lay*, since an important part of Rodger's argument depends upon the interpretation of this word.

The word *lay* is ambiguous in many contexts: it can be present-transitive or past-intransitive. The meaning of *lay* in the second line of the refrain is in doubt. Rodger claims that his analysis will help us to establish the meaning of the lyric. If we seek *lay* in the tables, we might expect to find assistance. In fact, such reference is in vain: the first table limits itself to registration of the ambiguity. We learn from our tabulation only what we have fed into it, and this is no more than Rodger or any 19th century philologist could have told us: that in Middle English, as in modern English, *lay* can be present-transitive or past-intransitive. As has already been remarked, when Rodger decides in favour of the former, he invokes the semic accompaniments of modern editors. Such a train of reasoning apparently entitles him to record the same word in Table III unequivocally as transitive.

It can be demonstrated that Rodger's tabulation is inferior as a technique in establishing the semantics of literature to many of the procedures which earlier editors took for granted. Rodger's final assertion, which I have quoted in full [LS:92], that to discover language and its modes of operation is to enter the world of literature by its front door, the texts, is an undue simplification, if by 'literary meaning' he implies the semantics of literature. He emphasizes the need for a linguistic approach which will supersede the intuitive methods of earlier writers. But by a hypothetical argument we may show that at least some of the earlier editors adhered more closely to the principles of the semantics of literature than Rodger does.

Let us restate the principle formulated [LS:93]: '...primary sources are preferable to secondary sources'. Let it be supposed, for the sake of argument, that the emendation 'robe' for 'robes' in line 7 were suggested. This would, if substantiated, reinforce many of Rodger's arguments concerning the meaning of the line: the case against an appositional *thay* would then, for this line, be overwhelming. But much of his discussion would equally be rendered superfluous: likewise, his tables would have to be altered. How could Rodger refute

this suggestion without examining Harley 7578, or a facsimile? And suppose
further it were argued that the MS actually substantiated the suggestion that
'robe' has erroneously been transcribed as plural by the earlier editors.[42] How
could this be refuted without recourse to palaeographical principles?

My argument is admittedly a hypothetical one; the word *is* 'robes' and
discussion of the ambiguity is therefore justified. We are, however, indebted
for the accuracy of our transcript, not to modern linguistic techniques, but to
the careful scholarship and palaeographical expertise of the earlier editors. As
far as the principles of the semantics of literature are concerned, this article is
an unintentional tribute to the soundness of the nineteenth-century philological
tradition.

Not until we move away from the semantics of literature and turn to semic
problems are the tables found to be useful. This is not to imply that analysis
can never be of service in establishing the semantics of literature. Statistical
analysis, which relies largely upon tabulations of this kind, is making rapid
progress.[43]

Empirical Semics and Linguistic Analysis

The first subdivision of semics which I shall consider is empirical semics. This
branch of literary semantics attempts to determine how far evidence collected
at the level of introspective semics as reported by subjects, correlates with
psychological and neurophysiological evidence. The empirical semicist is
interested, for instance, in whether a particular reading is **idiosemic** (peculiar to
one reader) or **parasemic** (experienced by all readers). More broadly, this might
extend to such questions as: What parallels are there in the neural processes of
an orienteer released blindfold in a strange location and a reader 'finding his
way' into a novel?

Let us repeat the **criterion of principles** for **empirical semics** [LS:87]: an
adequate principle is one which, having been defined and demonstrated, can be
operated independently by other linguists.[44] It does not follow of course that all
principles which satisfy this criterion will be useful.

Thus, given Rodger's tabulations of this lyric, I feel that I could carry
out analyses on the same lines of other texts. His tables operate at the level
of **empirical semics** and the **criterion of principles**. But when we come to
consider the inferences which the author draws from his tabulations, we find
ourselves in the domain of **introspective semics** and **theoretical semics**. To
give just one example of this: Rodger places emphasis upon the principle of
homogeneity of tense.[45] The occurrence of *lay* in line 7 is more likely to be

transitive-present, if we can establish that *lay* in the refrain is transitive-present. But there cannot be complete homogeneity of tense within the lyric, since *came* and *was* in lines 1 and 2 are as incontrovertibly in the past tense as *berith* in the refrain and *shines* in line 11 are in the present tense. The facts of language would lead us to suppose that two separate times are being referred to. If two different times are indicated by the tenses, how can we preclude the possibility that the place differs too? P says that she *was*, not that she *is*, in her mother's bower. What linguistic evidence is there that the glass window through which the sun shines is the window of P's mother's bower? Might P not now be in a church? And if so, the point which Rodger makes concerning the high social status of P is weakened. The analyst is taking his own selection of linguistic data and manipulating it according to his own semic accompaniment (**introspective semics**); there is nothing inevitable in his conclusions (**empirical semics**). In literary semantics there must be a level of accurate analysis; otherwise the supposedly linguistic analysis breaks off with Bateson to cavort with Apollo.

This lack of inevitability is even more clearly to be seen in the semantic equations. The refrain itself constitutes a recurrence: such a textually verifiable assertion belongs to empirical semics. But Rodger is, in effect, arguing that *the rose = red = the gold = the robes* and *maidens = I = lily = silver = white* are semantic recurrences. Now it may well be that in Rodger's semic accompaniment (and therefore justifying his comment at the level of introspective semics) there is a recurrent factor in these groups: virginity and whiteness are commonly associated concepts. But no linguist would regard them as strict synonyms; we have once more crossed the line of inevitability. There is slight difference in the later pages of Rodger's article between his symbol-suppositions and the subjective excesses of many literary critics. The exercise falls short of the claims made for it [LS:93].

I may now introduce the **method of concomitant variations**[46] at the level of empirical semics: this consists in the description of correlations between two associated patterns of observed phenomena. It is a linguistic fact, for example, that English-speaking people tend, on sultry days, to make such utterances as: 'Isn't it close!' By careful observation of the thermometer and hygrometer, we could work out a correlation between the reading of these instruments and the incidence of the utterances. We could then make predictions for the future on the basis of either set: given a certain T.H. Index, based on these readings, then the incidence of such exclamations will be high, or, conversely, given such utterances, then it is likely that the T.H. Index is such and such. Crude stimulus-response correlations at this level would be tedious to pursue and hard to find, given the teasing complexity of human discourse.

But there are such methodological possibilities at the level of empirical semics – indeed, some linguists are already exploiting them[47] – and I think that this is the real value of what Rodger himself is doing. Given certain linguistic data, what is the correlation between these and the judgments uttered by subjects when confronted by them? Academic critics have always been obsessed with dictating how people *ought to* read. Empirical semics attempts, as one of its central aims, to discover how they *do* read (see the discussion of Segers' book in chapter 11).

Relying, as far as may be seen, mainly upon **introspective semics**, Rodger asserts that the poem has an 'obscure simplicity'.[48] The **method of concomitant variations** would operate in the following manner. Firstly, it is necessary to decide whether we are to select the medieval or the modern printed version of the text. The criticism which was made [LS:94–96] applies only to the **semantics of literature**. At the level of **empirical semics** it does not matter which version we choose, providing that we do not use results gained from the modern version to reinforce arguments concerning the **semantics of literature** or **transmission semantics**. Secondly, if it can be established under rigorous experimental conditions that native English speakers who read the selected text are agreed in judging it *obscure* and *simple* (these adjectives selected from a non-weighted list), we can then begin to work out correlations between the judgments and the tables.[49] We can ask questions which desperately need answering: What degree of intersubjective variation is there in literary judgment, see chapter 5? What changes would we need to make in the text in order that the judgment 'obscure' might cease to be appropriate. I believe that Rodger has accounted, in his tabulated analysis, for certain phenomena within my semic accompaniment: it is easy to conceive of the further development of these methods.

Theoretical Semics and Linguistic Analysis

Theoretical semics is at the centre of all operations within literary semantics, never entirely absent, though sometimes unobtrusive. If the **analeptic component** aims to close the canon of the scriptures and the **kinetic** to keep it open, then in the structure of literary semantics it is the function of **theoretical semics** to mediate between the two, see the diagram [LS:101]. Given, for instance, a tabulation produced in research by an **empirical semicist** operating the Waring-Herdan formula,[50] it is the task of the **theoretical semicist**, who may of course be the same person, to provide an explanation of the results. Statements based upon the explanation will inevitably be less affident than those founded upon the tabulation. But as a result of the explanatory devices of theoretical semics, the empirical semicist may move towards new, and perhaps subsequently affident, descriptions.

During the latter part of his article, Rodger consciously makes increasing use of interpretation. What is the place of interpretation within literary semantics? Certainly, any function which it has will be at the level of theoretical (or introspective) semics. The theoretical semicist will consider an interpretation at least minimally justified if it demonstrates that an obscure text could be explicated, even though 'proof' of such an interpretation is inadequate at the level of empirical semics. Thus a detailed exegesis of *Finnegan's Wake* which presents a consistent view of the work as a whole is a contribution to **theoretical semics**, even though detail by detail it may be unsatisfactory at the level of **empirical semics**, or the **semantics of literature** (or **transmission semantics**). A more detailed analysis of this demarcation will be given in chapter 15. A study then that proves there is a *possibility of sense* may be theoretically vindicated. But there is an obvious danger in an academic pursuit which, at the expense of solid empirical achievement, devotes itself almost exclusively to stockpiling of remote theoretical possibilities. I take the view that the most important avenue for research in literary semantics is not the sort of pedantry I have indulged in with Rodger over this obscure text but the relation between the reading of texts and the activities of the brain. If we are going to speculate, let us speculate about something that is really worthwhile. The next two chapters will do just that.

B. KINETIC THEORY

CHAPTER 7

THEORETICAL SEMICS

Literature and Science

Recent years have seen growing interest in linguistic criticism of literature. Fowler's book, which provoked the controversy referred to in chapter 5, gives examples of such work, and many linguists are beginning to turn to this problem of literary language.[1] The assumption seems to be that the contribution of the linguists to the study of literature will be of this nature, and it is a prospect which the linguists appear to view with confidence, the critics with alarm.

With those critics who are anxious lest their humane pursuits become overrun by the analysis and statistics of the professional linguists I feel sympathy. As soon as the linguists turn to interpretation, they tend to become just as subjective as the critics, their conclusions, ostensibly the corollaries of their analytical tables, being far from inevitable. Evidence of this has been seen in Fowler's advocacy of linguistic analysis merely as a useful tool in literary criticism[2] and Rodger's failure to observe the principles of the semantics of literature. There is, however, a modal solution. One strength of the linguist lies in his awareness of the need to examine the sort of inference he is making and in his methodological tidiness. But my case for literary semantics, which has so far emphasized the linguists' tidy approach, is not confined to this brief. Literary semantics, in addition to being tidy, can also be imaginative.

The model I shall describe is as speculative as the work of most critics, but it differs in two important respects: firstly, it is labelled 'speculative' and located in the kinetic component of literary semantics; secondly, if, in the course of time, it were found to be more satisfactory than is at present claimed, the range of application would be wider than discoveries based on any single text would be likely to prove. Texts are important for literary semantics. Brains are even more important, for without *them* there would be no texts.

The **dynaxial hypersphere**, the model to be described, is accommodated within the diagram of the components of literary semantics as shown below. The claims that are made are small; the model is simply an indication of one of the directions theoretical semics might take, and theoretical semics is just one component in the analeptic structure of literary semantics.

What is literature? A consensus of texts acknowledged in academic circles to be 'literary' would doubtless show statistically a high degree of deviation from (a) the linguistic structures of 'everyday' speech[3] and (b) from the ontological commitments of 'ordinary-language' users.

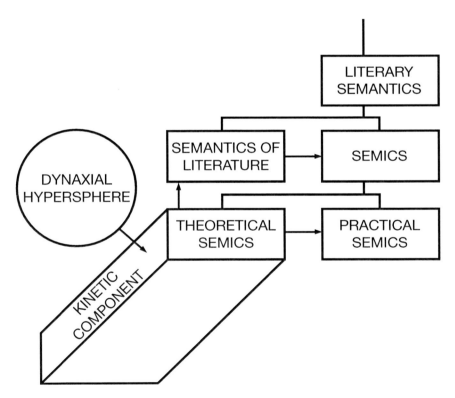

The above diagram shows the relation between the analeptic and the kinetic components of the science of literary semantics. A sub-section of the analeptic system, excised from the larger depiction [LS:52], projects downwards. Theoretical semics unites the recalcitrant functions of analepsis and kinesis. The dynaxial hypersphere, located within the kinetic component of theoretical semics is a speculative model and by the arrow labelled as such.

Figure 5.   Location of the Dynaxial Hypersphere Within the Kinetic Component.

Halliday, MacIntosh and Strevens suggest that it be regarded as a register. '... it is of the essence of creative writing that it calls attention to its own form, in the sense that unlike other language activity, written or spoken, it is meaningful as activity in itself and not merely as part of a larger situation: again, of course, without a clear line of demarcation'.[4] Phrases like 'creative writing' and 'calls attention to its own form' are unproductive: if it is true that the majority of grammatical sentences that we generate have never been used before, then most language is creative[5], and our *differentia* fails. 'Calls attention to its own form' introduces an appeal to aesthetics and invites the sort of critical subjectivity discussed in chapter 5.

It is doubtful whether delimitation of borders will ever be other than an involved and unrewarding labour. In the meantime, I wish to show that we can proceed from a widely acknowledged example of literary creativity to the formulation of a challenging question for theoretical semics [LS:108–126; chapter 8 *passim*]. In approaching the problem from the centre, we may discover the precise position of the margins to be without significance.

Transmission Semantics

'In Xamdu did Cublai Can build a stately Palace, encompassing sixteene miles of plaine ground with a wall, wherein are fertile Meddowes, pleasant springs, delightfull Streames, and all sorts of beasts of chase and game, and in the middest thereof a sumptuous house of pleasure, which may be removed from place to place.' This sentence from *Purchas His Pilgrimage* was probably the one which Coleridge was reading when, according to his own account,[6] he fell asleep in his chair. Coleridge places this occurrence in the summer of 1797.[7] He was unwell, and had retired to an isolated farmhouse near Porlock in Somerset where, on this important occasion, he sought relief in an anodyne.

'The Author continued for about three hours in a profound sleep, at least of the external senses, during which time he has the most vivid confidence, that he could not have composed less than from two to three hundred lines; if that indeed can be called composition in which all the images rose up before him as *things*, with a parallel production of the correspondent expressions, without any sensation or consciousness of effort. On awaking he appeared to himself to have a distinct recollection of the whole, and taking his pen, ink, and paper, instantly and eagerly wrote down the lines that are here preserved.'[8] At this fateful moment, Coleridge was interrupted by a visitor from Porlock. The visitor detained him for an hour, and when Coleridge returned to his room, he was able to remember only a minute portion of the poem.

In *The Road to Xanadu*, written shortly after the First World War and now a famous example of literary research (**semantics of literature/transmission semantics**), John Livingston Lowes attempted to trace the material with which Coleridge unconsciously worked in the production of *Kubla Khan*. Coleridge was an avid reader, and on one occasion announced in a letter to Thelwall that he had read almost everything.[9] What is more, he used to make detailed references in his notes to the reading he had been doing. Lowes' method was to retrace Coleridge's reading itinerary, in the hope of finding the raw material of poetic composition, '...it was inevitable that flashes of association should dart in all directions, and that images endowed with the potentiality of merging should stream together and coalesce'.[10] The results of this undertaking are remarkable. Lowes, with boundless dedication, read where Coleridge had read, and discovered many phrases which are undoubted analogues of phrases in *The Ancient Mariner* and *Kubla Khan*. Lowes' account belongs to the region where the **semantics of literature** and **transmission semantics** merge. These two analyses are subsumed within theoretical semics.

Whilst details of Lowes' argument may be questioned – for instance whether 'Abora' in line 41 of the poem is a coalescence of 'Abola' and 'Astaboras'[11] – the case which he presented seems, allowing for the difficulties inherent in establishing the semantics of literature,[12] to be broadly substantiated. And Lowes was aware that the implications of his research transcended the domain of the semantics of literature '...nothing is trivial which contributes to our understanding, on the one hand, of the strange working of the mind in dreams, and on the other, of the wakeful operations of the creative faculty'.[13]

Lowes' contention was that the dream which gave birth to *Kubla Khan* was induced by opium;[14] on the other hand, he argued that *The Rime of the Ancient Mariner*, although it may owe scattered images to indulgence in the drug, is too powerfully controlled to be essentially the product of a drugged mind.[15] But the more consciously regulated processes of poetic composition are nevertheless seen to be closely parallel to the fervid creativity of an opium dream.

Lowes' achievement is in his thorough analysis of the works which Coleridge had read. He was interested in the poetic processes which produced them, but his description of the cerebral events was unspecific – 'radiating streams of spontaneous association',[16] 'streaming processssion of linked images',[17] 'swift coalescence of the linked impressions,[18] 'subliminal reservoir'.[19] He came closest to raising the question which I would like to pose, and which, so far as I am aware, no one has seriously attempted to answer, when he asked, 'Where, indeed, at any given instant, are all the countless facts we know, and all the million scenes we have experienced?'[20] A highly speculative answer to this question is given in chapter 8 [LS:131–134].

The composition of *Kubla Khan*, if we can believe the details as presented by Coleridge himself,[21] constitutes a most astounding literary fact. We have all experienced the sense that in a given context a certain word is 'preferable' to another. But the system of choices which produced this scheme of preferences is almost beyond comprehending: a permutation of linguistic competence – phonological, lexical, syntactic, semantic and metrical. And this composition took place, so we are led to suppose, in sleep.

Two objections to my choice of *Kubla Khan* as an illustration may be anticipated. Firstly, the account given by Coleridge could not possibly be substantiated by external evidence. Secondly, in a chapter whose subject is theoretical semics, to offer a model which accounts for the composition of a poem rather than the experience of reading is to confuse **semics** with the **semantics of literature**. Dealing with the first point: the important issue here is not to establish whether Coleridge was telling the truth, but to accept his account tentatively as a most challenging and extreme portrayal of the capability of the brain. Any model which can cope with *Kubla Khan* should be able to accommodate any other 'literary' experience. Nor is there any confusion between semics and the semantics of literature. The semic machine is the same, whether composing or reading, and our model should be powerful enough to account for both operations in their chronological sequence: the **transmission semantics** of authorship and the **semics** of readership. The significance of the arrow drawn from theoretical semics to the semantics of literature/transmission semantics [LS:52] is to admit such speculations as these. Further, the dynaxial theory is applied briefly to the problem of semic accompaniment in the last section of chapter 8. Let us summarize the position in this manner: a semantic machine of such and such specifications would account for the alleged experiences of Coleridge, but it will not help us to establish the historical truth or falsehood of Coleridge's assertions.

The Rôle of Theoretical Semics as an Exploratory Tool

Lowes has analysed the input: there have been many analyses of the output.[22] Formulating the traditional linguistic concern for literary texts, we shall arrive at the following question: How can we produce an analysis of this text based on sound linguistic principles? Whilst this seems acceptable at one level – a linguistically unsound study of a linguistic text could scarcely be advocated – it avoids a more challenging question: What sort of machine is capable of generating this sort of output from that kind of input? A behaviourist machine? Brief consideration of the alleged experience will be enough to convince a fair-minded observer that if behaviourism is to explain such a phenomenon, we shall need a behaviourism distilled to a quintessence. Let us now elaborate the *analeptic-kinetic* theory of science touched upon on [LS:51–53] and then discuss the place of behaviourism within that structure.

The opposition between analepsis and kinesis may be seen at two levels: the **ontogenetic** and the **phylogenetic**. Each individual scientist has, internalized, a conceptual structure which more or less adequately represents the analeptic structures of the science.[23] Before he commits himself to publication, his material will already have been subjected to a filtering process: some of the criticisms which the analepsis traditionally raises will be anticipated, and attempts will be made to meet them in the processes of **reciprocal perspective**. Material which is thought by the individual scientist to be analeptically unacceptable may be modified or deleted. *The interchange between kinesis and analepsis takes place usually at the ontogenetic level prior to the phylogenetic.*

We may distinguish thus between a **science** and a **scientist**. Applying the definition of scientific health [LS:51–53] to these two levels – the phylogenetic level of the science and the ontogenetic level of the scientist – we may say that scientific health manifests itself at the phylogenetic (sociological) level in a balance between the theoretical and the empirical components (that is, for literary semantics, between theoretical semics and empirical semics); and at the ontogenetic (psychological) level in the same theoretical-empirical tension, as present in the mind of each individual scientist involved.

Reverting to the discussion of behaviourism – much depends upon how the basic tenet of behaviourism is formulated: (i) All psychic activity manifests itself in some form of observable behaviour; (ii) Propositions concerning psychic activity are more likely to beome affident if they are based upon observable behaviour. When (i) is expounded not as a procedural assumption but as a dogma, it is insidious: explanation gives way to description, and the experimenters tend to limit themselves to what they can adequately describe. Their endeavours become concentrated upon the bar-pressing activities of rodents. But (ii) seems to me wholly reasonable.

Chomsky has discussed at length the question of whether a mechanistic approach can account for the phenomenon of language acquisition[24] and he has spoken out polemically against the behaviourists and the empiricists. That he does at other times acknowledge a form of behaviourism[25] and does treat weak empiricism as self-evident[26] suggests that his reactionary tendencies are really only a shift in emphasis. In fact, the mechanistic-mentalistic controversy can never finally be resolved.[27] Consider the case of two disputants, one of whom, in order to refute his opponent's contention that the sap is transported up the tree by an invisible sprite, demonstrates experimentally at great length the botanical mechanisms whereby the sap is conveyed to the branches. The other – very patient and ostensibly open-minded – disputant tiresomely accedes, exclaiming, 'How wonderful are the ways of the sprite!'

Thus we may regard the progressive understanding of the psychological and neurophysiological mechanisms as increasing our awareness of the immanent mentalistic reality, or we can view it as a slow dismemberment of the cadaver, each mechanistic step forward entailing a mentalistic step backward, the inference being that at infinity mentalism would be left with no territory at all. Chomsky's discussion of the testable hypothesis that an artificial 'language' whose structures ran counter to the universals should prove harder to learn than a natural language does not affect this issue.[28] An innate linguistic faculty, even if proved to exist, could be just as mechanistic as an S→R model; that is to say, circularly speaking, if we were able to analyse its workings mechanistically, we should discover only mechanisms.

Crude behaviourism, pitched at rodent level, will not, it is true, account for the linguistic achievements of man. We are therefore faced with the alternative of modifying behaviourism, or of jettisoning it in favour of a neo-rationalist approach. Chomsky wished to abandon behaviourism altogether, even to the point of excising behaviourist terminology.[29] Are we therefore to change the squeaking wheel, or to oil it?

The rigorous experimentation of the behaviourists is basically well-conceived: the real complaint is that in concentrating their efforts upon situations where opportunities for scientific observation were possible, the behaviourists neglected the study of the human psyche. Whether the behaviourists were ever as naïve as Chomsky and Koestler[30] assert is debatable; what is certain is that they developed procedures which, within their limited sphere, were sound. The behaviourists evolved a rigorous analeptic system; they knew beforehand precisely what conditions their colleagues would demand should be fulfilled in the presentation of material. One of the two constituents necessary for scientific health is present. And, conversely, would it not be true to say that an 'explanatory' theory which did not lead to empirical discovery would be a scientific *cul-de-sac*?

The task of the literary semanticist is, profiting from the kinetic deficiency of the behaviourists and the analeptic failure of the literary critics, to provide a conceptual structure which builds in the rigour of the behaviourists at one level, and allows kinetic enterprise to flourish at another. Within this analeptic classification then, the **semantics of literature** (with **transmission semantics**) and **empirical semics** are rigorous and objective; **introspective semics** is subjective; but at the level of **theoretical semics** we may reformulate and speculate and imagine. One of its functions is as an exploratory tool. Chapter 4 of this book elaborated the analeptic structure outlined in chapters 1 to 3. Chapter

5 provided a confrontation of that structure with the position of academic critics. Chapter 6 analysed an article by a linguist, pointing out the strengths, weaknesses and pitfalls of linguistic criticism. The purpose of chapters 7 and 8 is to show that **literary semantics**, in embracing **analepsis**, need not reject **kinesis**, fertile speculation concerning questions of paramount importance for the future of literary studies.

Pure Science and Applied Science

At this point it will be useful to discuss the difference between a pure and an applied science. A metaphor which may illustrate this distinction is an echo chamber. The raw material of the empirical science is represented by the sounds, which are produced at the aperture of the echo chamber. In some cases, the sound, after reverberating through the echo chamber, emerges once more. Sometimes it never returns. The applied scientist, typically, stands at the entrance, making sounds in the hope that an echo will emerge to answer his problems. The interior of the echo chamber represents the pure science. Providing the path traced by the sound waves within the chamber has 'internal consistency', the demands of the pure science will have been fulfilled, though it may be that the echo is lost to the applied scientist for ever.

The applied and the pure science should be complementary. At the crudest kinetic level, the scientist has a corpus, and nothing more. At the highest degree of abstraction, the pure scientist becomes almost impervious to empirical data. Yet a corpus with neither explanation nor description is as unsatisfactory as a pure science, whose calculations are not predictive and are without application to a corpus. Some linguists, notably R. M. W. Dixon's *What is Language?*, insist upon the primacy of the corpus,[31] whilst others deliberately restrict the demands of the corpus by such devices as 'competence' and the 'ideal speaker-listener'. The danger is that the ones will be impeded by what, begging the question, is 'linguistically insignificant or misleading', e.g. utterances that the speaker would acknowledge to have been mistakes; and that the others may find, in basing their concept of 'grammaticality' upon an 'ideal' corpus, they have succeeded in formulating an algebra which neglects important empirical evidence.[32]

One of the shortcomings of linguistic considerations of literary works has been the concept of grammaticality. Many of the sentences in literary works are seen, by 'ordinary language' criteria, to be grammatically deviant: Dylan Thomas' 'A Grief Ago' is a famous example,[33] or the poems of e. e. cummings. But literary works are linguistic texts, and the linguist would like to deal with them. He is faced with a decision: is he perpetually to consign literary structures to an extra-grammatical limbo of deviation, or can he formulate a theory of grammaticality which reconciles the traditional concepts of grammaticality with the apparent waywardness of some literary works? We have reached the point we touched upon on [LS:101–102]; do we limit our corpus and regard some literature as deviant, or do we broaden our linguistics?

Semantic Models

Wim Bronzwaer, in a friendly review of my earliest work, first set me thinking in terms of the present model. I had postulated a semantic space on the lines developed by Osgood, Suci and Tannenbaum.[34] Bronzwaer wrote, 'It is at this point that the reader throws up his hands in despair, for who can imagine a Semantic Space comprehensive enough to accommodate all the categories of experience functioning in *King Lear*?'[35] My first reaction was that this was a justifiable criticism and, as Bronzwaer allows, this had never been my intention. As I have attempted, however, to work out the practical implications of my theories, it has become increasingly clear that if a scientific approach to literary experience is ultimately to be possible, a model of extreme complexity will be needed. A semantic space still seems to me as good a starting point as any.

Perhaps the most famous model for a semantic space was the one already mentioned, elaborated by Osgood, Suci and Tannenbaum [LS:4–6]. The underlying principle of their measurement was as simple as their derived models were complex.[36] A subject is given a graduated scale of seven possibilities, the extremes of which are bipolar adjectives. Between these bipolar adjectives, the subject is asked to locate various 'concepts'.

MOTHER

Hard							Soft
Strong							Weak
Good							Bad

The rationale of semantic differentiation is explained in Osgood et al. *The Measurement of Meaning* pp. 25-30.

When it comes to considering the semantic space of Osgood, Suci and Tannenbaum as a basis for a framework in theoretical semics, a difficulty immediately arises. The almost stately procession of concepts from a pathological to a healthful collocation may be ideal in psychiatric diagnosis, but it hardly does justice to the dynamic conceptual activity which would appear to take place when at least some works of literature are read (**semics**), still less to the turmoil of composition (**transmission semantics**) described by Coleridge, which produced *Kubla Khan*.

Secondly, there is an underlying assignment which I feel to be inelegant. We said that, according to the Osgood, Suci and Tannenbaum procedure, a concept, for instance 'mother', was assigned to a location somewhere between bipolar adjectives, for instance 'hard' and 'soft'. The question arises therefore that if 'mother' is a concept, what are 'hard' and 'soft'? The scale would seem to ascribe to them a separate status, which prejudges the very conceptual situation they are aiming to investigate. I am not blaming them for this, since, practically, we have to start somewhere, and wherever we start we shall be accused of arbitrary selection. In fact, the practical application of my theory [LS:116 and 118] would be very close to the Osgood conception.

Thirdly, the semantic space, although it claims to be conceptual, relies upon a linguistic gradation between bipolar adjectives, and a linguistic symbol as the 'concept'. This, of course, is inevitable, and admirably pragmatic. But there is a danger that in living with the politic we shall neglect the ideal.

My aim is to map out a semantic space which would eliminate these objections. I shall return to the Osgood, Suci and Tannenbaum conceptual space in order to illustrate the kind of model I have in mind. In any case, until we have a solution to the 'linking' problem, [LS:119], progress will necessarily be slow.

As the Osgood, Suci and Tannenbaum semantic space is extremely speculative, and as I am admitting at the outset that mine is even less practically based than theirs, perhaps we should consider briefly another venture into semantic space which, whilst it is also speculative, does at least attempt to encompass observable phenomena and relate these to the findings of neurophysiology.

The human cortex contains some 10,000,000,000 neurons, interrelated by means of dendrites and synapses. The mechanistic assumption is that what we call thinking consists in the chemical and electrical interaction of these neurons. E. C. Zeeman of Warwick University, a mathematician, postulates a cubic space consisting of 10^{10} neurons.[37] His aim is to prove a mathematical isomorphism between his space and the observed neurophysiological phenomena. Professor Zeeman is concerned to investigate activities which, compared to literary experience, are relatively simple. An example is the initial inability of patients blind from birth, who receive their sight as a result of an operation, to detect, when vision is possible, the difference between a triangle and a circle. A period of some months is necessary before most such patients can observe simultaneously this difference. What appears to us to be a 'natural' ability is thus seen to be a gradual acquisition.[38] Zeeman attempts to explain this phenomenon by means of a mathematical model.

I do not think his model, as it stands, would do justice to more complex semic phenomena. Isomorphism is, I believe, the clue to the connection between the speculative models. If Zeeman can prove an isomorphism between his cube and the activity of the brain, then it may be possible ultimately to provide a justification in isomorphic terms for more ambitious spaces. Despite the perhaps hypertheoretical tendencies of this chapter, I would regard ultimate isomorphism between the space and the neural phenomena as important. One other point should be mentioned which has consequences for my concept of a semantic space: Zeeman, speaking of the capacity of his model, observes that it is not infinite − 'the capacity is $10^{100,000}$ which is very high'.[39] This mathematical symbol is deceptively concise. With normal typesetting, the extended notation would fill many sheets of A4 paper with noughts. If a model based on the neurophysiological data will yield a capacity of this order, we need not be unduly economical in the dimensions of this speculative model for theoretical semics.

Professor Stephen Grossberg has set out in a similar direction.[40] He has constructed a mathematical machine capable, theoretically, of list-learning. His aim is to correlate the observed psychological and neurophysiological phenomena with the products of the machine. The more 'analogs' that can be discovered between the machine's functions and these phenomena, the more satisfactory the machine. What is more, predictions may be made on the basis of the machine's performance, which may then be tested. The phenomena which Grossberg examines are the result of behavioural research: 'bowing', 'anchoring', 'chunking', for instance. These are technical terms designating observed tendencies in the process of learning lists.

A difficulty which faces us in the construction of a model which will do justice to literary experience is the fundamental one of deciding precisely what the salient phenomena are. Zeeman's and Grossberg's data are relatively straightforward. If, for example, a subject is asked to learn a list, he has nothing to gain by providing untrue reports. When he has learnt the list, he will give the appropriate response, that is, repeat the list without hesitation or mistake, and the psychologist will fix criteria to determine when this point has been reached. But in literary studies, the avowed responses of students are less likely to be indices of their actual experiences. Grossberg's subject presented with a list will have two alternatives: learning the list, or not learning it: as there is a premium upon learning it, he will usually try to do this, and the responses he makes will be directly related to his learning performance. In literary studies, a student, faced with two possible evaluations or interpretations of a text, is likely to be influenced in recording his experience by what he knows to be the literary climate. He is conditioned by his literary 'training' to favour certain modes of response. If, perhaps, he truly responds to Kipling more readily than to Donne, he will tend to be reticent about this. He knows that Donne is highly thought of, and he does not wish to prejudice his career. But the student's true response is a literary fact, and as such, is more important semic material than his feigned response. In this way, academic criticism throws a blanket over valuable literary material. Introspective evidence, which at the best of times should be treated with caution, is rendered even less reliable.

The second difficulty is that the *langue-parole* dichotomy will be less useful here. Bateson develops a literary version of this, I believe unsuccessfully, for reasons I have tried to show. Grammaticality is by definition stable: literary response tends to be unstable. The search for a literary grammaticality or a rhetorical competence is destined, perhaps, never to succeed: as soon as we abandon 'verbal immobility' and make aesthetic response, we jettison linguistic convention and obey the rules of our own separate personalities. If Firth's dictum that 'the study of one person at a time seems amply justified as a scientific method' holds true of investigation into grammaticality,[41] how much more true is it of literary studies? Now, for all Bateson's emphasis upon *parole*, the concept of the 'right literary response' would appear to be an attempt to erect an aesthetic *langue*.

The Dynaxial Hypersphere

The requirements of a model for literary semantics are that it should be objective and neutral. By 'objective' I mean that there should be indisputable correlation between the model and the literary facts; by 'neutral' I mean that the model should not incorporate any preconceived notions concerning a poetic quality. Walter Koch is working towards this position when he distinguishes between an 'optimal' poem and 'good' poem; by 'optimal', I presume he means 'exhibiting in the highest degree those characteristics which constitute the criteria of a poetic work', as distinct from 'best', which has to do with the value judgment of a particular reader.[42] In theory at least, the objectivity and neutrality of our model could be established by means of an affidence test. A mathematical model would be admissible. I accept that a TG grammar with algebraically structured rules (analeptic constants) will detect algebraic patterns (also analeptic constants) in an example text. Unlike value judgment, this is circularity without whim. Our model is autonomous; we commit our data to it, and we accept its verdict whether we like it or not. My main aim is to exclude value considerations – as far as possible – from the model, but in this respect, see chapter 11.

My model is a geometrical one.[43] Envisage a multi-dimensional, semantic space, curved and finite, traversed by n-axes. Each axis represents a semantic potential xy, x and y being points on the axis. Each axis 'curves back' upon itself. The points x and y are polar opposites. This concept of curvature is perhaps difficult to grasp: I mean that a straight line, in this case, the axis, extending in a given direction, will ultimately join up with itself at the point at which it began. Imagine a map of the world with a slight overlap, so that, say, the British Isles appears twice, on the extreme right and the extreme left of the map. We place a ruler across the map and draw a line from London to London. The line is straight, and yet it has 'curved back' upon itself. The present microcosmology, then, postulates a finite semantic space, consistent with the finite storage capacity of the brain [LS:110]. This model aptly mirrors our subjective experience. In normal circumstances, however far, however fast and in whatever direction we move, literally or metaphorically, we return to our own consciousness.

Secondly, the points are adjustable; any adjustment of point y along the axis xy entails a corresponding adjustment of x, such that the spatial polarity between x and y still obtains. Thus all points on a given axis remain fixed in relation to one another, but are capable of movement relative to points on other axes:

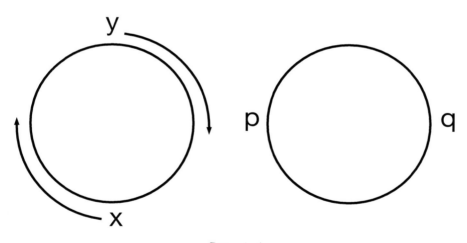

Dynamic Axes

Where the axes are represented as circles, the movement of y entails equal movement of x; x is still opposite y, but x is further away from p; and y is closer to intersection with p. The spatial polarity between x and y represents polarity of a semantic potential.

A third quality of this semantic space is that any point on any axis may coincide with any point on any other axis as a result of adjustment of either axis or both. When a point on an axis coincides with a point on another axis, this is known as **intersection**. In [LS:112], *y*, or any point on *xy*, can not only come nearer to, but potentially coincide with, any point on *pq*. We may then say that the two axes on which the points lie **intersect**. There is no theoretical limit to the number of axial intersections possible at any point within the space. The more intersections of axes at a given point within the semantic space, the more **intense** is the point. Any region of the space which contains many intense points is likewise said to be **intense**. A region with no **intense** points is **devoid**.

The region of the space in which at any given moment there is maximum adjustment of axes is said to be the **centre** of the semantic space. Let C be any region within the semantic space enclosing the centre at any given time. The smaller the volume of C (as in conscious thought?) the more **concentrated** the centre. The larger the volume of C (as in dreaming?), the more **diffuse** the centre. When an adjustment takes place for the first time, by this I mean that it bears no similarity to any previous adjustments, it is said to be **dynamic**. This is the **principle of dynamism**. Once a particular adjustment has taken place, it becomes statistically more likely that similar adjustments will take place in future; such adjustments are said to be **facilitated**. This is the **principle of facilitation**.[44] It seems to me possible that the principles of dynamism and facilitation may ultimately enable us to operate this model on foundations that are both neutral and objective.

The aim of the model is to provide a speculative account of the following facts: (A), (B) and (C) corresponding to **primary**, **secondary** and **tertiary dynamic-axial space**, or **dynaxial space**, respectively. The term 'dynamic-axial', or 'dynaxial', is chosen to distinguish it from the **conceptual-axial** space of Osgood, Suci and Tannenbaum, dynamic, because on disturbance it re-constitutes itself around a significant centre, consciousness.

(A)   Each person is born without the ability to use language, yet ultimately acquires a language. [**primary dynaxial space**]
(B)   The conceptual apparatus acquired by a human is stable enough to permit the person to communicate with others of the same linguistic community, more or less satisfactorily. [**secondary dynaxial space**]
(C)   The linguistic and conceptual patterns are constantly being modified by contact with the external world. [**tertiary dynaxial space**]

The observed fact (A) above represents the *potential* of any person's semantic space, let us say, at birth. This is the **primary semantic space**. We need to postulate this, whatever our assumptions concerning the problems of universals and the mechanistic/mentalistic controversy. In fact, it seems even the most primitive Watsonian Stimulus→Response behaviourism requires some sort of universal though not necessarily linguistic. A reponse is not, under any circumstances, a synonym for passivity. The passive response to a stimulus is no-response-at-all: even a blank slate *is* blank, and *is* a slate. It is the universal that determines the character of the response to a given stimulus. We would, however, be in good company nowadays if we were to make the assertion that there is more information built into the organism at the outset than the earlier behaviourists supposed.[45] Charles Hockett, replying to Chomsky's remarks about an innate system for the production of an indefinitely large set of grammars of 'possible' human languages, well sums up what I would take to be the minimum basic assumption: 'If we delete the metaphysics... and interpret it in the obvious way, it becomes simply a peculiar formulation of something that we have all known for a long time; that almost any human child can and, if he survives, almost certainly will learn a language...'[46]

What is certain, then, is that an English child is born without the ability to use, for instance, the linguistic symbol 'hot', presumably without a concept of 'hotness' (though with the necessary reflex mechanism to shun intense heat), and that by the age of five will normally have both the use of the word and possess the concept. We may therefore conclude that there is inbuilt in the human organism a conceptual (if not linguistic) potential which in normal cases is realised at a fairly early age.

Returning to the **primary semantic space**: I conceive of this as existing in an initial state of violent agitation; a state in which there is volatile adjustment and readjustment, but little intersection. Axes may be adjusted either by external activity (i.e. from outside the semantic space – Wittgenstein's 'objects' in his *Tractatus*), or internally by spontaneous dynamic activity, paralleled in the fact that all the cells in the cortex are firing even when not in use.

My concept of a semantic space suffers from the same disability as Wittgenstein's factual system, expounded in his early work, *The Tractatus Logico-Philosophicus*.[47] His view was that we move within a mosaic of propositions, and that somewhere 'beyond' are the 'objects' of the real world. Our destiny is never to comprehend this real and, it has been objected, metaphysical[48] sphere of the objects. The commonsense answer to this is that if we are going to postulate a system of propositions, which belong, after all, to the rather esoteric discourse of the logicians, why not proceed a little further and commit ourselves ontologically to the 'objects', which are familiar to everyone?[49]

In the same way, semantic space would appear to be incapable of 'receiving anything from the outside world', for any changes which take place are regarded as modifications of a primary semantic space which already possessed the capacity for being thus modified. We are moving towards an insoluble problem of the kind mentioned [LS:105–106]. In thus limiting the capacity of the space, I am restricting myself only at the kinetic level. The trichotomy theory, which is the all-embracing component of my analeptic theory, has not this deficiency: knowledge one, the possibility of 'being right', provides the theoretical escape route to the 'objects' we all can name but whose existence only the philosophers call in doubt. This illustrates the power of the overall approach: we can commit ourselves kinetically to a perhaps inadequate model, speculate, and then return to the analepsis to assess the results.

So far we have been dealing with potentials. The **secondary semantic space**, (B), represents the *actual* adjustments of the axes and the consequent *actual* modifications of the primary semantic space effected either by contact with the external world or causally by chain reaction as a result of previous adjustments. I must emphasize that this is not a different semantic space from the primary semantic space. It is simply what happens to the brain as a result of experience.

Of this secondary semantic space, language is a part. Here also belong the conceptual models of Osgood, Suci and Tannenbaum. The authors claim to deal with 'concepts', but these concepts can be referred to only linguistically. Language at this level comprises what Chomsky calls 'competence'. But it should be stressed that competence is not synonymous with secondary semantic space, for this space does not consist entirely of language.[50] I would assume that, within the space, there is a great deal of activity which is not linguistic, but that language directs, canalizes and condenses the non-linguistic activity (i.e. perhaps causes more stable alignment of the axes within semantic space).

Secondary semantic space is the primary space modifed and structured by the actual adjustments of the axes. We may say that the secondary semantic space is a realization of the primary semantic space. In the same way, **tertiary semantic space,** cf. (C) [LS:113], is the result of external interference causing redistribution of axes within secondary semantic space. Using the well-worn analogy of the game of chess, we can observe that the **primary semantic space** corresponds to the number of games which could, potentially, be played; the **secondary semantic space** to the observed tendencies in actual games, e.g. moving the knight at the commencement of the game; and the **tertiary semantic space** is whatever is happening in one particular game. Tertiary space is the point at which 'external reality' impinges upon the semantic space. Thus the experience of reality causes axial realignments at the level of tertiary semantic space. By a filtering process, **reciprocal perspective**, these are assimilated into, or modified or rejected by the secondary semantic space.

It is important to understand that this analysis belongs to the **psychological level**; the trichotomy theory is at the **philosophical level**. Summarizing then, we have a threefold analysis of semantic space. The space itself is flexible and dynamic, initially in a state of motion. The emphasis is not upon establishing concepts at a fixed distance from a neutral point (as in the Osgood model), but upon a dynamic field of axes shaped, into the consciousness we all know, by both internal and external influences. Intuitively, this seems to me better suited to coping theoretically with the complex experience associated with the reading of a work of literature.

According to my concept, therefore, the Osgood, Suci and Tannenbaum models are pedestrian (and I mean no disrespect) maps[51] of secondary semantic space. The semantic space is a metaphor, not a neural reality, conceived in order to explain the observed phenomena of the psyche.

Let us now consider a practical application of the theory. It was earlier observed that the models of Osgood, Suci and Tannenbaum were, according to the present theory, maps of secondary semantic space. *The Measurement of Meaning* was written with other purposes in mind, and my following account is an interpretation for my own purposes.

Consider the **semic accompaniment** of a **hypothetical reader** confronted by the following lines from *Antony and Cleopatra*. We assume that the reader identifies himself at least momentarily with Antony, and that he undergoes a conceptual reorganization which, on at least one level of commitment, he would take to represent the notional experiences of Antony himself.

(1)   *2nd Messenger*: Fulvia thy wife is dead.[52]

Figure 6.   Adjustment of Axes

Then, Antony's speech in reply to the Second Messenger makes explicit the conceptual reorganization which has taken place supposedly in Antony's mind, but in fact in the reader's. The letters (a), (b) and (c) correspond to the reorganizations mapped [LS:118].

(2)   *Antony*:

    (a)   There's a great spirit gone! Thus did I desire it:

    (b)   What our contempts do often hurl from us,
             We wish it ours again; the present pleasure
             By revolution lowering, does become
             The opposite of itself: she's good, being gone;
             The hand could pluck her back that shov'd her on.

    (c)   I must from this enchanting queen break off;
             Ten thousand harms, more than the ills I know,
             My idleness doth hatch.[53]

According to this model, shock such as might be occasioned by the announcement of someone's death is the result of violent conceptual activity: the concept of the person live runs the length of the axis to meet the concept death. The shock is lessened by allowing the concept to travel more slowly from x to the opposite polar extreme y; that is to say, we perhaps give the hearer a cup of tea, and hint at the truth, before finally breaking the news. The limitation is that the selection of bipolar adjectives somewhat arbitrarily, and one by one, fails to do justice to the dynamism of language which has infinite capacity for bringing diverse concepts into new relations. My own concept of a semantic space, though perhaps impossible to represent as a model, does attempt to accommodate the sometimes apparently volatile nature of literary experience. According to my notion, the axes themselves readjust, dynamically realigning and shifting the entire hypersphere of consciousness; whereas the models of Osgood, Suci and Tannenbaum are psychological 'stills', plotting at intervals the movement of concepts within a static cube whose centre denotes neutrality.

The following account is an attempt to transfer the (2) (a), (b), (c) reorganization into terms of my dynamic-axial semantic space. All concepts, 'Fulvia', 'Cleopatra', 'life', 'death', 'good', 'bad', 'love', 'politics' are the results of previous adjustments and consequent intersections of millions of axes. At the news of Fulvia's death, there is a sudden adjustment of large numbers of these axes, whereby the intersections now made redundant by this news separate violently from the conceptual centres represented by the axial intersections; they find new alignments and cause concatenations of vehement conceptual activity. [LS:118] is an attempt to describe the magnitude of the activity: the precise direction of the illustrated axes is without significance, for I have carried out no factor-analysis. Indeed, it is doubtful whether any factor-analysis based upon purely linguistic material can be satisfactory: what we really need is an analysis of the cerebral (conceptual) activity from which our linguistic measurements are inevitably several stages removed.

The diagrams of the conceptual activity which takes place during a reading of the passage from *Antony and Cleopatra* would be identical for a paraphrase of the same passage.[54] This is a shortcoming of the operation of the model as it has so far been demonstrated.

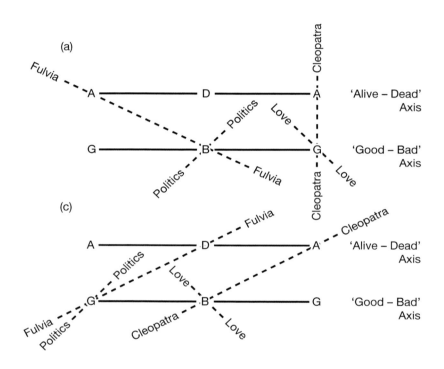

Figure 7.　*Dynaxial Impact in Semic Accompaniment.*

The (a) and (c) in the above diagram refer to the conceptual states of the reader prior to, and after, the verbal exchange between the 2nd Messenger and Antony [LS:116–117].

The conceptual reorganization which took place at a reading by a hypothetical reader of the *Faerie Queene* would certainly resemble the reorganization that occurred at a reading of a prose 'translation', though clearly there are differences; and these differences would be even greater, I believe, in a comparison between Donne's *A Valediction of Weeping*[55] and a prose paraphrase. But this deficiency is in the operation of the model, rather than in the model itself. To remedy this deficiency, we postulate further axes operating more delicately to differentiate such words in the passage as 'hurl', 'pluck' and 'hatch' and any syntactic or metrical deviations which might well be eliminated in a paraphrase. The model would thus work at two levels: 'broad mapping' which described the common ground in the conceptual reorganization of the original as compared with the prose version; and 'narrow mapping', which would account for the differences.

Dynamism and Facilitation

In speculations of the present sort, the theoretical problems may be classified under four headings: (i) Problems of the selection, acquisition and classification of the material with which the model is to operate; (ii) The 'linking' problem: how to render the material suitable for treatment by the model; (iii) the construction of the model itself; (iv) the problem of interpreting and evaluating the workings of the model. It is clear that the linking problem will be far more acute for narrow mapping than it is for broad mapping, but having admitted inadequacy, it will notwithstanding be useful to consider some of the problems of narrow mapping.

Earlier, in the description of the dynaxial space, a distinction was made between the **principle of dynamism** and the **principle of facilitation** [LS:113]. Consider the following sentences:

(3) [   ] is/are sold in the post-office.

    (i) *Syrup*

    (ii) *Stamps*

(4)   I've put cheese in the [   ]

    (i) *Mousetraps*

    (ii) *Mouseholes*

Dealing with these sentences at the level of the competence of a native speaker, we may judge that (3) (ii) has greater facilitation than (3) (i). This does not mean, of course, that the utterance is more probable. On the contrary, its very commonplaceness makes it improbable: a post-office which does not sell stamps is almost a contradiction in terms. The sentence is highly facilitated because, given a spatio-conceptual dictionary, it is to be expected that the concept 'stamps' would be located in the neighbourhood of 'post-office'. The range of lexical items which would fill the slot in sentence (3), and leave it facilitated, is virtually commensurate with the items normally sold in post-offices. When we widen the field of selection to items which are sold in shops but not normally in post-offices, the range of choice becomes enormously larger. The sentence 'Syrup is sold in the post-office' actually occurs in *Under Milk Wood*.[56] 'Syrup', in the hypothetical spatio-conceptual dictionary, must surely be much further from 'post-office' than is the concept 'stamps': it carries connotations of 'viscidity' entirely foreign to the dry orderliness and officialdom of a post-office. The axes which would be facilitated in the case of (3) (ii) are forced into readjustment by (3) (i). In that immediate context, 'syrup' is more dynamic than 'stamps'.

But there now arises the question: Why did the First Voice make this announcement at this point? This is a small Welsh town, very parochial, and a self-contained community. It is inevitable that functions fulfilled by separate units in a city will in this town be combined under one roof. Mrs. Organ Morgan's general shop, we are later told, sells everything: 'custard, buckets, henna, rat-traps, shrimp-nets, sugar, stamps, confetti, paraffin, hatchets, whistles'.[57] That syrup should be sold in the post-office is therefore quite in keeping with the image of the town that Thomas builds up. Let us postulate a reader for purely theoretical purposes, without prejudice as to what he *ought to* or even what he *does* experience, but simply as an illustration of what he *might* experience: let us call him a **hypothetical reader**. The concept of the hypothetical reader will belong to **theoretical semics**; the task of **instantiation** will belong to the **empirical semicist**. Thus, returning to the sentence from *Under Milk Wood,* what was, at a given **semic accompaniment** of our **hypothetical reader**, dynamic, becomes facilitated at the level of textual cohesion:[58] he is surprised briefly, but then he reflects that this is no surprise at all.

A more striking example of this is to be seen in the case of sentence (4). Sentence (4) (i), 'I've put cheese in the mousetraps', is both facilitated and probable. But what does 'probable' mean? Does it mean that, given the situation of a man, muttering under his breath, who has just put cheese in the mousetraps, this utterance is to be expected? But then, a man who has just put cheese in the mouseholes is likely by the same token to utter sentence (4) (ii).[59] Linguistic probability tends to keep pace with referential probability, and some of the linguistic 'deviation' is due to the ontological deviation of the 'literary' work. We have reached the point at which style and content are scarcely to be held separate. Because of this, any attempt to found a theory of literature operating at all levels upon a positivist ontolology will be unsatisfactory. We can adduce correlations between the events during a cricket match and the language used by a commentator, but in a typically 'fictive' composition, such correlation is much more difficult, and probably less rewarding. The correlation here is with the wiring of the brain. Nevertheless, the present theory provides ultimately for assessment by positivist standards at the level of empirical semics. Further, the traditional concept of grammaticality seems to invert the situation: it is not that literature disturbs the norms of grammar, but that grammar[60] represents a terminal point in the slowing down process of initially volatile axes, 'literature', in some cases, stimulating a return to this state of volatility.

The difficulty of definition and the ontological problem notwithstanding, I believe that the concept of dynamism is sufficiently objective to be useful in some circumstances. For instance, given sentence (3), and the four lexical alternatives 'Syrup', 'Stamps' 'Mousetraps' and 'Mouseholes' to be severally inserted in the slot and then arranged in order of ascending dynamism, can there be any serious dispute about the order? 'Stamps are sold in the post-office' is facilitated. 'Syrup is sold in the post-office' and, more or less equally, 'Mousetraps are sold in the post-office' are fairly dynamic. 'Mouseholes are sold in the post-office' is extremely dynamic, almost a semantic rupture, though not quite: in a different context it might be a semi-humorous hyperbole conveying the postmaster's powers of salesmanship.

The **dynamism** which has so far been discussed is **paradigmatic** (lexical choice on a vertical plane). But **syntagmatic dynamism** (lexical choice on a horizontal plane) is also possible. An instance of this would be a structure, apparently straightforward, which in the light of what follows turns out be to ambiguous. Consider sentence (5) in the light of its textual cohesion:

(5)   Syrup is sold in the post-office. A car drives to market, full of fowls and a farmer. Milk-churns stand at Coronation Corner like short silver policemen. And sitting at the open window of Schooner House, blind Captain Cat hears all the morning of the town.

So far I have interpreted 'is sold' as 'is for sale', that is, as a general statement about this post-office, a person who requires syrup can buy it there. But the verb in the following sentence, 'drives', would naturally be interpreted as indicating one particular, continuing action 'is being driven'. On one reading, by a quirk of my semic accompaniment (**introspective semics**), the verb 'drives' acted retrospectively, by **syntagmatic dynamism**, upon 'is sold', and an alternative interpretation was revealed, 'Syrup is being sold in the post-office at this moment'. And to press the textual cohesion further, we learn two lines later that Captain Cat, the blind, retired sailor who 'sees' everything that happens in the town, is sitting at the open window of Schooner House. Instead of a general statement about what is for sale in the post-office, we have an arresting description of a counter transaction which Captain Cat 'sees'.

It is not my purpose to argue that I have described something objective in the text, though literary critics often seriously defend even more outrageous interpretations than this, see, for instance, my discussion of Bateson's analysis of 'Papyrus' in chapter 5. Such moments of 'insight' seem to induce in literary critics a pleasurable rush, amounting to certainty. The danger is when, as academic critics, they convey this interpretation to their students as if it were at the level of empirical semics. Students in English departments should be trained to be critical of their own responses and to discriminate amongst the various modal levels of approach to literature. My evidence here belongs to introspective semics. Its value for theoretical semics is not that this is what the text means, but that, at a given reading by a given subject, such a semic accompaniment occurred. **Syntagmatic dynamism** (the backward or forward linking of textual items which leads to increased semic activity) is a theoretical possibility.[61] It is the task of the **empirical semicist** to determine under precisely what circumstances it takes place.

Returning to the point made concerning paradigmatic dynamism (sense of incongruity introduced in semic accompaniment as a result of unusual lexical choice), we may speculate concerning what, I trust, was there established. Given the context of sentence (3), we concluded that 'Stamps' is facilitated; 'Mousetraps' and 'syrup' are fairly dynamic; and 'Mouseholes' is extremely dynamic. The degree of dynamism is thus commensurate with the range of choice. The three stages in dynamism correspond to the increasing number of lexical members constituting the respective classes: (i) items normally sold in post-offices; (ii) items sold in shops; (iii) items not normally sold at all. But 'Mousetraps', 'syrup' and 'Mouseholes' are not always dynamic: their dynamism depends upon the context. In the context:

(6)   ☐‾‾‾‾‾‾‾‾‾☐ are frequently found in old houses.

'Mouseholes' would be as facilitated as 'stamps' is in (3). Part of the dynamism of 'Syrup is sold in the post-office' may consist therefore in the staged realigning of axes, proper to momentarily absent, facilitated contexts – (a) first semic reaction: *messy juxtaposition*; (b) second reaction: *normal transaction for small-town shop*; (c) my third (**idiosemic**) reaction: *Blind Captain Cat, who can't see, can see this*. A linear text thus gathers semic 'dimensions' in my own semic accompaniment (**introspective semics**).

A further observation may be made. Once the axes have been set into a state of volatile activity by the use of a dynamic item, and extra axes have been involved, a successive dynamic item offers possibilities of axial adjustment, not only with the immediate context, but with the whole range of dynamic activity which has already taken place. Relating this speculation to the **dynaxial theory**, I would suppose the **dynaxial centre** is **concentrated** in **facilitation** and **diffuse** in **dynamism**, cf.[LS:113]. Thus, a don upbraiding his student might intend to say, with facilitation:

(7)   You've missed all your history lectures.

but perpetrates the famous Spoonerism:

(8)   You've hissed all your mystery lectures.[62]

Adapting the sort of transcription used by G. N. Leech[63] to our present purposes, we may illustrate the 'snowballing' effect of dynamism: the number of potential dynaxial adjustments exceeds the number of dynamic lexical items :

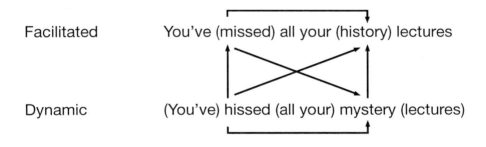

Syntagmatic Dynamism.

In grammatical terms, the intended surface structure of (7) constitutes an obvious variant of the surface structure of the actual utterance (8), and the two variants find resolution at a higher level of abstraction than the grammatical deep structure of either sentence taken separately and literally. In dynaxial terms, the intended straightforward (7) is neutral: the student's absence is not necessarily a sign of disapproval, but must be accounted for. This is the level of facilitation. At the dynamic level, the don unintentionally suggests that the student deeply disapproves, admits the obscurity of the lectures, and thereby supplies the student's motive for failing to attend, or even for showing open disapproval. The arrows above indicate the number of possible directions for extra axial adjustments. The facilitated version (7) involves fewer axial adjustments than (8); the dynaxial centre is concentrated. With the increase in dynamism in (8), there has been a loss of clarity, the utterance has significance, but it is not certain precisely what this is; the dynaxial centre is diffuse: a sudden neural collision within the dynaxial hypersphere of paradigmatic and syntagmatic axes.

An example of a passage which, intuitively, seems extremely dynamic, is the description of Mr. Pugh's gruesome reverie, its vocabulary contrasting with the quiet domesticity of School House and the polite, but frigid responses which Mr. Pugh has made to his wife's recriminations.

(9)   Alone in the hissing laboratory of his wishes, Mr Pugh minces among bad vats and jeroboams, tiptoes through spinneys of murdering herbs, agony dancing in his crucibles, and mixes especially for Mrs Pugh a venomous porridge unknown to toxicologists which will scald and viper through her until her ears fall off like figs, her toes grow big and black as balloons, and steam comes screaming out of her navel.[64]

That this passage has a tendency to initiate violent axial readjustment (or violent cerebral activity), receives behavioural support each time the passage meets with laughter in the live theatre. In fact, it may trivially explain at the lexical if not the neural level, how competent stand-up comedians keep audiences in a state of hysterical reaction for hours of a performance. Once the axes have become volatile and have been released from their grammatical and referential constraints, they intersect, separate and realign.

It is not the purpose of this book to identify the 'poetic dimension' with the principle of dynamism. Undoubtedly some of the texts which would widely be judged 'poetic' would show dynamic qualities. One of the important tasks for literary semantics is, having determined the criteria as objectively as possible, to plot the correlation between these criteria and the value judgments of individuals. But poetry also relies upon facilitation. Recurrence, for instance, cf. [LS:72], which would seem to operate according to the principle of facilitation rather than the principle of dynamism, occurs frequently in 'literary' texts: rhyme, alliteration, metric patterning, and so forth. Poetry is **dynamism**: poetry is **facilitation**: poetry is the **tension** between dynamism and facilitation. The **empirical semicist** were best to eliminate 'poetry' as a primary concept altogether.

Finally, in this discussion, let us briefly indicate some of the problems which arise in connection with the other principle, the principle of facilitation. I have just mentioned the tension between dynamism and facilitation. It seems unlikely that either principle ever operates entirely in isolation. Thus, in passage (9) from *Under Milk Wood* cited above, 'scald' and 'viper' are dynamic, in introducing new aspects of an unpleasant situation, but they are likewise facilitated in their reference to the underlying unpleasantness. It might reasonably be argued that, as they have axes in common, 'scald' and 'viper' constitute a semantic recurrence. How do we decide at what point there are enough common axes between two successive lexical occurrences to justify the use of the term 'recurrence'?

Then, there is the problem of interval. Antony's ironic reference, 'But Brutus is an honourable man'[65] is undoubtedly a recurrence. But this is a whole line of text, repeated at intervals of only a few lines. But does 'dangerous' in Act I, Scene II of *Julius Caesar*, used three times in the exchange between Caesar and Antony, line 192, 'such men are dangerous'... line 193, 'he's not dangerous'... line 207, 'therefore are they very dangerous' constitute a recurrence of the word as used by Cassius more than a hundred lines previously, line 77? In a text the length of a Shakespeare play, accidental lexical recurrence is just as likely as accidental phonological recurrence in a text the size of 'Papyrus'. We may find patterns in the tea leaves, but this does not mean they are significant.

Thirdly, there is the problem of interpretation: illustrating again from *Julius Caesar*.[66] In Act I, there are repeated references to omens: lions near the Capitol, men in fire, an owl shrieking at noonday, graves opening, and so forth. Then, in Act II, Brutus, in his orchard, is able to read the forged letters by the light of the 'exhalations' whizzing in the air. Shortly after this, the Conspirators enter, and whilst Brutus and Cassius whisper apart, Decius, Casca and Cinna have an apparently irrelevant conversation about the dawn:

(10) *Decius:* Here lies the east; doth not the day break here?
      Casca: No.
      Cinna: O, pardon, sir, it doth; and yon grey lines
                 That fret the clouds are messengers of day.
      Casca: You shall confess that you are both deceived.
                 Here, as I point my sword, the sun arises;
                 Which is a great way growing on the south,
                 Weighing the youthful season of the year.
                 Some two months hence up higher toward the north
                 He first presents his fire; and the high east
                 Stands, as the Capitol, directly here.

Why should the Conspirators indulge in a trivial dispute at this point of high tension? Shakespeare is fond of dawn imagery, and this may be nothing more than an interlude. Or, *Julius Caesar* being an early work, this may be simply a mark of immaturity. But Casca seems to know what he is talking about. The sun does rise in the winter to the south of due east, and in the summer, it rises to the north of due east. Can it be that his local knowledge is also accurate? He seems to know precisely where the sun will rise, and to be confident that

Decius is wrong. But if Casca is correct and the sun rises at a different point from the grey lines, then the grey lines cannot be the messengers of dawn. Perhaps these grey lines are a continuance of the 'exhalations' by whose light Brutus was earlier able to decipher the letters? And, if this is the case, does not this constitute a recurrence of the 'omen' theme? The alliteration in *Sir Gawain and the Green Knight* is a palpable instance of recurrence: in order to illustrate the opposite end of the spectrum, I have consciously slid into the discourse of literary criticism.

I shall now analyse the problem according to the **principles of literary semantics**: at the level of **introspective semics**, such an interpretation may enrich the reader's **semic accompaniment**, but it is close to the frontiers, where the discourse shades off into the domain of literary criticism and beyond towards **knowledge three**; at the level of **theoretical semics**, we may use it as an illustration of the sort of interpretation which undoubtedly does occur sometimes and constitutes, in this limited sense, a **semic** fact; at the level of the **semantics of literature** we shall regard it as an inherently tentative reconstruction of Shakespeare's purpose; at the level of **empirical semics**, because it hangs from a tenuous thread of speculation, we shall not accord it the status of recurrence. Intelligent analysis demands modal classification.

In this chapter, I have outlined a speculative model of a semantic space, and have tried to indicate the possible application of such a space in describing semic accompaniment. The claims made for this space are very small and it is always to be seen in relation to the analeptic framework outlined in chapter 4. The whole of the present chapter may be accounted as an exercise in theoretical semics. It is speculative. Even the most 'objective' concepts, recurrence, for example, are poor instruments for sounding the cerebral depths. Perhaps, ultimately, our primary concepts will emanate from the neurologists; if and when they are forthcoming, we should see to it that literary semantics is prepared to recognize and adopt them.

Chapter 8 will consider a range of other theoretical applications of the dynaxial hypersphere model.

CHAPTER 8

APPLICATIONS OF THE DYNAXIAL HYPERSPHERE

The Ontological Problem

We may use the model to provide a tentative ontology for fiction. Suppose that a reader finds the experience of reading a 'fictitious' or 'non-cognitive' work, *A Midsummer Night's Dream,* perhaps, worth while. During the course of a particular reading, his **semic accompaniment** has caused his **semantic space** to undergo **axial adjustment.**

Let P represent the **primary semantic space**, and P_1, P_2, P_3... P_n represent the potential states of P – the **secondary semantic space** – during the lifetime of an individual, P_n being death. Further, assume that at any given instant in the progress from P_1 to P_n, there is a state P^e_1, P^e_2, P^e_3... P^e_n, where e (= ethical) represents the 'ideal' state for that individual, in the light of **knowledge one**. Let P^a_1, P^a_2, P^a_3... P^a_n, where a (= actual) represents the given modifications of P in a given lifetime, P^a_n representing death. Let P be regarded as a machine for 'understanding', in the broadest cognitive (including ethical and aesthetic) senses, the universe; in other words, given a state, say, P^a_3, the machine's function is to locate P^e_4. In terms of this process, the Whorf-Sapir hypothesis,[1] and other such sceptical beliefs are self-annihilating, for, to assert that there is no means of locating P^a_4 is tantamount to claiming that man has no means of determining whether these very beliefs are true. Why have formulated the sceptical hypothesis in the first place? Maps, it may be averred, are useful, even though all they indicate is that there is no way through.

Instead of such negative assumptions, let us rather posit that man, and a man (and I use the term 'man' in the generic sense) has somewhere within the totality of his psyche the power to discern, at least partly, the relation between, say, P^a_3 and P^e_4. Assuming a gap between P^a_3 and P^e_3, then in order that P^a_4 and P^e_4 may coincide, a certain pattern of axial adjustment must take place within P. Would it not be possible that a reading of, say, *A Midsummer Night's Dream* might initiate such an adjustment? According to the tenets of the trichotomy theory and the dynaxial theory, such a reading might be as 'cognitive' as an experience of a more material (i.e. naturalistic) kind. An elaboration of this theory is given in chapter 14, 'The Chain of Modality': the intuitive experience of *valuing* (let's call it our **value-seeking faculty**) frequently bypasses 'cognitive' prudence. Here, the purpose is to offer an alternative to I. A. Richards' almost visceral theory of value (a balance of appetencies and aversions, see chapter 3) and his claim that the critic is bound to say 'I am better than you'.

This ontology of value places the individual at the ethical centre: a **knowledge three** in a quest for **knowledge one**, traversing **knowledge two** 'clockwise' cognitively and sociologically; yet with the potential to 'jump off', psychologically, 'anticlockwise', to seek knowledge one 'directly' through the ever-present knowledge three. He may choose to consult critics or not but certainly does not need to acknowledge their superiority. Our 'value-seeking' faculty is intuitive, immediate, unique in each individual and as integral an element in our epistemology as our sensory and logical endowment.

The Concept of Grammaticality

According to this model, the production of a sentence by a native speaker would be neither a compounding of engrams according to an S→R interpretation, nor an abstract computation essentially linguistic in its components. The one view lacks flexibility, the other tends to neglect the capacious garners of the brain.[2] A given situation is perceived through **tertiary semantic space**. Millions of **axes** readjust and the **dynaxial centre** is reconstituted. Any strict division of these axes into *linguistic* and *non-linguistic* is likely to misrepresent the operation, for in the process of conceptualization, the two have become inextricably entwined, mastery of language being partly the result of successful interpretation of perceptual experience, and this very experience in turn being infused and directed by the conventions of language. Far from being an 'algebraic computation', the production of a sentence is conceived of as a corollary of psychic reorganization.

Seen in this way, the feat of the child in mastering his or her native language so quickly becomes less surprising. He may be regarded as an epistemological machine whose task is to make sense of reality rather than as a linguistic machine designed to abstract algebraic patterns from linguistic substance. With the aid of language, the child stores away millions of **facilitations** which, though sifted by language, are not essentially linguistic, but a part of the child's reality. Further experiences evoke these facilitations and in the momentum of this coming to grips with reality there develops a mastery of language. As with many issues, the disagreement rests upon emphasis rather than principle, but it does seem that some of the difficulty experienced by writers on this subject is the result of viewing native language learning as an academic pursuit on the part of the child.[3] The more important question here seems to be not 'How does the child learn English in four years?' but 'How, in four years, does the child gain comprehension of reality?'

The present theory regards grammaticality as one of the terminal points in a process whereby the initial volatility of the dynaxial hypersphere settles into a more stable structure.

The Imagination of the Child

The dynaxial theory would accommodate the fact that children are more 'imaginative' than adults. Children's axes commence in a volatile state, adjusting arbitrarily, until a filtering process through tertiary and secondary semantic space brings them into more 'stable' adjustment. The adjective is marked because stability may itself be a mixed blessing.

Retardation of Language-Learning Ability in the Teens

The theory might be developed to account for the retardation in language learning ability experienced in the teens and later.[4] The **tertiary semantic space**, in the earliest years of the child, impinges directly upon the **primary semantic space**, without the interposition of the **secondary semantic space**. At this stage, the axes are adjusted by the contiguity of the phonetic data and the semantically related sense data. The linguistic experience of the child is an integral part of its process of **conceptualization**. As these adjustments are made, there is a decrease in axial volatility, and the secondary semantic space comes to play an increasing rôle. The child has learnt its native language.

But during the process of learning this first language, some of the initial volatility has disappeared; the primary semantic space has been permanently modified, that is to say, there is a secondary semantic space. The linguistic data of any 'second' language are in this case paired not only with the sense data to which they are appropriate at the tertiary level, but also with the linguistic data of the native language, now inexorably a part of the child's competence within the secondary semantic space. The linguistic facility has decreased.

The Centrality of Consciousness

The theory would do justice to the 'centrality' of consciousness, the fact that wherever the subject moves physically or mentally, he remains at the centre of his world of experience. In the Osgood, Suci and Tannenbaum space, concepts are seen in relation to a centre which in itself has no significance. According to the **dynaxial theory**, the most intense activity at any given moment constitutes the **centre** of the semantic space, consciousness.

Indistinct Recollection

The common experience of having something at the 'back of one's mind', of half recollecting an idea which becomes more elusive the more one attempts mentally to grasp it, would be dealt with in the following fashion.

Let us call the elusive idea the **target concept**. The **centre** establishes axial links with the target concept, but these are insufficient for **fusion** to take place (the question we ask ourselves would itself comprise some of the link **axes**: 'Now what *is* the name of the bright red star in Orion?'). The target concept is beyond the control of the axial centre (perhaps there has been no recent **facilitation**), and conscious efforts to recover the target merely **concentrate** the axial links, emphasizing their connection with the centre, rather than their attachment to the target. When we pursue some other interest and set the link axes free, we grant them the necessary autonomy. Our dilemma is that we have to let them out of conscious control in order that they may do their work. There then takes place a consequent non-central **intensification** as these axes cause an axial reorganization around the target concept. The **law of the dynaxial centre** then comes into operation: **Dynaxial space in the wakeful state will not tolerate a region of intensity equal to the centre**.

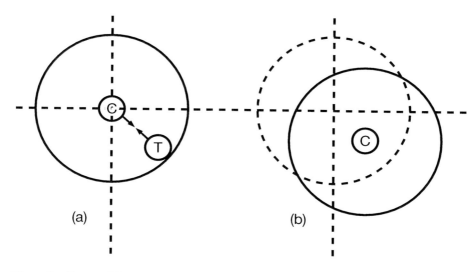

Figure 8. Dynaxial Fusion of C (Centre) and T (Target)

When the intensity of the target exceeds the level of toleration, (a) above, there is a sudden fusion of the target and the centre, even though the centre was not at the moment of realization consciously seeking the target. The answer, we say, comes in a flash. The two fused intense regions now constitute the centre of the dynaxial hypersphere (b).

It will also be observed that the centrality of the new centre is maintained not by its returning to the position of the old centre, but by the reconstitution of the entire hypersphere around it in its new position. The hypersphere is in permanent motion.

Dreaming and Poetic Creation: *Kubla Khan* (Transmission Semantics)

The dynaxial theory would explain the fact of dreaming as follows: the dreamer reverts to a more 'childlike' state where the axes abandon their more permanent adjustments. If the details related in *The Road to Xanadu* [LS:102–104], are substantially correct then only a model which allowed many simultaneous patterns of activity could adequately represent the semantic phenomena.

In order to accommodate such a complex phenomenon, I must elaborate, and further illustrate, the explanation which was given in my last section of the facts of indistinct recollection. For it would seem that the same principles are operating, though on a much larger scale.

Imagine a spherical amoeba, its nucleus at the centre. The nucleus is a large agglomeration of particles of matter. Outside the nucleus but within the cell wall, in a constant state of flux, are particles of matter with nucleus-forming potential. These particles are continually coalescing and separating; particle agglomerations are building up and being broken down. The nucleus itself is constantly receiving and losing particles. When an agglomeration of particles grows to the point where it equals the nucleus in size, the two are mutually attracted and they fuse at a point midway between their former positions. The amoeba is suspended in a fluid, and as the nucleus moves to its new position, the spherical walls of the cell reconstitute themselves, so that eccentricity never occurs. The amoeba moves. By a similar process of coalescence and separation, the nucleus returns to its normal intensity. We may similarly postulate subordinate fusions between non-nuclear agglomerations which, providing the sum total of the amalgamated particles does not equal the nucleus, leave the nucleus unaffected; these model the activity of the unconscious (or subconscious) mind.

The question we asked earlier concerning the genesis of *Kubla Khan* can now be discussed: 'What sort of machine is capable of generating this sort of output from that kind of input?' It was earlier stressed that the dynaxial space is not exclusively linguistic[LS:128]. I conceive of the hypersphere as being traversed by a number of atomic axes, and it is further assumed that there is a one-to-one relation between the axes and the storage potential of the neurons. As there is no way yet of 'linking' information on to my model [LS:119], with such precision, this is a theoretical nicety: one neuron firing, or failing to fire, would not be detectable, just as one pixel more or less on a television screen would pass unnoticed. We may therefore dispense with the concept of the 'atomic axis' for the time being, and regard the axis as a scale of alternatives whose presence or absence would affect significantly the process of thought.

Coleridge's own description of his dream makes it evident that he was aware of two levels of experience, linguistic and non-linguistic, 'all the *images* rose up before him as things, with a parallel production of the correspondent *expressions* [my italics]'. It would be a reasonable assumption that there is some **facilitated** proximity within the space between a word and its reference, a reciprocal relation between the **name** and the **sense**, as Ullmann puts it.[5] Thus, although the word 'chair' and the **referent**, or, pedantically, **reference**, *chair* are differentiated between by most sophisticated people, there is a close semantic tie. Having stressed that there are non-linguistic **axes**, we can, for present purpose, regard the linguistic axes as the primary ones.

The previous section, concerning the fact of 'indistinct recollection', discussed the possibility of the fusion of two regions within the space, one of the regions being the centre, the other an eccentric region which attained to equal intensity. On the analogy with the amoeba, we may now proceed further. Our semantic space contains millions of clusters of intense regions – and, by previous facilitation, potentially intense regions – the parallels of the agglomerations within the amoeba. Pursuing the similarity, we may infer that two neighbouring regions of equal intensity may coalesce, and providing the sum total intensity of the coalescence does not equal the intensity of the centre, the process will remain subliminal. I remind the reader that I am speculating.

Accepting Lowes' version of the sequence of events: the various semic accompaniments of Coleridge during his omnivorous reading were assigned to appropriate locations within his **semantic space**, and, for the most part, became 'decentralized'.

Now the process of (spontaneous?) composition begins. It may be that the coalescence and separation of intense regions within the semantic space had been proceeding for some time before Coleridge had the dream, so that the work was partially created prior to this experience. But this does not affect the mechanism of creation. Failing this period of prior reorganization, we must simply posit an even more rapid reorganization during the dream.

The generative grammarians map the generation of a grammatical sentence as a movement from deep[6] to surface structure through a hierarchy of alternatives. The degree to which this movement from depth to surface actually represents a psychic process is in dispute, but such analysis at least makes clear something of the structure of choices. The rules are extremely complex, even for so-called 'simple' sentences. If we are to believe Coleridge, he generated, spontaneously and effortlessly, a text which was two or three hundred lines long and which appears, from the surviving fragment, to be a carefully composed work. The hierarchy of alternatives, phonological, lexical, syntactic and metrical, which interposed itself between deep and surface structures is large. Poets have often traversed such hierarchies, but the normal state of affairs is for the choices to be made one, or a few, at a time.

Whether as a result of opium or not, Coleridge's semantic space was singularly volatile on this occasion. The axial activity was much more violent than usual, so that the acceptance and rejection of alternatives was expedited. Isaac Asimov, in *The Human Brain: Its Capabilities and Functions*,[7] discussing this composition, writes, 'Presumably, during the period of sleep his mind, unhampered by waking sensation and thought, played the more freely at this game of hit-and-miss.' We now have the same process which we discussed in the previous section, but on a far greater scale: thousands of smaller regions coalescing and separating as acceptances and rejections within the hierarchy are made, the resulting coalescences re-coalescing with a cumulative effect until the intensity of one of these regions, upon Coleridge's reawakening, equals the intensity of the centre. Just as in the previous section there came a moment of realization as the target concept fused with the centre, so Coleridge had this experience on an immeasurably heightened scale.

We may picture this as a computer with n components each of which is programmed to deal with a separate aspect of a complex problem. Thus, each component, whilst working on a separate aspect, is dealing with material ultimately relevant to the material of the other components. The components are so constructed that, according to the nature of the material being fed in, and the type of processing which is taking place, the 'rhythm' varies. Any number of components which are operating at the same rhythm at any given moment are automatically linked up, and they are able to 'share' information. The 'centre' of the computer at a given instant is the region which contains the largest number of components operating at the same rhythm. Such a computer would surely be an advance upon the 'dinosaur' machines recently denounced by Ivor Catt in *The New Scientist*.[8] It seems that if such a machine were practicable and operable it would possess many of the creative attributes of the human brain.

Deviation of Literary Language

The 'deviation' of literary language, far from being viewed as an eccentricity in danger of upsetting the apple-cart of grammaticality, may be seen as an intermediate stage between volatility without adjustment and adjustment without volatility in the process of modification which the **primary semantic space** undergoes during the course of a lifetime. This intermediate stage is natural in mythology, contrived in sophisticated literary expression.[9] In the discussion of the principle of dynamism [LS:119–124], an attempt was made to show that a function of one type of literary language is to stimulate the axes into volatile, pre-grammatical activity. Whether and how literary language is deviant is a question of subordinate importance to the questions: What are the axes of primary semantic space, and what are their properties? If we knew the answer to this, the concentration upon the problems of grammaticality and deviation might well prove to have hindered literary studies.

Tension

We may define tension as that process whereby scattered regions within the dynaxial space dynamically coalesce and become facilitated. In order to illustrate this point, we may take the following poem 'Nude Descending a Staircase', by X. J. Kennedy:[10]

(29)   Toe upon toe, a snowing flesh,
        A gold of lemon, root and rind,
        She sifts in sunlight down the stairs
        With nothing on. Nor on her mind.

        We spy beneath the banister
        A constant thresh of thigh on thigh
        Her lips imprint the swinging air
        That parts to let her parts go by.

        One woman waterfall, she wears
        Her slow descent like a long cape
        And pausing, on the final stair
        Collects her motions into shape.

Since this account is theoretical and we are describing what might happen rather than what does happen, the account need be neither precise nor exhaustive. Also, for the present purpose, a consideration of the first stanza will be sufficient.

(i)   The reading of the title raises certain expectations: any item which contributes to the fulfilment of these expectations will be facilitated. Thus, 'toe', 'flesh', 'she', 'nothing on' and doubtfully 'gold' are semantically facilitated; that is to say, in a poem entitled 'Nude Descending a Staircase', their occurrence is as much to be predicted as 'ohm', 'volt' and 'amp' in a set of electrical instructions.

(ii)   'Snowing' and 'lemon, root and rind' are more distantly located within the semantic space than the terms listed under (i). The dynaxial centre, as the semic accompaniment accommodates these words, undergoes extension. The centre is, as it were, 'stretched', becoming momentarily more diffuse. This is dynamism. But if, at the point where the poet first mentioned 'snow', he went on to an irrelevant description of snow, without relating this to the nude, then the tension would be lost. Tension consists not in the selection of dynamic items, but in their assimilation into the facilitated patterns. 'Snowing', the dynamic item, is followed by 'flesh', the facilitated item. In this way, the dynaxial space is restructured: distantly located concepts are evoked and then 'pulled together', and the space is axially reshaped.

(iii)   This process through which dynamic items become assimilated into the previously facilitated patterns is further assisted by phonological and metrical devices. Some phonological facilitations are the recurrences [ou] in 'toe' (twice), 'snow', 'gold'; [r] in 'root', 'rind' ; [ʃ/s/z] in 'she', 'sifts', 'sunlight', 'stairs'; [n] in 'nothing' 'on', 'nor', 'mind'. Likewise, we may observe metrical regularities – eight syllables per line, two stresses on either side of the caesura in each line, slightly reminiscent of Sievers' five types of stress pattern in Anglo-Saxon half-lines of verse.

Metaphor

The problem of metaphor, widely recognized as one of the central difficulties of poetic language, can be dealt with in the following manner. We shall employ the now widely accepted nomenclature[11] and call what is actually being referred to the **tenor**, and the term which figuratively presents this referent, the **vehicle**. In the third verse of the text quoted in the last section, there occurs the phrase 'one woman waterfall'. Here, the **tenor** is 'The Nude' or 'she' or 'woman': 'waterfall' is the **vehicle**.

The state of a **hypothetical reader's dynaxial space** immediately prior to a given reading may be called the **initial semic state** and, immediately after the reading, the **final semic state**. Any selected state during the reading is a **medial semic state**. In the initial semic state at a reading of 'Nude Descending a Staircase', there is a considerable distance between 'woman' and 'waterfall' within the dynaxial space; they are differentiated, for instance, on the animate-inanimate scale. Let us call the tenor T, the vehicle V, and the distance between them in the initial semic state d. The metaphorical process may be represented diagrammatically as below.

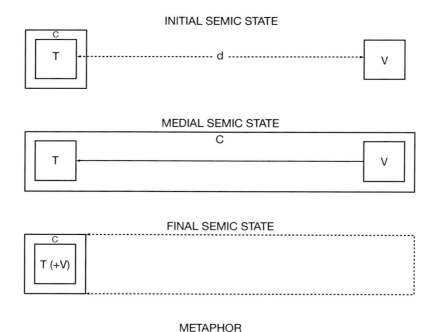

Figure 9.

According to the above diagram, the axes which constitute the 'tenor', the established concept in secondary semantic space, undergo vigorous readjustment, **dynamism**, to assimilate the recalcitrant axial adjustment of the vehicle as it is presented to the tertiary semantic space. There is a moment of dynamic activity as the two concepts are 'drawn together' and d is eliminated. The tenor is modified by its accommodation of the axial adjustments appropriate to the vehicle. It will also be observed that the centre C momentarily becomes more diffuse at the instant of dynamic activity and is, by means of a linguistic structure, **concentrated**. **Metaphor** may be defined as **a linguistic device whereby the dynaxial space of a hypothetical reader concentrates two or more distant regions**. In mythology, by animistic coalescence the **concentration** may be permanent – the sun 'becomes' Apollo; in literary experience, although the space is doubtless modifed, there is at least a partial reversion of the axes to their former state after the reading. This definition belongs, it should by now be no need to stress, to **theoretical semics**.

In the light of the **theory of metaphor** outlined above, I would predict that, should it ever be possible to carry out relevant experimentation, there are more neurons or 'neuron operations' involved in the medial semic state, at the instant of dynamic activity, as described, than in the initial and final semic states. I would further suppose that our 'metaphor experience' is the mutual reconciliation of those neuron operations appropriate to T with the different set appropriate to V.

Simile

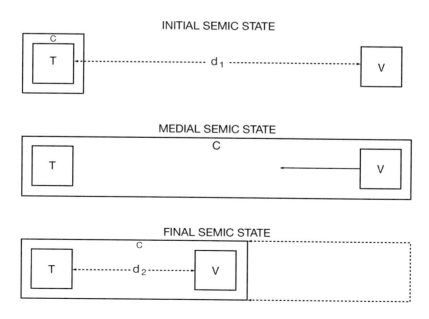

SIMILE

Figure 10.

The process for the simile is the same, except that in the **final semic state** the **centre** is more **diffuse** than in the corresponding metaphor. Textual signals such as 'like' and 'as' allow the two concepts to be linked and drawn towards each other without actually coalescing, d_2 being shorter than d_1, as indicated in Figure 10.

Semic Accompaniment

We may adumbrate the process which might take place when a work of literature is read: again, this is a speculative account. I return to Wim Bronzwaer's challenge [LS:108].

The initial semic state of a mature English reader has been structured by years of language experience. The actual graphic substance, visually perceived, immediately impinges upon the **tertiary semantic space** of this **hypothetical reader**. Even an intelligent and educated adult reader, approaching *King Lear* for the first time, would doubtless encounter unfamiliar words, perhaps *meiny* (2.4.35), *sectary* (1.2.157) or familiar words used in unfamiliar contexts, *addition* (1.1.136), *meat* (1.4.166). The linguistic context compensates for the unfamiliarity in some cases, but we may say that a totally unfamiliar word remains at tertiary level within the semantic space. Such words, however, will be in a minority, and as the semic accompaniment commences, a word is recognized, that is, it becomes linked with its semically appropriate concept within the secondary semantic space. The relevant concept is centralised.

But the act of centralization entails an axial redisposition. The word *meat*, for instance, in its non-central position within the secondary semantic space has thousands of axial facilitations that are irrelevant in the present linguistic context. 'Why, after I have cut the egg i' the middle and eat up the meat': the lexicographical entry 'flesh', for instance, is deleted in favour of 'yolk and white'. The corresponding axes are released, whilst the relevant ones receive facilitation. The semic accompaniment functions through a complex interaction – phonological, lexical, syntactic and semantic – between the secondary and tertiary levels of semantic space. Concepts are centralized, modified, reinforced, refined, and subsequently de-centralized, as the centre moves according as it is controlled by the visual stimulation at tertiary level.

The traditional notions of 'character' and 'plot' may be treated similarly. 'Kent', virtually without facilitation at the beginning of the play, is in the first scene axially structured into a concept by 'anger', 'loyalty', 'defiance', 'outspokenness', 'bravery', 'resignation'. An individual reader's concept of the character Kent is the result of the linguistic manipulation of the axes within secondary semantic space: they are realigned, and their configuration is the character. The facilitation has now taken place and the dramatist can allow the axes to decentralize, knowing that at a later point in the play he can evoke the axial complex once more. In terms of the amoeba metaphor [LS:132], we have an agglomeration of particles constituting Kent. Upon Kent's banishment towards the end of the first scene, this complex begins to recede outwards from the centre. The centre moves on: Cordelia agrees to marry France; Goneril and Regan discuss their father in disparaging tones; Edmund commences his villainous plot against his brother; Goneril orders Oswald to slight Lear. Then, in Act I, Scene IV, Kent enters disguised, and the Kent axial complex, which has slowly been drifting away from the centre, is recalled. This complex is now reinforced and extended. A similar departure and reappearance occurs in Chaucer's *Miller's Tale*, which might be thought to have an ending with four separate climaxes: Absolom is introduced, described and shelved soon after the beginning; then reintroduced after the first climax (Nicholas's bedding of Alison) as a necessary agent for the remaining three climaxes (Absolom's kiss of the 'nether eye'; the branding of Nicholas; the violent descent of the carpenter;), thus compounding the hilarity of the ending.

'Plot' thus consists of a succession of axial complexes, built out of the linguistic structures constituting the text – this without prejudice to the idiosemic content of literary experience – which are formed, developed and dropped, resumed and redeveloped in a mosaic of axial activity. By means of this process, the secondary semantic space is restructured until the **final semic state** is reached.

CHAPTER 9

THE CONCEPT OF MODALITY

The Use of Technical Terms

At the time *Theoretical Semics* was published in 1972 there went unheeded at the back of my mind a notion that a definition of *style* ought to be included in the lengthy glossary of terms. Since that book appeared I have resisted the impulse to publish my definition mainly because a note would scarcely have been intelligible without recapitulation at some length of my theories. Subsequent reviews have brought it home to me that, before the list be augmented by another term, the use of technical language in literary studies ought itself to be justified.

In a review published in *English Studies*, Robert St. Clair said of *Theoretical Semics*: 'In chapter four the model is described with the use of numerous diagrams and a battery of terminological explanations. These definitions, it should be noted, are recapitulated in the appendix of the book. Their effectiveness could be greatly enhanced by the addition of clear examples of just what they are supposed to convey. Unfortunately, in their present state they remain as an obstacle rather than an asset to communication.'[1] Then again, Roger Fowler in *Review of English Studies* says, 'Mr. Eaton has a flair for unprepossessing jargon. A casual browser in Mouton's catalogue might never suspect that this book has anything to do with literature; a critic flipping the pages would assuredly be discouraged by the ponderous (though fully glossed) terminology.'[2] Finally, H. G. Widdowson in *Modern Language Review* writes, 'The arguments in his book are expressed in a metalanguage which effectively prevents any overt comparison with other writings in the field so that correspondences with other views have to be worked out by the reader himself. What we in effect have in *Theoretical Semics* is a detached dialectic pattern which has a certain internal elegance but whose external significance is difficult to perceive. Mr. Eaton's theoretical design has something of the character of an abstract painting:

suggestive, perhaps profound, but ultimately enigmatic.'³ As I have read these and other reviews in scattered journals it has slowly dawned upon me that other workers in the field of literary studies do not understand why technical terms are necessary in the presentation of a metatheory.

In revising the material of this book, I have explained at greater length anything that might reasonably be regarded as, to use Widdowson's word, enigmatic. This may leave me open to a charge of repetitiveness. The terminology, which is a vital tool in conveying what I mean, stands.

In almost any other scientific sphere of endeavour no *apologia* would be deemed necessary. Your scientist would drily remark to anyone naïve enough to put the question, that he would rather be well understood by a few colleagues who had taken the pains to read what he had written than be misinterpreted by large numbers of readers inferring what they pleased from terms that were common currency. The retort is true *a fortiori* in literary circles. But there is a second reason for the use of technical terms. This, though it may be explained only at some length, can be expressed in one word: **modality**.

I shall explain what I understand by modality; then consider briefly some treatments of style; and finally in chapter 10 define **style** in the light of these discussions.

The Concept of Modality

Let us take as a sample of literary critical discourse the following passage by F. R. Leavis: 'The great English novelists are Jane Austen, George Eliot, Henry James, and Joseph Conrad to stop for the moment at that comparatively safe point in history. Since Jane Austen, for special reasons, needs to be studied at considerable length, I confine myself in this book to the last three. Critics have found me narrow, and I have no doubt that my opening proposition, whatever I may say to explain and justify it, will be adduced in reinforcement of their strictures. It passes as fact (in spite of the printed evidence) that I pronounce Milton negligible, dismiss "the Romantics", and hold that, since Donne there is no poet we need bother about except Hopkins and Eliot. The view, I suppose, will confidently be attributed to me that, except Jane Austen, George Eliot, James and Conrad, there are no English novelists worth reading.'⁴ I would like to draw attention, not so much to what this passage says, as to what Leavis *assumes*.

Firstly, it is implied that the study of literature is not to be held separate from the function of literary criticism. 'Jane Austen', he asserts, 'needs to be studied at considerable length'. He continues, with the weariness of a gentleman resigned to being misunderstood, 'It passes as fact (in spite of the printed evidence) that I pronounce Milton negligible, dismiss "the Romantics", and hold that, since Donne, there is no poet we need bother about except Hopkins and Eliot'. Leavis uses the word 'studied': but the context in which the word is used makes it clear he believes one of the purposes of the study of literature to be to make value judgments. He assumes that whether or not he pronounces Milton negligible, whether or not he dismisses 'the Romantics', that these are questions of some moment in the study of literature.

Secondly, it is assumed that the rules of academic discourse for the consideration of literature have been laid down. The laws of the game have been established: the reader can object to the way in which Leavis is playing this particular game, but – so imperiously and resolutely does he go about his task of persuasion – it does not occur to those who interpret him that the game might be played according to an entirely different set of rules. Thus the student may say, 'Dr. Leavis, I really do believe that your earlier essays on Milton did amount to a pronouncement that Milton was negligible'. But he is not likely to venture the opinion that what Dr. Leavis thinks one way or the other is of small relevance to the study of literature. Before pursuing this direction and asking what this different set of rules might be, I would like to discuss briefly just what it is that constitutes a scientific discipline.

Sir Karl Popper, in his famous essay, thinks back to the problem which was confronting him in 1919: How are we to distinguish between a science and a pseudo-science?[5] It had occurred to him that a most pressing task for the philosophy of science was to differentiate between those theories of predictive quality on the one hand and those theories on the other which are so flexible and broad that they can accommodate every contingent happening.

In the first category, the predictive type of theory, he places Einstein's notions of gravitation which led to Eddington's eclipse observations in 1919. To the second category he assigns the theories of Marx, Freud and Adler. These latter, Popper claims, can, by subtle recourse, be made to account for all possible outcomes.

'I may illustrate this,' writes Popper, 'by two very different examples of human behaviour: that of a man who pushes a child into the water with the intention of drowning it; and that of a man who sacrifices his life in an attempt to save the child. Each of these two cases can be explained with equal ease in Freudian and Adlerian terms. According to Freud the first man suffered from repression (say, of some component of his Oedipus complex), while the second man had achieved sublimation. According to Adler the first man suffered from feelings of inferiority (producing perhaps the need to prove to himself that he dared to commit some crime), and so did the second man (whose need was to prove to himself that he dared to rescue the child).'[6]

Popper therefore rejected the analyses of Freud and Adler. What makes a theory scientific, he concluded, is that it *forbids* certain things to happen. The more a theory forbids, the better it is. Thus the value of a scientific theory lies in the amount of risk it is prepared to take. Notice that, as Bateson, Popper is here making a value judgment; but his discussion makes it clear that the 'value' he is referring to is *instrumental* and not *intrinsic* (see my discussion of Segers' book in chapter 11), and he also makes clear that the criteria whereby his judgment is itself judged are empirical. Unlike Bateson, he has defined the scope of his own verdicts: predictive assertions which fail to predict are scientifically untenable.

Popper writes, 'Thus I was led by purely logical considerations to replace the psychological theory of induction by the following view. Without waiting, passively, for repetitions to impress or impose regularities upon us, we actively try to impose regularities upon the world. We try to discover similarities in it, and interpret it in terms of laws invented by us. Without waiting for premises we jump to conclusions. These may have to be discarded later, should observation show that they are wrong.'[7]

In the years since Popper was thinking these thoughts, induction has had a hard time. We find, for instance, Hempel writing in 1966, 'There are, then, no generally applicable "rules of induction" by which hypotheses or theories can be mechanically derived or inferred from empirical data. The transition from data to theory requires creative imagination.'[8] Then, a few years later, Medawar asserts, 'The idea, central to inductive theory, that scientific knowledge grows out of simple unbiased statements reporting the evidence of these senses is one that cannot be sustained.'[9]

Nowadays it has become a popular pastime to debunk the Baconian ideals of induction and to substitute for them the inspired – and only retrospectively controlled – flights of fancy sometimes alluded to as the 'hypothetico-deductive method'.

In a recent article, John M. Lipski makes these opening remarks: 'Corresponding to every level of discourse there is a metalevel which concerns itself with the first level... Within the realm of language, no matter what level or plane is considered, it is possible to define a metalevel which takes this plane or level as its object of interest.'[10]

English-speaking critics have not characteristically been preoccupied with the nature of critical discourse: they have perhaps been too busy engaging *in* the discourse to be seriously concerned with the problem of discourse itself. Lipski's article is moving in a welcome direction – though he does not venture so far up the ladder of literary discourse as might be wished. We can best illustrate the sort of **circumflexion of discourse** I have in mind by examining Popper's remarks.

The central assumption of Popper's essay seems to be: *a theory which is not refutable by any conceivable event is non-scientific*. But, subjecting this proposition to circumflexion, what is *its* status? Does it in fact constitute a theory of scientific theories? And, if so, is the proposition itself a scientific theory? Now if Popper's exposition, thus encapsulated, constitutes a scientific theory, it is appropriate in the interests of self-consistency to ask whether it is refutable by any conceivable event. Clearly, it is not. For, given some theory 'x', Popper's theory can only classify; it cannot predict except in a very weak sense. That is to say, Popper can predict beforehand that x will either be classified as scientific, or that it will not. But a subsequent decision that x is scientific or non-scientific will not falsify Popper's theory. The theory is not refutable by any conceivable event. It follows therefore that, if Popper's exposition has the status of a theory, it is not a scientific theory in the sense in which he has himself defined a scientific theory.

Presumably, Popper would reply that when he formulated this view he never intended it to be a scientific theory in itself. But nevertheless the standing of his own exposition is raised. If a philosopher of science is entitled to prescribe what constitutes a scientific theory, then in some sense his prescription is superordinate within the scientific system. Yet this superordinate statement lacks that very virtue of falsifiability which all good scientific theories should have.

It may seem that I am being critical and perhaps destructive at Popper's expense. That is not what I would wish: I am leading towards the point I made earlier about **modality**. What I am arguing is that the scientific machine functions on many levels, and that the philosopher of science has his place within, not outside, this machine. In other words, I am contending that Popper, as a philosopher of science, is just as much a scientist as the man who, like Einstein, makes falsifiable predictions. Theories of classification are as truly a part of scientific endeavour as theories of prediction. They belong, however, to different levels of scientific discourse. There is a further discussion of this contention in chapter 15.

Nor is the logician, even, free from the difficulties which occur when we switch from a given level to a metalevel. Consider E. J. Lemmon's proof technique[11] as a typical system of natural deduction in logic. Lemmon gives us the usual operators, such as negation, disjunction, material implication, which act on propositional variables; in addition to formation rules, he states, within the propositional calculus, ten rules of derivation. Now two of these rules enable us, at each instance of operation, to discharge an assumption: the rule of Conditional Proof and the rule of *Reductio ad Absurdum*. So, if a given line of our proof rests on three assumptions, and then we operate Conditional Proof (CP), the next line of our proof depends upon only two assumptions. A further application of CP reduces the number of assumptions to one. But, and here is the interesting phenomenon, there is nothing to prevent our operating CP a third time. This leaves us with a formula which *rests on no assumptions*. It *must* be true.

We will take as an example a proof which operates CP only once and in so doing produces one of the axioms of the Russell-Whitehead system:

$$\vdash Q \rightarrow (P \vee Q)$$

1	1	Q	A
1	2	P v Q	1 v1
	3	Q→ (P v Q)	1, 2 CP

This proof may be read as follows: It is a theorem that Q materially implies its own disjunction with P (i.e. the theorem above the line is what we are setting out to prove); at step 1 (cited between the 'chimney' lines) we introduce Q by the Rule of Assumptions (A in the right-hand margin) and the 1 in the left- hand margin indicates that it 'rests upon itself'; at step 2, the rule v-lntroduction (vI, for short − *v* itself is short for Latin *vel* = 'or' i.e. weak disjunction) enables us to disjoin Q with P (still resting on 1, indicated once more in the left-hand margin); finally, since P v Q was derived from Q, we can operate CP on steps 1 and 2, deriving in turn step 3, the required formula Q→(P v Q), and the blank space in the left-hand column signifies that, Assumption 1 having been duly discharged, the formula rests on no assumptions. The theorem has been proved.

This is a very simple example of proof in the propositional calculus. But if we start with a large number of assumptions and watch them, in the left-hand column, disappearing one by one, the process of elimination has an almost mesmeric effect upon the beholding mind. The final formula seems to be endowed with what can almost be described as a logical purity, a formal sanctity: because it relies upon no suppositions it cannot possibly be false.

What in fact we are overlooking, however, is that whilst we have faithfully observed the rules of the calculus, so that at *that* level we have eliminated all the assumptions, there is an extra hidden assumption, smuggled into the proof at the metalevel: namely, the assumption that the calculus itself with its variables, its operators and its rules, is a valid instrument of cognitive inquiry. And it is the same with an axiomatic system: we have to assume the axioms as self-evident – we cannot prove them *within* the system. Rationality, in order to function at all, has to assume the rationality of its own procedures.

With these sobering thoughts in mind, I turn now to **modality**, which may best provisionally be defined in terms of traditional grammar: *it is the determination on the part of the scholar never to use an indicative where he is strictly entitled to use only a subjunctive.* That is to say, I am using the term in a sense which is closer to the Hallidayan definition than it is to the sense in which it is widely used in modal logic. Rather than referring to an objectified scheme of necessity/possibility/impossibility, it has, as I employ it, to do with one's own attitude towards what one is saying not only in relation to possibility, but also with regard to what one believes to be the presuppositions of those with whom one is communicating. A stricter definition is offered [LS:152].

Consider the following two propositions:

(1)   The pressure of a fixed mass of gas at constant temperature is inversely proportional to its volume.

(2)   A deep depression moving slowly eastwards across Britain brings rain to Kent and Essex later this evening.

These propositions are both examples taken from scientific discourse. Both statements employ the indicative 'is', 'brings', but there is a great deal of difference in the degree of 'certainty', begging the question, of what is asserted. The first, Boyle's Law, is an inflexible expression of a law of the universe, though of course its field of reference is an idealized one. But the second, meteorological statement, is as likely as not to be inaccurate. It is very difficult to predict what English weather is going to do from one moment to the next, so many are the variables, though accuracy is now steadily improving.

Modality can be built into the assertion in two ways: firstly, at the level of the discourse itself 'A deep depression will *perhaps* bring rain…' or, alternatively, at the meta-level, the discourse as a whole can be presented with a modal qualification, at the meta-level, explicit or understood: 'any prediction made in an English weather-forecast is to be treated with caution' – a warning which 'narrows' the entire discourse. As far as weather-forecasting is concerned, even though the indicative is used, as in (2), we all know that the mood is really subjunctive: this latter course, labelling this entire book as **theoretical semics**, is the one I have chosen. Far from being an attempt to obfuscate the study of literature with technical terminology, the system I am outlining provides a means of bringing daylight to shine in regions where professional obfuscators like Bateson and Leavis have held sway for decades.

But let us now return to the opening statement in F. R. Leavis' book; 'The great English novelists are Jane Austen, George Eliot, Henry James and Joseph Conrad.' We have here the idiosyncratic view of one man presented as if it were on a level with Boyle's Law. What, for instance, is meant by 'great'? How is greatness to be computed? To what extent should the study of literature be concerned to assess greatness rather than undertake other tasks? Who, for that matter, is F. R. Leavis, that we should respect his opinion?

It is not my present purpose to embark upon a long critique of the writings of F. R. Leavis. What I am going to do is to summarize those respects in which he offends against what I believe to be the standards of academic discourse. I shall then go on to show how literary semantics attempts to put to rights the failings of literary criticism; for I believe that Leavis is typical, in the manner in which he pursues his discourse, of English-speaking literary critics.

(i)   Leavis shows no willingness to indicate the modality of his own assertions.

(ii)   Leavis fails to define his terms. Words like 'poetry', 'life', 'great', 'tradition', 'thinking', 'feeling', 'essential structure', 'creative genius' abound in his work. Even words like 'us' and 'we' are used tendentiously: 'Conrad', he says, 'is incomparably closer to us today than Hardy and Meredith are'.[12] Whom does he mean by 'us'? My interpretation is that he means 'F. R. Leavis and all sensitive and intelligent readers of literature'. By this apparently innocent pronoun, he places his student in a dilemma: he either agrees with the assertion, in which case the master wins his point, or he disagrees and is placed on the defensive, for Leavis' tone suggests that non-acceptance entails insensitivity.

(iii)   Leavis offers no operable principles of analysis. Thus, he will argue that the great poets are those who 'not only change the possibilities of the art for practitioners and readers, but are significant in terms of the human awareness they promote; awareness of the possibilities of life'.[13] But he gives us no viable criterion whereby we can determine whether a poet has actually achieved this promotion of awareness. Whose awareness is he referring to? As a human being, I am steadily gaining new awarenesses, but also reviving old ones and at the same time losing awareness. I am in a constant process of organic adjustment to the universe about me. Some of these changes are wrought by reading literature; others, by more direct perceptual experience.

And my pattern of awarenesses is quite different, I assume, from anyone else's. It seems facile to suggest that a reading of, say, *Emma*, is going to promote in all readers awareness of the possibilities of life. [On a personal level (**introspective semics**), I would say *Crime and Punishment, The Brothers Karamazov, The Idiot, The House of the Dead, War and Peace* and *Anna Karenina* did that for me during my (reluctant) National Service in the R.A.F.; *Emma* I found charming but comparatively trivial. I do not expect anyone to agree with me or care if they don't.]

(iv)   A refusal to tackle the difficult philosophical problems of literature; problems of the theory of knowledge and value. The reluctance of Leavis, verging on disdain, was brought out into the open in the debate with Wellek.[14]

(v)   Leavis' confusion of the *study of literature* with *morality*.[15] That is to say it seems inherent in Leavis' criticism that the study of literature is not just another academic or leisure pursuit: it is an activity to be regarded as intrinsically virtuous.

(vi)   The confusion of the rôle of the critic with that of the academic. It is in this respect, in my view, that the influence of Leavis has been most pernicious. Leavis, and English-speaking critics generally, whilst insisting upon the subjectivity and independence of judgment of the critic, have nevertheless been ready to accept office in academic institutions and to operate examination procedures, without any apparent awareness of the paradoxical nature of their task. Expressed briefly: if the purpose of reading literature is enjoyment, enlightenment, moral improvement and so forth, what evidence is there that sitting examinations enhances such experience? If on the other hand the aim of the study of literature is the advancement of knowledge, then why do not the academic critics take the necessary fundamental steps to establish their pursuit as an intellectual discipline?[16]

The purposes of literary semantics, as I conceive of it, arise by implication out of the objections I have made to Leavis and to critics like Bateson, Helen Vendler, Blackmur, Hough and even I. A. Richards. Although I have already implied what I believe the aims of literary semantics to be, it will be useful if at this point I briefly summarize them and, as I mentioned earlier, explain my concept of modality in relation to these discourse structures. The purposes are:

(a)   To tackle the philosophical problems of the study of literature including the theory of knowledge and the theory of value, attempting to relate the study of literature to adjacent disciplines.

(b)   To attempt rigorous definition of terms.
(c)   To formulate principles which can be operated with a high degree of objectivity (or at least intersubjectivity).
(d)   *To emphasize the need for modality in literary studies.*

The fundamental aim of literary semantics then is not to promote a new 'school' of literary criticism: it is rather to provide a stable framework within which the many activities that are already in being can function efficiently. For an extended statement, please see the first section of chapter 15, the document for discussion.

In order to do this, I have designed a metasystem which not only confronts the problems of knowledge and value, but also relates the various activities of literary students to one another and to the system as a whole by a division into levels. I call this an **analeptic system**. Only against such a system can modality satisfactorily be defined. A **science** is an academic pursuit which confronts a vigorous **kinesis** with an **analepsis** which is well-organized, vigilant, yet flexible.

The analeptic function is that process whereby the received structures of a science, the **analepsis**, reject or assimilate the fresh notions generated by the theorist at the level of the kinetic component. The **kinetic component** of a science, the **kinesis**, mediates between material from fresh observations and the analeptic structures (which often react in a recalcitrant fashion to the activities of the kinesis). In literary studies, the kinetic function may be visualized as being built into the analeptic component, within theoretical semics, at right-angles to the plane of the analeptic diagram [LS:101].

It is important to bear in mind about an analeptic theory that it is not predictive, in the Popperian sense, but classificatory. It is more likely to be effectively judged in terms of its usefulness, or lack of usefulness, rather than in terms of its predictive truth or falsehood. The claim is that the diagram includes everything that could ever be considered knowledge, truth, value and literature; and that it not only includes, but also organizes. I would like to suggest that the appropriate question to ask of it is: Does this analeptic system constitute a useful analysis? I can now proceed to recapitulate the details of my analeptic diagram: the underlying principles are simple, but the structure which emerges is of some complexity.

We commence with the rectangle, darkly shaded, at the top of the diagram. Knowledge is divided into three categories: knowledge one, knowledge two and knowledge three. **Knowledge one** is ultimate knowledge, where 'ultimate' implies a (property of) knowledge which, whether natural or supernatural, is unalterable. **Knowledge two** is that believed by the person possessing it to be communicable. **Knowledge three** is that believed by the person possessing it to be incommunicable. This threefold analysis of knowledge is referred to as the **trichotomy theory**. Within the trichotomy theory, **value** may be defined as a man's conviction (knowledge three) that he has access in some degree to knowledge one.

A **universe of discourse** is any discrete system of communication. All universes of discourse are associated with knowledge two and can arbitrarily be graded from high to low. **Affidence** is a sub-category of knowledge two, within the trichotomy theory; and a proposition universally considered true within the highest universe of discourse proper to the branch of learning concerned is said to be **affident**, or to have affidence. **Analepsis** may thus be viewed as a hierarchy, with **modal** dimensions, of affident propositions.

The various university disciplines are to be understood as being subsumed beneath knowledge two/affidence in the chain of boxes on the left of the diagram. The first divisions are trivial: 'linguistics' and 'other branches of knowledge'; 'literary semantics' and 'other branches of linguistics'; I take it for granted that literary semantics is subsumed beneath linguistics.

Literary semantics is subdivided into the **semantics of literature** (with **transmission semantics,** its experimental counterpart) and **semics**. The semantics of literature is the study of a 'work of literature' as an event in history; the attempt to reconstruct the meaning of a literary work by means of historical (biographical, textual, and so forth) research.[17] Semics is the study of **semic accompaniment** – that series of mediating reactions which a person experiences when he reads continuously at his normal speed a passage which contains for him no linguistic difficulties.

The remaining boxes on the left of the diagram are subdivisions of semics. **Theoretical semics** is that level of literary semantics at which the kinetic component functions. It is the task of the theoretical semicist to confront the problems of literary semantics and to 'stir up' the traditional concepts in the hope of finding solutions. There is thus a fundamental opposition between the **analeptic component** of which theoretical semics is a part, and the **kinetic component**, which transmits itself through theoretical semics. **Practical semics** subsumes **empirical semics** and **introspective semics**. **Empirical semics** is that part of semics which collates, classifies and describes evidence provided by subjects concerning their own semic accompaniments. The **empirical semicist** will also explore behaviourist evidence, psychological or neurophysiological, relevant to the semic accompaniment of an **instantiated reader**. **Introspective semics** is that part of semics which relies upon evidence provided by the investigator's own semic accompaniment. Introspective semics shades off into **practical criticism**. The investigator himself is thus an **instantiated reader** at the level of introspective semics. At the level of empirical semics an **instantiated reader** is one who provides evidence concerning his own semic accompaniment, whether by his own verbal description or by acting as a subject for behavioural experimentation – including electronic – to a scientific investigator. The instantiated reader is to be differentiated from a **hypothetical reader**, one postulated as experiencing a **semic accompaniment** of such-and-such a specification, so that the theorist (at the level of **theoretical semics**) may pursue a hypothetical argument.

I envisage the empirical semicist as adopting, at the level at which he operates, a rigorous positivist philosophy, expressing itself in behaviouristic and mechanistic assumptions. The theoretical semicist, not necessarily bound by such assumptions, is not precluded from enjoying the fruits of the empirical semicist's research, but he is given freedom to think imaginatively, to speculate, to 'turn things upside down'. The theorist will accuse his empirical brethren of being dull plodders; they him of indulging in fantasies. In an analogous fashion, optical and radio astronomers sometimes reproach the cosmologists for not wishing to be bothered with the facts.[18] In this way, the analeptic and kinetic components discipline each other. This is the built-in property of my modal structure: two or more components in **reciprocal perspective**, critically antagonistic – yet yoked with demur in a common endeavour. When the balance is good, the science is operating efficiently. It is important to mention that one person, the **scientist**, can assume the combined rôle of **theoretical semicist** and **empirical semicist**; in this case, the **analeptic-kinetic** opposition is between those two facets of his judicial self.

The trichotomy of knowledge of course includes everything; in fact the boxes, which are strictly included within the trichotomy, have been shown projecting downwards outside the rectangle for the sake of clarity: they belong to different **modal** levels, as a forward glance at the diagrams in chapter 14 [LS:213] and chapter 15 [LS:227] reveals. I wish to return briefly to the trichotomy and explain in what sense **modality** is bound up with it.

The realm of knowledge, as I have mapped it, is *absolutely* large. The traditional dichotomy between knowledge and belief has led to fruitless wranglings: '*x*, to which I am committed, is knowledge; *y*, which you hold, is belief'. Instead of a positivist demarcation line, which seems discourteous to many intelligent and educated men, my analeptic system draws two lines, above and below, as it were, of what a man believes himself capable of communicating [LS:12]. Whatever a man believes he experiences but cannot communicate is knowledge three. Whatever a man believes he can communicate to any other person is knowledge two. Whatever is 'correct' is knowledge one. My metatheory thus includes everything that could ever be considered knowledge – I challenge the reader to suggest something he considers to be knowledge which is not comprehended in this trichotomy – though it includes a great deal more than many would wish. The advantage we gain paying this price is that we begin with a broad scope which we can by mutual agreement reduce, should this seem necessary. The trichotomy theory thus embraces the three modal preconditions of civilized discourse: the possibility that *I* am right; the possibility that *you* are right; the possibility of *being* right. Far from murdering to dissect, the trichotomy theory throws us back on the old-fashioned virtues of courtesy and humility.

Another benefit to be gained by adopting the trichotomy theory is that it is neutral with regard to positivism. The traditional knowledge/belief dichotomy has always been uncompromisingly Procrustean for those who wished to devote themselves to serious academic consideration of what hard-headed colleagues in other disciplines dismissed as 'fairy-stories'.[19] Initially, the trichotomy theory is committed only to three types of 'knowledge-possibility'. But there is nothing to stop us building in a 'positive' philosophy at a lower level as I have shown in discussion of empirical semics – see also the diagram [LS:19], where Woozley's and Ayer's analyses are grouped together with the trichotomy at the level of knowledge two. At this level, the debate may continue but without the rhetoric of the 'absolute' claim.

Earlier in this chapter, modality was defined in terms of the traditional grammatical categories 'indicative' and 'subjunctive'. We can now redefine it in the light of what I have said about the analeptic system. An **affidence test** is a rigorously conducted investigation to determine whether a given proposition is **affident**. If all the participants in an affidence test are satisfied that they know what is meant by a term or sequence of terms, then that term or sequence of terms is said to be **secure**. The lower the security of a term, or sequence of terms, the more **insecure** it is said to be. An **analeptic constant** is a term **secure**, or a proposition **affident**, within a given **universe of discourse**. A **kinetic variable** is a term **insecure**, or proposition **inaffident**, within a given universe of discourse. My **principle of classification** states that **kinetic variables may not be transformed into analeptic constants**. **Modality** may therefore be redefined cf [LS:146] as *a determination to avoid violating the principle of classification.* **Reciprocal perspective** between scientific components is the means by which this may normally be achieved.

Applying this principle to the earlier examples from *The Great Tradition*, the sorts of statement which Leavis was making concerning the 'great' English novelists really belong to **introspective semics**. Although they purport to be about an objectified 'literature', **empirical semics**, they are better interpreted as statements to do with Leavis' own mental processes. Leavis has violated the **principle of classification**. In this case the **kinetic variables**, a set of Leavis' private responses, are presented as if they were incontrovertible, and about literature, **analeptic constants**.

One point remains to be cleared up. The criticism I made earlier [LS:143–144], applying the concept of the **circumflexion of discourse** to Popper's discussion of what constitutes a scientific theory, is a boomerang which I know is likely to return. I can, in short, imagine my readers quite properly asking me, 'To what modality does your present book belong?' The answer to this is that I am a theorist. All my published discussions of literary semantics are to be interpreted as exercises in **theoretical semics**. Nothing more is claimed for them than that.

CHAPTER 10

A MODAL THEORY OF STYLE

Some Treatments of Style

'Style' is a specific problem to which the analeptic divisions may be applied. The difficulties that have arisen in dealing with this slippery concept are occasioned, I believe, by a determination on the part of stylisticians to define 'style', in effect, as a primary concept within **empirical semics**, some immanent property sealed within the text; to turn a **kinetic variable** into an **analeptic constant**. It is just one more example of the type of theoretical instability which arises when the **principle of classification** is violated. By a simple dual definition, which makes it clear in each case precisely what is being defined, the concept emerges with a clearly delineated empirical version on the one hand and a theoretical version on the other. According to purpose, so the scholar may choose.

Leo Spitzer's Philological Circle

Leo Spitzer, in his article 'Linguistics and Literary History', outlined the method of stylistic analysis which became known as the 'philological circle'.[1] The method proceeds on the following lines:

(i)   The linguist, reading a work of literature, notices some usage which is aberrant.[2]

(ii)   This observation prompts him to vigilance, so that any similar usages in his subsequent reading of the author's work are also noticed.

(iii)   The features thus accumulated become the phenomenon to be explained and the linguist then seeks to establish a causal relationship between some posited pattern of the author's *Weltanschauung* and the features.[3]

(iv)   The circle which is involved here is that the features are themselves
            a part of the 'work of literature'. There can be no evidence within
            the work other than the language which constitutes it. Therefore
            an unknowable entity, the author's personality, is being called in to
            explain a phenomenon; but in order to supply the gap in our knowl-
            edge, we are using a selection of data from the phenomenon itself.[4]

(v)   Spitzer admits the circularity, but argues that it is not vicious:[5] the
            position of the reader in this situation is precisely analogous to that of
            the philologist who works backwards from his knowledge of living
            languages to the reconstruction of a protolanguage. Such philolo-
            gists use features of the languages they know to supply hypothetical
            details of the unrecorded language, the only test which is available to
            them being that of coherence.[6]

Now whilst I accept Spitzer's point about the circle – circles of this kind
are inherent in human reasoning, see my *caveat* concerning axiom and natural
deduction systems [LS:145–146], and the most we may hope to do is to remain
as finely-ordered as we can within our circles – there are three respects in
which the particular circle into which he would lead his reader are different
from the supposedly analogous relation between the Romance languages and
the hypothetical vulgar Latin prototype.

The first difference is in Spitzer's use of emotive-figurative language: 'Thus
we have made the trip from language or style to the soul';[7] 'the scholar will surely
be able to state…whether he has found the life-giving center, the sun of the solar
system';[8] (Spitzer means some mental reality causally related to the features);
'language motivation, plot, are only satellites of this mythological entity'.[9]

Secondly, and this emphasis overlaps with the first, Spitzer uses his illustration of the philological circle to present a moral perspective: 'we are given
insight into the soul of a writer';[10] 'A man without belief in the human mind
is a stunted human being – how can he be a Humanist? The humanities will
be restored only… when they become human again…';[11] 'the capacity for this
feeling is, again, deeply anchored in the previous life and education of the
critic';[12] 'in order to keep his soul ready for his scholarly task he must have
already made choices, in ordering his life, of what I would call a moral nature'.[13]

Of course there is nothing unusual in introducing metaphorical models
in scientific explanation,[14] so that Spitzer's language, with its propensity
for figures of speech, is not to be condemned on this account: where we are
describing what we cannot see, we may find it helpful to invoke what *is* visible.

But Spitzer's language is unnecessarily metaphorical. The use of such phrases as 'life-giving centre' and 'sun of the solar system' may be thought to provide the student with a sense of warmth. To feel the glow of humanism, he has only to adopt Spitzer's approach, see the problems through Spitzer's eyes. And this implication is reinforced when Spitzer goes on to speak of morality.

He concludes his chapter with these words: 'I have sometimes wondered if my *"explication de texte"* in the university classroom, where I strive to create an atmosphere suitable for the appreciation of the work of art, would not have succeeded much better if that atmosphere had been present at the breakfast table of my students.'[15] This implies that some of his students did not afford to the 'philological circle' the degree of fervour Spitzer would have wished. The phenomenon is by no means new. A literary critic rhetorically expounds a trivial device in such a way as to make it appear a pathway to moral deliverance. When it transpires that the audience is apathetic, he blames the lack of enthusiasm upon some limiting factor in their background. If a student challenges a point of detail in the philologist's reconstruction of a protolanguage, the only counter is refutation of the student's argument. But Spitzer's response to anyone so overweening as to question his method of analysis is apparently, in the name of humanism, to cast aspersions upon those with whom the student has taken breakfast.

The third respect in which Spitzer differs from the philologist is in illicit **modal** transposition (see my discussion of Leavis [LS:147–148]). Spitzer commences the account innocently enough: 'I had acquired the habit of underlining expressions which struck me as aberrant from general usage…'.[16] This is an unexceptionable statement concerning his own private practice (**introspective semics**). Before long, however, we encounter the following: 'And on this journey we may catch a glimpse into a historical evolution of the French soul in the twentieth century'[17] (observe the Leavis-like use of 'we' – Spitzer and all other sensitive readers?); 'And the individual *mens Philippina* is a reflection of the *mens Franco-gallica* of the twentieth century: its ineffability consists precisely in Philippe's anticipatory sensitivity for the spiritual needs of the nation'[18] (observe the way in which Spitzer, by the use of 'precisely' and taxonomic Latin, assigns to his questionable categories, **kinetic variables**, the status of Linnaean classes, **analeptic constants**); 'The reason that the clues cannot be mechanically transferred from one work of art to another lies in the fact of artistic expressivity itself'.[19]

What began as a trivial observation of Spitzer's personal custom has been transformed in the space of a few pages into the most rampant generalization concerning the soul of Philippe, the soul and spiritual needs of the French nation during the twentieth century and the uniqueness of artistic expression. Despite Spitzer's protestations, his circle is different from the method of the 'proto-philologists'. If a student accepts Sir William Jones' hypothesis, he is committed to the existence of some proto-language. That is all. But it appears that the corollary of his accepting the Spitzerian circle is his subscribing to facile universals concerning the needs of the French soul.

Michael Riffaterre's Style Analysis

Michael Riffaterre's article, 'Criteria for Style Analysis',[20] shows a much greater **modal** awareness than Spitzer's discussion in the article I have dealt with: 'subjective impressionism, normative rhetoric and premature aesthetic evaluation have long interfered with the development of stylistics as a science, especially as a science of literary styles'.[21] Riffaterre is anxious to reduce the rôle played in stylistic analysis by personal responses. He imports into stylistics the linguistic technique of eliciting information from informants, whose responses will draw attention to linguistic features of the text. His method differs from Spitzer's in that there is a clear theoretical separation between the 'psychological and cultural conditioning of the perception'[22] and the textual stimulus. This is a step towards making stylistics a science by the elimination of subjectivity.

The problem which Riffaterre's analysis does not solve is: What is the relation between a stylistic fact and a linguistic fact? Having made a strict theoretical division between the textual stimulus and the reader's perception, having shifted the analysis from the investigator's own reading experience to that of an informant, we still do not know what style is. His definition does not help us very much: 'Style is understood as an emphasis (expressive, affective or aesthetic) added to the information conveyed by the linguistic structure, without alteration of meaning. Which is to say that language expresses and that style stresses…'.[23] But, given a linguistic feature, how are we to determine whether it is also a stylistic feature? Do we need the concept of style at all? Perhaps style is an excrescent entity?

Bennison Gray's Excision of 'Style' by Occam's Razor

Bennison Gray in his book *Style: The Problem and its Solution*[24] proposes cutting the Gordian knot.

(i)   All agree, says Gray, that there is a phenomenon 'style', but there is no consensus of opinion as to what the entity is.[25]

(ii)   The interest in 'style' is an example of *conceptual realism*: it is assumed that style must exist because there is a word for it. 'Stylistic' is not a defining characteristic of literature.[26]

(iii)   Gray attacks George Miller's definition of 'style' as expressive behaviour. The study of literature is not to be subsumed under psychology.[27]

(iv)   All methods of study which propose to relate the attributes of a literary work to its author are circular. The work is seen as an index of the author's personality, and then deductions based upon this are used to make unwarranted conclusions concerning the surface structure of the text.[28]

(v)   Neither psychologist nor student of style is justified in inferring from a product of human behaviour anything except that there must have been a human being to produce it.[29] [I find this an astounding affirmation.]

(vi)   All stylistic comparisons resolve themselves into comparisons of *meaning*.[30]

(vii)   For if we define meaning, and then define style as meaning, we will still have to justify the additional term 'style'.[31]

(viii)   Even stylistically minded linguists on both sides of the Atlantic have never clearly demonstrated that style exists and is something that can be studied. They are condescending towards the intuitive stylists, like Spitzer, whom they rightly regard as unscientific. But they regard tabulation (which rests, as Spitzer points out, upon subjective judgments as to which images are the most characteristic of authors) as indisputable. 'We know simply what the author said; we do not know what he knew that he might have said.' Either two words or syntactical constructions mean the same thing – in which case it does not matter which one the author chooses, the choice is meaningless; or, if there are no synonymous words and syntactical constructions, then a difference between two words or phrases is a difference in meaning.[32]

(ix)   Gray's conclusion is that 'style' is an unnecessary entity. 'There often comes a time when it is necessary to ignore the terminology, to find out for one's self what the phenomena have in common, and to define them according to this common characteristic. This is the principle of economy in literature, in science, and in almost any other human activity; it is the principle, in short, of Occam's Razor: do not multiply entities unnecessarily.'[33]

(x)   Thus, Bennison Gray's solution to the problem of style turns out to be a rather drastic one: abolish the notion altogether. He ends his book: 'To be able to discard the concept of an entity which is not necessary and whose existence can be neither empirically established nor logically deduced – this is to be truly scientific.'[34]

A concept which has proved so protean as style may be the result of a wrong analysis of the problem and we would do well to try and manage without it. But Gray's book, published in 1969, has done nothing to stem the flow of publications in style. New books wholly or partly devoted to the concept are published by the score; new journals spring up all over the world.[35] If Gray has laid the ghost of style, how can this be?

An Anthropological Aside

Although this chapter is not meant to be an exercise in anthropology, perhaps I may be permitted at this point to venture an anthropological suggestion as to why the concept of style persists. It is simply this: that man's physical survival has often depended upon an ability to distinguish between very small features within alternative behaviour patterns. As Hrothgar's coastguard, who hailed Beowulf and his men when they landed in Denmark, observed, 'It is the duty of the smart shield-warrior, the truly perceptive one, to know the difference between words and deeds' [my translation]. The heroic behaviour of friendly visitors – or hostile invaders, who might be dissimulating – is not easily interpreted. The ceremonial disembarkation of Beowulf and his men might look broadly the same, whether it boded well or ill: the coastguard must find quickly, perhaps intuitively, some clue in the behaviour of the newcomers. The same action, a man coming at me with a knife, may signal hostility or jest. We need to decide almost instantaneously which alternative **psychological frame** matches the confronting **external frame** (see chapter 13 and Glossary). The wink, the turn of his lips, may be a portent for me that it is the one or the other. In matters of life and death, we would like more information before making a decision; but our survival or, less seriously, our success, often depends upon our ability to 'read the personality' of our acquaintances from a few minute clues. Style awareness may therefore be a vestige of a defence mechanism and style would be nothing more than those personal indicators that men keep their eyes open for in order to survive or succeed. The phylogenetic habits are transferred from the spoken to the written word. Despite the ontological problem, scholars continue to look for style in language because they cannot help themselves. This is, however, a hypothesis that it would be very difficult to put to the test. A similar evolutionary conjecture, it may be noted in passing, can be made to explain the phenomenon of **fictionality,** see [LS:234].

Returning then to the problem of style in literature, whether or not they are justified in making inferences from a subset of linguistic features to the personality of the author, there is evidence that this is what a large number of readers incorrigibly do. Men make stylistic judgments even if style does not exist. I suspect that **Occam's Razor** can never be successfully employed upon the concept, in the manner in which Gray wielded it, for this reason. But there is an empirical path through.

Occam's Razor and the Concept of Style

Occam's Razor is an important scientific principle. Curiously, Occam himself does not seem to have been responsible for formulating it in the sentence which convention preserves: *'E(sse)ntia non sunt multiplicanda praeter necessitatem'*. So far as I am aware, the earliest recorded occurrence of this – in the form *'non sunt multiplicanda entia sine necessitate'* – is in a commentary upon the *Liber III Sententiarum* of Duns Scotus by a seventeenth century scholar, John Ponce of Cork.[36] Occam's works do contain a fair number of references to the spirit, if not to the letter, of the received sentence: for instance *'frustra fit per plura, quod potest fieri per pauciora'*. But in fact the Razor, in various guises, was approved of and applied by a number of medieval divines, including Duns Scotus, and analogues can be found even in Aristotle.[37]

Occam's Razor, misnamed though it may be, has been widely accepted by philosophers of science, who have sometimes referred to it as the Principle of Economy, or the Principle of Parsimony. It has met with theoretical acclaim, but has frequently been found wanting in practice. The difficulty arises over *precisely what entities are necessary*. It is not conducive to useful discussion to argue that one's opponent's two entities should be reduced to one, if he thinks that both are needed. My own solution is a modal refinement, in keeping with my anthropological analysis of style in the previous section. The two parallel, self-consistent definitions hold out the possibility of empirical testing in one mode and yet preserve the spirit of Buffon's famous dictum 'Le style est l'homme même' in another.

To return therefore to Gray's contention: the pressures upon the human psyche are too many and great for us to be troubled with bogus entities. Gray argues that style is redundant. But, for all that, when I read a book or a letter, I cannot help seeing some parts of the meaning as being more obvious indicators of the author's personality than others. And I am not able to get this awareness out of my mind. This, I suspect, is the case with most readers: they are sensitive to an apparent level of meaning which seems to betray some aspects of the personality of the author. Now this suspicion that a correlation exists between a subset of linguistic features and the mind of the writer may not be an important piece of scientific information, but it has at least something of the status of the remark made to Ludlow, the surgeon of Sodbury in Gloucestershire, by a dairymaid. She told Ludlow that the pustular infection which she had contracted could not possibly be smallpox, for she had already had the cowpox and nobody ever caught the smallpox after that. Ludlow passed this story on to Edward Jenner, the eighteenth-century doctor, who went on to discover the wonders of vaccination.[38]

The dairymaid's remark becomes important only with hindsight. In the structures of science there are many mansions: a casual statement by an unskilled person is not necessarily to be despised. Nor are readers' intuitions. What we need is a **modal** system which will enable us to assign some status to those concepts which, whilst they seem worth pursuing, have not yet been attested. If the problem of style is thus modally 'reduced', an experimental stylistics, with empirical rigour, becomes easily attainable.

Occam's Razor, in its received form, proves to be too crude for the problem of style. If we fail to use it the concept of style remains and we have to come to terms with the theoretical difficulty of trying to disentangle style from language – an impossible task, since whatever stylistic feature we seize upon turns out to be a linguistic feature; and similarly, whatever feature of language we select may well be argued by someone to manifest style. Alternatively, we wield Occam's Razor and leave just language. But in this event we excise an important element in human awareness of literature.

A Modal Theory of Style

It is in order to find a way out of this dilemma that I suggest a corollary to **Occam's Razor**: the **principle of subsumption**. In empirical semics, according to the criterion of principles, an adequate principle is one which, having been defined and demonstrated, can be operated independently by other linguists. Now my principle of subsumption does not meet this criterion. But then, as we saw [LS:159–160], nor does Occam's Razor. This does not preclude, however, their being regarded as useful tools at the theoretical level.

The **principle of subsumption** may be formulated as follows: *whatever pluralities necessity dictates subsume if you can*. This directive, for which no originality is claimed, can be applied to the problem of style. Instead of having the two entities *language* and *style* at the same theoretical level, we allow style to be subsumed beneath language. This we do simply by defining style, not relative to language as a whole, but in relation to a given person's semic accompaniment: in other words, we use psycholinguistics to provide research with a determining factor. We arrive at the following dual definition of style, the second of which provides a firm basis for an experimental stylistics:

(I)   In *theoretical semics*, given two passages A and B and a hypothetical
           reader's semic accompaniment to the two separate passages, then the
           stylistic features of A are those linguistic features which would lead
           the hypothetical reader to suppose, rightly or wrongly, that A and B
           are, or are not, written by the same person.

(II)   In *empirical semics*, style is the totality of the linguistic features in a
           given passage which can be experimentally demonstrated (by means of
           instantiated readers) to lead to correct predictions concerning passages
           where all relevant details of authorship are known by the investigator.

Definitions I and II may be employed in two typically different types of enquiry.

To illustrate Definition I, I will take as an example a stylistic analysis
recently performed upon Aristotle's *Nichomachean* and *Eudemian Ethics* by
Anthony Kenny.[39] Kenny's paper is only one of hundreds of computer analyses[40] which are being carried out on authorship problems, but it is, I believe, an
interesting sample of its type.

The *Nichomachean Ethics* and the *Eudemian Ethics* are separate works but
three books are common to both: books 5, 6 and 7 of the *Nichomachean Ethics*
being identical respectively with books 4, 5 and 6 of the *Eudemian Ethics*.
'Scholars have argued both ways on the question whether, as regards style and
doctrine, the affinities of the common or disputed books are with the other
books of the NE or with the other books of the EE,' writes W. F. R. Hardie.[41]

The question to which Kenny addresses the Oxford computer is: Do the
regularities which can be observed in the disputed books resemble more closely
those to be found in the *Nichomachean Ethics* or those in the *Eudemian Ethics*?
He has carried out a number of measurements, with extensive tabulation, of
lexical frequencies: particles, connectives, prepositions, adverbs, pronouns and
so forth are subjected to statistical scrutiny. He comes to the conclusion that the
common books resemble the *Eudemian Ethics* more than the *Nichomachean*.

The results of this particular piece of research are not my present concern.
What I am arguing is that this is a Definition I type of stylistic exercise within
theoretical semics. The experiment is of some empirical interest, but the structure of suppositions in the features Kenny selects is too tenuous for us to say
that any firm conclusion he might reach on the basis of such data has been
empirically established. We do not look in vain in the version of the paper which
Kenny has kindly sent me for the appropriate **modal** indicators: 'Altogether the
tests, which cover some sixty per cent of the total word usage of the treatises,
present an overwhelming weight of evidence *for the view that the common
books resemble* the Eudemian Ethics more than the Nichomachean. *The most*

economical explanation of the evidence presented in this paper is that the common books, *as they now stand,* belonged originally to the Eudemian Ethics. *It would no doubt be rash to claim that* stylometric methods have solved a problem which has occupied scholars for centuries:...' (my italics). The careful modality of this exercise in theoretical semics is in stark contrast with the illicit modality of Leavis' pronouncement in *The Great Tradition* and in the operation of Spitzer's Philological Circle [LS:147–148; 154–157].

Turning now to Definition II, I have not yet come across an example of the sort of empirical study I am advocating. The nearest proposals in spirit are contained in a recent article by Eugene R. Kintgen.[42] My own method may be outlined as follows. The investigator takes a batch of ten essays written by one person and ten written by another; he knows for certain the authorship of each essay. He has them typed out, omitting all reference to the name of the author (and any included biographical clues, which we might agree to regard as 'unfair', non-stylistic clues). Chosen subjects are then asked to read the essays and, without conferring, to decide which ten essays are by the same person. They are instructed to note down the linguistic features they took as indicators. If there is a high correlation between the judgments and, what is more, a fair degree of accuracy in assessment, then we are beginning to make progress in our quest for style. The investigator can begin to extrapolate to cases where the authorship is unknown. The modal structures of theoretical semics, which are contingent upon the experimental demonstrations of the empirical semicists, are progressively refined. The study of stylistics, as a result of this modal restructuring, is becoming empirical and predictive in the Popperian sense. My present proposals within Definition II are crude, but it is easy to conceive of many developments and modifications.

Subsumption

By employing the **principle of subsumption**, the theorist can deal with the concept of style more efficiently (see also **subsumption** of knowledge/belief within **knowledge two** [LS:19]). The notion is defined relative to the semic accompaniment of a given reader within theoretical semics or within empirical semics. Within empirical semics, where authorship of a work is known for certain, predictive experimentation is shown to be possible. Results within empirical semics can then be used to further investigations within theoretical semics. Modal style definitions will vary, within empirical demands, according to the scholar's purpose. But the most important aim of this chapter has been to suggest strongly that literary discourse would profit greatly if its proponents would devote serious attention to the problems of modality.

CHAPTER 11

EMPIRICAL SEMICS

Segers' Treatment of Value

In an article published in 1978, which with some minor revision formed the basis of chapter 10, I advocated dealing with the problem of 'style' by modal reduction. The same year Rien T. Segers published a book which I believe was a landmark in literary semantics: he had bravely undertaken a rigorous empirical investigation into the problem of value. He quite independently approached the topic by a form of **modal reduction**: the named object of his enquiry was *evaluation*. The review article I subsequently wrote forms the basis of this chapter.

Segers' new book had the short title: *The Evaluation of Literary Texts*. First, I will summarise his work, and then critically discuss his analysis.

Drawing upon the theories of Nauta, Eco, Jakobson, Lotman, Wienold and Siegfried Schmidt, Segers assembles the theoretical material for his definition of a literary text. The following page references are to his book. Having affirmed that literary texts are embedded in a communication process between author and reader (page 13), the author develops a model, based upon the work of Eco and Jakobson, of the literary communication process. The definition of a literary text is, he says, of extreme importance in literary theory (page 28). To this end, he begins with Miller's definition of a code (page 18), extends this to encompass a literary code (page 25), finally arriving at a specification of a literary text: an explicit, limited and structured set of verbal signs, of which the aesthetic function is found dominant by the reader (page 31). As the defining characteristic of a literary text, the dominance of the aesthetic function as adjudged by the reader is preferred to the frequently submitted candidates: *deviance* and *fictionality*. The present investigation is to concentrate upon text-reception; specifically, upon the relation between value judgments and text function.

Segers goes on to consider the aesthetics of reception (*Rezeptionsaesthetik*). Russian Formalists had concentrated almost exclusively upon the aesthetic function (page 38), but the Prague Structuralists, whose interests were wider, provided the source of inspiration for the aesthetics of reception: literature was seen by them as a communication process, a dynamic force within society (page 40). There follows a review in some detail of the work of Jauss and Iser, the main proponents of *Rezeptionsaesthetik*, which had its origin in the late 1960s. He sees as the most important concepts Jauss's *horizon of expectations* (page 401) and Iser's *indeterminate section* (page 41). More important to Segers' study than these theoretical notions have been the methodological proposals which have resulted from the application of psychological techniques to measure the reader's realization of a text. These most clearly emerge in the discussion of Norbert Groeben's 'empirical' approach (page 43). Segers believes practical investigation to be essential but observes that, because the aesthetics of reception is a recent branch of literary studies, very little experimental work has been accomplished (page 49). The concepts of *ideal*, *implicit* and *real* reader are introduced (page 52): it is the last which is the most important instrument for the aesthetics of reception. There follows a warning: the aesthetics of reception, in focusing upon the concretization of the text, must not lose sight of the text itself. The disciplines of semiotics, sociology and psychology can open up new ways of studying literature; at the theoretical centre of this endeavour should be the triad: reader-text-author (page 55).

Attention now turns to the problem of value itself. A *criterion* is a standard of judgment employed in a particular situation (page 59). *Norm* has a more generalized application, denoting a complex of criteria. A *normative proposition*, one which implies a norm as opposed to a descriptive proposition depends both on the norm system of the evaluating subject and on the structure of the object to be evaluated (page 60). Segers, arguing that it is impossible to find objective grounds on which to justify an evaluation, defines value: a value represents a formula capable of providing the *rationalization* of an action. By rationalization is meant an attempt using one or more criteria, to justify a value-judgment (page 60). A normative proposition which attaches value to an entity without revealing the criterion (e.g. I like playing tennis) is called a *preference*. A *value judgment* is a normative proposition, based on an intellectual appraisal, which rationalizes an action and enables us to infer a value (page 61). A *literary value* can be defined as a formula capable of providing the rationalization of a reader's reaction (page 62). The author then produces the following model as a (non-mentalistic) description of the literary evaluation process:

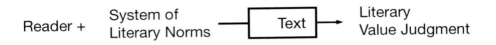

Segers' Model: Literary Evaluation Process.

Given this theoretical apparatus, Segers provides the justification for the experiment he subsequently describes: that it is possible to investigate values by means of questionnaires. He then considers the attempts of Beerling and others to present a parallelism between epistemology and **axiology** (pages 63-5). Taking Helmut Seiffert's deductive and inductive epistemological schemes, Segers constructs analogous models first for general axiology and then specifically for literary axiology (page 67). Although claiming that the ways in which value judgments are related to evaluation criteria are, within the framework he presents, laid open to scientific investigation, he stresses that there is not a perfect analogy between the axiological and epistemological models. In evaluation, the rôle of the subject is of paramount importance and the scientific aspiration to intersubjectivity can have no part (page 67). The sociology and psychology of literature are dealt with next. Reception research falls within the domain of the sociology of literature. There is a mutual dependency between the aesthetics of reception and experimental aesthetics, the former providing the theoretical basis, the latter the framework for investigation (page 78).

Segers now compares the intrinsic and the relational concepts of literary value. Proponents of the intrinsic view regard value as an independent entity present in, or absent from, a text (page 84). Those who hold the relational theory believe that value exists in the relation between the reader's norm system and the structure of the text (p. 84). The former view precludes scientific enquiry. The author commits himself to the relational view, abstracting three objects of investigation: (i) the textual structure and code; (ii) reader's horizons of expectation; (iii) an analysis of the mutual relations between (i) and (ii). The present volume is concerned with the investigation of the value judgments of groups of readers inductively to establish the norm systems of these groups (page 89). The value judgments of informed, actual readers (an *informed* reader is one possessing 'literary competence') are more interesting than judgments based upon little knowledge of the valued object (page 90). Informed readers are the respondents in his research.

Having completed these theoretical preliminaries, Segers turns to his experimental inquiries.

The research was conducted at the University of Indiana (Autumn 1974) and at the University of Yale (Autumn 1975). On the basis of an exploratory questionnaire completed by a group of Indiana graduates, a list of literary criteria for evaluating short stories was compiled. A questionnaire incorporating these twelve criteria was completed by three Indiana University groups: undergraduates; graduates (not the ones who completed the exploratory questionnaire); and faculty members. Four short stories, reprinted in an appendix to Segers' book, were read by the respondents and provided the objects for their responses: for instance, '.... this short story leads me to some kind of personal involvement in the characters and action', then, p.190, follow seven choices, in the manner of Osgood's semantic differential [LS:4–6], from 'strongly agree' to 'strongly disagree'. In addition, the reader was asked to give an overall impressionistic value-judgment, the polar terms being 'very good'... 'very bad', of the story as a whole. By correlating the overall impression with the list of choices, it is possible, Segers argues, to examine how far overall literary value judgment is determined by specific criteria and to decide upon the relative importance of the criteria. At Yale, three parallel groups were chosen and they completed a modified form of the Indiana questionnaire.

Segers carries out a factor analysis on the Indiana graduate questionnaire (the one used in the experiment proper), discovering three factors which seem to form the basis for their evaluation of short stories: novelty, impact and design. These factors provided an adequate description for the choices of the Yale graduates also, and for the Indiana and Yale faculty members, but were not on the whole suitable for the groups of undergraduates. It was found generally that the novelty factor provided the highest correlation with the overall evaluation.

Finally, the author discusses the results and limitations of his experiments. He briefly lists fields into which research on the lines he has carried out could be extended: Jakobson's theory of poetic function, aesthetics of identity, the concepts of Jauss and Iser, – dealt with in his second chapter – shifts in norm systems, comparative literature and education. He finally asks whether a new paradigm, in Kuhn's sense, has arrived in literary studies. To this, he gives a guarded affirmation, but he sees interdisciplinary techniques and theories as a complement to, not a substitute for, the activities of literary critics. A very lengthy bibliography is appended.

Value and Style

In chapters 9 and 10, I argued in favour of a modal reduction of the concept of style: instead of defining style as a subset of the linguistic features of a text, we distance the concept and define it in relation to one reader. In theoretical semics, given two passages, A and B, and a hypothetical reader's semic accompaniment to the two separate passages, then the stylistic features of A are those linguistic features which would lead the hypothetical reader to suppose, rightly or wrongly, that A and B are, or are not, written by the same person. In this way, **theoretical semics** prepares the way for style to become an object of empirical research: the investigator, in **empirical semics**, can take texts of whose provenance he is certain, submit them to an **instantiated reader** and test the reliability of the reader's textual predictions based on style awareness. If, for instance, given one hundred texts, the instantiated reader sorts them accurately into five separate authorship piles and is able to specify the linguistic features which enabled him to do this, then the investigator would feel justified in allowing some credence to these as stylistic features.

Although such accuracy is unlikely, the argument stands. Whether the results are positive or negative, the investigator is tackling a problem which is open to enquiry: how reliable an indicator of the authorship of a text is the instantiated reader's style awareness? If the success rate is no better than random, then we are moving towards Bennison Gray's position: expunge 'style' from the lexicon. Yet the quest is still empirical. An enquiry only ceases to be empirical *if it is impossible to conceive of* an experiment or observation which would answer the query one way or the other. This approach to the problem of style has the advantage of opening up an elusive concept to investigation; it also has the attraction of interpreting the concept in a commonsense manner – the traditions of Buffon's assertion, 'Le style est l'homme même'. An extension of the experiment mentioned in my previous paragraph would be to take essays written by several people well-known to the subject. He would be asked to determine which of his acquaintances wrote which essay and to list the linguistic features which led him to his decisions. If style *is* the man, then given 'style', it should be possible to make predictions about the man, and *vice versa*. Empirical semics provides the scholar with a prolific source of research into the concept of style.[1]

Segers' book takes the concept of value and, in my terms, executes a modal reduction, reformulating the concept at the level of empirical semics. Published in 1978, it was a book I had been waiting for since, in 1964, I wrote the words 'Semics can be either empirical or introspective' [LS:38]. Not only had he taken on a full-scale empirical 'literary' investigation, but he had chosen the most virulent nettle in the wild wood of literary studies: **value**. Furthermore, he undertook an *analysis of the concept 'value'* in a way that would have seemed repugnant, I guess, to Bateson and many of the critics I discussed in the earlier chapters of this book. My reaction was and is that literary semantics is beginning to make real progress. Segers' approach to **value** and mine to **style** are similar, though it should be repeated that he produces a full-scale investigation in **empirical semics**, whereas the only claim I make for my writings is that, apart from sections used in illustration, they belong to **theoretical semics.** *Literary Semantics* is, so far as I am aware, the first book published on the subject of literary studies that **modally reduces** the academic claims of its own comprised discourse.

It is my contention that, although what Segers has done is extremely interesting, a treatment like his of value, which makes no attempt at constructing an epistemological metatheory – he adopts the *relational* view but never comes to grips philosophically with the *intrinsic* view – entails a distortion.

A literary value, he says, can be defined as a formula capable of providing the rationalization of a reader's reaction. Thus, instead of defining value as a property of a text, we *distance* the concept by defining it in relation to one reader. Secondly, he subjects the concept to investigation at the level of **empirical semics,** though, of course, he does not use this term. Empirical semics incorporates the positivist assumptions of scientific experimentation, notably the **method of concomitant variations**. This may be expressed: if, given any two events A and B such that variation in A is matched commensurately by variation in event B, then some causal connection from A to B or from B to A – or from event C to both – may, at least tentatively, be inferred. The method can be redefined in terms of set theory. The author's fifth chapter is entirely devoted to such a study: chiefly, a correlation between the overall evaluations of the short stories and factors extrapolated from the scale items.

The underlying model which Segers aims to vindicate proposes that a reader's literary value judgment is based both upon the read literary text and upon the reader's system of literary norms. Such a model is simple almost to the point of triviality. Any act of judgment presupposes on the one hand an entity to be judged and on the other a set of criteria whereby the decision is arrived at. For instance, my possible judgment 'x has the property *green*' will be determined by (at least) two variables: (i) the colour of x; and (ii) my norm for deciding the limits of green in the spectrum. Radically change either the colour or my norm and it is almost certain that my judgment will change. Hence, it is hardly surprising when the author demonstrates that 'Two reading groups using two different literary norms in judging the same literary text, will give completely different value judgments about that text' (p. 151). A more serious criticism is that, for all Segers' emphasis upon the text in his model and his care in relating his study to semiotics and linguistics, the texts themselves – though reproduced in an appendix for the benefit of the reader – are almost entirely neglected.[2]

No quantitative linguistic analysis is carried out: the author mentions research into the correlation between textual features and arousal as a problem to be considered in future experiments (p. 160).

In his theoretical treatment, the author rejects the intrinsic conception of value (which implies that literary value is an independent entity present in or absent from a text) on the grounds that no objective justification for a value can be found (p. 60). He espouses instead a relational view: literary value is dependent on the norm system of the reader and the structure of the text. This compromise is perplexing. Segers rejects the intrinsic conception because, if there is such an entity as an independent value, no objective justification can be found: it is a rejection which rules out any empirical enquiry into value; with this I agree. Value is essentially different from style.

The difference between style and value is this: that style is an *indicator*, whereas value is not.[3] To argue within my **trichotomy theory** that it is an indicator of **knowledge one**, is tautologous: that assertion is equivalent to contending that it is an indicator of itself.

When we define something as being an indicator of *something else*, we immediately have two sets available for correlation, say A and B, which represent, at the level of **empirical semics**, the supposedly *indicating* and the possibly *indicated*. Style is an indicator (of the author's personality, or of the literary period, or so forth) or it is nothing. The **method of concomitant variations** can establish a constant conjunction, or its absence. But, leaving on one side the question of *instrumental* values, which *can* be probed empirically, **value** is an entity which may or may not have objective existence; and, if it does so exist, it may or may not yield identifying indicators.

Its nebulousness is such that whatever we settle upon as a possible indicator cannot by any of the canons of inductive enquiry be steadily correlated with **value**, the entity. The most we can do is to tie one supposed indicator in with other indicators. 'Ninety-nine men value x' may lead us to predict that the hundredth man will value x, but even if the prediction proves true, this will not demonstrate that x is valuable. All we can say is that in this study, at the level of **knowledge two**, propositions affirming the value of x have **affidence**. Affidence is **truth two**; not necessarily **truth one**. Such studies as Segers' are interesting in that they focus upon an area where **science**, for all its acclaimed impressive and tangible performances, becomes inadequate.

Now it is only fair to point out that Segers is fully aware of all this; indeed, his title proclaims that he is concerned with evaluation rather than with value. But his discussion of the relational conception and his frequent references to value seem to suggest that he envisages his empiricism groping towards **value** 'itself'. The obvious alternative to the intrinsic conception is a subjective view – value is in the mind of the evaluating subject. The consequences of this for empiricism are unequivocal: the object of study is evaluation, not value. But the relational view must demand the two entities to be related; if we place value in the relation between the reader's norm system and the text and if the value is not entirely encompassed within the reader's norm system, then it must in some sense and to some degree be located in the text. To the extent that this is so, we are surely back with an *intrinsic* conception.

Despite his relational view, Segers pursues an uncompromising empiricism. Value is defined as a formula capable of providing the rationalization of an action. The definition centres upon a formula which finds expression in observable behaviour. The presence of a value, given a co-operating subject, can be verified. But the value remains firmly located in the subject. Nor does Segers' elaborate correlation of overall evaluation and factors change this: all it shows is that certain sets of judgments have an internal coherence. Furthermore, the enquiry raises a dilemma.

The Limits of Empiricism

The dilemma I am referring to arises frequently, though not usually in quite such clear focus as in Segers's study. In general terms, it may be stated in this manner. A scholar uses the techniques of a positivistic philosophy to examine the attitudes and beliefs of people who do not subscribe to this philosophy: either the scholar operates the procedures rigidly, in which case he fails to do justice to the non-positivistic beliefs of those he is investigating, or he takes those beliefs seriously, in which event he calls in question the adequacy of his own techniques. A form of this dilemma may be seen in the Klaeber edition of *Beowulf* which contains in its Introduction an exposition of 'The Fabulous or Supernatural Elements' (16 pages) followed by a treatment of 'The Historical Elements' (20 pages). The positivistic inference is clear: the poem can be effectively divided into two categories – the parts which we can believe to be true and the parts which we reject as false. But it is more than open to doubt that such a dichotomy would have any interpretative significance for those in the oral tradition who comprised the audience of *Beowulf.*

And it is the same with analyses carried out on, for example, Firthian lines. A cricket commentary provides a better text for a 'dimensional' analysis than a transcript of a prayer meeting: if prayer be an effectual instrument for enquiry into the universe, then new dimensions are called for. There does seem to be more than a trace of cultural overweening in the frequent assumption of sociologists that empirical techniques represent a *terminus ad quem* for all men for all time. Segers comes near to recognizing this problem with reference to author/reader, in his discussion of Lotman's aesthetics of opposition (page 26), but he does not transfer this to the metalevel of investigator/subject.

The relevance of such a dilemma for the present book is this: the author rejects the intrinsic conception of value, at least ostensibly, but there is no evidence that the subjects who provided the material for this enquiry would themselves reject the intrinsic view. Indeed, whatever standpoint a man may take retrospectively, at the moment of 'valuing', his commitment is surely to an intrinsic value: it seems paradoxical to assert 'x is valuable but its value consists solely in my valuing it'. If this be the case, then empirical analysis is bound to miss an essential element in the object of study. Segers himself makes a rare lapse. Throughout most of the book he attempts to subject **value** to a **modal reduction**. But when at the end he comes to consider the relevance of his research for the teaching of literature, he falls to the language of value commitment for instance, '…high school students also *have the right* to profit from the modern theory of literature' (my italics) (p. 165). There is no modal reduction here – the statement suggests a writer strongly committed to an intrinsic concept of value. The position may be summed up in this way. The valuing subject places the value in the object. The investigator can inquire into the object but this inquiry tells him nothing about the value of the object. If he inquires into the subject, he learns only about evaluation, not value.

It would not be fair to give the impression that Segers neglects the episte-mological aspects of his study. In his third chapter, he discusses the relation between axiology and epistemology. He constructs an axiological model analo-gous to the epistemological model of Seiffert, which works from axiom through to derivation and demonstration – it is, in fact, the well-attested construct of an axiomatic system. Segers' analogy for a deductive model in axiology is from norm to evaluation criterion to value judgment. But in such a scheme (and the same is true of his inductive model), value is always bound to be at a disadvantage. An axiom is typically contemplated within an axiom system: we can operate the transformational rules upon the axioms, yet the axioms still remain axioms.

But as soon as we place a 'value' into a deductive system, we tear it out of its proper environment: what we are now contemplating within the system is a 'formula' or 'norm' closer ontologically to an axiom than to a value. Seiffert produces an epistemological model for epistemology: Segers' solution is to devise an epistemological model for axiology. The currency of ratiocinative argument – 'descriptive' utterances, mathematical symbols, and structures – is always several stages removed from the attitude of mind in which we contem-plate 'valuable' objects. Thus, any attempt to feed value into an axiom set violates the concept.

An Alternative View of Value

We cannot do justice to value by building it into a positivistic epistemological construct. We need a metatheory which analyses knowledge in a new way; which, whilst accommodating a positivistic component, allows value to by-pass the positivistic concept of knowledge and become an 'epistemological' (using the term in an extended '**trichotomy**' sense) tool in its own right.

Again analysing the problem of value in the light of the trichotomy theory, this can be effected by a division of knowledge into three categories: knowledge one, knowledge two and knowledge three (which respectively may be labelled ultimate, communicable and incommunicable knowledge).[4] Value is then defined as a man's intuition (knowledge three) that he has access in some degree to knowledge one. It is a definition which remains neutral to the intrinsic and relational concepts of value: if the man's intuitions are 'justified', then the value is intrinsic.

The trichotomy analysis of value comprehends both naturalistic and super-naturalistic views – it may be remarked in passing. For suppose a woman with a large family receives conflicting advice from her utilitarian psychiatrist and her parish priest concerning the use of contraceptives: the psychiatrist arguing that failure to use them will almost certainly increase the sum total of human unhappiness, the priest contending that their use is contrary to the will of God. Since knowledge one is ultimate knowledge, it accommodates whichever of these views is 'correct', that of the psychiatrist (naturalistic) or that of the priest (supernaturalistic). The conflicting views are analeptically assimilated within the definition of value: a man's intuition (knowledge three) that he has access in some degree to knowledge one. The example also illustrates one of the ways in which an analeptic theory proceeds. At the higher level, we aim at a definition which will include everything. **Kinetic** exploration of more specific definitions takes place lower down – for instance in **empirical semics**, as in Segers' inquiry.

This strategy accords to **value** full epistemological status. I argued [LS:146], that 'rationality', in order to function at all, has to assume the rationality of its own procedures. Value is in the same circular position: we presuppose that our values provide us with an intuitive 'hold' upon the universe. We can rationalise and inquire into symbolised abstractions derived from these values. But our value awareness – *and aesthetic awareness* – will always remain in the pre-linguistic, pre-symbolic domain of knowledge three. This is illustrated in Figure 11 overleaf:

Segers' study thus necessarily concentrates upon those aspects of value which fall within the domain of knowledge two/affidence (b); and that is the realm where *value* is least at home.

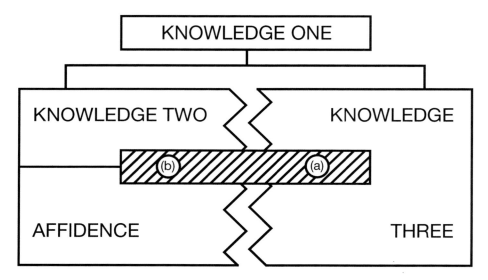

(a) Value awareness/aesthetic awareness
(b) Norm systems and other communicable formulations related to value
    (and within aesthetics)

Figure 11.   Value Within the Trichotomy Theory.

Now the question arises: in what sense is it true to say that literary semantics can accommodate value more successfully than can the tradition to which Segers belongs? The answer lies, I believe, in the carefully constructed metasystem. Sociological approaches to literature suffer from the disadvantage of inflexibility. If positivistic techniques fail to capture the essence of what most of us mean by **value**, then some readers may be left with a sense of the barrenness of the exploit and a disillusionment with empirical analysis. If, however, we consign such endeavours to the category **empirical semics**, just one of a number of levels of inquiry in a meta-system which provides other, non-positivistic possibilities for inquiring into the truth, then we shall keep positivistic techniques in perspective.

As with style, it is again a matter for modality. I regard Segers' book as a very important contribution to the problem of value in literature: as a thorough and serious treatment of one the most teasing problems in literary theory. It is easy to envisage undergraduate courses based upon the sort of techniques he is employing. My main criticism is that the author provides no way of compensating for the distortion of the concept of value which such useful studies necessarily entail. He modally reduces **value**, but he fails to design a meta-system capable of modally reducing his own empiricism. This view of **value** is further explored in chapter 14, 'The Chain of Modality'.

LITERARY SEMANTICS

PART III
THEORY AND PRACTICE

Ce n'est pas seulement le coeur
qui brûle – mais l'intellect même.

Anon.

CHAPTER 12

LEVELS OF MODALITY

Modality Within and Beyond Discourse

Knowledge Two Modalities: Logic to Natural Languages

The discussion of modal statements goes back to the *Prior Analytics* and *De Interpretatione* of Aristotle. On the one hand it has led to the development in modern philosophy of modal logic, concerned with such concepts as necessity, possibility and impossibility. Linguists, on the other hand, with one eye on developments in modal logic, have naturally concentrated upon modal statements in ordinary language. In English, this has meant systematic treatment of the so-called modal verbs.

Von Wright (1951: 12) established the alethic/epistemic/deontic classification, which has been influential in linguistic treatments. The alethic category, which concerns the necessary, the contingent and the possible, is frequently mentioned in linguistic discussions but dismissed as being of little importance in its application to ordinary language (see, for instance, Palmer, 1979: 3).

Rescher, working within the discipline of modal logic, added temporal, boulomaic, evaluative and causal modalities to the list. His definition of modality is worth quoting at length since it forms the basis for my own definition of textual modality, upon which in turn my notion of frame-profiling (see chapter 13) is based:

(1)   'A proposition is presented by a complete, self-contained statement
             which, taken as a whole, will be true or false: the cat is on the mat,
             for example. When such a proposition is itself made subject to some
             further qualification of such a kind that the entire resulting complex
             is itself once again a proposition, then this qualification is said to
             represent a modality to which the original proposition is subjected'
             (Rescher, 1968:24).

Thus, 'It is possibly true that the cat is on the mat' represents a modality of
'The cat is on the mat'. The logician is seen to have a considerable advantage
over linguists in that he can contrive his own forms. He takes a sentence like
'The cat is on the mat', devoid of any explicit reference to a particular state of
affairs and time, assigns to it the propositional variable letter 'p', then prefixes
this with a possibility operator 'M'. The resulting 'Mp' is then adjudged to be
a well-formed formula (wff), in conformity with a set of formation rules (see,
for instance, Lemmon, 1965: 44-6; Hughes and Cresswell, 1968: 133-4). In
systems of this kind, both the wff and the formation rules are created by the
logician.

Such systems profit the linguist by giving him insights into types of
modality, but they do not help him with the practical problems which natural
languages present. English modal verbs, the Greek optative and Latin subjunctive are examples of morphological systems whose meanings and functions
are related to one another. It is sometimes possible, as with the English
modals (Huddleston, 1984: 164), to define the formal characteristics of such
systems. The difficulty is, having determined the forms, to relate them to the
semantic notion of modality, which is vague and elusive. Is modality to do
with possibility and necessity, as some logicians maintain, or with attitudes
and opinions (Lyons, 1977: 452), illocutionary acts (Searle, 1979: 12-29;
Lyons, 1977: 725), or subjectivity or non-factuality, as discussed in Palmer
(1986: 16-18)? Palmer himself follows Lyons, treating 'grammatical main
clause modality, in which speakers express opinions and attitudes as basic'
(Palmer, 1986: 15). He takes the view that modality is a grammatical category
similar to aspect, tense, number and gender (1986:1). For the purposes of this
chapter, **modality** will be defined as **reciprocal perspective**. This is aestheti-
cally caught in *Earthrise*, a photograph of the nascent earth taken from the
Moon's surface. Moonrise, a phenomenon familiar since the dawn of life, is
abruptly displaced by orbital reality. And Man alongside is at once translated
from the rôle of static witness to the stirring duality of beholder-and-beheld
(NASA; *Apollo 11*; 20th July 1969). A derived concept will be seen to work
at all three levels of my theory – **psychologically** in **reflective modality**,
sociologically in **component modality** and **philosophically** in **knowledge
one modality**.

Perkins (1982, 1983) adopts a lexicalist (in the sense of emphasising the 'primacy of lexical units over the syntactic relations which exist between them' (1982: 245)) approach to modals, aiming to isolate the core meaning of each in turn by means of a formula. He takes CAN, MAY, MUST, WILL and SHALL as the primary modals and COULD, MIGHT, OUGHT TO, WOULD and SHOULD as secondary' (1982: 248; 1983: 29). Early forms of all these, except OUGHT TO, occur in *The Miller's Tale*, which is the text chosen to illustrate my own argument; there are, however, only epistemic examples of MIGHT and only one occurrence of CAN. Perkins provides formulae for determining the 'core meaning' of modal verbs.

An example of one such formula is:

(2)   MAY: K (C does not preclude X)

                    where:
        (i)   K = social laws/rational laws (typically)
        (ii)   C = deontic source/evidence (typically)
        (iii) X = the occurrence of e/the truth of p
               (Where K, C, X are variables; e is an event and p is a proposition)

If a given occurrence of a modal verb provides a satisfactory instantiation of the variables, then the occurrence accords with the 'core meaning' of the modal as depicted by Perkins.

The definitions of Rescher and Perkins thus represent two extremes of the spectrum of modal analysis: Rescher's is a theoretical formal construct based upon the logical notion of *propositions* rather than the linguistic concept of *utterances*; Perkins' formulae are semantic models against which raw instances of natural language may be measured. It should be noted in passing that logic systems, far from being mere academic constructs, frequently provide useful models for investigating ordinary language: a derivation in predicate calculus may present the logical form of an infinite number of arguments in everyday language. Indeed, Rescher's definition of modality, (1), will be extended and modified, *in tandem* with frame theory, to provide a more flexible analysis of English modal verbs.

I shall refer to both the modal structures devised by logicians, for instance, Rescher, on the one hand, and the modal devices occurring in natural languages, on the other – as **knowledge two modalities** – because they, as discourse, all belong to human communication.

Knowledge One and the Glass Ceiling

(a) Possible Worlds

The esoteric character of modal logic formulation, as opposed to the ordinary language utterances Perkins is aiming to represent, may be seen in the following examples:

(3)   Necessarily p is logically equivalent to not possibly not-p
(4)   The United Kingdom decides to secede from the EEC

That these are commonly held to be fundamentally different kinds of assertion may be seen by the following modifications:

(3a)   There exists a possible world in which not-(3)
(4a)   There exists a possible world in which not-(4)

Whereas (3a) would be regarded as inconsistent, (4a) is acceptable because it simply asserts a state of affairs contingent upon the real world (although the United Kingdom has not yet decided to secede from the EEC, there is nothing inconsistent in asserting (4a) or (4)).

　　　The problem arises when we ask: what is a possible world? As an earth-bound human, I have a high regard for logic systems and believe that inconsistency is, where possible, to be eschewed. But this is a guiding principle for the universe that I happen to find myself in. Philosophers who argue that (3) is true in all possible worlds and that (3a) is false in all possible worlds seem to me to be using a formula of words to legislate for something which is entirely beyond man's ken. We are acquainted only with the world we inhabit. I simply do not know whether there exists a universe in which the fundamental meta-assumptions of logic do not obtain. Notice also how (4b), below, brings out a curious aspect of modal usage in ordinary language: even when attempts to modalise discourse are made, there always remains a level at which statements are categorical. Thus (4b):

(4b)   The United Kingdom may decide to secede from the EEC

may be paraphased without distortion or contradiction as:

(4c)   It is certain that (4b)

Or, invoking the axiom of the Lewis system S5 (see Hughes and Cresswell, 1968: 237)

(4d)   If possibly (4b), then necessarily possibly (4b)

Our discourse is so fashioned that man's natural dogmatism informs with certainty all our statements, however uncertain we try to make them. We may be uncertain, but we are certain about our uncertainty. What is really needed is a metalevel of modality which builds in uncertainty as an integral part of the discourse. The very language we use, be it natural or artificial, is an uncertain cognitive tool and needs labelling as such, see [LS:146–147].

(b) Mathematics and Logic

There is a sense in which discourse seems to create its own reality. This is true even of the discourse of mathematics and logic. Mathematical entities take on for their exponents a concreteness which appears to transcend the intensity of the world of physical objects: they are analeptic constants and statements based upon them are affident [LS:145].

Take, for instance, the reification of the null set. Sets are of course abstractions, analeptic devices, which provide isomorphism with other logical constructs, for instance, propositional calculus and switching theory. It is possible, using the axiom of extensionality, to prove that there is only one null set. The *axiom of extensionality* states that, if two sets contain exactly the same members, then those two sets are identical (Lemmon, 1968: 26-27). But, if two sets contain exactly no members, that is to say, we postulate for the sake of argument two null sets, then it follows from the axiom that those two sets are identical: that is, there is only one null set. The mathematician thus employs the concept of identity to justify the uniqueness of the null set. But the concept of identity is itself a source of perplexity. What can it mean to say that one entity is identical to another? What sort of a proof is it that postulates two entities and then proceeds to demonstrate the paradox that these two entities are one and the same? If two abstract entities are identical, how was it possible to differentiate between them in the first place? The answer is: by using an *axiom*, which is yet another mathematical abstraction. *Proof* is sometimes treated as having almost transcendent authority. But no proof is more powerful than the deductive (or inductive) system within which it is derived.

The tenacious intellectual hold which mathematical concepts can exert over some philosophers is well documented in the life of Bertrand Russell (Russell, 1967: 152). A set may be defined as any collection of entities: a set of five chairs; the set of natural numbers; the set of sets containing exactly five members; the set of sets which include themselves. Members of sets, then, may be physical objects like chairs, abstract objects like numbers or sets themselves.

Even more esoterically, if there is no restriction upon set membership, and we take the mathematical view, we may conceive of a set which is a member of itself, or contains itself. If, for instance, everything is a member of the universal set, then the universal set must be a member of the universal set: it must contain itself. So we are faced with two types of set: those which contain themselves and those which do not. And this is where set theory runs into difficulty. By a simple proof it can be shown that allowing sets to 'feed back' into themselves leads to contradictions, see, for instance, Jeffrey (1981: 159-160).

It was Russell who was eponymously credited with this discovery. He perceived both its triviality and at the same time the threat it posed to the mathematical foundations he had worked so hard to lay. So disturbed was he by this, and by other related paradoxes, that he sank into depression, on occasion actually contemplating suicide.

The very concept of a set 'containing itself', if the reader will for a moment allow mathematical discourse to recede to such distance as will afford decent perspective, is faintly absurd. And if the aim of set theory was to devise a system which would not allow inconsistencies to be derived, the fabrication of a universal set was decidedly a false move. Mathematicians accept, apparently without intellectual difficulty, the prospect of a set containing itself. But consider a concrete object:

(5)   Builder Jarvis's bucket contains itself.

Sentence (5), judged by the standards of ordinary language, verges on the nonsensical: *a priori*, the contained is smaller than the container. If buckets, which are relatively simple to cognize, stretch credulity to breaking point in this context, why should it occasion surprise that a theory of sets which defies this rule yields inconsistencies? Should such extravagances happen to bear fruit it is there for the enjoying, but I see no reason to accept fictions simply because they are mathematical: *e falso sequitur quodlibet*. In any case **reciprocal perspective**, by offering alternating vantage points, avoids the self-containment problem.

My present purpose is not to pursue a disquisition into the views of Russell, but to focus upon him as a man trapped within his own discourse. It is a common phenomenon and one which, in my view, results from an inadequate view of modality specifically in this instance, knowledge one modality or absolute modality. There is a curious parallel with Wittgenstein, who having invited his reader to climb the ladder, obliged him to abandon it in mid-air [LS:21].

There is the same problem, see [LS:144–146], with the system of logic known as natural deduction. We can proceed with a proof eliminating assumptions one by one, until the point is reached that we derive a well-formed formula (wff) resting upon no assumptions. But the miracle is achieved only by a mathematical sleight. The extra assumption is there: we have simply failed to declare it. I believe that the creation of natural and artificial (logical and mathematical) languages is man's supreme intellectual achievement, but it does not transcend knowledge two.

The trichotomy theory of knowledge draws a line across between knowledge one and knowledge two: it is a sort of glass ceiling. Communication takes place within knowledge two: logic and mathematics, within knowledge two, may be regarded as our most reliable providers of affidence.

Knowledge One Modality

Russell believed that he was on the way to a definitive solution of the most difficult problems of mathematics (1967: 145). The discourse he engaged in possessed a 'solidity' and logical consistency and this philosophical pursuit in conjunction with the discoveries of science was destined, he believed, to lead to the establishment of certainties concerning the universe. The realisation that these cherished systems allowed contradictions at the most fundamental level was almost too much for him to bear. The faith in any mode of discourse which, when thwarted, prompts serious thoughts of suicide or even leaves the reasoner stranded up a ladder whose removal is inevitable, is dubiously placed. What I tried to do with my theory of knowledge, described in chapter 1, was to tackle this problem, which seemed to bedevil most levels of discourse. What the theory did was to build in knowledge one at the highest level as the *sine qua non* of all discourse: the possibility of being right, which implies, of course, in our universe, the possibility of being wrong.

No other theory of knowledge, so far as I am aware, takes this meta-modality as its starting point; it has the added gain of leading naturally into a theory of value (chapter 3). A further point should here be added. My analeptic theory has been criticised for neglecting the aesthetic dimension of literary experience. There are no grounds for such criticism. Experimental aesthetics is accommodated at the level of **empirical semics** (chapter 11). And the personal aspects of aesthetic experience are located within the **trichotomy theory** in the direct (intuited) relation between **knowledge three** and **knowledge one**, which short-circuits, as it were, **knowledge two**. Artistic pleasure and delight from reading books in no way depend upon the activities of university English departments. I have argued at length that the principle of humanism within an examination system centred upon the study of English is self-baulking [LS:42–46].

The paradox of introducing knowledge one into the analysis of knowledge is that, having instituted it, we ignore it and work entirely at the levels of knowledge two and knowledge three. Knowledge one is there simply as a meta-modal category: we hope we may in some degree attain to it; indeed, it is the only ultimate validation of our endeavours at the level of knowledge two and knowledge three, but as academics we avoid claiming it. It is, to put it crudely, as meta as you can get.

The advantages of building knowledge one into the theory are that, firstly, it modalises all knowledge: awareness of the possibility of being wrong, on the one hand, discourages dogmatism, while awareness of the possibility of being right wards off scepticism, as prevalent nowadays as dogmatism. Knowledge one, then, is whatever is ultimately true about the universe; whatever is the case. And as far as conflicting philosophical views are concerned, natural v. supernatural, empiricist v. rationalist, nominalist v. realist, and so forth, knowledge one, as a cognitive device, is neutral.

The problem of academic dogmatism has been discussed with regard particularly to Bateson, Blackmur, Leavis and Spitzer. But modal distortion is also to be observed in exercises in linguistic analysis, as I pointed out in chapter 6. Furthermore, it is inherent in the world view of Hallidayan linguistics. Varieties of language are viewed as situational types with distinctive sets of features. Crystal and Davy seek to isolate 'those features which are restricted to certain kinds of social context' (1969: 10). Consecutive chapters in that book analyse the 'language of unscripted commentary' upon a cricket match – and the 'language of religion'. Discussing the latter, the authors write, 'We have already noted under the heading of vocabulary the way in which this variety makes use of a single concept, "God", as a semantic cornerstone, this being primarily established through the meaning relations operating between specific items of vocabulary in certain grammatical structures, especially apposition' (1969: 10). I accept that this is a textual comment making no claims about the status of God as a referent. It seems implicit, however, in the two analyses that cricket commentary and liturgy are mere functions of the physical situations in which they are produced. This doubtless does justice to sports commentary; but one may fancifully envisage Crystal and Davy being one day nodded through the Gates as a celestial voice with feigned severity intones 'Semantic cornerstone indeed!'

This last example illustrates one of the advantages of a modal structure: modality defined as **reciprocal perspective**. In a materialist analysis, the genuine beliefs of non-materialists are distorted. We may wish to proceed in this way, but the theoretical structures should be in place to declare that this is what we have done. The trichotomy of knowledge allows the dissection at the semic level of **semics** and **transmission semantics** but preserves the integrity of the work at the metalevel (**knowledge one modality**).

Knowledge one therefore represents absolute modality, acknowledging the problem inherent in human discourse: man's natural dogmatism. Knowledge one modality builds into all human discourse the possibility of being right (and being wrong) at the metalevel. It thus introduces a stabilizing force into the collective search for good sense, which from time immemorial has been beset with polemics, antagonism and bigotry.

It is important at this point to mention the vital monitoring rôle played by the empirical function, which is the necessary precondition of scientific endeavour, though much more is needed to ensure the health of a science. In disciplines like linguistics and education, where the object of enquiry is itself language, I believe the satisfactory operation of the empirical function can be achieved only through the sorts of complex modal structure which this book outlines. *Just as knowledge one stands in* **reciprocal perspective** *with* **knowledge two** *and* **knowledge three**, *so, within* **literary semantics**, *does* **empirical semics** *stand in relation to* **theoretical semics**.

Knowledge Two Modalities in Literary Semantics

Literary Semantics as a Science

Scientific enquiry, within my scheme, is located within **knowledge two**.

We may distinguish two functions within a science: the **kinetic** and the **analeptic**. The **kinetic function** mediates between the received structures of the scientific discipline and the raw material of fresh observation. These traditional structures themselves constitute the **analeptic function** [LS:51].

The **kinetic function**, coping with the unpredictability of kinesis, raw observations, is inherently unstable. The **analeptic function** assimilates into received scientific belief the new material supplied by the kinetic function. Mathematics, logic and, at the other extreme, literary criticism are examples of analeptic structures. Scientific enquiry is aided by clear definition. Thus 'A contradiction is the conjunction of a wff with its negation' enables the logician to determine on sight whether any one of an infinite set of wffs (well-formed formulae, themselves built up according to a rigorous set of formation rules, and therefore **secure**) is or is not a contradiction. Clarity of definition is achieved through the **principle of security** [LS:16]. Many terms employed within the analeptic structures of academic critics: 'poetry', 'novel', 'good' are not secure. Academic criticism, whilst exuding the confidence of a university discipline, thus fails a fundamental test of scientific discourse.

Next, I would differentiate between a **science** and a **scientist**. A **science** is defined as **an academic pursuit which confronts a vigorous kinesis with an analepsis which is well-organized, vigilant, yet flexible**. A science comprises a **theoretical component** and an **empirical component**, groups of academics who work together for the health of the science in adversarial co-operation. These two components overlap, are mutually aware and critical, self-correcting and with interchangeable rôles. But if either component becomes weak, the science suffers. A **scientist** may be seen as a microcosm of this tension between the theoretical and the empirical. **The 'good' scientist (internalizing this scientific opposition) is continually aware of the importance of both components abstractly represented within his or her own psyche**.

To put the programme more specifically, the theoretical and empirical components have to address the problems of, and to refine such working concepts as, descriptive adequacy, logic, observation, measurement, mathematical accuracy, definition, inductive principles, explanatory adequacy, hypothetico-deductive principles, controls, models, methods, experiment, elimination of variables, detection of a common cause, prediction, refutation, communication and modality itself. The organization of these matters and of the structure of, and interaction between, the components is the domain of **component modality** (defined earlier in this book simply as modality).

The relation between the theoretical and empirical components varies from science to science. Literary semantics and education, where frequently the object of enquiry is itself language, require a complex structure of components. It is not possible, nor even desirable, to make education itself into a branch of science, but I think that educational theory would profit greatly from analysis on scientific lines (Eaton, 1982: 82-5). Passmore, for instance, analyses the process of teaching as a triadic relationship (Passmore, 1980: 22). For the teacher, this may well be the case: but when the educationalist intervenes, and Passmore is writing in the guise of an educationalist, it becomes at least a pentadic relationship, see Appendix Four.

Educationalists are prone to project themselves 'into' the teaching rôle, reducing the real teacher to the status of a nonentity. But in fact it is the real teacher who is entrusted with the task of teaching and s/he may have a different set of ethical commitments from the educationalist. The result is that, in my experience of the English educational system, educationalists are held in almost universal contempt by practising teachers. The problem would be solved by acknowledging the pentadic relationship and admitting that, *for the educationalist, pedagogic theory must be teacher-centred*. Teachers, judiciously appointed, are naturally pupil-centred; indeed, those who are not do not last long. Passmore's is an elementary error (a violation of the **principle of**

classification) and results from a failure to identify educationalists and teach-ers as separate components within education. Even philosophers are prone to make unjustified simplification when they turn their minds to the problems of teaching.

Component Modality

Component modality is the determination on the part of a scholar to avoid violat-ing the principle of classification: **kinetic variables** may not be transformed into **analeptic constants**. A recapitulation of the concepts already discussed may be useful at this point.

The **theoretical** and **empirical components** of science are realised in **literary semantics** as **theoretical semics** and **empirical semics**, **semics** itself being defined as the study of **semic accompaniment**. **Semic accompaniment** is defined as **that series of mediating reactions which a person experi-ences when he or she reads continuously at normal speed a passage which contains for that person no linguistic difficulties**. Semic accompaniment presupposes readers' diversity of experience and makes no commitment to an aesthetic object, unlike Iser's concretization (Eaton 1980: review of Iser in *Style*). Similarity between readers' response may be established through experimentation at the level of empirical semics. **The empirical semicist is concerned with how people do read, not how they should read.**

Literary semantics, then, comprises the **semantics of literature** and **semics**, this division stemming naturally from the **transmission/reception** divide, fundamental in all language theory. The **semantics of literature** is the *study of a text as an event in history; the attempt to reconstruct the meaning of the text through historical research*. The semantics of literature, as **transmis-sion semantics**, is the *study of transmission*, the psychological processes of composition, with the author as experimental subject; **semics**, concerned with **semic accompaniment**, is the study of **reception.**

Semics comprises **theoretical semics** and **practical semics**, the latter being subdivided into **empirical semics** and **introspective semics**. This proliferation of components is occasioned by the subject matter of literary semantics. As has been pointed out, **the object of enquiry** is itself **language**. A scientist studying beetles or molecules is concerning himself with events which take place outside his own brain. Though conceptual and linguistic habits may sometimes distort, they can with self-discipline be held separate from raw observations. When language itself is the object of enquiry, the researcher needs a 'distancing' device to enable him to separate objective from subjective events.

Empirical semics is that part of semics which *collates, classifies and describes evidence provided by subjects concerning their own semic accompaniment.* The empirical semicist will also explore behaviourist evidence, psychological or neurophysiological, relevant to the semic accompaniment of a subject. **Theoretical semics** is *that level of literary semantics at which the kinetic function comes into play.* This component is thus the organizing force within literary semantics as a whole, Figure 5, constantly monitoring the other components and indicating possible new directions. *The guiding force* is the **principle of classification**. It was the operation of this principle which led me, in my capacity as a theoretical semicist, to devise the analeptic structure of literary semantics.

It simply did not make sense to have one sprawling academic subject, responsible for the study of 'literature' – its proponents unaware or contemptuous of the many better ordered, adjacent disciplines – which made no distinction between **transmission** and **reception**, nor between the scholar's own reading processes and the reading processes of pupils, which processes, by reason of academic superiority and control of examinations, they were in a position with some ruthlessness to manipulate. The direction of this silent control has shifted over the years. I think specifically of political outpourings inspired by ideologies such as Marxism and feminism. These trends, in my view, have a place in literary semantics – indeed they were reflected in *JLS* under my editorship – but no doctrine based upon tendentious premises should be allowed to *dominate* an academic discipline, still less to dictate the criteria of success and failure within an education system.

The components themselves, their number, interrelation and interaction, are a matter for component modality. Nor is this present arrangement sacrosanct. The number of components might be added to or subtracted from and their configuration rearranged in the light of new findings and the needs of research.

I mentioned in the previous paragraph that one of the tasks of theoretical semics is to provide imaginative possible new directions. To illustrate the kind of work I have in mind, I shall develop the notion of textual modality. The strength of the semic approach should become clear: not only is a new method, based upon frame theory and Rescher's definition of modality, explored but the structures of discourse are provided which allow the analysis to be seen in perspective. **Textual modality** (*an analytical instrument in* **practical semics**) is *modalised* within **component modality** (by **theoretical semics** which examines the **reciprocal perspective** between pairs of **semic components**) which in turn is *modalised* within **knowledge one modality** (the level of the trichotomy which may remind the researcher that in all human enquiry, even scientific, as well as the possibility of being right, there lurks also the possibility of being wrong). *Instead of monolithic discourse, literary semantics provides a system of components against which endeavours at particular levels may be judged.*

To the objection that the system I have created is mind-taxingly complex, I would reply that this complexity just reflects the subject matter of literary semantics. The task of devising a structured discourse capable of remaining stable and confronting the phenomenon of 'literature' is one of the most difficult that theoretical linguists face.

Textual Modality

The following is a definition of textual modality presented at the level of theoretical semics as an analytical instrument for use within practical semics: in this instance, **introspective semics** – my own readings, as projected on to a **hypothetical reader**. The definition is an adaptation of Rescher's (1) and I shall use it in conjunction with a version of frame theory to tackle some practical 'literary' problems. There is no reason why this instrument should not be employed at the level of **empirical semics**, but to claim that it is being so used in the present study would be to violate the **principle of classification**. The strength of this approach is that I can use the theoretical and introspective semic components to explore a text without making exaggerated claims for the findings (see chapter 6). The semic method would not itself be impugned by the refutation of a particular investigation.

(6)   When speaker S truthfully utters, or potentially truthfully utters, U, concerning some direct and immediate experience of S, U is said to be a primitive (potential) utterance; when U is made subject to some further qualification whereby the directness and immediacy are removed or diminished, then this qualification is said to represent a textual modality to which U is subjected. Textual modality is a subdivision of reflective modality, which is not my concern here. [LS:177; and chapter 14 *passim*].

The present study is purely linguistic and cognitive: the text is viewed as a corpus with no greater and no less claim to attention than any other assembly of linguistic material. It is the processing by the reader of the text as a piece of language which is my concern. Therefore I assume that there is an intelligent reader, as competent in Middle English as possible, but without any extra level of 'literary' competence. The reader is simply attempting to 'make sense' of the text and is not aiming to derive ingenious interpretations, to make aesthetic commentary or value-judgments.

Let us call the conceptual experience of such a reader processing such a text his semic accompaniment. There are three levels at which this may be treated. **Practical semics** comprises the first two levels: **empirical semics** (where the reader is a subject for experimental psychology) and **introspective semics** (the reader is the analyst himself). The third level is **theoretical semics** (where the concept of a **hypothetical reader** and explanatory models – the theoretical devices of scientific explanation and prediction – are employed). Analysts often conflate these approaches: for instance many a commentator does not make clear whether a given observation about a text is a statement about his/her semic accompaniment (**introspective semics**) or about an imagined response on the part of some ideal or supposedly typical reader (**theoretical semics**).

It should be noted that my own classification differs from all others, whether or not primarily devised to treat literature, that I have come across in that (unlike, say, theories of relevance, of speech acts, of possible worlds, of text-reception, of literary pragmatics) literary semantics, and its derived semic theory, is not primarily intended to be a tool for dealing with literary texts. To pursue this metaphor, semic theory is rather a classification of the tools which are already in use. An example would be the literary application of relevance theory (see, for instance, Sperber and Wilson, 1986: 237-243).

I do not expect that my own readings of the text will be controversial, but it is acknowledged at the outset that they are based in introspective semics. The theory of external and psychological frames belongs to theoretical semics.

There is an advantage to be gained from this kind of 'semic classification'. Frames are not strictly definable in terms of formal linguistic features; as Metzing says, such models are nothing more than 'working concepts' (1979: xi). Yet it is my view that interesting analyses may be conducted using frames as theoretical devices. Studies of this sort are in contrast with work being carried out in empirical semics (see, for instance, Carroll, 1960: 283-92; van Peer, 1983: 3-18; Segers, 1978; Ruth Eaton, 1988; Hanauer, 1995). By assigning expositions in semics to one level or another, **component modality** may be achieved.

CHAPTER 13

AN EXERCISE IN PRACTICAL SEMICS

The Inadequacy of Modal Verb Classification

Modal Verbs in *The Miller's Tale*

Chaucer's *Canterbury Tales* purports to depict a medieval pilgrimage setting out from the Tabard Inn in Southwark, in the late fourteenth century, for the famous shrine of St.Thomas à Becket in Canterbury. Chaucer describes some thirty pilgrims, under their self-appointed leader, Harry Bailly, Host of the Tabard Inn, telling tales to pass the time as they proceed on horseback to Canterbury. When the Knight, the first pilgrim to tell a tale, has completed his courtly romance, the Miller, a drunken churl, demands the right to tell his story. It turns out to be an extremely vulgar *fabliau*, having analogues in German, Italian, Flemish and English. The Miller's purpose is to insult the Reeve, his fellow-pilgrim and enemy, who is a carpenter by trade. The Tale concerns the ingenious scheme of Nicholas, student-lodger of John, an ageing Oxford carpenter, to seduce John's young wife, Alison. Nicholas deceives John into believing that God has decided to drown all mankind in the greatest flood since Noah's time. John's only hope of escape is to secure three tubs in the rafters of his house for himself, Alison and Nicholas. When the floods arrive, the three of them can break out through the gable, float away to safety and become lords of the world. Nicholas' real intention is for John to fall asleep with the effort of preparation and thus provide opportunity for adultery. The plot, further complicated by the intervention of Absolom, also suitor to Alison, culminates in four climaxes, each compounding the hilarity of the ending.

Chaucer wrote in the East Midland dialect of fourteenth-century Middle English, sometimes employing Kentish forms. Anglo-Saxon was highly inflected and Chaucer's language represents a transitional stage in the development of English morphology between Anglo-Saxon and today's English. This erosion of inflections is particularly true of the verbs: distinctive endings, such as *-an*, were gradually being weakened and lost.

The most obvious differences in Chaucer's English for the modern reader are the -(e)st, -(e)th inflections in the indicative. Loss of inflections meant that subjunctive forms began to coalesce with the indicative, so that in many contexts it is not possible to determine whether Chaucer was employing a subjunctive or not.

As the subjunctive mood declined, a class of modal combinations, whose origins were in Anglo-Saxon, emerged in Middle English and remain in the language today. Anglo-Saxon had two infinitive forms. Since in origin the infinitive was treated as a *nomen actionis*, the West Germanic infinitive was inflected as a noun. This practice survived in Anglo-Saxon, so that we find the plain infinitive, e.g. *bewerian*, 'to defend', alongside the *dative*, or *inflected infinitive*, '*to bewerienne*', which is the forerunner of our modern infinitive with 'to', in origin a preposition always separate from the verbal element – a fact which confounds the arguments of those who, on analogy with other languages where schism is unthinkable, condemn split infinitives.

The Middle English ancestors of the modern modal verbs comprise a *strong-weak* verb, such as *conne*, *mowe* or the irregular verb *wil(le)* in combination with a plain infinitive. The modal usually preceded the infinitive. Sometimes the modal was fused with its subject pronoun: *shaltou*, *shaltow* for *thou shalt*.

If Perkins' formulae [LS:178] for examining the core meaning of modal verbs are applied to the 107 examples of modals in *The Miller's Tale*, the results suggest that Chaucer's employment of these verbs was remarkably similar to modern usage. The most difficult of Perkins' variables to operate turns out to be 'K', see (2) in the previous chapter, where it is realised by what he calls 'rational laws', which he glosses, somewhat tautologously, as 'the laws of reason' (1983: 12). The schema is useful but not specific enough for me to match the variables to the text.

To take a specific example – line references to Robinson (1933):

(1)   Men *may dyen* of ymaginacioun (1.3612)

(NOTE: I have followed the practice of italicizing both the modal and lexical verb, since discussion of the context usually involves both).

A paraphrase for (1), overleaf, on the basis of Perkins' schema on page [LS:178] might run as follows: 'It is the case relative to K (= rational law?) that the set of circumstances C (= ?deontic source: imagination) does not preclude X (= the occurrence of e: death)'.

But when the same schema is applied to:

(2)   In which we *moue swimme* as in a barge (1.3550)

the paraphrase might be: 'It is the case relative to K (= natural law?: specifically, Archimedes' principle?) that the set of circumstances C (= ?evidence or ?deontic source: the embarkation of John, Alison and Nicholas into their respective tubs and the subsequent rising of the flood water-level to the point where the tubs would, if they failed to rise, begin to fill with water?) will not preclude X (= the truth of p: that the tubs will float with us inside them?).' It is in what Perkins regards as the typical assignment of variables that a discrepancy is found: if I have understood him, K is here a natural law rather than a social or a rational law, and C is the empirical circumstance of the embarkation, not a deontic source. In fact, the formula Perkins provides for CAN (1983: 34) seems more appropriate for (2):

(3)   K (C does not preclude X)
           where:
(i)   K = natural laws
(ii)   C = an empirical circumstance
(iii)   e = an event
(iv)   K(x) = x is the case relative to K

It seems to indicate that Perkins' schema on page [LS:178] should include natural laws as well as rational laws in the schema for MAY: he does indeed discuss this (1982: 255, footnote, and 259).

Although Perkins has undoubtedly contributed by his analysis to an understanding of the core meaning of the modals, and although the formulae generally do prove themselves to be remarkably adaptable to the usages of a Middle English text, there are dimensions of textual modality which are left untouched by classification on the lines he has proposed.

(4)   Yet *shal* I *saven* hire and thee and me (1.3533)
(5)   Thy wif *shal* I wel *saven* (1.3561)

These lines are uttered by Nicholas as he assures John that the household can escape the flood. The modal complexes are ambiguous between *epistemic* and *volitional*, with possible *deontic* overtones. The ambivalence arises from the two points of view of the interlocutors Nicholas and John. For John, the force is *epistemic* and perhaps *deontic*: he believes that Nicholas knows (*epistemic*) that God has given orders (*deontic*) to save Alison. For Nicholas, whose purpose is to seduce Alison, the force is *volitional*: the modality is complicated by the fact that Nicholas is lying: he knows there is not going to be a flood – he just wants John to be asleep with exhaustion, so that he can have his way with Alison. Within the fictional context, any operation of Perkins' schemata is going to become unwieldy, since the ambiguity of perspective for the two characters will either demand two core analyses for one modal, which will call in doubt the 'core' concept, or conflate the two perspectives and thus fail to convey the modal ambiguity.

Then there is the problem of the two instances of *shaltow* (graphological variant *shaltou*):

(6)   Than *shaltow hange* hem in the roof ful hye (1.3565)
(7)   Thanne *shaltou swymme* as myrie, I undertake,
         As dooth the white doke after hire drake. (1.3575-6)

In the case of (6) and (7), the inadequacy of the traditional analysis of SHALL is even more patent. The two phonologically identical forms are understood by Nicholas and John at one level in very different ways. All the traditional semantic classification can say about these is that (6) is *deontic* and (7) is *epistemic*. But, with (6) Nicholas really does want John to hang the tubs in the roof, and John understands this as an instruction he is 'really' to act upon. (7), however, is understood by John as something which is in reality going to happen, providing he follows Nicholas's instructions; for Nicholas, it is a fabrication: he knows there is to be no flood and that John will 'really' be asleep in his tub. Yet at another level, as the inverted commas indicate, the reader knows that both John and Nicholas are fictional characters. The hypothetical reader therefore is aware with (7) of the two different perspectives of the characters and with (at least) two different fictional levels: Nicholas, himself a fictional character, is describing a situation which he knows to be fictional. How does the reader manage with ease to process a message of such complexity? Certainly neither the *epistemic/deontic* differentiation nor any core schema on the lines described by Perkins is going to explain such occurrences, which are commonplace in fiction. Perkins, however, never intended his schemata to be applied to *The Miller's Tale*.

If a modal verb is to have multiple interpretations according to the points of view of different fictional characters, and if these are further compounded in the point of view of the reader, who perhaps processes all these interpretations simultaneously, then a new approach is called for which will allow theoretical differentiation of these perspectives. We could at this point introduce a new level of analysis and argue that this is an activity which takes place outside semantics altogether (the 'pragmatics' recourse, which seems inelegant on the grounds of **Occam's Razor**). Or we can say that, if your semantics fails to deal with these phenomena, which doubtless have to do with the meaning of language, then your semantics is too small. It is this latter view which I have always taken.

A Theory of Fictionality

Textual Modality and Frame-Profiling

At this point I introduce a theoretical device which has had much attention in recent years: the *frame*. 'Frame conceptions' as Metzing calls them, were first developed by Winograd (see e.g. 1972, 1983) and others at MIT and applied to vision and language processing; then to story processing (Shank and Riesbeck, 1981: 141 ff.); see also Metzing (1979: vii-viii).

Minsky, who has been influential in developing the notion, sees the frame 'as a data structure for representing a stereotyped situation like being in a certain type of living room or going to a child's birthday party. Attached to each frame are several kinds of information. Some of this information is about how to use the frame. Some is about what one can expect to happen next. Some is about what to do if these expectations are not confirmed' (Minsky, 1979: 1). For practical applications of frame theory, see Weber (1982), Reid (1988) and Tannen (1993).

A **frame** I will define as: *an arbitrarily delimited set of entities static (frozen) or dynamic (moving), which are spatially, temporally or spatio-temporally located*. A frame may be **external**, actually *existing in the 'real world'*, or **psychological**, *an individual's representation of an external frame*. A psychological frame may be **adequate**, that is, *truly corresponding with the external frame it purports to represent*, or **inadequate**, *failing to correspond with such an external frame*. Psychological frames are models which in some small measure cope with the **linking problem** raised in my description of the *dynaxial hypersphere* [LS:119]. The *frame-set*, which I shall define in due course, may be seen as plotting axial adjustments within the **semantic space,** which is a more volatile model dealing with the same cerebral activities.

The frame, as defined, begs epistemological and ontological problems: what is the 'real world'? how are we to ascertain the adequacy of a given psychological frame when, as individuals, we can view external frames only 'through' intervening psychological frames? These problems, while not 'solved' by the **trichotomy theory of knowledge**, are at least accommodated within it. **Knowledge one** provides us with 'the possibility of being right'. On the one hand, it is best to avoid claiming direct access to knowledge one and allow discourse to proceed at the more manageable levels of **knowledge two** (with **knowledge three**); on the other, without the possibility of some access to knowledge one, there is no point in discoursing at all. Though these questions are ubiquitous and often seem insoluble, I hope to show that the distinction between external and psychological frames can be applied to problems of fictionality within literary texts. They also provide a definition and theory of **fictionality,** which, with more careful drafting than I have carried out, would be operable at the level of **empirical semics**.

A **frame-set** is *a group of psychological or external frames sharing similar features. Frames* and *frame-sets may be linguistic or non-linguistic.* To illustrate, I shall begin with an example of a **non-linguistic frame-set**. The term **formal representation** will be used to convey the fact that the original experience of the *subject* in (8), the driver-conductor, not put into words at the time it happened, is here expressed formally in language.

In the example on the next page, the external frames comprise a number of entities spatio-temporally located. They are **dynamic**, in that they actually, or potentially, move. An example of a **static** frame-set is the London Stock Exchange closing FTSE share index on any given day.

The non-linguistic frame is in each case given a **formal representation** in words on the printed page, propositions representing **external frames** being printed in capitals. The **second-level formal representation** for frame 1 may be read as follows. 'There is an external frame within which X actually does believe and X's belief is a frame such that the card is genuine season ticket. Underlying this compound frame (i.e. a frame comprising two or more sub-frames) is a compound external frame within which X believes card to be genuine and it really is.' The small square brackets mark X's external and psychological frames. The large square brackets indicate that the entire structure comprises my psychological frame: since this is at one stage removed from X's actual experience (which was at first level), I call my analysis second level. For the reader of this chapter, the conceptualizing of X's experiences will be at third level. According to this analysis, a definition of a **fictional notion** would be: **a lower-case (psychological frame) representation which is not underlain by a corresponding representation in capitals**. An example may be seen in [LS:196]: the second level formal representation of frame 2, where the capitals

(8)

Frame-Set: Season Ticket Inspection
Subject: East Kent Driver-Conductor X
Dynamic Entities: Omnibus halted at 'bus stop; driver-conductor
        admitting new passengers; fare transactions etc.

EXTERNAL FRAME 1:

Man enters 'bus and quickly shows card (card is a valid season ticket)

X'S PSYCHOLOGICAL FRAME 1:

X accepts man's card as valid and nods him on.

Second-Level Formal Representation of Frame 1:

[[X BELIEVES [card is genuine season ticket]]
  [X BELIEVES [CARD IS A GENUINE SEASON TICKET]]]

(Capitals indicate external frame)

EXTERNAL FRAME 2:

Man enters 'bus and quickly shows card (card is poor forgery of season ticket)

X'S PSYCHOLOGICAL FRAME 2:

X accepts man's card as valid and nods him on.

Second-Level Formal Representation of Frame 2:

[[X BELIEVES [card is genuine season ticket]]
            [CARD IS NOT GENUINE SEASON TICKET]]

(Capitals indicate external frame)

(Shortly afterwards, an inspector joins the 'bus, discovers the forgery, and reprimands X for not detecting it)

The above representation extends the Ogden-Richards account of external and psychological contexts conjoining it with frame theory and with Rescher's definition of modality. The result is a theory of fictionality, which is further explored in this Chapter in an analysis of Geoffrey Chaucer's *Miller's Tale* and in Appendix Three of the *Merchant's Tale*.

Figure 12.   Formal Representation of Frame-Set.

negate the lower-case clause 'card is genuine season ticket'. A **fictional statement is one which asserts an external frame to exist where none does**. This definition and theory is offered at the level of **theoretical semics**, which is my present purpose. It begs many questions which, in particular cases, could doubtless be answered by an **empirical semicist** who had clearly specified the purpose and scope of an experimental inquiry.

It is now possible to link the definition of an **external frame** [LS:194] to the definition of **textual modality** within **practical semics** [LS:188]. It may be inferred from what has been said that the **presence of a first level external frame is a necessary, though not sufficient, condition, for a primitive (potential) utterance.**

At this stage, it should be unequivocally pointed out that frame-sets and frame-levels are *ad hoc* concepts. Psychological frames can proliferate indefinitely and it is hard to see how formal criteria may be laid down to restrict them [LS:210–211]. This is because they are models of what *does* take place in the human psyche: there is no end to the number of ways in which humans may allocate and re-allocate their psychological representations; and what does take place should be *a priori* within the scope of scientific inquiry. Two principles for dealing with frames may, however, be laid down. Firstly, for all the difficulties inherent in operating **Occam's Razor** [LS:161], it may be accepted that unnecessary proliferation of frames should be avoided. Secondly, we can make explicit the following rule, which follows from what has already been said: **no first level frame can be fictional**. Alternatively, this may be expressed in terms of the definition of textual modality [LS:188]: **no utterance can be both fictional and primitive.** This **theory of fictionality** is thus derived from Rescher's (1) [LS:177], via the definition of textual modality (6) [LS:188].

We may now consider some linguistic examples in the light of what has been said concerning external and psychological frames. These will be dealt with informally, dispensing with the frame-set representation exemplified by Figure 12.

(9)   I see the moon!

(10)   I can see the moon.

(11)   If I moved to the window, I could see the moon.

(12)   John said that he could see the moon.

(13)   John aboard the 'Canberra', slowly traversing the Red Sea, throb of the band beating in his ears, exclaimed, 'I can see the moon'.

(14)   I assure you that John said last week that, when he was aboard the 'Canberra' in April, he could see the moon.

(15)   John says he can see the moon, but I know him to be lying.

The first two examples, taken from Palmer (1974: 117), though I have added the exclamation mark to (9), are by him regarded as being semantically identical, the modal *can* adding 'nothing that is not indicated in the non-modal form'. The exclamation mark has been added to suggest that (9) expresses a primitive utterance. It presents a **first level psychological frame** underlain by a corresponding **external frame**: the moon is actually visible here and I am at this moment seeing it. (10) could appropriately be uttered in the same circumstances, but equally it could be said on the telephone from a hotel bedroom when my back was turned towards the window through which the moon was visible to me some moments before: it is no longer a primitive utterance.

Now suppose that a pedant in the room was eavesdropping on my telephone conversation and observing the direction of my gaze. He could effectively counter to (9),

(9a)   No you don't!

But in the case of (10), were he to retort,

(10a)   No, you can't!

he would not vitiate my claim, which would be pressed home by my repeating:

(10b)   I *can* see the moon!

In other words, the truth condition for the modal is fulfilled by my being in a position to see the moon, even though my glance is not at present directed at it. A frame analysis brings out a linguistic fact which the traditional semantic grid employed by Palmer obscures: 'Although I am not at this moment actually seeing the moon, there is an easily accessible external frame within which I see the moon'. The insertion of an extra frame-level just for the sake of argument does draw attention to the distancing effect which modals tend to have.

The supposition that there might be two frame-levels involved in (11) does not seem so extreme: 'I posit a conditional psychological frame within which I move to the window and then there is an external frame in which I see the moon'.

Returning to definition (6) [LS:188] and its concept of qualification, examples (9), (10), (11), (12) and (13) may be seen as arranged in a cline of increasing textual modality. When I read (10) in normal circumstances (as opposed to analysing it to make a semantic distinction), I do not seem to cross from one frame-level to another. When I read (13), I do: John's exclamation is a primitive utterance and the rest of the example is an elaborate qualification. This illustration shows at once the 'slipperiness' of the concept of psychological framing and at the same time its usefulness in tackling informally the practical aspects of modality.

A contrast may now be drawn between (14) and (15). Let us assume that (14) comprises three frame-levels: John sees the moon from the 'Canberra' in April; John last week reports this experience; I assure you that John made this report. We have here a progression from a first level external frame (assuming John's report to have been true: a primitive (potential) utterance), to an adequate psychological frame (John's experience of seeing the moon) also at first level, to a second level psychological frame (John's report last week of his experience), to a third level psychological frame (my report of John's report). I shall call this phenomenon **sequential framing**. Sequential framing may be **serial**, i.e. *passing from one frame to another of the same level*, or **hierarchical**, *passing from one frame to another of a different level*. In some analyses, this distinction will not need to be made; in others, for instance in the discussion of the Sir Topas episode in the penultimate paragraph of this section, the explanatory power is derived from **hierarchical sequential framing**: the whimsicality results when the **hypothetical reader** discovers 'two Chaucers' – one a self-effacing pilgrim and incompetent poet, the other simultaneously penning a timeless masterpiece – at two different levels.

On the other hand (15), as with all situations where deliberate lying is involved, requires **simultaneous framing**. (15) may be roughly paraphrased: 'John was aware of two psychological frames, in one of which the moon is shining and in the other of which the moon is not shining; John asserts that the former is *adequate*, knowing it to be *inadequate*' (see Werth's discussion of linguistic 'double vision' (1977: 3-25)).

Frame level, in sequential framing, provides controls over perspective in a literary work. Firstly, we can avoid the danger of becoming involved in discussion of fictional characters as if they were real. *Fictional characters never exist at the level of the first level external frame.* The semic modal categories are a constant reminder of that fact. This may seem so obvious as not to need to be said. But, in an all-girls' secondary school some years ago, as a professional performer of Chaucer's *Tales*, I made what I thought was a harmless but disparaging remark about the Wife of Bath's propensity for lying; really I was just playing the literary-critical game, providing the pupils with ideas for a possible 'A' level question. To my surprise a female teacher, with palpable fury, leapt to the Wife's defence as if she were present and in that very room, 'Well! She *had* to!' she shouted. The irony is that not only is the Wife of Bath a *fictional* character, but that any shortcomings she may have had were bestowed upon her by a *real* man – in contrast with fictional characters, all living humans always exist, at least in their consciousness, at the level of the first level frame. I report that encounter as a primitive (potential) utterance on my part. Could this experience be construed as an argument for the wider dissemination of literary semantics?

Secondly, we can, at levels other than first level external frames, distinguish the 'real world' from the 'imaginary world' within fiction. It makes sense to say of lines 3671-4 in *The Miller's Tale* that at this point in the story Absolom believes John is not at home, whereas in fact he is. Yet, seen from a different perspective, John cannot in fact be at home, as he is a fictional being. Thus, to take another example, in the fictional world of *Romeo and Juliet*, which cannot be a first level external frame, we may say that Friar Lawrence, Act V, Scene 2.1.28, conceives the possibility of preventing Juliet's suicide. The external frame 'Friar Lawrence fails to prevent Juliet's committing suicide' is presented in Act V, Scene 3. This may be assigned the following formal representation:

(16)

$$\left[\begin{array}{l} \textit{[FRIAR LAWRENCE BELIEVES [he can prevent the suicide]]} \\ \qquad\qquad\qquad \textit{[HE CANNOT PREVENT THE SUICIDE]} \end{array} \right]$$

where the italicized capitals and lower case letters indicate frames which are not at first level. Both the external and psychological frames here represented are fictional. Historical fictional characters, such as Napoleon, in *War and Peace*, may be treated as first level or second level, according to the purpose of the analyst.

The third control may be illustrated by turning once more to *The Miller's Tale*.

(17)   Geoffrey Chaucer writes *The Canterbury Tales* (**first level**)
(18)   A Geoffrey Chaucer *persona* is presented as the teller of *The Canterbury Tales* (**second level**)
(19)   This *persona* claims to be reporting a tale told originally on a pilgrimage to Canterbury by a Miller (**second level**)
(20)   This Miller describes in his tale several characters, among whom are Nicholas, the Oxford student, and John, the carpenter (**third level**)
(21)   Nicholas (third level) predicts that there will be a great flood (**fourth level**)
(22)   John (**third level**) hears himself described by Nicholas as emerging safe from the flood and greeting Nicholas with the words 'Good morwe, I se thee wel, for it is day (l.3580) (**fourth level**)

Thus, a character at third level, John in (22), already fictional, hears himself projected to the fourth level of fiction. (17)-(22) may be seen as a progression through levels in a sequential frame, see discussion of (14). Who utters the words quoted in (22)? Is it John, or Nicholas, or the Miller or the Chaucer *persona* or is it Chaucer himself? The answer must surely be that, in the semic accompaniment of a hypothetical reader it is all or any of them. And if that is the case, we are here confronted by a textual modality of great complexity. There is no point in saying that semantics just cannot cope here. The reason it cannot cope is that linguists have concentrated traditionally upon contrived sentences, rather than the richness of language as it may be, and sometimes is, used.

That Chaucer is not only aware of this complexity but consciously exploits it may be seen in the humorous episode which follows hard upon the *Tale of Sir Thopas*. The pilgrim who tells this Tale is abruptly cut short by the Host 'Thy drasty rymyng is nat worth a toord!'(1.930). The rueful response is, 'it is the beste rym I kan'. But this Tale is being told by the Chaucer *persona*, Chaucer the Pilgrim (**second level**). Chaucer's *Tale of Sir Thopas* (**level three**) is thus pilloried by Harry Bailly for its poor literary quality, 'Your worthless rhymes are not worth a turd!' At **first level**, however, Chaucer wrote the entire *Canterbury Tales* including the Host's criticism of *The Tale of Sir Thopas*. The paradox which results is rather like that which arises from an Escher design: the water conduits serially flow downhill but defy gravity by arriving at source. Chaucer the confident and gifted storyteller makes fun of Chaucer the reciter of doggerel romance. Chaucer urbanely dismisses his own 'best' work as worthless. The paradox is that the **hypothetical reader**, in **semic accompaniment**, follows the perspectives through from **first level** to **third level** and suddenly realises that, having been induced to accept **level three** (Chaucer as an incompetent storyteller), he is simultaneously obliged to reject it, **level one**; the very pretence of incompetence is itself achieved through competence. We have here a very early illustration of Russell's Paradox: the set of fictional Canterbury pilgrims includes a member who created the set of fictional Canterbury pilgrims. Unlike Russell, however, Chaucer saw it was the stuff that jokes are made of.

One final theoretical refinement is needed before the concepts of simultaneous and sequential framing are applied to a specific passage in *The Miller's Tale*. **Psychological frames** may be located on a fictional timeline: a 'dimension of the narrative world in which the events occur' (Dry, 1983: 19). We sub-classify them as **past-**, **present-** and **future-frames**. Lines 3833-39 present a **past-frame** at this point in the text; Nicholas and Alison refer back in the timeline (untruthfully) to the Carpenter's self-delusion and preparations for the flood. Lines 3366-69 provide an example of a **present-frame**: John and Alison, in the dark, are aware of Absolom's serenading Alison outside their window. The passage I have chosen for analysis, lines 3547-3600, is a **future-frame**. Nicholas is telling John of the imminent, terrible flood.

Simultaneous Framing

Alison has agreed to commit adultery with the student Nicholas, providing he can devise a plan to remove her husband, John the Carpenter, from the scene. In this passage, Nicholas, see Appendix One, pursuing his purpose, presents in vivid detail to John the 'revelation' of God. There is to be a flood which will overwhelm the earth. John, Alison and Nicholas are to be the sole survivors but only if John agrees to carry out a preposterous sequence of preparations. Nicholas, then, is lying: he claims divine prediction, knowing that he has received no such revelation. This requires (at least) two simultaneous psychological frames on the part of the liar [LS:199]: one frame representing reality as it is, or as the liar believes it to be, and a second representing the deliberately distorted view of reality. For the **hypothetical reader** [LS:120], processing a text where he knows one character to be lying and another to be being deceived by the lies, the framing is even more complex. He is aware of the simultaneous frames of the liar and of the single frame of the dupe. Awareness of these different perspectives must contribute to the textual modality of the passage: the reader has to keep before him the alternative sets of consequences for each character.

Nicholas's psychological future-frame at this point in the Tale may be represented diagrammatically:

EXPECTED	NOT EXPECTED
1. *Preparation for the Flood.* A. John obtains three large kneading troughs, or similar vessels. B. John hangs these in the roof of his house. C. John furnishes the troughs with sufficient victuals for one day. D. John will reveal these preparations to no one. E. John will exhaust himself in these preparations.	3. *During the Flood.*
2. *Waiting for the Flood.* F. John, Alison and Nicholas will climb into the troughs on Monday night - John's trough being some distance from Alison's. G. John will attempt no sexual intercourse with Alison. H. None of the three will communicate among themselves.	4. *After the Flood.*
5. *Adultery with Alison.*	

Figure 13. Miller's Tale: Example for Frame Analysis

The diagram shows that Nicholas' **psychological future-frame** may be regarded as comprising five sub-frames. I shall in fact refer to sub-frames as 'frames' in future, except in cases where ambiguity might arise. The plus markers under columns I.1-5 in the Appendix give the textual references for all these frames: 1, 2 and 5 constitute what Nicholas wants to, and expects will, happen; 3 and 4 consist of fabrications. These have nevertheless considerable importance in the modality of the passage: Nicholas derives great deontic force from them.

Nicholas, in his attempt to seduce Alison, will need John's extensive co-operation. John is not going to provide this unless he is motivated through some deep deception. Frames 1 and 2, therefore, are differentiated from 3 and 4 not only in terms of expected/not expected (i.e. does Nicholas really expect X to happen/not to happen?), but in the interpersonal relations which they entail between the two men. Frames 1 and 2 must fill John with fear and despair, at the same time establishing Nicholas' authority over him. Frames 3 and 4, entirely fictitious, must hold out the hope of salvation from the flood. To persuade the Carpenter to carry out instructions based on A-H [see LS:202], Nicholas must induce him to see them in the light of the reward frames 3 and 4. Thus the deontic force exerted by frames 3 and 4, mentioned earlier, is achieved by the juxtaposition of frames which threaten and frames which offer release. For Nicholas, frames 1 and 2 are the preconditions of frame 5, his adultery with Alison, no allusion to which, of course, must appear in his exhortation (though note the ambivalence of 1.3561, and the earlier explicit mention by the narrator, 1.3405-7).

A hypothetical reader is aware at a first reading of all the circumstances modelled by the five frames and of the two different perspectives of Nicholas and John. At a second reading, he is also conscious of the four climaxes of the Tale – the bedding of Alison, Absolom's kiss, Nicholas' singed behind and John's headlong plunge – the last three of which are not foreseen even by Nicholas.

The columns in the Appendix are based upon a list of questions which I have, as it were, asked myself concerning the passage (1.3547-3600). Although such questioning takes place at the level of introspective semics, there is no reason why the list should not be used with co-operating subjects in empirical semics. To obtain valid results it would be assumed that, as indeed I have, they had all read the text many times.

The questions, numbers corresponding with the numbered headings in Appendix Two, are as follows:

I   Does the verb complex (*in its linguistic context*) refer most directly to: 1, 2, 3, 4, 5, M; A, B, C, D, E, F, G, H? (where 1-5 are the sub-frames (with listed stages A-H); M is 'meta-discourse'-utterances devoted to the regulation of the immediate dialogue, e.g. L.3557-3560, where Nicholas's main aim is to forestall John's objections

II   Does the verb complex (in its linguistic context) have a different relevance (cf Sperber and Wilson, 1986: 125) for Nicholas and John? I take *relevance* here to be the relating of the information conveyed by the verb complex in context to the respective beliefs of Nicholas and John.

III Does Nicholas   really 'mean' the verb in context?
                       expect the action/state indicated by the verb to happen?
                       expect the directive in the verb complex to be obeyed?

IV   Does the verb complex lay particular emphasis upon Nicholas' authority?

V   Does the verb complex have a relevance beyond what either Nicholas or John conceive?

The questions are thus confined to the verbs used in the passage under examination. It is certainly the case that other lexico-grammatical and cohesive features contribute to textual modality. Also, there are doubtless many further tests which could be used to bring out textual modality. What does emerge is that the **modality** of the passage is by no means a function of the use of modal verbs alone (cf. Palmer, 1986: 21-3).

The profiles in the Appendix contain no more information than a **hypothetical reader** in **theoretical semics** (extrapolated from my own response in **introspective semics**) would have absorbed after a careful reading of the Tale. Questions which elicited aesthetic or evaluative judgments were deliberately avoided, the purpose being to focus upon the semic processes which take place when a reader conceptualizes a passage conveying complex fictional modality. As far as this passage is concerned, we may draw very tentative conclusions concerning simultaneous framing and sequential framing (in a fictional text of this kind the two are often intertwined) under three headings: authority, fictionality and relevance. These brief expositions are at the level of **introspective semics** and **theoretical semics;** like all such interpretations, they should be treated with reasoned scepticism.

Authority

In a text which focuses upon the interpersonal relations between characters, as is the case with this passage, the establishing of authority can be an important element in **textual modality**. The hypothetical reader is aware of the absurdity of, and of Nicholas's awareness of the absurdity of, frames 3 and 4. The Carpenter approached the interview with Nicholas, assuming that he himself was to take the dominant rôle, 'He shal be rated of his studiyng' (1.3463).

Having emerged from his feigned trance, Nicholas intimates that the world is to be destroyed. Before John has had the chance to comprehend this, Nicholas peremptorily sends John downstairs for a drink (1.3492). The Carpenter returns with a quart of ale. They drink it and Nicholas mysteriously shuts the door (which – a rare *non-sequitur* on Chaucer's part – has minutes before been wrested off its hinges). Chaucer writes, 'doun the Carpenter by hym he sette'. Nicholas sits the Carpenter down beside him: a paralinguistic gesture which, since John does not demur, establishes for Nicholas the interpersonal ascendancy, to borrow a Hallidayan phrase. His account of the flood is so harrowing that, by the commencement of the selected passage, John is distraught.

This securing of authority is important in the **textual modality** of the passage and of the Tale as a whole. The **hypothetical reader** knows, and perceives that Nicholas is aware, that the story is preposterous. The problem for the teller seems to be to make the Carpenter's gullibility credible. Whether or not the reader finds it so may be established within **empirical semics**.

Column IV of Appendix Two has 'plus' markers to indicate verbs which seem to lay particular emphasis upon Nicholas' authority – typically, imperatives, deontic modals, performatives and compound tenses with auxiliary 'have' (used to recapitulate instructions e.g. 'but when you have obtained these three kneading troughs' (1.3563)). It will be observed that there is some degree of correlation of 'plus' markers in column IV with entries I.1-2 (i.e. the frames concerning the preparation and waiting for the flood). The plus markers represent my retrospectively recalled semic accompaniment and would doubtless show some changes, on different occasions of self-testing. No attempt has been made to meet the psychological criteria of reliability and validity, which formal investigations in empirical semics would often demand.

Thus in column I.1 we find the imperatives *go* (1. 3547), *looke* (1.3549), *han* (1.3551), *go, speed* (1.3562), *go* (1.3596), *go, save* (1.3600); deontic modal verbs *may nat wite* (1.3555), *shaltow hange* (1.3565); the perfects (Huddleston, 1984: 133) *hast ygeten* (1.3563-4), *hast doon* (1.3567), *hast yleyd* (1.3568); in column I.2 the deontic modal verb *moote hange* (l.3589); in column I.M the imperatives *axe* (1.3557), *be avysed* (1.3584); – notice how four subjunctives are subordinated to this imperative, doubtless reinforcing the directive: *speke* (1.3586), *clepe, crie, be* (1.3587), *go* (1.3596); the deontic *may nat save* (1.3556); the volitional/deontic *wol nat tellen* (1.3558); the perfect *have seyd* (1.3567); the performatives *undertake* (1.3575), *warne* (1.3583); the passive indicative *is seyd* (1.3592) – indicating vaguely God's authority?; the subjunctive with imperative force *speede* (1.3592).

The only imperative to occur in I.3-4 is *be* (1.3578), in the exhortation 'be merry'; there are no deontic modals or performatives. Yet epistemic modal verbs do occur, perhaps suggesting Nicholas' confidence in his own predictions both with regard to God's intervention and the natural processes which will both threaten and avert the disaster.

Fictionality

Meanwhile, as Nicholas steadily establishes his authority and instils in John the attitudes of fear and hope which will prompt him to carry out I.A-H, there is, for the **hypothetical reader**, a steady awareness of Nicholas' own expectations concerning the actions/states conveyed in the VPs. The values under III indicate what Nicholas' view with regard to future 'factuality' is. The two modal contractions *shaltow hange* (1.3565) and *shaltou swymme* (1.3575) provide a useful contrast here. Nicholas does want John to hang the tubs in the rafters, so that the former is used as a directive (*deontic* modal *shalt(ow)* 1.3565). The latter, however, is a fanciful observation (*epistemic* modal) emphasizing the happy outcome of a state of affairs which Nicholas has described but does not believe in. The phonological forms of the verbs are identical. The modal function and the modal consequences are a product of the contexts in which they occur. They belong to different **future sequential frames**; *shaltow hange* takes as object *hem* (1.3565), cohesive by reference (Halliday and Hasan, 1976: 335) with *knedyng-tubbes thre* in the previous line; this in turn is lexically cohesive (Halliday and Hasan, *ibid.*: 338) with *knedyng-trogh* (1.3548), itself the object of *go gete* (1.3547), a VP with imperative force (*go* is actually an imperative, *gete*, an infinitive) – thus belonging to frame 1, with consequences for frame 2. By a similar chain of reasoning, *shaltou swymme* (1.3575) is related to the events which 'will take place' during the escape – which belong to frame 3, with consequences for frame 4; Nicholas 'believes in' frames 1 and 2, but not in frames 3 and 4.

An examination of Appendix Two will reveal that the 'plus' markers under columns I.1-2 show some correlation with the 'plus' markers under column III; the exceptions are *may not save* (1.3556) and *shal saven* (1.3561), where the actions are not tied to specific frames. Nicholas does not believe that he '*may not save*' Gille: he does not in fact believe her to be in any danger. He does believe that he '*shall save*' Alison, but her salvation will not be from the flood. This frame analysis is very complex – much more complex than traditional modal verb categories can cope with. But the medium of *The Miller's Tale* is language and these are linguistic/semantic problems. The Perkins' schemata are fairly simple and have their uses but the necessities of literary semantics strain their application to breaking point. Do we dismiss these deviant patterns as irksome complexities, undermining a received wisdom which is admittedly useful in teaching English as a foreign language? Or do we investigate the cerebral evidence that **literary semantics** presents us with and focus upon the underlying problem of *fictionality* itself?

Relevance

Another factor which is at work in the textual modality of this passage is the respective relevance of the VPs (in context) for Nicholas and John. The striking difference between the two is brought out in column II of the Appendix, which abounds in 'plus' markers: the VPs do have different relevance for Nicholas and John. This was anticipated at various points in the earlier discussion, but the Appendix brings this out very clearly.

Firstly, there is a difference between Nicholas's and John's conception of the deontic sources acting upon them both. For Nicholas, the deontic modals, imperatives and performatives already referred to [LS:205], are motivated by his own will: the result of his desire to go to bed with Alison. For John, they are injunctions from God himself through his mediator Nicholas.

Secondly, the purpose of the instructions is differently conceived. 'The subjunctives *speke*, *clepe*, *crie* (1.3586-7), which in context prohibit discourse on the Monday night prior to the flood, are Nicholas' way of ensuring that the Carpenter will go to sleep as quickly as possible. For the Carpenter, silence is a fitting spiritual preparation for that terrible moment when he must commit himself to the mercy of the Lord. Similarly, keeping Robyn in the dark (1.3555) will ensure that Nicholas' planned seduction of Alison does not become discovered and therefore prevented; John sees it as a corollary of God's decision to save only three people from the flood. And the same is true of the meta-discourse. Nicholas' protests that John should not question him further and that he has no time to discuss the reasons for the plan (1.3557-8) are subterfuges for avoiding awkward questions; for John, they are a part of God's deep designs.

Thirdly, for Nicholas, sub-frames 3 and 4 are deliberate manipulations of the Carpenter (the *wyle*, 1.3403) to produce the motivation to effect frames 1 and 2. When, for instance, he assures John that he needs provisions for only one day because the water will subside, Nicholas knows that that is all the time he needs to seduce Alison. John presumably regards the time duration as a mysterious caprice of the Lord.

Sequential Framing

Resuming now the discussion of sequential framing [LS:199] we may consider the following examples:

(23)   I expect you will enjoy these strawberries tomorrow.

(24)   I see you, sitting in the punt tomorrow, serenaded by Fernando, willows of the Cherwell brushing your hair – 'I am enjoying these strawberries!' you say.

(23) comprises a main clause *I expect* and a dependent clause *you will enjoy these strawberries tomorrow*, containing the modal verb complex *will enjoy*. In (24), there are two main clauses whose verbs are both indicatives, *see*, *say*, and a dependent clause complement of *say* whose verb is also in the indicative, *am enjoying*. If modality has to do with 'the meanings that are usually associated with mood' (Palmer, 1979: 4), then it has to be explained how this degree of modality is achieved with indicatives. Part of the explanation seems to be the result of the adverbial *tomorrow* used to modify the present tense *see*. We cannot literally be perceiving with our eyes today anything which will not take place until tomorrow. But another factor may well be psychological and contextual. Because, let us assume, you know that you are not in the punt now; you know also that I cannot literally see you in the punt. *I see you* cannot therefore be a **primitive utterance**, as defined [LS:188]. The use of the indicative in this way initiates a **sequential psychological frame** at the **second level**. There are thus two frames: (i) I now having a (metaphorical) visual experience; (ii) you, tomorrow, in the sensuous surroundings described.

The modality of fiction often works in this way, through **sequential framing**. When the reader has, as it were, passed in his semic accompaniment through to the second level frame, the indicative can be used, as here, *am enjoying*, with the effect of a modal. This is **reciprocal perspective** at the level of **textual modality**: I addressing you here now am instantaneously aware of you addressing me there tomorrow. The rhetorical force of the indicative is to conceal from the addressee, though not from the hypothetical reader, the emotive subterfuge of the verb. The application of these examples to *The Miller's Tale* will become clear in due course.

In addition to the simultaneous frames described [LS:202–204], *The Miller's Tale* also provides examples of sequential framing. *Hast yleyd* (l.3568) takes as object *vitaille*. This is straightforward and has been dealt with in the Appendix under column I.1 – part of the preparations for the flood. But *yleyd* also takes a second object an *ax* (1.3569). What possible relevance has this for Nicholas? His main purpose is to ensure that John is snoring away in the tub on Monday night; his possession of an axe is of no import. From Nicholas' point of view, the instruction can only be to lend colour and realism to the Carpenter's plight – i. e. to make coherence within sub-frames 3 and 4; there really will be a flood and John will need to cut the rope and break a hole in the gable.

But the axe comes, in the fulness of time, to have a significance within the structure of the Tale, which Nicholas himself does not foresee. There are, as was earlier stated, to be four climaxes to the story: the seduction (1.3650-3656); the humiliation of Absolom (1.3730-3743); the burning of Nicholas' behind (1.3806-3815); and the fall of the Carpenter from the rafters (1.3816-3823).

The plus markers in column V against *hast yleyd* and *to smyte* (see Appendix Two) indicate a relevance beyond the immediate level at which Nicholas and John are interacting. The **hypothetical reader**, at a first reading, may simply assume that the significance of the lines is to make the threat seem more immediate. At a second reading, it is apparent that the axe is an important feature in a different frame-level: an intrusion into the **fourth level** discourse of Nicholas (22), of Chaucer's **first level** structure (17), the author contriving the dangerous tumble of John to the ground. Similarly, the hanging of the tubs '*ful hye*' may be seen to have a triple relevance: for Nicholas at **third level** (21) (i.e. the practical, as opposed to the fabricated, level) to prevent the scheme from becoming public knowledge, by obscuring them high up and to make John exhausted so that he will sleep; for John at **fourth level** (22), to maintain God's secrecy; and again at **first level** Chaucer can ensure that John's humiliation will be compounded by the precipitate, though not tragic, descent.

But, by the same token, the axe and the hanging of the tubs in the rafters are also relevant at **second level**. The Miller is, after all, the putative teller of the Tale. He is the sworn enemy of the Reeve, who is a carpenter by trade (Robinson, 1933: 26, line 614). Thus the modal complexes (a) *shaltow hange* and (b) *shaltou swymme* not only contrast with each other in **simultaneous framing**, but also in **hierarchical sequential framing** [LS:199]: (a) functions as a step in the story at four different levels of discourse (Chaucer's intention to set up the fourth climax (**first level**); the Miller's intention to humiliate the Reeve, who is a carpenter by trade (**second level**); Nicholas' purpose in getting the Carpenter out of the way during the seduction (**third level**); and John's concept of the act of emerging safe from the flood (**fourth level**); (b) seems to have little significance beyond Nicholas's fabrication (**fourth level**, i.e. deception, and therefore **simultaneous frame**).

Shaltou swymme does, however, introduce a very interesting feature of this passage. Nicholas, moving in his description towards the fictional simultaneous sub-frame 3 (see Figure 2), proceeds as follows: temporal clause (1.3563-4) followed by instruction (1.3565) and reason for the instruction (1.3566). A second temporal clause (1.3567) raises expectations of a further instruction (i.e. within sub-frame 1). But instead of this Nicholas launches into a series of dependent clauses: a third temporal clause (1.3568), a non-finite clause of purpose (1.3569), a fourth temporal clause (1.3570), a second clause of purpose (of result) (1.3570), a co-ordinate clause of purpose (1.3571-2), to which is subordinated yet another clause of purpose (1.3573), itself subordinated to a fifth temporal clause – leading finally to the main clause *thanne shaltou swymme* (on this interpretation, the clause *I undertake* (1.3575) is parenthetical and does not dominate *thanne shaltou swymme*). Instead of another deontic to parallel *shaltow hange*, this succession of loosely connected clauses leads into the epistemic modal complex *shaltou swymme*, and then a description of John and Alison triumphant after the flood. After this breathless succession of dependent clauses Nicholas 'quotes' John's surprised utterance on emerging from the flood:

(25)   Good morwe, I se thee wel, for it is day (1.3580).

The parallel between (25) and (24) can now be drawn. A defining characteristic of quotation – 'repeating words which have already been uttered' – is, in both cases, ignored. Both speakers contrive to project an utterance into the future. It is almost a hypnotist's trick: to lead the listener through sequential frames, in Nicholas' case, of labyrinthine complexity; and then omnisciently supply John with words to say. But the most striking point in (25) is that, as in (24), the present indicative is employed, representing, ostensibly, a **primitive utterance**. It is almost as though, in his cognitive manipulation of John, Nicholas has reached a semantic plateau of modal 'reality'. Textual modality, here, the simultaneous awareness (or reciprocal perspective) of the visual immediacy of the greeting and its fictionality, is achieved through the use of the present indicative verbs *se* and *is*.

Formal Criteria for Establishing Frames

For reasons I have already outlined, I believe it is impossible to lay down formal criteria determining the presence or absence of a frame, or of a transition from one frame level to another. A word processor copies texts with ease and the operator cannot tell by looking at the screen whether any given display is an 'original', a copy, or a copy of a copy. So it is with the imaging of the brain. Frames, as I define them, are models which attempt to plot the relations between texts and the meanings brains ascribe to them. I see them as coming within the scope of linguistic study.

It would be possible to formulate principles of framing, e.g. a sentence comprising two clauses is more likely to 'need' two frames than a sentence consisting of just one clause; or, modal verbs are more likely to initiate extra frames than indicatives. But these simply state tendencies. We can find textual signals, for instance (1.3514-5) '*I have yfounde in myn astrologye… that…*' to suggest that a future frame (see 3.2) is about to be introduced. The use here of the present perfect tense (suggesting, perhaps, immediacy of importance), the lexical choice of *find* and *astrology* (together implying mysterious prescience) are frame signals but we know this only because a frame (announcement of the coming rains and floods) actually follows. If Nicholas had said 'I have yfounde in myn astrologye – nothyng' the apparent signal would be there but no frame would follow.

The position is a circular one: textual modality is at once the product, and yet modifies the significance, of the lexico-grammatical and cohesive features of the text. *Shaltou swymme* is one indicator, I have argued, of a transition to a new frame-level, but it is the frame-level itself which tells us that the meaning of *shaltou* (1.3575) is different from its identical (phonological) form *shaltow* (1.3565). The hypothetical reader knows that *shaltou swymme* expresses an expectation that John will float rather than a directive to John to swim, because he knows that Nicholas has entered upon sub-frame 3 and that sub-frame 3 is a fabrication.

It may be objected that the analysis of this passage from *The Miller's Tale* is no more than a presentation of what might take place in a literary critic's head. I accept this. The point I am making is that the passage is a linguistic text which has caused a cerebral reaction in an **instantiated reader**: me. I feel certain that any respectable theory that emerges in the course of time will not rely for its insight upon the present taxonomy of English modal verbs.

CHAPTER 14

THE CHAIN OF MODALITY

The Chain of Modality

In chapter 10, I pointed out that one of the strengths of a modal approach is that alternative definitions can be made at different levels of disquisition. Thus, in defining **style**, I differentiated between **theoretical semics** and **empirical semics**:

(I)   In **theoretical semics**, given two passages A and B and a **hypothetical reader's semic accompaniment** to the two separate passages, then the **stylistic** features of A are those linguistic features which would lead the hypothetical reader to suppose, rightly or wrongly, that A and B are, or are not, written by the same person.

(II)   In **empirical semics**, **style** is the totality of the linguistic features in a given passage which can be experimentally demonstrated (by means of **instantiated readers**) to lead to correct predictions concerning passages where all relevant details of authorship are known by the investigator.

By thus separating the reader's own intuitive sense of style from the data amassed from investigation into psychological subjects, the concept of style is refined and enquiries in theoretical semics and empirical semics become mutually supportive. (I), to put this another way, is what style has for a long time generally been supposed to be [LS:161–163]; (II) offers the possibility of empirical substantiation.

And the same is true of modality itself. According to my analysis, **modality** has a natural beginning (**knowledge three**) and a natural end (**knowledge** one). The beginning is known: it is the **primary semantic space** and it is known to each one of us in consciousness individually and severally only. The middle, **knowledge two**, is what we all share. The goal, knowledge one, is best regarded as being above a **glass ceiling**. If we believe that at some stage we have attained to knowledge one, 'ultimate knowledge', then it is best in the interests of civilised discourse not too loudly to proclaim it. Dogmatism is the worst enemy of mankind – and that is the only thing I would be dogmatic about.

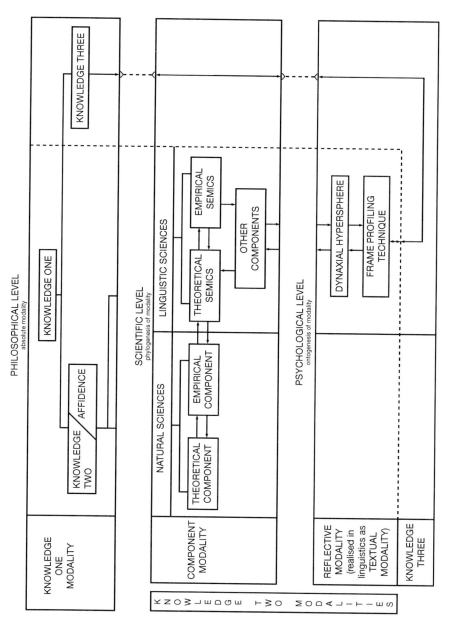

Figure 14.   The Chain of Modality

The Figure 14 [LS:213] should be read in conjunction with the Figure 4 [LS:52]. Both diagrams represent the trichotomy of knowledge, but Figure 14 has been laid out in three tiers to bring the different levels of modality into relief. As with most diagrams, there is some distortion: the three levels are not really to be held separate; nor is knowledge three to be excluded from the genesis of modality, as indicated by the small rectangular box in the bottom left-hand corner. Knowledge two, it should again be stressed, comprises all human discourse and communication, not just science.

Firstly, attention should be drawn to the knowledge three element involved in all human experience. I may convey to you the fact that I have toothache, but I cannot convey my toothache. And if through some empathic channel I do manage to transmit toothache to you, the ache ceases to be mine and becomes yours. And the same is true if I persuade you that a particular entity is valuable: as soon as I succeed, your act of valuing becomes separate from mine, though you can talk about it and may share it with me or others at the level of knowledge two. A part of each human experience belongs inalienably to the individual. The process of valuing is innate in us: it is part of our consciousness as human beings.

Secondly, the only reason that the empirical component is ascribed such high status in scientific investigation is that man judges intuitively that the evidence of the senses is (with *caveats*) to be relied upon. However reasonable this assumption may be, it is still an assumption, and it is impossible to differentiate epistemologically the status of an intuition concerning sense data (the existence of a chair, for instance) from an intuition ascribing value to some entity [LS:173]. Our search for value and our acts of valuing come as part of our cognitive apparatus. Intuition is an inextricable part of all human knowledge. In this way, at trichotomy level, epistemology seamlessly comprehends both ethics and aesthetics.

The chain of modality begins, then, with the knowledge three input, the arrowed line descending from the knowledge three box (top right) in the trichotomy of knowledge, into frame profiling technique. This technique, devised to throw light on literary texts, is seen to have broader psychological implications: the movement from **external frames**, through successive **psychological frames**, **simultaneous** and **sequential**, constitutes the **ontogenesis of modality**. The first step for a human being is from primitive experience of an external frame to experience of a second, different, but intuitively similar, external frame: the corresponding second psychological frame provides an **alternative perspective** to the first **psychological frame**. As each subsequent alternative perspective is facilitated, a new frame for the full **reciprocal perspective** of modality is established. The individual progresses from raw **percept** to double and treble and *n*-ary vision: to the **concepts**; the multi-faceted grasp on the world which enables us to function as individuals. It is possible to conceive of this ontogenesis of modality as having both linguistic (**textual modality**) and non-linguistic elements. **Textual modality** and **non-linguistic modality** may be regarded as co-hyponyms of **reflective modality**.

Frame-profiling technique is a derivative of the concept of the **dynaxial hypersphere**, the model devised to map on to the neuron activities of the brain, see chapter 7. The problem with brain models is that, in order to be manageable, their movements need to be slow and observable. The dynaxial hypersphere, which relates to the volatility of the brain, is a gravitational model with billions of adjusting axes. The region of maximum intersection of axes, the centre (or consciousness), automatically coalesces with any other region where a similar aggregation of axes occurs. The growth of computer graphics in recent years has brought nearer the day when such a model may be viable. In the meantime, we have to make do with more sluggish versions like the semantic differential and frame-profiling, see Appendix Two.

Indeed when it comes to dealing with the problems of modality, where even a complex work like *The Canterbury Tales* generally demands no more than four levels – at least for the analysis which was undertaken in chapter 13; 'The Merchant's Tale' needs six, see Appendix Three – frame-profiling copes quite well, demonstrating informally that fictionality may be analysed as a kind of modality. It might be mentioned in passing that even metaphor [LS:136], may be analysed as a modal phenomenon, the **T** and **V** being examples of **simultaneous framing**. I would make this prediction for empirical semics: when, eventually, it becomes possible to correlate semic accompaniment with neuron firings, simultaneous framing entails a significant increase in neural activity, as compared with single framing.

Ascending within the diagram to the scientific level, we move to **component modality**: [LS:186–188]: the interaction between groups of activities, or groups of people, within the science; science itself being a small subset of the world's sociological network. But, as an academic, it is science that concerns me primarily in this book. Within the linguistic sciences, **theoretical semics** and **empirical semics** are fixed in co-operative, but mutually critical tension, with each other and with the other components: **practical semics**, **introspective semics** and the **semantics of literature** (with **transmission semantics**). This last component employs historical evidence in my original conception of it, but now, renamed in its *alter ego* as **transmission semantics**, it can assume the rôle of research into the psychological processes of poetic composition: **semantic generation** (transmission), as opposed to **semic accompaniment** (reception).

The arrows between **theoretical semics** and the **empirical component** of the natural sciences reflect the fact that all sciences are interrelated. At this level the **ontogenesis of modality** has become part of a vast **phylogenetic structure**, where the components interact, correct one another, stimulate one another and work corporately towards grappling with the unsolved problems of the universe. This level may be regarded as the **phylogenesis of modality**. But, for all the amazing apparent success of scientific discovery, it should never be forgotten that 'science' itself takes philosophical sides: a view of the universe which is essentially naturalistic and empirical. The presence of an **empirical component** is a necessary, though not sufficient, condition for the existence of a science. Chomsky's onslaughts against empiricism do not change this: rationalism without empirical component has no place in science. Furthermore, man cannot exist without **values**: whatever deliberate activity we undertake presupposes some act of valuing even if we change our minds and desist. And whereas science can help to clarify the nature of (sets of) alternative **instrumental values**, **intrinsic values** lie beyond its domain, see chapter 11.

That is why the diagram [LS:213] ascends yet further to the level of **knowledge one modality**. At this level, even the mighty machine of science, **knowledge two**, with all its physical achievements, is brought into **reciprocal perspective** against **knowledge one**, *the possibility of being right*. **Knowledge three**, our intuition, may bypass the dogmatic claims of human discourse, and seek knowledge one direct. **Art and music and fiction are in this way accorded equal epistemological status with logic, mathematics and science.**

The chain of modality begins at knowledge three and aspires to knowledge one either by proceeding clockwise through the analeptic systems of human discourse or, directly, anticlockwise through intuition. This is an elegant simplification of the human quest for truth.

CHAPTER 15

A MODEL FOR THE HUMAN SCIENCES

Literary Semantics – an academic discipline: a Document for Discussion

The following is an exposition of the discipline of Literary Semantics as submitted to the International Association for Semiotic Studies (IASS-AIS), which kindly invited the International Association of Literary Semantics (IALS) to apply for membership of IASS-AIS. This description was written by Trevor Eaton and does not necessarily represent the views of the Committee or even individual members of IALS.

LITERARY SEMANTICS

Reading a work of literature is one of the most complex activities of which the human brain is capable. Linguistically, all the phonological, lexical and syntactic devices of referential language may be called upon, with the addition of whatever deviations from 'normal usage' the author, who may choose his own rules, employs. Psychologically, the task is immense: the brain is required to cope with all the usual demands of referential language as employed in the 'real' world, but with the addition of fanciful dimensions beyond the scope of the spatio-temporal universe. Philosophically, the reader has to contend with an instance of the phenomenon Paul Werth called 'double vision' (Werth,1977:9): a fictional universe which he almost simultaneously believes in and yet does not believe in. Then there are such further complications as historical and sociological divergences between the author and the reader and the ubiquitous problems of ethics and aesthetics.

And this brief discussion has begged an important question. It seems to suppose that 'literature' is a clearly defined set of texts. Yet many acknowledged literary texts are discursive, grammatical and non-fictional. Despite this, most attempts to solve the problems which I take to be within the domain of literary semantics have set out to define literature, or at least have assumed that such definition is possible and desirable. As Dieter Freundlieb has recently expressed it: 'A discipline called "literary semantics" must be based, it seems, on the idea that (a) there is a reasonably well-defined set of objects called literary texts; (b) there either is or can be a systematic study of the meanings of such texts; (c) the construction of meaning in literary texts is sufficiently different from that found in non-literary texts; and (d) the systematic study of the meanings of literary texts is something that differs from, and is perhaps superior to, ...other more hermeneutical approaches to the study of literary texts' (Freundlieb, 1998:61).

I quote Freundlieb at length because his words represent a widespread view amongst writers on literary semantics and because they betray a curious difficulty which arises in tackling the problem of literature. If 'literature' presupposes some special mode of existence, or even proper characteristics for literary works, then the tools, procedures and assumptions of linguistic semantics, insofar as they were developed for dealing with referential language, need to be re-examined. Literary semantics cannot both aver that literature is different and at the same time assume that linguistic semantics will be adequate to deal with it.

The scepticism I have for the view that the set of literary texts is well-defined has left me free to ignore the problems of definition (Eaton:1996:2) and to concentrate upon what I regard as the really important task of constructing a metatheory which will encompass and clarify the many endeavours of students of literature which are already in existence.

To take a parallel and important case: Karl Popper's contribution to the philosophy of science is widely acknowledged. The question I would raise is: was Popper, in that very act of propounding his theory of science, himself being a scientist? Was his own work part of scientific activity? My own answer to this is *yes* (Eaton: 1978:8). And by the same token, I would argue that literary semantics is not only concerned with literary texts but also with its own function in relation to the texts it purports to study.

For those who are still not happy with a professed science which refuses to define its object of concern, let the explication be framed in this way: literary semantics is *that branch of linguistics which studies (a) those texts (in relation to their readership) which are from time to time deemed 'literary' and (b) draws from this study meta-theoretical implications for linguistics as a whole.* (As a definition this has no greater indeterminacy than a definition of, say, plant ecology: *the study of plants in relation to their environment:* environment in turn defined as *whatever physical conditions happen to support plant life.)*

Indeed, I believe that a metatheory is a *sine qua non* for all linguistic sciences. Man's subjective standpoint may interfere in the pursuit of truth within even the natural sciences. On yet stronger grounds it impedes linguistic sciences. Without the brain there would have been no language. Where the brain circumflects to observe its own behaviour, it needs distancing devices to ensure observational accuracy. The problems of the 'ideal speaker-listener' are frequently encountered in linguistics. In the study of literature, where aesthetic sensitivity and ethical viewpoint tend to come into play, a stable discipline can only be attained through a many-levelled modal analysis (Eaton, 1978:8-15; 19-21; 1996:47-51).

The complexity of the problems of literary semantics seems to demand a new philosophical structure for literary studies. What follows is my own solution, doubtless arguable, but I believe that any alternative theory must at least tackle the problems my system addresses, even if that theory attempts to solve them by other means.

(1)   Literary semantics defines its terms and principles as clearly as possible (Eaton, 1996:55-65).

(2)   An exception to 1. is the term 'literature' itself, which cannot be satisfactorily defined (Eaton, 1996:2).

(3)   Literary semantics is a science (Eaton, 1996:16-23).

(4)   No science can exist without an empirical component (Eaton, 1996:51).

(5)   No science can operate effectively without a theoretical component (in tension with the empirical component) (Eaton, 1979: 114-115; 1996:19-21).

(6)   A theory is needed that at the highest theoretical level assigns epistemological status to works of literature which, in the worlds they represent, themselves defy empirical principles (in other words at this highest level of the metatheory, even the scientific commitments we make as linguists are avowed not to be absolute) (Eaton, 1996:114-115;47-51).

(7)   My metatheory begins with the theory of knowledge which, at its highest level (knowledge one), is neutral to scientific commitment (Eaton, 1966:20-26; 1972: 20-23; 1996:7-16, 51).

(8)   The empirical and theoretical components (4.and 5. above) are built in at the level of knowledge two (Eaton, 1996:16-21).

(9)   Aesthetic and ethical constituents are seated in, but not confined to, knowledge three (1979: passim; 1996:14).

(10)   The concepts 'transmission and reception' are fundamental to
            literary semantics. Within the trichotomy theory and the theory of
            science I have expounded (Eaton, 1972:93-106; 1966:passim), these
            are realised as the *semantics of literature* (an historical study, or
            transmission semantics, a psychological study of authors' creation
            of texts); and *semics*, the study of *semic accompaniment* (readers'
            experience), subdivided into *theoretical semics, practical semics,
            empirical semics* and *introspective semics* (Eaton, 1972:13-33,
            1979:passim; 1996:21-46).

Responses to the Document for Discussion

Freundlieb, Dieter. (2000). 'What is Literary Semantics?'. *Journal of Literary
      Semantics*. 29/2:135-40.
Pollard, Denis E. B. (2002). 'Literary Semantics as an Academic Discipline'.
      Journal of Literary Semantics. 31/1:77-82

Freundlieb's Critique

Dieter Freundlieb and Denis Pollard responded to 'Literary Semantics – an
Academic Discipline: A Document for Discussion'. (1999). The former wrote
a brief, trenchant critique of my views as reprinted above. I accept his contention that literary semantics is faced with a very difficult task but believe that
'literature' is too important and challenging a branch of linguistics to be denied
status as a scientific discipline. First, I shall summarise his critique.

     Freundlieb, doubting whether literature can be precisely defined, sees this
vagueness as an obstacle to scientific treatment: a literary semantics concerned
with an indeterminate cluster of entities may neither be held separate from other
branches of semantics nor will it yield explanatory laws.

     Furthermore, he argues that philosophical reflection does not constitute an
integral part of scientific activity; this entails that the philosophy of science and
scientific investigation are distinct activities. A science must have an object
domain – and textual meanings are not observable entities.

     Semantics is either translational – by this he means the reducing of meanings
to formalised algebraic notations – or it tries to give an account of how our
intuitive capacity to understand meaningful signs works. But he is sceptical
about the possibility for literary semantics to become a systematic description
and explanation of the cognitive processes that humans engage in when they

produce and read literary texts. On the other hand, he regards literary criticism as having a useful and moral rôle, though as a systematic academic discipline it is intellectually dubious.

I shall, for the sake of convenient treatment, reduce my reply to discussion of two problems which he raises; at the same time referring to Denis Pollard's response, whose view of literary semantics appears to overlap generously with mine. I am grateful to them both for their responses.

The Problem of the Object Domain

One point upon which Freundlieb and I are agreed is that no satisfactory definition of literature is possible. Indeed, I would go further: formal delimitation of the scope of the term 'literary' simply introduces fresh problems (see Pollard's six negative affirmations (Pollard 2002: 77-79)). We end up with scholars taking different ethical and aesthetic stands and the result is demarcation disputes (Eaton 1972: 14-15). Defining *literature* is not a cerebral task like defining language: partiality is built into any attempted formulation; as Pollard says, 'it is ambiguous as between a descriptive/classificatory and a normative sense' (2002: 78). If I define literature as *X* and thereby exclude *Y*, what happens if an author claims that his work *y* lies within the domain *X*? We are back to the literary equivalent of Tracey Emin's unmade bed. And it is at this point that Freundlieb loses heart. How can you have a science of a domain which cannot even be determined and specified?

By object domain, I take him to mean a clearly defined set of related entities upon which the scientific research is centred. So the argument runs: no satisfactory definition of literature can be devised, therefore no science of literature is possible.

'The proper study of mankind is man', wrote Alexander Pope. Such a sweeping assertion of equivalence may profitably be reshaped: *all aspects of man's experience are proper subjects for scientific investigation. The Journal of Linguistics*, to which I have been subscribing for 36 of its venerable 37 years has, on a careful count and at the time I am writing, published during those 36 years 430 articles (excluding review articles). Of these, on a generous assessment, only 9, about 2%, may be said to be centrally concerned with 'literary' language. Yet there is no need to carry out extensive research to support the view that 'literature' figures large among human preoccupations: the proportion of 'fictional' books in public libraries, the number of students taking literature courses in universities and schools, casual observation of the number of commuters on public transport reading novels, are but three simple indicators of this. One may say almost without fear of contradiction that, globally, many billions of man-hours are spent reading texts which the readers themselves would regard as 'literature', or its hyponym 'fiction'. Literature has stood the test of time and its very survival suggests that this tangle of human concern is worthy of serious study. If we ever succeeded in unravelling it, we might well be left with multiple object domains. Why should that be a problem?

The classic refutation of Freundlieb's insistence upon the prior establishment of an object domain is Linnaeus' taxonomy of the plant and animal kingdoms, which worked scientifically *back to front*, the received wisdom being *descriptive adequacy* followed, it may be hoped, by *explanatory adequacy*. He *began* with *explanation* – genera and species differed because God had so ordained them. By his contemporary standards, this was *explanatory adequacy*. As Stearn put it, 'Linnaeus could excusably believe himself God's chosen instrument for revealing in an orderly way the divinely ordered works of Creation, and he did not spare himself in that task', (Blunt, appendix, 1971: 242). A supernatural entity was assumed by him to constitute, or to be integral with, the object domain. He then proceeded to *descriptive adequacy*, his Linnaean taxonomy, but unwittingly set in chain a mode of sceptical enquiry which in the course of a century or so displaced the deity from scientific reckoning, thus supplanting his original explanation in a way he could never have foreseen.

To pursue this line of argument chronologically, one of the most notable scientific achievements of the twentieth century was the emergence of the science of genetics, the undisputed founding father of which was Gregor Mendel, a nineteenth-century monk, the breadth of whose vision contrasted with the narrowness of his focus – a fact which might explain why his achievements lay dormant for over 30 years.

He was a genius in the sense of a man with a capacity to take almost infinite pains. But the domains of entities which comprise the concern of present-day genetics – chromosomes, genes, genomes – were beyond his horizon and became demonstrable only with the development of microscopic techniques. He spent painstaking years measuring and classifying and nursing seedlings of the humble pea and would perhaps have regarded these as (a subset of) his object domain. His paper *Versuche ueber Pflanzenhybriden*, published in 1866, was brought to international notice in 1900 by three botanists, de Vries, Correns and Tschermak von Seysenegg, who each cited it independently. There can be no doubt that his scientific concerns far transcended garden pulse. He had chosen peas because he believed that they were the ideal species to answer fundamental questions about the plant and animal kingdoms and, indeed, about heredity itself.

But, for one moment, let us assume counterfactually that Mendel had been concerned solely with the propagation of peas: that he was just a plant grower commercially interested in the mechanics of pea-breeding. Suppose that he had written his *Versuche ueber Pflanzenhybriden* totally unaware of any implications for genetics beyond the practical problems of plant breeding. Posit too that de Vries, Correns and von Seysenegg had stumbled upon the publication and that it had contained no reference to the wider implications for heredity – for instance, by omission of Section 10 and a reshaping of sections 1 and 11 (these section headings, absent from the original, were later edited into Mendel's publication). Is it not highly probable that the history of the 20th century science of genetics would have been substantially the same, these scientists perceiving and pointing out the significances which Mendel had missed? Science marches on many legs and may still arrive though one be amputated. What made Mendel's work important was not his undoubted insight into the object domain, the problems of heredity in general, but his minute attention to the particular (Gribbin and Gribbin 1997: 64): the thousands of pea plants he patiently observed and experimented with. If this argument holds, it implies that prior establishment of an object domain is not a necessary precondition for the founding of a science.

Furthermore, it is inherent in scientific research that the perception, if not the assumed 'reality', of the object domain, changes: if it does not, nothing has been discovered. The history of science gives many examples of researchers who began by supposing they were studying one thing and ended up realising that they were dealing with something else. Even given that Mendel's burning interest was heredity and that this was his object domain, it was no more than a distorted glimpse, as I hinted earlier, of what the 20th century brought to fruition: the double helix model of Watson and Crick, the advances in microscopic techniques, molecular biology, the subsequent corroborative photographing of DNA molecules, the charting of the human genome and such offshoots as genetic fingerprinting, with all its social and forensic implications, and the 'reproductive' science which has made IVF treatment possible.

Mendel was fortunate in having a steady, measurable, classifiable set of objects, bio-organisms, to observe. Had he chosen literary semantics with all its attendant problems, he might have abandoned the task in despair. But this does not entail that he would have been right to do so. Mendel proved that scientific progress can result not exclusively from studies of a broad Darwinian scope but also from a narrowly focused methodology based upon mathematics and patient observation of a limited domain. And this, in essence, is an appropriate heuristic approach for literary semantics, as I shall argue [LS:228–236].

Again, although I have made it clear that there is no point in listing characteristics of literature as defining properties, such texts continually display distinctive features which demand, and are now receiving, investigation: fictionality, style, deviance, figurative language, genre, narrative, ambiguity, modality; or they engage readers' responses in treatments and portrayals not centrally associated with referential texts: humour, nonsense, myth, ethics, morality, religion, aesthetics, emotion, consciousness, dreams. These widely scattered paths lead researchers into philosophy, psychology, linguistics and, the most exciting track of all, I believe, neurophysiology.

Literature is, for all the chameleon properties which comprise it and which it depicts, a focal point for human activity. I believe that as such it deserves scientific study in its own right. But it is clear, and Freundlieb has drawn attention to several of the problems, that the methods and assumptions of scientific endeavour need to be redrafted. To put the problem crudely: how is such a diversity and vagueness of object domain to be tolerated without sacrificing the empirical rigour which is a defining characteristic of all science (see, for instance, Popper (1972: 25-61). And to give the answer just as briefly: by consigning the endless round of thesis-antithesis that is the stuff of so-called literary studies to a subordinate position within a meta-theoretical synthesis [LS:227]: a domain which includes and organises everything which could ever be considered knowledge (Eaton 1966: 25; 1972: 21), yet which remains, at its highest, **knowledge one** level, uncommitted to any particular view.

The Problem of Metatheory

Freundlieb refers to 'the unavoidable difference between science and the philosophy of science' and writes of Popper's notion of falsifiability as a technical term 'with a very circumscribed area of application' (2000:136-137). Similarly, Pollard distinguishes between the theory of, and the philosophy of, a discipline, arguing that when Logical Positivism was dominant 'Much of the physics in the same period was conducted successfully with blissful indifference to the positivist picture and its failure to achieve semantic reduction of specimen scientific statements to more "primitive" ("protocol") statements about immediate experiences' (Pollard 2002: 82). There are teasing distinctions here which escape me. A practising scientist does not have to be an academically competent philosopher skilled in semantic analysis in order to be philosophically aware. And it is unavoidable, the further the move is made from the natural sciences towards the human sciences, that the line between science and the philosophy of science becomes harder to draw: the objects of enquiry are often themselves subjective, thus blurring the comfortable scientific distinction between observer and observed.

While, admittedly, it sometimes is convenient to stress the theoretical difference between science and the philosophy of science, on other occasions it frequently becomes almost impossible to hold them separate. Statements that scientists make concerning observation and explanation are also commitments to perception and causality: experimental level and philosophical metalevel are conterminous. To assert scientifically 'event B because A' is simultaneously to state that there exists a causal connection between A and B; and this is a philosophical proposition presupposing a whole structure of 'scientific' commitments.

Furthermore, when Mendel might have asserted 'I see before me two pea hybrids: a round yellow hybrid and an angular yellow hybrid' – he would as a scientist have found no reason to raise such questions as to whether the peas actually existed or were angular or whether he was really seeing them. Certainly, he would not have been forced to devise such a concept as a set of 'ideal-pea-observers', naming himself as an instantiated member: since he did not himself create the peas, their objectivity was assured. He accepted his observations as scientific facts to be used inductively and deductively in his attempt to arrive at explanatory adequacy. Yet such questions might have been important in not dissimilar conditions, as we shall see. And the same is true of Popper's concept of falsifiability. You cannot have falsification *in vacuo*: there is always the further question, 'falsified in relation to what system of proof?' Whatever physical experiment is devised as a test and whatever principles and criteria are formulated, they all belong within a logical and empirical and therefore philosophical system.

Although this line of reasoning, applied to the natural sciences, may sound pedantic and without consequence, a recent unfortunate occurrence in research into BSE might be mentioned as a *caveat*. A team of British scientists at the Institute for Animal Health in Edinburgh, but actually experimenting at Compton in Berkshire (Coghlan 2001: 15), spent four years of research into the spread of BSE only to discover that the sheeps' brains they thought they were working on were in fact cattle brains (Balter 2002). Whatever the outcome of a current inquiry into what went wrong, the time was wasted and the experiments vitiated by uncertainty, if not by error. These scientists had fulfilled Freundlieb's criterion by establishing the respective object domains (*animal kingdom*: sheeps' brains/cattle brains) but failed to ascertain at the outset the answer to the philosophical question: '**Are we sure**: *that our sample is ovine and not bovine?*' One scientist, Chris Bostock, voiced the concerns that were felt amongst the team and counselled caution but, mitigating if not excusing the seriousness of the error, the pressure to determine whether traces of BSE could be found in sheep was too urgent. It was a rare lapse on the part of a team whose record otherwise has been exemplary (Balter 2002).

Even in the natural sciences, scientific investigation and philosophical awareness go hand in hand: the practising scientist should always be alert to the ancient scholastic warning: *e falso sequitur quodlibet* – if your premises are flawed, there will be no safeguarding your conclusions. The same holds for the Piltdown hoax, where a mandible of an orang-utan had been mischievously fixed into a human cranium, thus distorting scientists' conception of the anthropological object domain for several decades. In science, positive identification of the investigated substance is more important than cognizance of an abstract domain.

But when we reflect that within linguistics for the past 40 years a central tenet in the 'empirical' treatment of grammaticality and other aspects of language has been the concept, explicit or implicit, of the ideal speaker-listener, the analogy is plain. In the natural sciences, you open your eyes and you know you are looking at a pea plant. In linguistic science, you open your eyes and in order to be certain you are beholding a grammatical structure – even in a printed corpus – you adopt the stratagem of idealising yourself. We have come full circle to the point where I. A. Richards betrayed his own scientific principles: 'He [the literary critic] is forced to say in effect, "I am better than you" ' (1960[1924]:26). In linguistics, subsets of the object domain, notably (putative) grammatical structures, are being subjectively generated and instantaneously subjectively monitored. One of the marvels of post-1965 linguistics is how any self-proclaimed science could have emerged scatheless from such blatant circularity. The point in the present argument is also plain: Freundlieb objects to a literary semantics in which the object domain is unspecified; yet in linguistics itself an empirically questionable concept has become accepted currency and practice. The door to scientific laxity, with this essentially speculative device, is already open.

Literature exists as an indeterminate complex of related processes and activities, linguistically mediated. The parts of this complex defy rigid specification on the lines Freundlieb might wish, but may be roughly tabulated to provide *ad hoc* domains, textual, psychological, neurological, educational, for empirical research into some of the most challenging problems that science can ever be called upon to tackle. And the prime question for literary semantics is not 'Where are we going?' but 'Are we clear, experiment by experiment, where we are starting from; and what immediate questions the present experiment is designed to answer?' As Tudge puts it, 'Mendel's method, and his strength, was to identify problems that he knew were probably soluble and then move step by step into more difficult areas' (Tudge 2002:37).

In short, I do not see the rigid separation of science from the philosophy of science as possible; nor, to revert to the question dealt with earlier, do I see an agreed, defined object domain as anything more than a luxury we have to learn to do without; what is of paramount importance is to attempt *to separate the empirical from the non-empirical and to safeguard the former without losing respect for the latter*. We may thus, even as scientists, retain and cherish non-empirical constructs (such as the ideal speaker-listener, invaluable as a theoretical device). Context-sensitive definitions of 'empirical' are, however, needed.

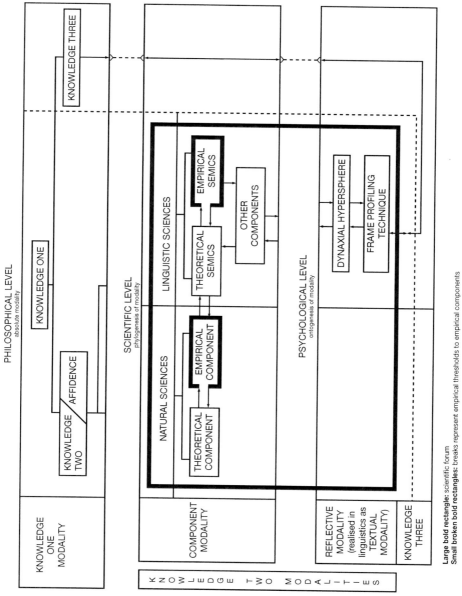

Figure 15.   Scientific Forum and Empirical Component.

To recapitulate, such an indeterminate but nevertheless important region of human endeavour and experience, as 'literature' undoubtedly is, deserves serious scientific study. It demands a scientific framework different from the natural sciences and the only solution that I can see is to allow a variety of domains and a many-levelled modality, building in the rigour, which is a *sine qua non* of all sciences, *within* the metatheory. In other words, it is an inclusive science, tolerant of a great deal of 'non-scientific' activity; but answerable, exclusively, at the core, to rigorous empirical challenge.

The Scientific Integration of Literary Studies

This book has been a long journey both through time, from 1962 to 2010, and through concepts. A massive raft of terminology has been created which I believe is necessary if the study of literature is ever to become a serious intellectual endeavour, disjoined from the sheer delight in, and enjoyment of, literature for its own sake. The Figures, produced over decades of wrestling with the problem of separating the one activity from the other, while doing justice to both, go far beyond the scope which is normally allotted to literary studies – necessarily so. In the remainder of this chapter, I shall explain the significances and further implications of the two figures 14 and 15.

Psychological Level: the Ontogenesis of Modality

Another way of viewing **knowledge three** as opposed to the various explanations I have made earlier is to say that it is what we humans ontogenetically start with and in a sense retain throughout our lives: that part of our being which we believe to be necessarily private.

The child moves from raw **percept** through the process of **conceptualization** [it attains to **reflective modality**], simultaneously into the socializing discipline of language and, normally, in parallel awareness, from the sheer discovery of a real world of given objectivity to an accruing structure of belief and questioning and doubt. He or she begins to **modalise** experience. The process is described in my account of **frame-profiling technique** [LS:chapter 13 *passim*] and the **dynaxial hypersphere** [LS: chapters 7 *passim* and 8 *passim*]. It should be mentioned that intuition, which is omnipresent in human experience, plays a part even in our initial acceptance of the actuality of sense-data; though it is logically absurd to imagine a pre-linguistic child saying to itself 'Perhaps the breast which I appear to see is illusory'. So, the child moves from the **ontogenetic** to the **phylogenetic** level; it steadily becomes a social animal and the knowledge three it was born with is structured by shared, communal, linguistic experiences of the community into which it has been born. It moves gradually towards **knowledge two**. Perhaps the climax of this transition often comes during the period between the child's second and third birthday: 'the terrible twos', as it has now widely become known.

Sociological (Scientific) Level: Phylogenesis of Modality

This is the stage, occurring gradually, at which the child's **knowledge three** becomes increasingly to be shaped by the social and physical environment into which he or she has been born. Science, in its loosest etymological sense – the 'wisdom' of the receiving community – begins to shape and inform its world view. In literate societies, **reflective modality**, the result of learning to speak, edges into **textual modality** as the infant learns to read. In 'advanced' – I use the word with hesitation – societies, the child gains some knowledge of **component modality**, and may even become active within a scientific component.

    Knowledge two is that which is believed by any individual to be communicable. The range is vast: the whole of human discourse, encompassing at one extreme uttered and even unuttered thoughts, ideas, arguments; then casual conversations; and at the other extreme, disciplined academic dialogue and, specifically, the sciences.

Philosophical Level: Meta-Modality

The trichotomy of knowledge, a philosophical metatheory, at the head of the diagram includes everything that could ever be considered knowledge. The trichotomy has been described in detail in earlier chapters; it comprises knowledge three, knowledge two and knowledge one, this last category constituting a (hypothetical) validation for the other two. To put it briefly, knowledge one represents in man's ratiocinations, whatever his philosophy or field of inquiry, the possibility of being 'right'. By common consent we consign knowledge one to an 'upstairs attic, viewed from knowledge two, through a glass ceiling' and agree to work at the levels of knowledge two and knowledge three. But without the possibility of being right as held out by knowledge one, there would be little point in engaging in discussion at the level of knowledge two; indeed, 'knowing' *anything*, even at the level of knowledge three, would be paradoxical and without point.

Insofar as we humans may gain exit from this straitened terrestrial discourse, knowledge one is the *terminus ad quem* of our endeavours. It is, in sum, 'as meta as you can get': the supreme modality to which all human discourse aspires.

The Tracks within the Chain of Modality

Value within this system, or at least *intrinsic* as opposed to *instrumental* value, is a man's conviction (knowledge three) that he has access in some degree to knowledge one. By this analysis, value (which has always been at a disadvantage in the logical and empirical scheme) is accorded an equal epistemological status with ratiocination: we may track clockwise round the diagram from knowledge three to knowledge two in ratiocination, but this process will not 'reveal' value. At any point in our clockwise tracking, value dawns upon us – or rather perhaps was present unnoticed with us continually – through knowledge three: this not in any mystical sense, but in as immediate a fashion as our perceptions convince us of the existence of the physical objects around us, so described in the section on the **Psychological Level**. I find the notion that science and philosophy should on principle be held separate from one another hard to comprehend. Value is another case in point. Any sentient being, faced with a choice, makes a value judgment in choosing; and scientists, in embracing science and in selecting one experiment as opposed to some other, are making ethical decisions, yet often being more aware of the decisions than of the value which they attach to them.

Figure 15 [LS:227] it is true, does portray philosophy and science as separate entities but this is a distortion to which most diagrams are prone, murdering to dissect. Philosophy is to be seen as 'in-built' into the model and much depends on the level we happen to focus upon. To take an example track which develops my discussion of knowledge three: (a) the child's ontological development is represented, from inside, as a subjective phenomenon within **reflective modality**, as in **frame-profiling technique** (Eaton 1996: 28-46); (b) then, from outside, as an objective occurrence for scientific research at the level of component modality in the natural and linguistic sciences [neurophysiology, psychology, psycholinguistics, and so forth] (see for instance Ruth Eaton 1988); and, at the head of the diagram: (c) in turn, modalising science itself, as a process involving philosophical categories: a movement from knowledge three to knowledge two, whose ultimate validation rests with knowledge one. Scientific enquiry is a form of philosophical investigation and the two should be prised apart only when it is safe, convenient and useful to do so.

But, in yet another parallel track, the same clockwise movement traces both (a) the ontogenetic and (b) the phylogenetic aspects of **science**, whilst (c) modalising science itself as described in my previous paragraph. The **scientist** (a), within **reflective modality**, is seen as a microcosm of **science** as a whole at the **psychological level**: the competent scientist is constantly and simultaneously balancing theoretical and empirical demands within his own mind (cf. Eaton 1972: 101-102); this is an individual counterpart of (b) the scientific, confrontational-cooperative **theoretical component** and **empirical component** as depicted at the level of the phylogenesis of modality, that is, the level of interacting scientists; yet (c), science itself, is **modalised**: it is not in my system treated as absolute truth, but subject, as all knowledge, to **knowledge one**, the absolute modality, the possibility of being right.

Pollard's criterion

This reply to Dieter Freundlieb is no more than a sketch. How could a science which is as yet unformed be described in detail? All that is possible is to present to a favourably disposed readership a case that there is something here worth trying to make a science of.

The answer is, I believe, clearly stated by Denis Pollard when he broaches the question 'can literary semantics be a science?' For it to succeed, it must be, he argues, systematic, explanatory and precise. He goes on to describe what I take to be one of the rôles of theoretical semics: 'careful elucidation of what counts as testability or what could count as the analogue of "empirical" data in physics, chemistry or biology' (Pollard 2002: 80). A fine aspiration, but if I had pedantically insisted upon this in 30 years of editing *JLS*, I doubt if I would have been left with more than three years' material. It would also have excluded scores of articles I believed to be of importance or interest.

Taking Pollard's lead as the cue, let me suggest a resolution.

Exclusive and Inclusive Science of Literary Semantics

Exclusive View: the Empirical Threshold

We assign to literary semantics an inclusive scientific forum but, within that generously extended region, establish an *exclusive* enclave within which conclusions follow logically and empirically from research into a chosen sub-domain. Scholars working within this empirical component would declare that this was what they were about and demonstrate how their work fulfilled empirical criteria. I make a critical distinction between this large *scientific forum* and an *empirical threshold to a smaller empirical component*, represented in Figure 15 by 'broken' rectangles, this component being one defining characteristic of science. It will be clear from this account that my system substitutes for Freundlieb's object domain (an abstraction drawn from a set of objects or processes in the material world) a duality of *function domains* [components, as I call them] theoretical/empirical. The advantage of this is that these function domains, unlike object domains, persist unchanged, though their modes of procedure would be context sensitive, appropriate to each particular subject matter as long as science may last. The diagram could be adapted to describe any science and, judging from the BSE example I gave earlier, even the natural sciences might profit from a friendly confrontation between cautious theorists who were philosophically aware and colleagues so keen, or under such pressure, that they embarked upon experiments without having ascertained precisely what they were experimenting on.

This brings me to the main thrust of my argument. I believe that the traditional oppositions within linguistics – synchronic/diachronic, transmission/reception, spoken/written, sound/meaning, competence/performance, for instance – all have their place. But I believe the most important determining division should be between the **empirical** and the **non-empirical**. This is the significance of the broken rectangles inserted in the diagram: it represents a co-operative confrontation between the theoretical (semicists) and the empirical (semicists) – an opposition which is all too often lacking.

Insofar as there is a stable object domain for literary semantics it is language, or a subset, not necessarily proper subset (Eaton 1996: 2) of language: and the objects of study are texts, spoken or written, creators of texts and readers of texts. See also Pollard's Catechism no. 9, which amounts to the same claim: if a discipline cannot be demonstrated to have relevance for language it has no relevance for literary semantics (Pollard 2002: 80). No attempt is made to define 'literature' but researchers will tend to concentrate upon, though not exclusively, those texts which linguistics has traditionally neglected. An informal illustration of what I mean by a scientific forum, the inclusive scope, of literary semantics, would be the collective writings in *JLS* volumes, past and present. I will give an example, which I have already dealt with in some detail, to illustrate what is meant by empirical semics.

Rien T. Segers: The Evaluation of Literary Texts

This volume, published in 1978, was important in my view because it was an empirical study which centred on one of the most vexing, and least amenable to scientific treatment, of all aspects of literary semantics: value. Segers takes what he calls a 'relational' view of value, which may suggest that he believes that the study is confronting the problem of intrinsic value – a standpoint I dissented from in chapter 11. Nevertheless, he claims to be studying *evaluation* and his methods are rigorous. The book is therefore important at the level of research into texts, at the level of research into responses, and also at the philosophical metalevel of revealing the Achilles' heel of dogmatic and absolute commitment to science: the problem of determining what entities are intrinsically valuable. Nothing I have read since seems to present a braver step from the scientific forum into the empirical component. It is a book which deserves to be reissued, if only as a milestone in literary semantics.

The discipline I am proposing is 'generous' at two levels: firstly the scientific forum for literary semantics is inclusive and open, its boundaries self-regulating and delimited by common consent; and secondly, within these boundaries any scholar can 'cross the empirical threshold', choose a subject for empirical research and devise experiments. A pattern of cohesion amongst diverse experiments might be difficult to discern, but I would submit that the various diagrams in this book, explained in the structured Glossary, do include, separate and tackle the most important constituents. In any case, all attempts to classify what Freundlieb might term the 'object domains' of the human sciences will confront similar recalcitrant material. The principle will be: a rigorous empirical component within a generous theoretical component, which would include even literary criticism, should its exponents evince any desire to join in.

The classic procedure might be that the empirical semicist chooses a domain or sub-domain, devises a procedure for investigation and a context-sensitive definition of 'empirical'; the theoretical semicist then presents a critical assessment of the project and determines whether the proposed definition of empirical is adequate in the context of the investigation. Such a dialectic may be unnecessary in the natural sciences; but for reasons I have explained, philosophical awareness is essential in the linguistic sciences.

Inclusive View; the Scientific Forum

Returning to Figure 15, the diagram is based upon others I have presented over the years, but most directly upon Figure 14, of which it is a slight modification. It may be seen as a loose cartographical sketch, not just of literature itself, but of the disciplines, as outlined in my conclusion, which are relevant to, or concern themselves with, literature. I have allowed, in Appendix Four, theoretical semics to make a brief foray into the theory of education.

The thick black frame in Figure 15 marks the scientific forum. To literary semantics, and *mutatis mutandis* to the linguistic sciences, instead of a clearly determined object domain, are assigned the core components: **theoretical semics** and **empirical semics**. The other components, specified and described with the earlier diagrams, are **semantics of literature** (**transmission semantics**) and **practical semics** – which subsume the components **empirical semics** and **introspective semics**. The division **transmission semantics/semics** is based upon **transmission** (including the creative processes involved in producing a literary work together with the historical reconstruction of this, cf. *The Road to Xanadu* (Lowes 1951), and **reception** (the experiences, or **semic accompaniments**, of readers, who may be centuries removed from the processes of creation and transmission). Grammarians have sought to abstract underlying general features of language and in doing so have avoided literary works as being particular and perhaps even idiosyncratic. Hence, literary works have been neglected by linguists. It is my view, however, that idiosyncratic language deserves at least as much attention as referential language.

Let us look at this from a different point of view. A child, by the time it is 4 years old, has attained to an amazing degree of awareness about its environment. I remember my older daughter asking me out of the blue many years ago, when she was about four years old, 'Can forget-me-nots change their minds?' Perhaps such rapid cerebral adjustment can be achieved only by a device (the brain) capable of generating a very high number of 'world hypotheses': a system which is highly wasteful.

Think of a child removed from its native English-speaking parents and fostered abroad by native speakers of any one of three thousand and more languages belonging to any linguistic grouping in the world. The infant has no prior warning of what language is going to be sprung on it. By the time the child is four he or she will be speaking with some fluency this 'non-native' language. Like **style** [LS:159], **fictionality** may be a straightforward consequence of a capacity to survive. The child is innately generating billions of abstract linguistic/non-linguistic hypotheses or fictions – part of the equipment it needs for its survival – in parallel with the sensory-motor data it experiences. The abilities (a) to make sense of its environment; (b) to master the facilitating linguistic keys to this: these twin evolutionary tracks weld into one. That is to say, the acquisition of linguistically structured concepts.

The child is thus endowed as a natural entailment with a conceptual apparatus capable of generating an infinite number of fictional frames (Eaton 1972:

136-138; 1996: 28-31). According to this analysis, fictionality in literature might be seen as a vestige of this conceptual endowment. **Fictionality**, rather than grammaticality, may thus be the innate norm (Eaton 1972: 136-145). It is also worth noting at this point that the search for an object domain may have been one of the reasons for linguists' obsession with grammar and non-deviant usage. Reliable, referential discourse has provided a fairly stable object domain. But a case may be made out that communication takes place also through 'deviant' structures and through non-referential use of language: why should these problems be less interesting to scholars than non-deviant and referential usage? Perhaps quite the reverse.

The scientific forum includes, and is in complementary relationship with, the empirical component. If this model were adopted, both empirical and non-empirical theoretical research would continue as at present. What I hope would emerge is a code of good practice on both sides: theorists would feel bound to assess and state the empirical implications, if any, of their notions; conversely, the empiricists would acknowledge the importance of non-empirical theorising and come to regard the scientific forum at large as a provider of insights which, selectively, merited empirical investigation; they would also seek to choose projects for research which met the following two criteria: (i) they were not simply verifications of the obvious and (ii) they furthered human knowledge.

The Justification for Literary Semantics

In this discussion, I have tried to respond specifically to the two fundamental objections Dieter Freundlieb made in his critique: that a science must begin with an established object domain; and that philosophical reflection does not constitute an integral part of scientific activity.

That cluster of activities we call literature is of vital human importance. I believe that the immense obstacles which debar scientific investigation should be overcome. I take an inclusive view: comprehending within the scientific forum even such activities as speculation, conversation, chance and chance remarks. Colin Tudge makes the case for an inclusive view of science provocatively: 'Some scientists affect to dislike speculation, but if nobody speculated there would be no science at all' (Tudge 2002: 271). I regard research which relies upon such a speculative device as the ideal speaker-listener as belonging, within the inclusive domain of science, to introspective semics (descriptive statements based upon the linguist's own intuitions) and theoretical semics (hypothetical arguments based upon introspections or upon other non-empirical evidence).

Instead of excluding the device *speaker-listener* absolutely or including it and assigning to it a higher status than it theoretically deserves (as happens at present), we should modalise it. It is not unscientific to say *may*; it becomes so only when we use *is* in circumstances which permit only *may*. The *is* awaits the mutually negotiated sanction of theoretical and empirical semics: it results from crossing over the **empirical threshold**. And even then, when sanction is granted, it is true, attested to and as yet not falsified, only in the sense of **affident** (Eaton 1966: 28; 1972: 22): 'truth, in this sense, constantly changes' (Eaton 1966: 63). Instead of modal verbs, literary semantics has modal compartments. And, to pursue his metaphor, practitioners of the human sciences would do well to commit to memory, as a sacred text, Catechism 8, **Pollard's Criterion**.This calls for 'careful elucidation of what counts as testability or what could count as the analogue of empirical data in physics, chemistry or biology' (Pollard 2002: 80).

Some readers question the usefulness of the complex system I have outlined. I can only reply that the sorts of cognitive problems raised by literature – philosophical, logical, epistemological, ethical, aesthetic, ontological, moral, religious, neurological, linguistic, psychological, sociological, anthropological, historical, educational – warrant such complexity. No model can attain to simplicity *and* take account of all the manifestations of human activity and experience that literature embraces. My trichotomy of knowledge comprehends all this.

NOTES

CHAPTER ONE NOTES

1. Charles Ogden and I.A. Richards (1945). *The Meaning of Meaning.*
2. C. E. Osgood, G.J. Suci and P. H. Tannenbaum. (1957), *The Measurement of Meaning.* See also C. E. Osgood, 'Studies on the Generality of Affective Meaning Systems', *American Psychologist*, January 1962.
3. Osgood *et al.* (1957), pp. 5-6. For a further discussion of the behaviourist-mentalist controversy, see C.W. Morris, (1955). *Signs, Language and Behavior*: pp. 27-31.
4. Osgood *et al., Measurement of Meaning*, pp. 318-9.
5. I am not sure that the Ogden and Richards' view is mentalistic. A cursory glance at the Basic Triangle, [LS:10], might lead to this conclusion but the authors are careful to eliminate any 'mysterious extra entity' in knowledge, see, for instance, *The Meaning of Meaning*, p. 81.
6. Osgood *et al., Measurement of Meaning*, p. 29.
7. *Ibid.*, see beginning of chapter 8.
8. *Ibid.*, see end of chapter 2.
9. See *The Measurement of Meaning*, chapter 8, p. 320 ff. 'In what sense is the Semantic Differential a Measurement of Meaning?' Uriel Weinreich, however, 'Travels through Semantic Space', *Word*, 1958, pp. 358-9, suggests that the authors' discussion of such theoretical questions is hindered by inadequate reading in elementary semantics and consequent inadequate terminology. Weinreich believes that the authors have been reluctant to distinguish meaning from affect. Osgood's reply includes a careful definition of connotation and denotation, 'Semantic Space Revisited', *Word*, 1959, pp. 192-201.
10. Osgood *et al.* chapter 5.
11. Max Black. (1949). *Language and Philosophy.* Note p. 192.
12. Stephen Ullmann. (1962). *Semantics, an Introduction to the Science of Meaning*: pp. 57-8.
13. Ogden and Richards. (1945), p. 58.
14. *Ibid.*, p. 56.
15. *Ibid.*, p. 56.
16. *Ibid.*, p. 52, 'the residual trace of an adaptation made by the organism to a stimulus'.

17.   *Ibid.*, p. 52.
18.   *Ibid.*, p. 59.
19.   *Ibid.,* p. 62.
20.   *Ibid.,* p. 73.
21.   *Ibid.*, p. 73.
22.   *Ibid.*, p. 76.
23.   *Ibid.*, pp. 106 and 188.
24.   *Ibid.*, p. 88.
25.   *Ibid.*, p. 9.
26.   *Ibid.*, p. 9.
27.   *Ibid.*, p. 188.
28.   *Ibid.*, Chapter 5.
29.   *Ibid.*, p. 88.
30.   *Ibid.*, p. 102.
31.   *Ibid.*, p. 102.
32.   *Ibid.*, p. 115.
33.   *Ibid.*, p. 115.
34.   *Ibid.*, pp. 186 ff.
35.   *Ibid.*, p. 11 ff.
36.   *Ibid.*, p. 206.
37.   *Ibid.*, p. 205.
38.   *Ibid.*, pp. 226-7.
39.   *Ibid.*, p. 223.
40.   *Ibid.*, p. 235.
41.   Cf. D. Daiches. (1956). *Critical Approaches to Literature*, pp. 155-7.
42.   Ullmann. (1957), pp. 72-3; also (1962), p. 58. For The Basic Triangle see Ogden and Richards (1945), p. 11.
43.   Bertrand Russell. (1956). *Human Knowledge: Its Scope and Limits*, p. 13.
44.   Even a naturalistic view of the universe would support this statement. Cf. Hoyle. (1957), *The Nature of the Universe*, 'we are already observing about half as far into space as we can ever hope to do. If we built a telescope a million times as big as the one at Mount Palomar we could scarcely double our present range of vision. So what it amounts to is that owing to the expansion of the Universe we can never observe events that happen outside a certain quite definite finite region of space.'
45.   See C.S. Lewis. (1960). *Miracles*. Chapter 2 and *passim*.
46.   See John Passmore. (1957). *A Hundred Years of Philosophy*, Chapter 16.
47.   See W.V. Quine. (1967). *Word and Object,* p. 235.
48.   Cf. A.J. Ayer (1956) *The Problem of Knowledge*, p. 29, where Ayer says it would not be correct to say of a superstitious person who had walked under a ladder and felt convinced that he was about to suffer some misfortune that he *knew* this was going to be so. His process of reasoning was not generally reliable even if the expected misfortune befell him. But if Ayer were himself a superstitious person then he might consider the process of reasoning which the superstitious person employed reliable, and might concur in the opinion that this premonition was a form of knowledge. Within the trichotomy theory, Ayer's contention remains the same, but is treated at the level of knowledge two.

49.   For further arguments on these lines but with reference to the power of language to shape thought, see Whorf, B.L. (1956). *Language, Thought and Reality: Selected Writings of Benjamin Lee Whorf*; also Max Black. (1962). *Models and Metaphors: Studies in Language and Philosophy*, Chapter 14.

CHAPTER TWO NOTES

1.   By 'universe of discourse' I mean any system of human communication. A university is an example of a high universe of discourse; two members of a primitive tribe making signs is an example of a low universe of discourse. The distinction between high and low must be arbitrary – some degree of arbitrariness is inherent in all scientific process. This usage of 'universe of discourse' may be thought eccentric but the character of the present trichotomy theory justifies the slight shift in application; cf. W.M. Urban. (1951). *Language and Reality*, pp.197-9; also pp. 203-4.

2.   See L.J. Cohen. (1962). *The Diversity of Meaning*, p. 311 ff., where Cohen discusses the possibility of defining the measure of confirmation enjoyed by a given hypothesis at a given time. The present system would approach the problem by defining the measure of acceptance.

3.   L. Armour. (1962). 'Value Data and Moral Rule', *Philosophical Quarterly*, pp. 228-38.

4.   See, for instance, J. Harrison. (1963). 'Does Knowing imply Believing', *The Philosophical Quarterly*, 13:322-32.

5.   A.D. Woozley. (1957). *Theory of Knowledge*, p. 178.

6.   *Ibid.*, p. 192.

7.   A.J.Ayer. (1956). *The Problem of Knowledge*, p. 34. It should be noted that Ayer does not consider his statement to be a definition of knowledge.

8.   See L.J. Cohen. (1962). *The Diversity of Meaning*, pp. 88-9, where Cohen gives an admirable illustration of the sort of impasse which is reached.

9.   See W.M. Urban. (1951). *Language and Reality*, p.168.

10.   See B.L. Whorf. (1956). *Language, Thought and Reality*, p. 246, where Whorf asserts that what we call 'scientific thought' is a specialization of the Western Indo-European type of language.

11.   W.M. Urban. (1951) *Language and Reality*, Chapter 7.

12.   A.J. Ayer. (1953). *Language, Truth and Logic*, p.34. Ayer was not the first to expound this view; it stemmed from the 'Vienna Circle' led by Moritz Schlick in the 1920s. See John Passmore. (1957). *A Hundred Years of Philosophy*, pp. 369-98.

13.   Max Black. (1949). *Language and Philosophy: Studies in Method.*

14.   Ludwig Wittgenstein. (1955). *Tractatus Logico-Philosophicus.*

15.   Ogden and Richards. (1945). *The Meaning of Meaning*, p. 149 ff.

16.   I.A. Richards. (1959). *The Principles of Literary Criticism*, Chapter 34. See also I.A. Richards. (1954). *Practical Criticism*, pp. 213-24, where Richards makes some observations concerning the emotive use of words.

17.   G.L. Kittredge. (1960). *Chaucer and His Poetry*, p. 211.

18.   For a discussion of such problems, see M.R. Cohen and E.Nagel. (1957). *An*

Introduction to Logic and the Scientific Method, Chapter 17, and particularly pp. 343-4.

19.   I.A. Richards. (1955). *Speculative Instruments*, p. 4.
20.   C.W. Morris. (1955). *Signs, Language and Behavior*, p. 74.
21.   *Ibid.*, p. 2.
22.   See W.M. Urban. (1951). *Language and Reality*, pp. 92-4.
23.   C.W. Morris. (1955). *Signs, Language and Behavior*, p. 125.
24.   *Ibid.*, p. 62.
25.   *Ibid.*, p. 125.
26.   For a discussion of some of these problems see Max Black, C.L. Stevenson, and I.A. Richards, 'A Symposium on Emotive Meaning', in *Philosophical Review*, March, 1948, pp.111-57. See also the Additional Notes in Max Black. (1949). *Language and Philosophy, Studies in Method*, p. 254-57; C.L. Stevenson. (1950). *Ethics and Language*.
27.   See I.A. Richards. (1955). *Speculative Instruments*, p. 49. Chapter 3 of that book is a reprint of the Paper by Richards in the Symposium mentioned above, in note 26.
28.   T.S. Kuhn, *The Copernican Revolution* (New York, 1959; copyright 1957, p. 172)..

CHAPTER THREE NOTES

1.   *Ibid.*, I.A. Richards. (1959). *The Principles of Literary Criticism*, p. 60.
2.   *Ibid.*, pp. 83-4
3.   *Ibid.*, p. 176 (footnote).
4.   *Ibid.*, p. 39.
5.   *Ibid.*, p. 41.
6.   *Ibid.*, p. 8.
7.   *Ibid.*, p. 10.
8.   *Ibid.*, p. 23.
9.   *Ibid.*, p. 24
10.   *Ibid.*, p. 86.
11.   *Ibid.*, p. 86.
12.   *Ibid.*, p. 87.
13.   *Ibid.*, p. 47.
14.   *Ibid.*, p. 48.
15.   *Ibid.*, p. 51.
16.   *Ibid.*, pp. 52-5.
17.   *Ibid.*, p. 52.
18.   *Ibid.*, p. 56.
19.   *Ibid.*, p. 56.
20.   *Ibid.*, p. 57.
21.   *Ibid.*, p. 58.
22.   *Ibid.*, p. 59.
23.   *Ibid.*, p. 60.
24.   *Ibid.*, p. 246.

25. *Ibid.*, p. 37.
26. *Ibid.*, p. 114.
27. *Ibid.*, p. 117.
28. *Ibid.*, p. 132.
29. *Ibid.*, p. 112.
30. *Ibid.*, p. 109.
31. *Ibid.*, p. 110.
32. *Ibid.*, p. 68.
33. *Ibid.*, p. 70.
34. *Ibid.*, p. 96.
35. *Ibid.*, p. 114.
36. *Ibid.*, p. 75.
37. *Ibid.*, chapter 29.
38. *Ibid.*, pp. 275-6.
39. *Ibid.*, p. 175.
40. *Ibid.*, p. 177.
41. *Ibid.*, p. 26.
42. *Ibid.*, p. 181.
43. *Ibid.*, p. 194.
44. *Ibid.*, p. 61.
45. *Ibid.*, p. 26.
46. *Ibid.*, p. 27.
47. *Ibid.*, p. 28.
48. *Ibid.*, p. 204.
49. Leslie Armour. (1962). 'Value Data and Moral Rules', *Philosophical Quarterly*, pp. 228-38.
50. R. Wellek and A. Warren. (1961). *The Theory of Literature,* p. 4.
51. I.A. Richards. (1954). *Practical Criticism*, p. 310.
52. *Ibid.*, pp. 299-300.
53. *Ibid.*, p. 302.
54. *Ibid.*, p. 302.
55. *Ibid.*, p. 303.
56. *Ibid.*, p. 305.
57. *Ibid.*, p. 351.
58. *Ibid.*, p. 321.
59. *Ibid.*, p. 179.
60. *Ibid.*, p. 315.
61. *Ibid.*, p. 351.
62. Max Black. (1949). *Language and Philosophy*, p. 210.
63. C.C. Fries. (1957). *The Structure of English*, see p. 76 onwards; also chapter 6.
64. Cf. Helen Gardner. (1959). *The Business of Criticism*, pp. 32-5.
65. J.L. Lowes. (1956). *Geoffrey Chaucer.*
66. G.C. Coulton. (1963). *Chaucer and his England.*
67. G.L. Kittredge. (1960). *Chaucer and his Poetry*, p.218.
68. *Ibid.*, p.217.
69. W.C. Curry. (1960). *Chaucer and the Medieval Sciences*, p.28.
70. *Ibid.*, pp. 28-9.
71. Compare, for further illustration of this point, the method of J.C. Pope.

(1942). *The Rhythm of Beowulf*, with A.J. Bliss. (1958). *The Metre of Beowulf*. Pope relies on semic accompaniment to a greater extent than Bliss.

72.   D. Daiches. (1956). *Critical Approaches to Literature*, p. 391. Also R.S. Crane. (1957). *The Languages of Criticism and the Structure of Poetry*, p.191.

73.   T.S. Eliot's statement that the only critics worth reading are those who actually practise the art they criticize is worth noting in this respect. He later withdrew this remark: *Selected Essays*. (1953), p.31.

74.   I.A. Richards. (1959). *The Principles of Literary Criticism*, p. 176; see also p.116 ff.

75.   *Ibid., passim.*

76.   *Ibid., passim* – most saliently p. 37.

77.   John Passmore. (1957). *A Hundred Years of Philosophy*, p. 392.

78.   L.J. Cohen. (1962). *The Diversity of Meaning*, p. 311.

79.   M.R. Cohen and E. Nagel. (1957). *An Introduction to Logic and Scientific Method*, p. 403.

80.   R.W. Chambers. (1955). *Man's Unconquerable Mind*, p. 91.

81.   *Ibid.*, p. 94.

82.   E.M.W. Tillyard. (1958). *The Muse Unchained*, pp. 136-7.

83.   R. Wellek and A. Warren. (1961). *The Theory of Literature*, p. 157.

CHAPTER FOUR NOTES

1.   Cleanth Brooks. (1949). *The Well Wrought Urn*, pp.229-230.

2.   John Crowe Ransom. (1941). *The New Criticism*.

3.   William Empson. (1956). *Seven Types of Ambiguity*.

4.   R.P. Blackmur. (1954). *Language as Gesture*.

5.   W.K. Wimsatt, Jr. (1958). *The Verbal Icon: Studies in the Meaning of Poetry*.

6.   Philip Wheelwright. (1959). *The Burning Fountain*. Also (1962) *Metaphor and Reality*.

7.   Marcus B. Hester. (1967). *The Meaning of Poetic Metaphor*.

8.   William Righter. (1963). *Logic and Criticism*.

9.   Richard Foster. (1962). *The New Romantics*.

10.   *Ibid.*, p. 180. 'This, we shall see, involves the poetic imagining of a whole religion of poetry, complete with worshippers, images and holy objects and a corps of spiritual fathers'.

11.   Isabel Hungerland. (1958). *Poetic Discourse*; see particularly Chapter 1, 'Language and Poetry'.

12.   Winifred Nowottny. (1962). *The Language Poets Use*, p. 72, 'the chief difference between language in poems and language outside poems is that the one is more highly structured than the other...'

13.   Shakespeare, Sonnet No. 129.

14.   R. P. Blackmur. (1954), p. 18.

15.   *Ibid.*, p. 6.

16.   *Aristotle on the Art of Poetry*, tr. by Ingram Bywater (Oxford, 1954), p. 35.

17.   Graham Hough. (1966). *An Essay in Criticism*, p. 19.

18. W.W. Robson. (1966). *Critical Essays*, see chapter 3, 'English as a University Subject', p. 38.

19. There is a discussion of this inherent conflict in T. S. Kuhn. (1962). *The Structure of Scientific Revolution.*

20. *Neophilologus.* April 1968, pp. 192-3.

21. See, for instance, Roman Jakobson. (1960). 'Closing Statement; Linguistics and Poetics': 'Since linguistics is the global science of verbal structure, poetics may be regarded as an integral part of linguistics', *Style in Language*, ed. Sebeok, p. 350.

22. It also implies an overlap with critical interests – cf. Bateson's use of the term in his discussion with Fowler, chapter 5. The way is thus opened for subjective discussions of this sort, 'And a limited and tentative definition of "style" could be that use of language as a result of which we are compelled, while listening or reading, to see ourselves as the ultimate object of exploration – however fantastic the events narrated', David Daiches. (1948). *A Study of Literature*, p. 35. Such definitions fail to measure up to the **criterion of principles** (see Glossary).

23. T. Sebeok ed. (1960). *Style in Language.*

24. Roger Fowler ed. (1966). *Essays on Style and Language.*

25. John B. Carroll. 'Vectors of Prose Style', pp. 283-292 of *Style in Language*, T.Sebeok ed.

26. Dorothy Whitelock. (1951). *The Audience of Beowulf.*

27. G.C. Coulton. (1963). *Chaucer and his England.*

28. E.M.W. Tillyard. (1943). *The Elizabethan World Picture.*

29. J.L. Lowes. (1951). *The Road to Xanadu.*

30. Malcolm Bradbury ed. (1971). *Contemporary Criticism.*

31. Trevor Eaton. (1966). *The Semantics of Literature*, p. 57.

32. Walter Koch. (1966). *Recurrence and a Three-modal Approach to Poetry.*

33. See Malcolm Bradbury, ed. (1971).

34. T. Sebeok, ed. (1960), pp. 283-292. *Statistics and Style*, ed. Lubomír Doležel and Richard W. Bailey, is an excellent collation of articles illustrating in general the application of the principles of empirical semics.

35. Particularly pp. 81-2 but cf. p. 88 where, if their first comment is carried to its logical conclusion, they would appear to be arguing in favour of investigating the situation of a modern contemporary secondary encoder (e.g. the priest, in the case of liturgical language) rather than the original encoder. For further discussion, see [LS:183].

36. William Righter. (1963). pp. 91-100.

37. Richard Foster. (1962), see chapter 8.

38. Graham Hough. (1966), p. 8.

39. David Lodge. (1966). in *The Language of Fiction*, discusses briefly the relation between literature and linguistics, touching upon this point, p. 57, '... values are not amenable to the scientific method.'

40. F. W. Bateson. (1950). *English Poetry: A Critical Introduction*, pp. 7-9.

41. A similar ambiguity occurs in Chaucer's reference to the Prioress's rosary: *Amor vincit omnia* (see *General Prologue* line 162). Is it devotional or romantic? Readers' interpretations may be fed by prior mind-sets.

CHAPTER FIVE NOTES

1.   The Bateson-Fowler Controversy, p. 457.
2.   *Ibid.,* p. 460.
3.   *Ibid.,* p. 459.
4.   *Ibid.,* pp. 460-1.
5.   *Ibid.,* p. 461.
6.   *Ibid.,* p. 462.
7.   *Ibid.,* p. 457.
8.   *Ibid.,* p. 460. See also Roger Fowler's article (1966). 'Linguistics, stylistics, criticism?' in *Lingua*, Vol. 16:153-65.
9.   *Ibid.,* p. 458.
10.   *Ibid.,* pp. 460-1.
11.   *Ibid.,* p. 460.
12.   *Ibid.,* p. 463.
13.   *Ibid.,* pp. 464-5.
14.   *Ibid.,* p. 328.
15.   *Ibid.,* p. 464 of *Essays in Criticism*, October 1966.
16.   P. 330 of *Essays in Criticism*, July 1967.
17.   *Ibid.,* p. 327.
18.   P. 168 of *Essays in Criticism*, April 1968. Mr. Fowler has pointed out to me that his main purpose here was to emphasize that the distinction between science and art is a false one.
19.   P. 328 of *Essays in Criticism*, July, 1967.
20.   *Ibid.,* p. 331.
21.   *Ibid.,* p. 331.
22.   *Ibid.,* p. 332.
23.   *Ibid.,* pp. 333-4.
24.   *Ibid.,* p. 336.
25.   *Ibid.,* p. 340.
26.   *Ibid.,* p. 337.
27.   *Ibid.,* p. 338.
28.   *Ibid.,* p. 336. But cf. my note 18, above.
29.   *Ibid.,* p. 338.
30.   In note 2, p. 346, Bateson makes it clear that he himself locates the value of literature in the response of the reader and not on the printed page.
31.   Pp. 338-9. There is a discussion of the place of syntax in poetry in Donald Davie, *Articulate Energy* (London, 1955), see particularly the account of T. E. Hulme's views in chapter 1.
32.   P. 340 of *Essays in Criticism*, July, 1967.
33.   Pp. 82-93, 'The Application of Linguistics to the Study of Poetic Language'.
34.   Ezra Pound, 'Papyrus'; see *Personae: Collected Shorter Poems of Ezra Pound* (London 1952), p. 122. (1) [LS:66] is not an extract, but the entire text as published by Pound. I omit the title 'Papyrus', as Bateson's exegesis is confined to the text itself.
35.   P. 341 of *Essays in Criticism* (July, 1967).

36.   *Ibid.,* p. 342.
37.   *Ibid.,* pp. 343-4.
38.   *Ibid.,* p. 345.
39.   P. 458 of *Essays in Criticism*, October 1966.
40.   Pp. 165-6 of *Essays in Criticism*, April 1968.
41.   See for instance, Isabel Hungerland, *Poetic Discourse* (Berkeley1958), p. 5; 'I have rejected the descriptive-emotive dichotomy as being an ineffective instrument for the task'. This question is also discussed in chapter 2 of this book.
42.   *Ibid.,* p. 169.
43.   P. 172; Fowler observes that he is here using the term 'style' with some misgivings. A theory of this concept (without the term) appeared in *Linguistics* (November 1970), 'Against Idealization'.
44.   *Ibid.,* p. 173.
45.   *Ibid.,* p. 173.
46.   *Ibid.,* p. 174.
47.   *Ibid.,* p. 177; Fowler informs me that he deliberately refrained from commenting upon Sinclair's analysis as there was then a possibility that Sinclair might himself reply to Bateson.
48.   *Ibid.,* pp. 178-9.
49.   Fowler observes that he has avoided formal analyses as a matter of strategy. He has never advocated linguistic analyses of literary texts as a substitute for critical analyses, but only critical analyses informed by a formal knowledge of how language works.
50.   P. 181. Mr. Bateson has kindly drawn my attention to an article 'Linguistics and Literary Criticism' which he contributed to *The Disciplines of Criticism* (New Haven, 1968), ed. Peter Demetz *et al.* He there elaborates his conception of the literary transaction, following de Saussure's *circuit de la langue*, and introducing extra stages in the process of literary communication. Basically, however, his above analysis still stands, and for the sake of simplicity I will preserve this, since I believe my own comments will apply equally to the later account. Bateson makes further comments on the *langue/parole* dichotomy and the inadequacy of stylistics in 'Stilus, An Iron Implement' pp. 264-8 of *Essays in Criticism* (April, 1970).
51.   *Ibid.,* p. 182.
52.   G.N. Leech expresses a similar view, '... linguistics and literary criticism, in so far as they both deal with poetic language, are complementary not competing activities', p. 60, *A Linguistic Guide to English Poetry*, (1969) p. 60.
53.   See, for instance, Marcus B. Hester, *The Meaning of Poetic Metaphor* (1967), p. 128. W.K. Wimsatt, Jr., in *The Verbal Icon* (1958), devotes two essays to discussion of these 'fallacies'; this part of the book was written in collaboration with Monroe C. Beardsley.
54.   George Watson in (1969). *The Study of Literature*, p. 151, makes much the same point. Watson is, however, more sanguine concerning the possible eventual collaboration of linguists and literary historians than is Bateson.
55.   P. 341 of *Essays in Criticism*, July, 1967.
56.   See, for instance, Walter Koch. (1966). *Recurrence and a Three-Modal Approach to Poetry*.

57.   Cf. Noam Chomsky. (1965). *Aspects of the Theory of Syntax*, p. 16: 'This system of rules can be analyzed into the three major components of a generative grammar: the syntactic, phonological, and semantic components'. Of course, 'grammar' can be used in the narrower sense, but in that case the linguist's concern is much wider than grammar. Bateson cannot be allowed to equate 'linguist' and 'grammarian' and then to argue that since the latter is concerned with grammar in the narrow sense, there are some linguistic utterances beyond the scope of the linguist.

58.   Robert Graves. (1949). *The Common Asphodel*, p. 148.

59.   G.S. Fraser. (1960). *Ezra Pound*, p. 111.

60.   P. 335 of *Essays in Criticism*, July, 1967.

61.   Geoffrey N. Leech. (1969). *A Linguistic Guide to English Poetry*, p. 220.

62.   *The Explicator*, Feb. 1951.

63.   *Notes and Queries*, June, 1958, pp. 265-6.

64.   *Literary Essays of Ezra Pound*, ed. T.S.Eliot (1954), p. 25.

65.   [LS:35].

66.   C.K. Ogden and I.A. Richards, *The Meaning of Meaning* (London, 1923).

67.   I.A. Richards. (1924).*The Principles of Literary Criticism*, p. 246.

68.   *Ibid.,* p. 37.

69.   See Chapter 1, 'On the Teaching of Modern Literature', in Lionel Trilling. (1966). *Beyond Culture*.

70.   *Essays in Criticism* (July, 1967), pp. 342-345.

71.   See F.R. Leavis, '"English" – Unrest and Continuity', an opening address at a Colloquium on 'English' held by the University of Wales at Gregynog' reprinted in *The Times Literary Supplement,* 29th May, 1969; '...the problem of acquiring something coherent, meaningful and organic, a living reality that he [the student] can carry away with him (or *in* him)...' p. 570 – square brackets mine. Leavis further discusses the rôle of English at universities in 'Literature and the University: the Wrong Question', pp. 39-60 of *English Literature in our Time and the University* (London, 1969).

72.   John Holt. (1964). *How Children Fail*, p. 174.

73.   W.W. Robson, though with some reservations, acknowledges the need for this, 'I would urge the importance, as a criterion of university studies, of some reference to a *genuine body of knowledge*'(his italics): (1966). *Critical Essays*, p.27.

74.   P. 344 of *Essays in Criticism*, July 1967.

75.   In this respect, see George Kane. (1965). *The Autobiographical Fallacy in Chaucer and Langland Studies* 'We can then, as things are, have no biography of Langland, only speculative "lives", without historical necessity', p. 17.

76.   Final Examination Schools, University of Oxford, 1947.

77.   W.W. Robson, *Critical Essays, op. cit.*, p. 44.

78.   F.R. Leavis, *op. cit., T.L.S.,* p. 569, hints at this possibility: 'I know I can't assume that everyone who holds a post in "English" believes intensely that English Literature matters – believes that it ought to be a potent living reality in the present, so that to succeed in making it that would be to do something important towards remedying those disorders of civilized society which frighten us'.

79.   *Essays in Criticism*, October, 1969, pp. 420-6.

80.   *Theory of Literature* (1961), R. Wellek and A. Warren, p. 157. 'The work

of art, then, appears as an object of knowledge *sui generis* which has a special ontological status. It is neither real (like a statue) nor mental (like the experience of light or pain) nor ideal (like a triangle). It is a system of norms of ideal concepts which are intersubjective. They must be assumed to exist in collective ideology, changing with it, accessible only through individual mental experiences, based on the sound structure of its sentences'.

81.   P. 423 of *Essays in Criticism*, October, 1969.

82.   Pp. 426-433 of *Essays in Criticism*, October, 1969.

83.   *Ibid.,* p. 427.

84.   *Ibid.,* p. 428.

85.   *Ibid.,* p. 428.

86.   *Ibid.,* pp. 49-52.

87.   P. 431 of *Essays in Criticism*, October 1969.

88.   P. 433. E.B. Greenwood writes a brief note in support of Bateson's position. Greenwood re-asserts the objectivity of what is communicated in criticism – *Essays in Criticism*, April 1970, 'The Sceptical Dane: A Note on Cay Dollerup's Doubts about the Objectivity of Criticism', pp. 271-3.

89.   Cf. [LS:41].

90.   P. 432 of *Essays in Criticism*, October, 1969.

91.   In fairness to Dollerup, I do not think he ever claimed that such communication was impossible, cf. [LS:82] Dollerup's quoted assertion in the penultimate summary of his argument.

CHAPTER SIX NOTES

1.   The second of two articles contributed by Rodger to Hugh Fraser and W.R. O'Donnell eds. (1969). *Applied Linguistics and the Teaching of English*, pp. 176-216.

2.   Rodger includes both the above medieval version and a modern printed version of the lyric, his references being to the latter. In my own summary of his argument, the references will for the sake of convenience be adjusted to (1), [LS:89]. MS Harley 7578 is in the British Museum, see Frontispiece reproduction.

3.   *Ibid.,* p. 178.

4.   *Ibid.,* p. 194.

5.   *Ibid.,* pp. 180-1.

6.   *Ibid.,* pp. 181-2.

7.   *Ibid.,* p. 183.

8.   *Ibid.,* pp. 183-6.

9.   For discussion of 'cohesion', see M.A.K.Halliday. 'The Linguistic Study of Literary Texts', pp.217-223 of *Essays on the Language of Literature*, pp. 217-23, (1967) ed. Seymour Chatman and Samuel R. Levin; also 'Descriptive Linguistics in Literary Studies' in *Patterns of Language*, pp.56-69, (1966) ed. M.A.K. Halliday and A. McIntosh. Paper No. 7 of the *Programme in Linguistics and English Teaching* (Communications Research Centre, London 1968). 'Grammatical Cohesion in Spoken and

Written English' by Ruqaiya Hasan might also be noted.

10.   P. 187 of Rodger's article.
11.   *Ibid.*, p. 192.
12.   *Ibid.*, pp. 192-3.
13.   *Ibid.*, p. 194.
14.   *Ibid.*, p. 195.
15.   *Ibid.*, p. 197.
16.   For a discussion of 'foregrounding', see G.N. Leech. (1969). *A Linguistic Guide to English Poetry*, pp. 56-58.
17.   S = Subject; P = Predicator (i.e. verb/verbal complex); C = Complement (object); A = Adjunct (i.e. adverbial, prepositional or conjunctive group).
18.   Pp. 199-200 of Rodger's article.
19.   *Ibid.*, pp. 201-2.
20.   *Ibid.*, pp. 202-4
21.   *Ibid.*, p. 204
22.   *Ibid.*, p. 205.
23.   *Ibid.*, p. 206
24.   *Ibid.*, pp. 207-9
25.   *Ibid.*, p. 209
26.   *Ibid.*, p. 210.
27.   *Ibid.*, p. 210. See also his discussion in chapter 6, 'Linguistics and the Teaching of Literature', pp. 88-98.
28.   *Ibid.*, pp. 210-211.
29.   *Ibid.*, p. 177.
30.   *Ibid.*, p. 178.
31.   *Ibid.*, p. 180.
32.   *Ibid.*, p. 180.
33.   *Ibid.*, p. 180
34.   *Ibid.*, p. 182
35.   *Ibid.*, p. 186.
36.   *Ibid.*, p. 213, Rodger's footnote 7, 'In my view, Chambers and Sidgwick instinctively supplied the correct punctuation, and it is significant that no later editor has punctuated this line to give appositional function to its three nominal groups'. It might be mentioned that there occur in the musical notation accompanying the lyric, clusters of vertical lines, indicating rests in the music. These rests always coincide with clause boundaries, though at the end of each line preceding the refrain we find clause boundaries unmarked by a musical rest. Perhaps it is not entirely true to say that the manuscript is without punctuation.
37.   *Ibid.*, p. 194.
38.   On this point, see N.E. Enkvist, J. Spencer and Michael Gregory, *Linguistics and Style* (1964), 'An Approach to the Study of Style' by Spencer and Gregory pp. 82-3.
39.   P. 194 of Rodger's article.
40.   *Ibid.*, p. 195.
41.   *Ibid.*, p.187.
42.   Anyone who deciphered this word in the manuscript relying on modern orthographical conventions would, I believe, almost certainly decide in favour of a singular. See Frontispiece.

43.   See Lubomír Doležel and Richard W. Bailey, eds., (1969). *Statistics and Style*, particularly the article by Bailey, 'Statistics and Style: A Historical Survey', pp. 217-36.

44.   The two quantitative principles stated in David Crystal and Derek Davy, (1969), *Investigating English Style,* p.21, are of this sort, '...the more important stylistic feature in a text will be (a) that which occurs more frequently within the variety in question, and (b) that which is shared less by other varieties'.

45.   *Ibid.,* p.186.

46.   For brief elementary accounts of this method, see S.H. Mellone. (1966). *Elements of Modern Logic*, pp. 235-38; J.G. Brennan. (1957). *A Handbook of Logic*, pp. 195-97; L. Susan Stebbing. (1943). *A Modern Elementary Logic*, pp. 173-9.

47.   See John B. Carroll. (1960). 'Vectors of Prose Style', in *Style in Language*, pp. 283-92.

48.   P. 194 of Rodger's article.

49.   See John McH. Sinclair. (1968). 'A Technique of Stylistic Description', pp. 215-42 of *Language and Style*, Autumn. Sinclair is working towards this kind of analysis – see his Section 5, p. 223.

50.   See Charles Muller, 'Lexical Distribution Reconsidered: TheWaring-Herdan Formula', pp. 42-56 of *Statistics and Style*, ed. Lubomír Doležel and Richard W. Bailey (1969), originally published in *Cahiers de Lexicologie VI* (1965).

CHAPTER SEVEN NOTES

1.   See, for instance, Walter A. Koch. (1966), *Recurrence and a Three-Modal Approach to Poetry*; also M.A.K. Halliday and Angus McIntosh. (1966). *Patterns of Language*. A more recent attempt by John Mc H. Sinclair, which counters the allegation that linguistic critics concentrate upon the Thomas/ cummings' type of poem, appears in *Language and Style*, Autumn, 1968, 'A Technique of Stylistic Description', pp. 215-242.

2.   It should be noted that Fowler's definition of linguistic analysis envisages an explanation of the psychological processes underlying the experience of reading literature – see [LS:68]. In practice, however, linguistic analysis falls short of this.

3.   Michael Riffaterre. (1967). 'Criteria for Style Analysis' in *Essays on the Language of Literature*, reprinted from *Word*, April 1959, expresses part of the problem in stylistic terms, thus, '...on the one hand, *stylistic facts can be apprehended only in language, since that is their vehicle*; on the other hand, *they must have a specific character, since otherwise they could not be distinguished from linguistic facts'* (his italics), p. 412.

4.   M.A.K. Halliday, Angus McIntosh and Peter Strevens. (1964). *The Linguistic Sciences and Language Teaching*, pp. 97-8.

5.   Noam Chomsky. (1966). *Cartesian Linguistics*, pp. 27-8, where Humboldt's work is criticized for failing to observe this distinction.

6. The sentence which Coleridge quotes in his own account is a rough paraphrase of the sentence above. Presumably Coleridge was writing from memory and did not trouble to check his reference. For actual reference see *Purchas his Pilgrimage* (London, 1626), p. 418, Book IV, chapter 13.

7. John Livingston Lowes. (1927). *The Road to Xanadu*, argues that Coleridge made a mistake and that the incident did not take place then, but in 1798; p. 357.

8. These prefatory lines were written for the publication of *Kubla Khan* in 1816. See p. 296 of *The Poetical Works of Samuel Taylor Coleridge,* ed. E.H. Coleridge.

9. *Letters of Samuel Taylor Coleridge*, ed., Ernest Hartley Coleridge, Volume 1, p. 180, 'I am, and ever have been, a great reader, and have read almost everything – a library cormorant.' (November 19th, 1796).

10. *The Road to Xanadu, op.cit.*, p. 359.

11. *Ibid.,* p. 376.

12. Cf. [LS:56].

13. *Ibid.,* p. 376.

14. Chapter XXI.

15. *Ibid.,* p. 424.

16. *Ibid.,* p. 411.

17. *Ibid.,* p. 411.

18. *Ibid.,* p. 412.

19. *Ibid.,* p. 401.

20. *Ibid.,* p. 430.

21. William Empson. (1964). 'The Ancient Mariner', in *Critical Quarterly*, Winter, pp. 317-8, suggests that Coleridge was lying.

22. See Elizabeth Schneider. (1966). *Coleridge, Opium and Kubla Khan*, chapter 5, and her references pp. 353-7. Also, Marshall Suther. (1965). *Visions of Xanadu*, particularly chapter 5 and the Bibliography pp. 289-90.

23. An attempt on the part of an individual to formulate such a structure is Louis Hjelmslev. (1963). *Prolegomena to a Theory of Language*, tr. Francis J. Whitfield.

24. Noam Chomsky. (1966). *Cartesian Linguistics*, p. 6 ff.

25. Noam Chomsky. (1968). *Language and Mind*, p. 58, and p. 64, 'There is an obvious sense in which any aspect of psychology is based ultimately on the observation of behavior'.

26. Ernest Gellner, 'On Chomsky', *New Society*, 29th May, 1969, p. 832.

27. John Lyons sums up neatly the standpoint of the linguist, 'The position that should be maintained by the linguist is one that is neutral with respect to 'mentalism' and 'mechanism'; a position that is consistent with both and implies neither.'(1968). *Introduction to Theoretical Linguistics*, p. 408.

28. Discussion on the B.B.C. Third Programme; See *The Listener*, Thursday, 30th May, 1968, 'Noam Chomsky and Stuart Hampshire discuss the study of language' pp. 687-691, 'I think that we could show this empirically: we should be able to show that there would be a qualitative difference in the way I would interpret and master this material [i.e. a structure-independent code] as compared with the way I would master and interpret the material from a normal human language'. For further discussion on these lines, see (1965), *Aspects of the Theory of Syntax*, pp. 47-59.

29. First John Locke Lecture delivered at University College, London, on April 29th 1969. The Lecture is excerpted in *The Times Literary Supplement*, 15th May, 1969, pp. 523-525. 'I would only suggest that we now also abandon the terms "association", "conditioning", "reinforcement" and "behaviourism" now that they have been deprived of whatever content they have in the psychological literature, and now that all the characteristic assumptions of behaviourism have been abandoned'.

30. Arthur Koestler. (1967). *The Ghost in the Machine, passim.*

31. R.M.W. Dixon. (1965). *What is Language?* pp. 105-7. Dixon's position has since been considerably modified.

32. See R.M.W. Dixon's criticisms of Chomsky's mathematical logical approach, particularly (1963). *Linguistic Science and Logic,* pp. 81-85: 'Chomsky's "description" is of language not as it is but as it might be, the "might be" being deducible from Chomsky's own theory!' – p. 82. Thomas Pollock (1942). *The Nature of Literature*, p. 56, discussing the question 'What is Literature?' writes, 'There have been, are, and presumably will be an uncounted – *n* – number of actual speech transactions. The problem which any study of the uses of language faces, therefore, is the determination of the useful classifications which can be made of these uncounted speech transactions'.

33. See the discussion in Chapter Two of G. N. Leech (1969). *A Linguistic Guide to English Poetry*. Samuel Levin's discussion of grammaticalness may be noted in this respect – particularly the generative rules he formulates for cummings' 'he danced his did' – 'Poetry and Grammaticalness', pp. 224-30, of *Essays on the Language of Literature*, ed. S. Chatman and Levin.

34. C.E. Osgood, G.J. Suci and P.H. Tannenbaum. (1957). *The Measurement of Meaning.*

35. W.J.M. Bronzwaer. (1967). *Journal of Aesthetics and Art Criticism*, Winter, pp. 262-4.

36. Stephen Ullmann. (1964). *Language and Style*, p. 2l.

37. E.C. Zeeman. (1962). 'The Topology of the Brain and Visual Perception', in *Topology of 3-Manifolds*, ed. M.K. Fort, pp. 240-56. Also, (1965).'Topology of the Brain', *Mathematics and Computer Science in Biology and Medicine* (Medical Research Council) and E.C. Zeeman and O.P. Buneman, *Tolerance Spaces and the Brain* (Mimeograph, no date).

38. 'The Topology of the Brain and Visual Perception', *op.cit.*, p. 244 ff.

39. *Ibid.*, p. 247.

40. Stephen Grossberg. (1969). 'On the Serial Learning of Lists', *Mathematical Biosciences 4*, pp. 201-53.

41. J.R. Firth. (1957). *Papers in Linguistics, 1934-1951*, p. 187. Thomas Pollock, *The Nature of Literature*, *op. cit.*, p. 165, writes, 'The response of any particular reader to any particular series of symbols will depend, not only on the symbols themselves, but also on the reader's psycho-physiological characteristics at the moment of reading. This is a fact which theorists often overlook...' Similarly, David Lodge, *The Language of Fiction*, *op. cit.* p. 58, 'The paradoxical relationship between the formally fixed artefact and the necessarily variable human responses to it is one of the grounds for asserting that literary criticism can never be a science'.

42. Walter A. Koch. (1966). *Recurrence and a Three-Modal Approach to*

Poetry, p.34, 'Thus, a poem which is commonly held to be of an extremely high value may evince a low degree of poeticalness according to the criteria put forward so far'.

43.   For an example of a geometrical model, employing the principle of symmetry, used in anthropological research, see G.B. Milner. (1969). 'Siamese twins, birds and the double helix' in *Man* Volume 4, No. 1, March, particularly pp. 17-23.

44.   E.C. Zeeman, 'Topology of the Brain', *op.cit.*, p. 281.

45.   See Arthur Koestler. (1967). *The Ghost in the Machine, passim*, where Koestler attacks the naiveté of the early behaviourists. George Miller expresses some disillusionment with behaviourism in his Foreword to *Language in the Crib*, (1962) by Ruth Weir, pp. 13-17. Jerrold J. Katz. (1966). *The Philosophy of Language*, p. 269, claims a high content for the 'Language Acquisition Device', including, for instance, 'a methodology for choosing optimal linguistic descriptions'; and Chomsky. (1965). *Aspects of the Theory of Syntax*, p. 30 ff. argues similarly. D. McNeill, 'Developmental Psycholinguistics', pp. 15-82 of *The Genesis of Language* ed. Frank Smith, actually goes so far as to refer to an innate *faculté de langage* – p.65. There has been much discussion of the question in recent years, cf. Colin Fraser's amusing parody of the Chomskian view in (1966). *Psycholinguistics Papers*, ed. J. Lyons and R. J. Wales p. 116: 'Metaphorically speaking, a child is now born with a copy of *Aspects of the Theory of Syntax* tucked away somewhere inside'.

46.   Charles Hockett. (1966). *The State of the Art*, p. 79.

47.   L. Wittgenstein. (1955). *Tractatus Logico-Philosophicus*.

48.   Alexander Maslow. (1961). *A Study in Wittgenstein's 'Tractatus'*, pp. 11-12, comments upon the 'metaphysical strain' in Wittgenstein's treatment of the 'object' – at least as implied in his terminology. Maslow originally wrote this book as a positivist in 1933, but has since changed his views.

49.   Willard Van Orman Quine.(1960). *Word and Object*, p. 3, says, 'On the face of it there is a certain verbal perversity in the idea that ordinary talk of familiar physical things is not in large part understood as it stands, or that the familiar physical things are not real, or that evidence for their reality needs to be uncovered'.

50.   See, for instance, Winifred Nowottny. (1962). *The Language Poets Use*, p. 85, 'Indeed, many of the problems of discussing structures of meaning originate in the very fact that words provoke unverbalized processes, such as the apprehension of relationships, and they refer us to objects in real life which as it were express in shorthand the long stream of our consciousness of process.' **In this statement, she comes close to communicating the, by my definition, incommunicable: at least a small part of the cerebral activities of what is meant by the term** *knowledge three*.

51.   For a discussion of maps and models, see S. Toulmin. (1953). *The Philosophy of Science: an Introduction*, Chapter IV, pp. 105-39.

52.   *Antony and Cleopatra*, Act I, Scene II.

53.   Cf. Arden ed., lines 181-2, 'Sextus Pompeius hath given the dare to Caesar'.

54.   For a brief discussion of the 'paraphrastic heresy' see G.N. Leech. (1969). *A Linguistic Guide to English Poetry*, pp. 39-40. See also Cleanth Brooks. (1949). *The Well Wrought Urn*, pp. 176-196.

55.   Herbert Grierson, ed. (1956). *Metaphysical Lyrics and Poems of the*

Seventeenth Century, Herbert Grierson, p. 11.

56.   Dylan Thomas. (1967). *Under Milk Wood*, p. 37.

57.   *Ibid.*, p. 44.

58.   The study of the relations that hold amongst sentences within a given text.

59.   *Under Milk Wood, op. cit.*, p. 27.

60.   'Grammaticality' is defined as what those structures have in common that are maximally secure.

61.   A less disputable example would be the proverbial, 'God helps those who help themselves, providing they don't steal', where the first unambiguous context of 'helps' veils the ambiguity of the reflexive 'help', and this in turn is brought to light through syntagmatic dynamism by the use of 'steal' in the appended clause of condition.

62.   For this example, I am indebted to Mr. G.B. Milner, who discussed its possibilities at a recent meeting of The Linguistics Association of Great Britain.

63.   G.N. Leech. (1969). *A Linguistic Guide to English Poetry*, pp. 134 and 154.

64.   *Under Milk Wood, op.cit.*, p.63.

65.   *Julius Caesar*, Act III, Scene 2 (Arden ed.). See Walter A. Koch. (1966). *Recurrence and a Three-Modal Approach to Poetry*, p. 18.

66.   The Editor of the Arden edition observes, 'Not only does this realistic little discussion "cover" the whispered conversation of Brutus and Cassius, but it illustrates admirably how men will conceal pent-up feelings by talking about trivial things'. The extract occurs in Act II, Scene 1 (commencing line 101 in the Arden edition).

CHAPTER EIGHT NOTES

1.   See John B. Carroll, ed. (1956). *Language, Thought and Reality: Selected Writings of Benjamin Lee Whorf*, pp. 134-59.

2.   The issue of 'computation' versus 'storage' is raised in 'Reflections on the Conference' by James J. Jenkins. See (1966). *The Genesis of Language* ed. Frank Smith and G.A. Miller, p. 355.

3.   Noam Chomsky. (1965). *Aspects of the Theory of Syntax*, p.25, '... the child constructs a grammar...'.

4.   See, for instance, *The Genesis of Language, op.cit.*, pp. 246-7.

5.   Stephen Ullmann. (1957). *The Principles of Semantics*, p. 70.

6.   Two papers have recently been delivered at Conferences of The Linguistics Association of Great Britain calling in question the concept of 'deep structure': Dr. E.C. Fudge, 'Grammar and Deep Structure' (November, 1968); and Mr. P.H. Matthews, 'Some Queries concerning Deep Structure' (November, 1969). In this talk Matthews made out an 'advocate's case' against the usefulness of the deep structure concept. The issue here, of course, does not affect my argument.

7.   Isaac Asimov. (1965). *The Human Brain: Its Capabilities and Functions*, p. 304.

8.   Ivor Catt, 'Dinosaur among the data', *The New Scientist*, 6th March, 1969,

pp. 501-2.
9.   In an account of Potebnja's poetic theory, Krystyna Pomorska expounds, 'From poetic language, which, as in folk poetry, is the primary mode of expression, to the "prosaic" language of communication and back to poetic language – such is, according to Potebnja, the path of linguistic development'. (1968). *Russian Formalist Theory and its Poetic Ambiance*, p. 63.
10.   This poem is discussed by Nancy Sullivan. (1968). *Perspective and the Poetic Process*, pp. 14-16.
11.   See, for instance, Geoffrey N. Leech. (1969). *A Linguistic Guide to English Poetry*, pp. 150-1.

CHAPTER NINE NOTES

1.   *English Studies*, April 1975, pp. 174-6.
2.   *Review of English Studies*, August 1975, pp. 361-3.
3.   *Modern Language Review,* July 1975, pp. 579-81.
4.   F. R. Leavis, *The Great Tradition* (London, 1948), p. 1.
5.   Karl R. Popper. (1969). *Conjectures and Refutations: The Growth of Scientific Knowledge*, p. 33: '*I wished to distinguish between science and pseudo-science*; knowing very well that science often errs, and that pseudo-science may happen to stumble on the truth.' (His italics.)
6.   *Ibid.*, p. 35.
7.   *Ibid.*, p. 46.
8.   Carl G. Hempel. (1966). *Philosophy of Natural Science*, p. 15.
9.   P.B. Medawar. (1969). *Induction and Intuition in Scientific Thought*, p. 41.
10.   John M. Lipski. (1976). 'On the Metastructures of Literary Discourse'. *Journal of Literary Semantics*, 5/2, p. 53.
11.   E. J. Lemmon. (1965). *Beginning Logic*.
12.   *The Great Tradition*, *op.cit.*, p. 22.
13.   *Ibid.* p. 2.
14.   René Wellek, 'Literary Criticism and Philosophy', *Scrutiny* Vol. V/4, March 1937, pp. 375-383: 'I could wish that you had stated your assumptions more explicitly and defended them systematically', p. 376. Leavis' reply appeared in *Scrutiny* Vol. VI, June 1937, 'Literary Criticism and Philosophy: A Reply', pp. 59-70: '...Dr. Wellek is a philosopher; and my reply to him in the first place is that I myself am not a philosopher, and that I doubt whether in any case I could elaborate a theory that he would find satisfactory...I have pretensions – pretensions to being a literary critic... Literary criticism and philosophy seem to me to be quite distinct and different kinds of discipline...'.
15.   See also my discussion of Spitzer, [LS: 154–157] in chapter 10.
16.   See (1966). *The Semantics of Literature* and (1972) *Theoretical Semics*, *passim*.

17. For a short critique of my concept, see A.P. Foulkes. (1975). *The Search for Literary Meaning.*
18. For confirming what I had long suspected on this point, I am indebted to Dr. David Dewhirst of the Institute of Astronomy, University of Cambridge.
19. For a book devoted to this problem, discussing fictive propositions against the background of modal and many-valued logics, see John Woods. (1974). *The Logic of Fiction.*

CHAPTER TEN NOTES

1. Leo Spitzer (1962). *Linguistics and Literary History: Essays in Stylistics.* A briefer statement appears in '*Explication de Texte* applied to three great Middle English poems'. *Archivum Linguisticum*, 3:1-22;137-65. In a footnote, pp. 2-3, Spitzer writes, 'In reality, my procedure involves two separate movements (both of which, taken together, serve to complete the "philological circle"): I first draw from one detail (which need not always be linguistic or stylistic, but may also be compositional in nature) of incontrovertible factual evidence, an inference as to the (at this stage still hypothetic) psyche of the author or the period, which hypothesis is then, in a second movement controlled by a scrutiny of (to the degree that this is feasible) *all* other striking details (stylistic or compositional) which occur in the same author or period.' For a defence of the 'humanity' of his method against the onslaught of Bloomfieldian mechanism, see *Language* 20:45-55;245-51, 'Answer to Mr. Bloomfield'.
2. *Loc. cit., Linguistics and Literary History*, p. 11.
3. *Ibid.*, p. 13.
4. *Ibid.,* p. 19, 'There is no shadow of truth in the objection raised not long ago by one of the representatives of the mechanist Yale school of linguists against the "circularity of arguments" of the mentalists: against the "explanation" of a linguistic fact by an assumed psychological process for which the only evidence is the fact to be explained.'
5. *Ibid.*, p. 19.
6. *Ibid.*, p. 20.
7. *Ibid.*, p. 14.
8. *Ibid.*, p. 19.
9. *Ibid.*, p. 14.
10. *Ibid.*, p. 14.
11. *Ibid.*, pp. 24-5.
12. *Ibid.*, p. 28.
13. *Ibid.*, p. 29.
14. See Mary B. Hesse. (1970). *Models and Analogies in Science, passim.* Also Norman Campbell. (1952). *What is Science?*, p. 84, says, 'And so by tracing a relation between the unfamiliar changes which gases undergo when their temperature or volume is altered, and the extremely familiar changes which accompany the motions and mutual reactions of solid bodies, we are rendering the former more intelligible; we are explaining

them.' John Hospers. (1970) in *An Introduction to Philosophical Analysis* also discusses 'invisibility' in explanation; p. 244.

15. *Linguistics and Literary History*, loc. cit., p. 29.
16. *Ibid.,* p. 11.
17. *Ibid.,* p. 14.
18. *Ibid.,* p. 14.
19. *Ibid.,* p. 28.
20. 'Criteria for Style Analysis' (1959) *Word* 15:154-74.
21. *Ibid.,* p. 154.
22. *Ibid.,* p. 163.
23. *Ibid.,* p. 155.
24. (1969). *Style: The Problem and its Solution.*
25. *Ibid.,* p. 7.
26. *Ibid.,* pp. 13-15.
27. *Ibid.,* Chapter 2.
28. *Ibid.,* pp. 52-3.
29. *Ibid.,* p. 66.
30. *Ibid.,* p. 87.
31. *Ibid.,* p. 90.
32. *Ibid.,* pp. 98-106.
33. *Ibid.,* pp.83-4.
34. *Ibid.,* p. 110. Gray's later book (1975). *The Phenomenon of Literature*, pp. 33-4, gives evidence that Gray has not relented. 'In *Style: The Problem and its Solution* (The Hague, 1969) we have gone into great detail to show that style is an empty concept and that it never has had nor can have any systematic application in literary study. Moreover, in "Stylistics: The End of a Tradition" we have tried to give an historical accounting of why style should seem to literary scholars such a self-evident concept despite its manifest conceptual and analytic inadequacies.' The present chapter demonstrates, I believe, that Gray's 'solution' is both wasteful of a useful concept and unnecessary.
35. See, for instance, James R. Bennett. (1976). 'A Stylistics Checklist'. *Style*.10/3:350-401.
36. W. M. Thorburn, having appealed to readers of *Mind* for information, published an article in that Journal: Vol. 27, 1918, pp. 345-53, 'The Myth of Occam's Razor'. In this he argued, p. 350, '"Occam's Razor" is a modern myth. There is nothing mediaeval in it, except the general sense of the post-mediaeval formula...'. C. Delisle Burns in a Note, *Mind*, Vol. 24, 1915 puts forward the view that the formula, strictly interpreted, is contrary to the spirit of Occam's philosophy: he would never have supposed it possible to multiply 'real things'.
37. See W.D. Ross ed. (1936). Aristotle's *Physics*, ed. W.D. Ross; Book I iv, line 17; 'and it is better to assume a smaller and finite number of principles, as Empedocles does'.
38. See Dorothy Fisk. (1959). *Dr. Jenner of Berkeley*, pp. 20 and 122.
39. Anthony Kenny. (1978). *The Aristotelian Ethics*. The paper I heard was read at Cambridge in May, 1977.
40. See, for instance, *passim* in the *Association for Literary and Linguistic Computing Bulletin* (Stockport,1973) and *Computers and the Humanities*

(New York, 1966).
41.   W.F.R. Hardie. (1968). *Aristotle's Ethical Theory*, p. 8.
42.
        42.   Eugene R. Kintgen. (1977). 'Reader Response and Stylistics' *Style*, 11/1: 1-18; particularly p.14.

CHAPTER ELEVEN NOTES

1.   See, for instance, George L. Hogben. (1977). 'Linguistic Style and Personality', 10/4:270-84, Autumn; *Language and Style*.

2.   Compare Segers' approach with John B. Carroll, 'Vectors of Prose Style', pp. 283-92 of *Style in Language*, ed. Thomas A. Sebeok, M.I.T. Press, Cambridge, Mass., 1960.

3.   I am here excluding of course mystical examples – for instance, transubstantiation. In those cases, a natural substance is valued as an indicator of some indwelling supernatural entity: there, whatever may be indicated is beyond empirical enquiry.

4.   This is an abridged and inadequate statement. The theory was originally expounded in (1966). *The Semantics of Literature* and developed in (1972). *Theoretical Semics*. These two monographs form the foundation for the earlier chapters of this book.

GLOSSARY

A DISCOURSE STRUCTURE FOR LITERARY SEMANTICS

The following glossary collates and revises terms used in LITERARY SEMANTICS by Trevor Eaton. Secondary sources are cited in square brackets. These entries and definitions are compiled as a working foundation for literary semantics: to be modified, extended and deleted according to context of research and purpose of investigation.

absolute modality See *knowledge one modality*.

academic critic A literary critic committed to a *syllabus* (q.v.).

academic criticism Literary criticism as practised at departmental level within universities.

accidental phonological (lexical, syntactic, semantic) recurrence See *recurrence*.

adequate In *frame theory* (q.v.), a *psychological frame* (q.v.) is said to be *adequate* to the extent that it accurately corresponds to the *external frame* (q.v.) it purports to represent.

adjustment A term used within the *dynaxial theory*, see *dynamic-axial space*. A movement of a point along any given *axis* (q.v.) such that, although the distance between that point and any other point on the same axis remains constant, its position relative to points on other axes is altered.

affidence In *empirical semics* (q.v.): a sub-category of *knowledge two* (q.v.) within the *trichotomy theory* (q.v.). A proposition universally considered true within the highest *universe of discourse* (q.v.) proper to the branch of learning concerned is said to be *affident,* or to have *affidence.*

affidence assessment In *empirical semics* (q.v.): an individual's putative judgment of *affidence* in the absence of an *affidence test.*

affidence test In *empirical semics* (q.v.): a scientifically controlled investigation to determine the *affidence* (q.v.) of a proposition or propositions within a *universe of discourse* (q.v.).

affident See *affidence.*

alternative perspective An intermediate step in the establishment of *reciprocal perspective* (q.v.). See *primitive (potential) utterance* and *reflective modality.*

analepsis The *analeptic function* is that process whereby the received structure of a science, the *analepsis* (Greek ἀναλαμβάνω: I take up), rejects or assimilates the fresh notions of the theorist at the level of the *kinetic* component; *kinesis* (q.v.); see also *science* (q.v.).

analeptic See *analepsis.*

analeptic component The received structure of the concepts of a *science* (q.v.).

analeptic constant A term *secure* (q.v.) or a proposition *affident* (q.v.) within a given *universe of discourse* (q.v.). See also *kinetic variable* and *science.*

analeptic function See *analepsis.*

analeptic theory See *science.*

appetency [Richards] A favourable reaction of an organism to a stimulus. See *aversion.*

applied scientist A scientist, *science* (q.v.), whose interests and endeavours are dictated primarily by *kinetic* (q.v.) exigencies. See also *pure scientist.*

atomic axis An *axis* (q.v.) whose operation corresponds to the electrochemical activity of single neurons, rather than to semantically significant aggregates of neurons.

aversion [Richards] An unfavourable reaction to a stimulus. See *appetency.*

axial adjustment See *adjustment.*

axiology [Segers] A term often used in the sense of *ethics*. For further discussion of *axiology* and *ethics*, see dictionaries by Flew, Lacey and Angeles. See *value*, in this Glossary, for an epistemological (as opposed to axiological) analysis.

axis A *curved* (q.v.) line, representing a semantic factor, traversing *dynaxial space* (q.v.).

basic triangle [Richards] See Figure 1.

broad mapping In *semics* (q.v.), an analysis of a literary text treating those aspects which would not be eliminated in a (prose) paraphrase. See also *narrow mapping*.

centrality of consciousness The *knowledge three* (q.v.) phenomenon: wherever a subject moves physically or mentally s/he always remains at the *centre* (q.v) of his/her world of experience. According to *dynaxial theory* (q.v.), the most intense activity at any moment constitutes the *centre* (q.v.) of the *hypersphere*. See *dynaxial space*.

centre That region of *dynaxial space* (q.v.) in which there is maximum *adjustment* (q.v.) of *axes* (q.v.).

chain of modality theory Within *trichotomy theory* (q.v.), (see Figure 14.), *ontogenetic* and *phylogenetic* movement through *psychological frames* (q.v.) in quest of *knowledge one* (q.v.) either directly and intuitively (*knowledge three* (q.v.) and *value* (q.v.)) or, sociologically, by way of *knowledge two* (q.v.). See also *philosophical level, sociological level and psychological level*.

child's ontological development Within *frame-theory* (q.v.): (a) a subjective phenomenon within *reflective modality* (q.v.), moving by *reciprocal perspective* (q.v.) from *percept* (q.v.) to *concept* (q.v.). Then (b), transferring gradually from the *ontogenesis of modality* (q.v.) to the *phylogenesis of modality* (q.v.). See Figure 14.

circumflexion of discourse In the *human sciences* (q.v.) as opposed to the *natural sciences,* man's scientific investigation is directed upon man himself and, specifically, his own activities. The subjective distortion which sometimes occurs in the natural sciences is more likely to occur in the human sciences.

component modality A *knowledge two modality* (q.v.) at the phylogenetic (*phylogenesis of modality* q.v.) stage: the *reciprocal perspective* (q.v.) between groups of people or centres of activity. Within a *science* (q.v.), *component modality* results from the tension between the *theoretical component* and the *empirical component*. The function of the *theoretical component* (q.v.) is to monitor the *empirical component* (q.v.), making necessary adaptations in direction and priority, proposing new methods of solving problems. The *empirical component* (q.v.) is based in experiment and relies upon tried scientific methods, see the brief summary on [LS: 185]. The *principle of classification* (q.v.), which matches the natural and artificial languages of the *theoretical component* to the *kinesis* (q.v.), typically, the data of observation and experiment, is an important instrument in achieving component modality.

Within *literary semantics*, component modality relates *theoretical semics* (q.v.), *empirical semics* (q.v.), *introspective semics* (q.v.) and the *semantics of literature* (q.v.) / *transmission semantics* (q.v.) one to another and to the natural sciences.

compound frame A frame which is not a *primitive (potential) utterance* (q.v.).

concentrated Within *dynaxial theory* (q.v.), the smaller the volume of the region containing the *centre* (q.v.),the more *concentrated*, as opposed to *diffuse* (q.v.), it is said to be.

concept A *percept* (q.v.) occurs within an individual's experience. Subsequent similar percepts in *reciprocal perspective* (q.v.) become modified and reified (through a process of intermittent *serial framing* (q.v.)) into an abstract notion: a *concept*. This process of *conceptualization* (q.v.) is usually, or frequently, shaped by language.

conceptual-axial A semantic space in which the '*concept*'(q.v.) and '*axes*' (q.v.) are assigned separate status is *conceptual-axial*, as opposed to *dynamic-axial* (q.v.).

conceptualization Within the *ontogenesis of modality* (q.v.), the movement from the *psychological level* (q.v.) to the *sociological level* (q.v.). See also *concept,* above.

criterion of principles In *empirical semics* (q.v.), an adequate principle is one which, having been defined and demonstrated, can be operated independently by other linguists.

curvature In *dynaxial theory* (q.v.), any *axis* (q.v.) extending in a straight line in a given direction will ultimately join up with itself at the point where it began. The joining is known as *curvature*, and such an axis is *curved*. This property of the finite model, the *hypersphere*, reflects the finiteness of the brain.

curved See *curvature*.

dance A form of *non-linguistic modality* (q.v.) within *reflective modality* (q.v.). This is not a definition of *dance* but simply locates it within the *trichotomy theory* (q.v.).

decentralization In *dynaxial space* (q.v.), the movement of any given region away from the *centre* (q.v.).

devoid The fewer *intense* (q.v.) points contained by any region of the *dynaxial hypersphere* (q.v.), the more *devoid* it is said to be.

diffuse The larger the volume of the region containing the *centre* (q.v.) – or some *non-central* region – the more *diffuse*, as opposed to *concentrated* (q.v.), it is said to be.

domain [Freundlieb] See *object domain* and Chapter 15 *passim*.

double vision A concept which I relate to my version of *frame theory* (q.v.), but which derives from Paul Werth. An underlying psychological process whereby two or more different frames combine to produce a frame (q. v.) distinct from both. The phenomenon, belonging to *theoretical semics* (q.v.), may be observed in metaphor, simile, irony, satire and, universally, in humour.

dynamic See *dynamism* (a) within *dynaxial theory* (q.v.); (b) within *frame theory*, see *dynamic frame*, immediately below.

dynamic-axial (dynaxial) space In *theoretical semics* (q.v.), *dynamic-axial (dynaxial) space* is a model representing the human psyche. The aim is to construct a model which is self-consistent, and will show stable correspond-ence with observed behaviour. Since all the *axes* (q.v.) traversing the space are *curved* (q.v.), the present model may be imagined as a multi-dimensional sphere, or *hypersphere*.

dynamic frame Within *frame theory* (q.v.), a frame *external* (q.v.) or *psycho-logical* (q.v.) which moves.

dynamism Within *dynaxial theory* (q.v.), any *adjustment* (q.v.) within the *dynaxial space* (q.v.) bearing no similarity to any previous adjustment is said to have *dynamism* or to be *dynamic*.

dynaxial theory The theory of *dynamic-axial space* (q.v.).

empirical component Within a *science* (q.v.), that set of activities/functions (or that group of people) which is primarily concerned with observation, description, experiment and reasoned explanation. It is in critical tension (*reciprocal perspective* q.v.) with the *theoretical component* (q.v.).

empirical semicist See *empirical semics*.

empirical semics That part of *semics* (q.v.) which collates, classifies and describes evidence provided by subjects concerning their own *semic accompaniment* (q.v.) The *empirical semicist* will also explore behaviourist (including electronic) evidence, linguistic, psychological or neurophysiological, relevant to the semic accompaniment of a subject. The empirical semicist will also be concerned with *semantic generation* (q.v.) and *transmission semantics* (q.v.). See also *method of concomitant variations*.

empirical threshold Within *theoretical semics* (q.v.), a notional entrance line to the *empirical component* (q.v.), beyond which a *scientist* (q.v.) accepts the rigorous standards of investigative science.

engram [Ogden and Richards; earlier R. Semon, *Die Mneme* 1904] A neural imprint, resulting from experience, which modifies subsequent experience and behaviour.

ethics See *value*.

external context [Ogden and Richards] Certain sets of entities occur in experience and are similar to other sets of entities. Such a set is called an *external context*.

external frame See *frame theory*. This is analogous within my frame theory to the Ogden-Richards' *external context*, above.

facilitated Any *adjustment* (q.v.) within *dynaxial space* (q.v.) similar to any previous adjustment is said to be facilitated. The process is *facilitation*.

facilitation see *facilitated*.

fictionality See *fictional statement*.

fictional statement In *frame theory* (q.v.), (within *theoretical semics* (q.v.)), a *fictional statement* is one which asserts an *external frame* (q.v.) to exist, where none does. *Fictionality*, within *frame theory* (q.v.), is thus subsumed (*principle of subsumption* q.v.) as a form of *modality* (q.v.).

final semic state In *semics* (q.v.), the disposition of the *axes* (q.v.) – see *dynaxial space*, or some other equivalent semic model – at the end of a given *semic accompaniment* (q.v.).

first-level frame Within *frame theory* (q.v.), within *theoretical semics* (q.v.), an *external frame* (q.v.), or corresponding *adequate psychological frame* (q.v.). Although this is a theoretical tool, it has important implications in *empirical semics* (q.v.): conclusions in academic discourse (and, specifically *academic criticism* (q.v.)) should not go beyond the premises on which they are argued to depend – see, for instance, the discussions of Blackmur, Bateson and Spitzer in this book.

formal representation of frames A schema setting out particulars of a *frame-set* (q.v.) for the purpose of analysis within *textual modality* (q.v.) or *reflective modality* (q.v.). See Figure 12.

frame See *frame theory*.

frame level An arbitrarily graded progression through layers of *fictional statement* (q.v.). See also discussion, pages 194–211 and also Appendix Three (*Merchant's Tale*).

frame-profiling Within *semics* (q.v.), the correlation of specific textual features with readers' awareness of narrative progression or of narrative structure as abstracted in a series of frames. *Frame-profiling* has a wider cognitive application, see *ontogenesis of modality* and *phylogenesis of modality*. See Appendix Two.

frame-set A group of *frames* (*frame theory* (q.v.)), regarded as sharing similar spatial or temporal features.

frame theory A frame is an arbitrarily delimited set of entities, still or moving, which are spatially, temporally or spatio-temporally located. Frames may be *external*, objectively existing, or *psychological*, individuals' *adequate* (q.v.) or *inadequate* (q.v.) representations of external frames. *Formal representations* (q.v.) of frames may be used in analysis of *textual modality* (q.v.). See page 197. Frames may be *simultaneous* (q.v.), as in deliberate lying, or *sequential* (q.v.), as in narrative. Sequential frames may be *serial* (q.v.), on the same level, or *hierarchical*, on at least two levels. Within *semic accompaniment* (q.v.), given a fictional time-line, *present frames* refer to the fictional time of the point in the narrative at which they occur; *past frames* and *future frames* refer backwards and forwards respectively. Frame theory, more widely, underlies the concept of *reflective modality* (q.v.) and the *ontogenesis of modality* (q.v.).

function domain For example *theoretical semics* (q.v.) and *empirical semics* (q.v.), which are context-sensitive and therefore more flexible than Freundlieb's *object domain* (q.v.).

fusion In *dynaxial space* the coalescence of two or more *intense* (q.v.) regions, either in accordance with the *law of the dynaxial centre* (q.v.), or of two or more *intense, non-central* regions.

future frame See *frame theory*.

glass ceiling In *trichotomy theory* (q.v.), the entire region of knowledge is divided into three levels by two transverse lines (see Figure 2.). The lower line is notionally drawn by each individual between private, *knowledge three* (q.v.) experience and shared *knowledge two* (q.v.) experience. The upper line may metaphorically be regarded as a *glass ceiling* between man's shared experience, *knowledge two*, and knowledge which is absolute, *knowledge one* (q.v.). See Figure 2.

grammar see *grammaticality*.

grammaticality In the *trichotomy theory* (q.v.), what those sequences of terms have in common which are maximally *secure* (q.v.). Alternatively, in *dynaxial theory*, (q.v.), a terminal point in the process whereby those *axes* (q.v.) basic to language settle into the structures necessary for stable communication.

hierarchical framing See *frame theory*.

hortative obligation Within the theory of the *syllabus* (q.v.), a view, philosophical or methodological, communicated prescriptively to the teacher by his employer, which the teacher may, without detriment to his professional position, disregard. See also the *principle of humanism* (q.v.) and the *principle of information* (q.v.).

human sciences For the purposes of this book, and specifically the final chapter, the *human sciences* are those such as psychology, psycholinguistics and linguistics, and it is argued in this book, literary semantics, where *circumflexion of discourse* (q.v.) may cause distortion and hinder objectivity (see page 224).

hypersphere See *dynamic-axial space*.

hypothetical argument In logic, a derivation whose conclusion contains one or more conditionals.

hypothetical reader In *theoretical semics* (q.v.), one who is postulated as experiencing a *semic accompaniment* (q.v.) of such-and-such a specification, in order that the theorist may pursue a hypothetical argument. It belongs to *empirical semics* (q.v.) or *introspective semics* (q.v.) to furnish evidence of an *instantiated reader* (q.v.).

idiosemic Those parts of *semic accompaniment* (q.v.) which are demonstrated within *empirical semics* (q.v.) to be due to an individual's personality, rather than to language as a stable vehicle of communication, are *idiosemic*. See also *parasemic*.

inadequate In *frame theory* (q.v.), a *psychological frame* (q.v.) is said to be *inadequate* to the extent that it fails to correspond to the *external frame* (q.v.) it purports to represent. The underlying philosophical problem of identifying *inadequate* frame properties is overcome, though not solved, by the *knowledge two* (q.v.) sleight: we can see through the *glass ceiling* (q.v.) to view the *knowledge one* (q.v.) 'reality' of the *external frame*. As humans, all we 'really' have is a pair of alternative psychological frames, one of which may have preferred 'objectivity'.

inaffident The lower the *affidence* (q.v.) rating of a proposition, the more *inaffident* it is said to be.

initial semic state In *semics* (q.v.), the disposition of the *axes* (q.v.) within the *dynamic-axial space* (q.v.) – or some other equivalent semic model – at the commencement of a given *semic accompaniment* (q.v.). See also *medial semic state* and *final semic state*.

insecure The lower the *security* (q.v.) of a term, or sequence of terms, the more *insecure* it is said to be.

instantiated reader In *empirical semics* (q.v.), a subject whose *semic accompaniment* (q.v.) is established. In *introspective semics* (q.v.), one who provides evidence concerning his own *semic accompaniment*.

intense In *dynaxial theory* (q.v.) any point at which many *axes* (q.v.) intersect (q.v.), is *intense*. The same term is used of any *region* (q.v.) within the *dynaxial space* (q.v.) which contains many intense points.

intensity See *intense*.

intersect In *dynaxial space* (q.v.), two *axes* (q.v.) with coinciding points are said to *intersect*. There is no theoretical limit to the number of axial intersections possible at any point within the space.

intersection See *intersect*.

introspective semicist See *introspective semics*.

introspective semics That part of *semics* (q.v.) which relies upon the evidence provided by the investigator's own *semic accompaniment* (q.v.). *Introspective semics* shades off into practical criticism. The difference between a 'practical critic' and an *introspective semicist* is that the latter modally reduces his claims by labelling them as *introspective semics*.

jussive obligation Within the theory of the *syllabus* (q.v.), any rule the proven infringement of which will lead to disciplinary action being taken against the offending teacher. See also the *principle of humanism* and the *principle of information*.

kinesis See *kinetic*.

kinetic The *kinetic* (Greek κῑνέω: I stir up) *component* or *function* of a science, (q.v.), the *kinesis*, mediates between material from fresh observations and the received structure of the concepts of the science, the *analepsis* (q.v.). See also *science* and Figure 5.

kinetic component See *kinetic*.

kinetic function See *kinetic*.

kinetic variable Within the theory of *affidence* (q.v.), a term *insecure* (q.v.) or proposition *inaffident* (q.v.), within a given *universe of discourse* (q.v.). See also *analeptic constant*.

knowledge one In the *trichotomy theory* (q.v.), absolute or ultimate knowledge, where 'absolute' or 'ultimate' imply a knowledge which, whether natural or supernatural, is unalterable. The term occupies a paradoxical position in *trichotomy theory*: on the one hand *knowledge one* is philosophically (ideologically) neutral; on the other, it provides a theoretical validation for whatever may constitute 'truth' at the level of *knowledge two* (q.v.) and *knowledge three* (q.v.). See also *reciprocal perspective*.

knowledge one modality The possibility of being 'right', in an absolute sense. It is in *reciprocal perspective* (q.v.) with *knowledge two* (q.v.) and *knowledge three* (q.v.).

knowledge two is knowledge believed by the person possessing it to be communicable.

knowledge two modality See, for instance, *reflective modality* and *component modality*.

knowledge three Is knowledge believed by the person possessing it to be incommunicable.

laughter in *theoretical semics* (q.v.), a psychological reaction, often linguistically induced, explicable within *dynaxial theory* (q.v.) by the *law of dynaxial increase* (q.v.) cf [LS:124], or within *frame theory* (q.v.) by the experience within an individual of two or more recalcitrant and simultaneous psychological (or external) frames.

law of the dynaxial centre This law states that *dynaxial space* (q.v.) in the wakeful state will not tolerate a region of *intensity* (q.v.) equal to the *centre* (q.v.).

law of dynaxial increase This law states that the number of potential *dynamic-axial adjustments* (q.v.) is in excess of the number of *dynamic* (q.v.) lexical items within any given text. See Dylan Thomas illustration, for instance, page 124.

linguistic transaction [Ogden and Richards] '…a language transaction … may be defined as a use of symbols in such a way that acts of reference occur in a hearer which are similar in all relevant respects to those which are symbolized by them in the speaker.'

linking problem The organization (i) of linguistic material into well-defined entities which will provide a mathematically viable input for a model of the *dynaxial* (q.v.) type and conversely, (ii) the refinement and modification of the model itself to the point where this input may be accommodated. The aim is to develop a model viable at the level of *empirical semics* (q.v.).

literary semantics The broader task of literary semantics is to examine philosophically the relation between literature and the disciplines of linguistics, mathematics, psychology, neurophysiology and other relevant subjects. There is a fuller, documented statement of the aims of literary semantics at the beginning of chapter 15 of this book. On a more restricted level, it is that branch of the linguistic sciences which aims to describe the totality of the meaning and this would subsume the phonetic, lexical, syntactic and metrical elements of a work of 'literature'.

local affidence A proposition which receives a low *affidence* (q.v.) rating in the highest *universe of discourse* (q.v.) might find universal acceptance in a *lower universe of discourse*. This proposition would be said to have *local affidence*.

medial semic state In *semics* (q.v.), the disposition of the *axes* (q.v.) within the hypersphere or some other equivalent semic model at a selected instant between the *initial semic state* (q.v.) and the *final semic state* (q.v.) of a *semic accompaniment* (q.v.).

metaphor In *dynaxial theory* (q.v.), a linguistic device whereby two or more distant regions within the *dynaxial space* (q.v.) of a *hypothetical reader* (q.v.) are *concentrated* (q.v.) Metaphor is also analysed as a device within *textual (reflective) modality* (q.v.), involving *simultaneous framing* (q.v.). See pages 136 and 215.

method of concomitant variations (John Stuart Mill's notion, which subsumes his other scientific methods of induction). The method turns upon the following assumption: given a situation containing two elements A and B, such that when A varies, B also varies (commensurately), then A is causally connected with B. In *empirical semics* (q.v.), this method is used, for example, to investigate the correlations between the input of linguistic data and the output of literary judgment (chapter 11 *passim*).

modality Specifically, a *scientist's* (q.v.) determination to operate the *principle of classification* (q.v.). *Modality* is the most important mediating device at all levels of the discussions in this book, operating as it does at the *philosophical level* (q.v.), *sociological level* (q.v.) and *psychological level* (q.v.), within the *trichotomy theory* (q.v.). See also *principle of subsumption* and *reciprocal perspective*.

modal reduction See *principle of subsumption* (q.v.). Lack of a modal structure is what, in my own analysis, vitiates much of *academic criticism* (q.v.). Assertions are often made as if incontrovertibly factual, with knowledge one authority: [e.g. Blackmur, page 49 '…an arrow aimed at the Almighty, carrying, in its gesture, the whole church with it'; Spitzer, page 155 'Thus we have made the trip from language or style to the soul'; Bateson, page 85 'Their function in fact turns out to be merely to set off the one good line in the poem'.] Such statements, and many others still being made in 2000+, may be subsumed within *knowledge one* (q.v.) to the level of *knowledge two* (q.v.), to the level of *science* (q.v.), to the level of *linguistics,* to the level of *literary semantics* (q.v.), to the level of *semics* (q.v.), to the level of *theoretical semics* (q.v.) (the level at which, incidentally, this Glossary operates), to the level of *practical semics* (q.v.), to the level of *introspective semics* (q.v.). They are thus stripped of pretence and bogus authority and modally reduced to a commonsense level within literary semantics. [***Personal note***: **Such academic analysis is entirely independent of the pursuit of pleasure for its own sake in books and oral performance, which pursuit I wholeheartedly embrace.**]

music A form of *non-linguistic modality* (q.v.), though subsuming a linguistic subset, e.g. opera, within *reflective modality* (q.v.). This is clearly not a definition of *music* but simply locates it within the *trichotomy theory* (q.v.).

name [Ullmann] Roughly corresponds with *symbol* (q.v.).

narrow mapping In *frame theory* (q.v.), an analysis treating those aspects of a text which would be eliminated in a prose paraphrase. See also *broad mapping*.

non-central intensification In *dynaxial theory* (q.v.), an increase in *axial adjustment* (q.v.), which – though it may lead to *fusion* (q.v.) of lesser regions – is not sufficiently *intense* (q.v.) to trigger the *law of the dynaxial centre* (q.v.).

non-linguistic modality Subsumed with *textual modality* (q.v.) within *reflective modality* (q.v.), includes *music* (q.v.), *dance* (q.v.), *visual arts*, etc. These are naturally seated within *knowledge three* (q.v.) and *value* (q.v.).

object domain [Freundlieb] A defining precondition for any (scientific) discipline: the existence of a delimited, distinctive and agreed set of objects comprising the scope of that discipline; this set of objects being open to systematic study. (My interpretation based on Freundlieb *JLS* 1998 and 2000.)

Occam's Razor Important scientific principle conventionally attributed to medieval scholar William of Ockham (c.1285-c.1349) in the form '*E(sse) ntia non sunt multiplicanda praeter necessitatem*' – but see the discussion on [LS:161–163]; (q.v. *principle of subsumption*).

ontogenesis of modality Within *dynaxial theory* (q.v.) and *frame theory* (q.v.): the growth of *reciprocal perspective* (q.v.) within individuals. See also *child's ontological development*.

ontogenesis of science The inner representation of the *analepsis* (q.v.) of *science* (q.v.) within an individual.

ontogenetic Pertaining to the *psychological level* (q.v.).

paradigmatic dynamism Within *semic accompaniment* (q.v.), the experience resulting from the use at a given point in the text of a lexical item different from the items the reader <u>might</u> (in *theoretical semics* (q.v.)) or <u>would</u> (in *empirical semics* (q.v.)) have predicted had his reading ceased immediately prior to the item.

parasemic Those aspects of *semic accompaniment* (q.v.) which are demonstrated to be due to language as a stable vehicle of communication are *parasemic*. See also *idiosemic*.

past-frame See *frame theory*.

percept In *frame theory* (q.v.), a sense experience which precedes *conceptualization* (see *concept*).

philosophical level One of three levels of analysis within the *trichotomy theory* (q.v.), the other two levels being the *sociological level* (q.v.) (which subsumes *science* (q.v.) and scientific investigation) and the *psychological level* (q.v.). These three levels of analysis are presented as a first step to solving the problem which I. A. Richards famously tackled and abandoned: how to reconcile literary studies with scientific theory.

phylogenesis of modality The growth of *reflective modality* (q.v.) and *component modality* (q.v.) amongst groups of individuals. The term clearly also includes the growth of 'non-scientific' modality, despite the implication in the use of the term 'component'.

phylogenesis of science The growth of *component modality* i.e. excluding 'non-scientific' modality.

phylogenetic Pertaining to the *sociological level* (q.v.).

plot In *theoretical semics* (q.v.) and *frame theory* (q.v.), a *continuum* of frames represented in a text – or iconic equivalent of a text – which is judged to 'cohere' by an *instantiated reader* (q.v.) at the level of *practical semics* (q.v.); in *empirical semics* (q.v.), experimental investigation of such *continua*.

practical semics The component of *semics* (q.v), which subsumes *empirical semics* (q.v.) and *introspective semics* (q.v.).

present-frame See *frame theory*.

primary semantic space In *theoretical semics* (q.v.), which subsumes *dynaxial theory* (q.v.), this represents the (presumably infinite) innate potentials of an individual's *dynaxial space* (q.v.) at birth.

primitive (potential) utterance In *frame theory* (q.v.), within *theoretical semics* (q.v.), an utterance made, actually (or potentially), by a speaker concerning some direct and immediate experience. See *textual modality* and *reflective modality*.

principle The principles in this glossary are of two sorts: theoretical and methodological. They are all defined at the level of **theoretical semics** (q.v.). The theoretical principles (*dynamism* and *facilitation*) are a fundamental classification of the possible modifications of *dynaxial space* (q.v.). Within *chain of modality theory* (q.v.), they are analytical devices in *theoretical semics* (q.v.), at the level of *reflective modality* (q.v.). That is to say, they offer tentative hypotheses not just for *semic accompaniment* (q.v.) and *transmission semantics* (q.v.), but also for such topics as retardation of language learning in the teens, centrality of consciousness, indistinct recollection, dreaming, laughter, metaphor and simile (see chapter 8).

The other principles are methodological, their purpose being to organize (*classification, objectivity, security, semantics of literature, subsumption*) or, within the theory of education, to clarify (*humanism, information*), the material of literary semantics.

principle of classification A methodological principle. *Kinetic variables* (q.v.) may not be transformed into *analeptic constants* (q.v.).

principle of dynamism A theoretical principle. In *theoretical semics* (q.v.), within the *dynaxial theory* (q.v.), any axial *adjustment* (q.v.) which is *dynamic* (q.v.) is said to operate according to the *principle of dynamism*.

principle of facilitation A theoretical principle. In *dynaxial theory* (q.v.), any *axial adjustment* (q.v.) which is *facilitated* (q.v.) is said to operate according to the *principle of facilitation*.

principle of humanism A prescriptive educational principle, inherent in many books by academic critics, that academic criticism is concerned to educate the 'full man', to make the student capable of mature response to literature, and to enrich his/her life by developing that human perceptiveness and sensibility whereby s/he becomes, in some moral or aesthetic sense, the better – *value* (q.v.) – for that training.

principle of information A prescriptive educational principle, widely rejected by academic critics, that the function of a university course is to impart a body of 'essential' knowledge, so that the student may be the better equipped to live intelligently in today's world and be a useful member of society.

principle of objectivity In *empirical semics* (q.v.): empirical semics recognizes only those entities which are textually signalled. For examples of the application of this principle, see, for instance, the discussion of Blackmur, [LS:49; 58–60]; Bateson, chapter 5 *passim*.

principle of security Within the theory of *affidence* (q.v.): no proposition can be *affident* (q.v.) if it contains terms, or sequences of terms, which are not *secure* (q.v.).

principle of the semantic gap [Bateson] An example of a principle which violates the *criterion of principles* (q.v.) within *empirical semics* (q.v.), see discussion [LS:87–88]. See also *principle* (q.v.).

principle of subsumption A corollary to *Occam's Razor* (q.v.): *whatever entities necessity dictates subsume if you can.* See *modal reduction.*

principles of the semantics of literature Examples of such historical principles are: *ceteris paribus*, primary sources are preferable to secondary sources; *ceteris paribus,* an interpretation informed by a knowledge of the historical background of the author is preferable to one written in ignorance of these facts (see discussion of Rodger's linguistic analysis, pages 92–98); an interpretation of a text which is in accordance with the known dialect and date of the text is superior to one which is not.

psychological context [Ogden and Richards] The 'mnemic effects' of a compound set of stimuli. More clearly expressed: an individual's memory of some perceived *external context* (q.v.).

psychological frame An individual's subjective perception of an *external frame*. See *frame theory* and *psychological context*.

psychological level One of three levels of analysis within the *trichotomy theory* (q.v.), and *chain of modality theory* (q.v.), the other two levels being the *philosophical level* (q.v.) and the *sociological level* (q.v.). See Figures 14 and 15.

pure scientist Within the analeptic-kinetic theory of *science* (q.v.), a *pure scientist* is one whose interests and endeavours are not primarily dictated by the exigencies of the *kinesis* (q.v.), but by intellectual inquiry.

reception See *transmission-reception.*

reciprocal perspective Alternating viewpoint (a) between *frames* (q.v.) in *textual (reflective) modality* (q.v.); (b) between *components* in *component modality* (q.v.); (c) between *knowledge one* (q.v.) versus *knowledge two* (q.v.) and *knowledge three* (q.v.), within the *trichotomy theory* (q.v.). See also *principle of subsumption* (q.v.) and *concept* (q.v.).

recurrence In *introspective semics* (q.v.), the repetition of any linguistic feature which an *instantiated reader* (q.v.) judges to be deliberate.

reference [Richards] Act of referring (roughly equivalent to *thought*, but with no *mentalistic* presuppositions). I have adopted some of Richards' terms from time to time where I was making use of his analyses. The *trichotomy theory* (q.v.) as outlined in this Glossary is as neutral to all broad philosophical alignments (e.g. mechanistic/mentalistic) as it is possible to be; see *glass ceiling*. See also discussions throughout the book of *knowledge one*.

referent [Richards] An entity or an occurrence in the external world.

reflective modality The first stage in the *ontogenesis of modality* (q.v.). A second *psychological frame* (q.v.) provides an *alternative perspective* (q.v.) to a first. With the *facilitation* (q.v.) of this alternative perspective, *reciprocal perspective* (q.v.), is initiated and gradually develops with further experience. *Reflective modality* comprises linguistic (*textual modality* (q.v.)) and *non-linguistic modality*, e.g. *music* (q.v.), *dance* (q.v.), *visual arts* (q.v.) – development of *concepts* (q.v.) aside from language, insofar as this is possible. See also *knowledge three*.

region Any selected location within a *hypersphere*. See *dynaxial space* and *intense*.

relevance two Within **literary semantics** (q.v.), that which is in accordance with certain agreed principles, for instance **principles of the semantics of literature** (q.v.). Relevance is analysed as a corollary of the **trichotomy theory**: for brief discussion of **relevance one** and **relevance three**, see pages [LS: 29-30;73].

science An academic pursuit which confronts a vigorous *kinesis* (q.v.) with an *analepsis* (q.v.), which is well-organized, vigilant, yet flexible.

scientist An academic dedicated to reconciling *analepsis* (q.v.) with *kinesis* (q.v.).

secondary semantic space Within the *dynaxial theory* (q.v.), which in turn belongs within *theoretical semics* (q.v.), this represents the actual *adjustments* (q.v.) of the *axes* (q.v.) and the consequent actual modifications of the *primary semantic space* (q.v.), effected either by contact with the 'external world', *tertiary semantic space* (q.v.), or by chain reaction as a result of previous adjustments.

secure If all the participants in an *affidence test* (q.v.) are satisfied that they know what is meant by a term or sequence of terms (occurring in the proposition under consideration), then that term or sequence of terms is said to be *secure*, or to have *security*. See also the *principle of security*.

security See *secure*.

semantic generation The processes of linguistic creation. *Semantic generation* is the *transmission* counterpart (see *transmission-reception*) of *semic accompaniment* (q.v.), which is a *reception* process.

semantics of literature The study of a 'work of literature' as an event in history; the attempt to reconstruct the meaning of a literary work by means of historical research. The division between the *semantics of literature* (q.v.) and *semics* (q.v.) is based upon the Ogden-Richards' definition of a language transaction, now more usually referred to as *transmission-reception* (q.v.). See also *transmission semantics*, *semantic generation* and *principles of the semantics of literature*.

semantic space A device introduced at the level of *theoretical semics* (q.v.): a metaphorical representation of the human cognitive faculty. See *dynaxial space*.

semic accompaniment That series of mediating reactions which a person experiences when he reads continuously at his normal speed a passage which contains for him no linguistic difficulties. See also *semantic generation*. [*Semic accompaniment* is used in a neutral sense, as opposed to terms such as Iser's *concretization* which presupposes that 'competent' readers' reconstructions are 'sound' in an aesthetic sense. *Semics*, at the level of *empirical semics* (q.v.), assumes diversity of interpretation until uniformity is proven. See Eaton (1980), review of Iser, and discussion of Spitzer's 'philological circle' pages 154–155].

semics The study of *semic accompaniment* (q.v.). *Semics* and the *semantics of literature* (q.v.) (including *transmission semantics* (q.v.)) are the subdivisions of literary semantics. *Semics* is in turn subdivided into *theoretical semics* (q.v.) and *practical semics*, the latter itself subsuming *empirical semics* (q.v.) and *introspective semics* (q.v.).

sense [Ullmann] Roughly corresponds to *reference* (q.v.).

sequential framing See *frame theory*. In *theoretical semics* (q.v.), *sequential framing* is needed to deal adequately with moving and/or intermittent, as opposed to static, situations.

serial framing See *frame theory* and *sequential framing*: framing appropriate for simple (*one level*) moving or intermittent yet similar occurrences (see page 199).

simile In *dynaxial theory* (q.v.), a linguistic device whereby two or more distant regions within the *dynaxial space* (q.v.) of a *hypothetical reader* (q.v.) are *concentrated* (q.v.), the degree of *diffuseness* in the *final semic state* (q.v.) being greater than in the corresponding *metaphor* (q.v.).

simultaneous framing See *frame theory*. *Simultaneous framing* takes place, for instance, in cases of deliberate lying, metaphor and humour, where at least two partly separate frames are needed to explain the processes.

sociological level See *knowledge two*. One of three levels of analysis in the *trichotomy theory* (q.v.), the other two levels being the *philosophical level* (q.v.) and the *psychological level*. The *sociological level* subsumes scientific investigation: *science* (q.v.). See Figures 14 and 15.

static frame One which is without movement, as opposed to *serial* and *sequential frames* (q.v.).

style An example of *modal* definition, (*modality* (q.v.)). Such definitions may be operated usefully at different levels of enquiry.

(a) In *theoretical semics* (q.v.) given two passages A and B and a *hypothetical reader's* (q.v.) *semic accompaniment* (q.v.) to the two separate passages, then the stylistic features of A are those linguistic features which would lead the hypothetical reader to suppose, rightly or wrongly, that A and B are, or are not written by the same person.

(b) In *empirical semics*, style is the totality of the linguistic features in a given passage which can be experimentally demonstrated (by means of *instantiated readers* (q.v.)) to lead to correct predictions concerning passages where all relevant details of authorship are known by the investigator.

Direct clues as to the authorship of the passages in (a) and (b) should of course be deleted prior to the reading.

syllabus In education theory, that system of obligations, both *jussive* (q.v.) and *hortative* (q.v.) which will best enable the teacher to reconcile with the ethical drive — *value* (q.v.) — of his/her own personality the needs of the community, on the one side, and the exigencies of the classroom situation, on the other. It follows that, from the educationalist's viewpoint, the syllabus should be teacher-centred – see Appendix Four.

symbol [Ogden and Richards] Roughly corresponds to a *word* or *linguistic utterance*, spoken or written, designating a *referent* (q.v.).

syntagmatic dynamism *Dynamism* (q.v.) which occurs when the *semic accompaniment* (q.v.) refers backwards (or forwards) within the text from the textual item(s) concerned, rather than to other items which might have replaced the item(s). See *paradigmatic dynamism*.

target concept See *Indistinct Recollection* [LS: 130–131].

tenor The *final semic state* (q.v.) of a *hypothetical reader* (q.v.) differs from the *initial semic state* (q.v.) in that the *dynaxial space* (q.v.) has been restructured by a *metaphor*: (a) The *tenor* is the *centre* (q.v.) or that part of the centre, which was present in the initial semic state and was restructured by the metaphor; alternatively, (b) the tenor is that part of the *text* appropriate to the *tenor* in sense (a).

tension In dynaxial theory (q.v.), that process whereby, during *semic accompaniment* (q.v.), scattered regions within the *dynaxial space* (q.v.) dynamically coalesce and become *facilitated* (q.v.).

tertiary semantic space That point at which external reality impinges upon *dynaxial space* (q.v.). See also *primary semantic space* and *secondary semantic space*.

textual modality A *knowledge two* (q.v.) *modality* (q.v.). When speaker S truthfully utters, or (potentially) truthfully utters, U, concerning some direct and immediate experience of S, U is said to be a *primitive (potential) utterance* (q.v.); when U is made subject to some further qualification whereby the directness and immediacy are removed or diminished, then this qualification is said to represent a *textual modality* to which U is subjected. This definition is based upon Rescher (1968: 24). Textual modality is a subdivision of *reflective modality* (q.v.).

theoretical component That set of imaginative activities within a *science* (q.v.), which is in *reciprocal perspective* (q.v.) with the *empirical component* (q.v.).

theoretical semicist See *theoretical semics*.

theoretical semics That level of *literary semantics* (q.v.) at which the *kinetic* (q.v.) *component* functions. It is the task of the theoretical semicist to confront the problems of literary semantics, and to 'stir up' (Greek κῑνέω 'I stir up', whence *kinesis*) the received concepts, the *analepsis* (q.v.), in the quest for solutions.

transmission-reception A fundamental classification of a linguistic transaction, as in speaker/hearer, writer/reader.

transmission semantics An extension of the scope of the *semantics of literature* (q.v.) to include the study of *semantic generation* (q.v.). The emphasis of the former is linguistic and historical; of the latter, neurolinguistic and experimental.

trichotomy theory The analysis of knowledge expounded in chapter 1 of this book, dividing knowledge into three categories: *knowledge one* (q.v.), *knowledge two* (q.v.) and *knowledge three* (q.v.). The theory constitutes the *philosophical level* (q.v.) of the discussions in this book.

universe of discourse Within the theory of *affidence* (q.v.), any discrete system of communication. It differs from the logicians' use of the same term, which is an abstract mathematical concept in set theory. Instead of set theory, the term used in this book refers to communicating *people*.

value Within the *trichotomy theory* (q.v.), *value* is a man's conviction, *knowledge three* (q.v.), that he has access in some degree to *knowledge one* (q.v.). This conviction may be (a) unconsciously accreted; (b) consciously induced; or (c) a combination of these two processes.

vehicle The distant region which in *metaphor* (q.v.) coalesces with the *tenor* (q.v.); alternatively, the part of the *text* appropriate to that region.

visual arts See *modal reduction*, *reflective modality* and *non-linguistic modality*. This is not a definition of *visual arts* but simply locates them within the *trichotomy theory* (q.v.).

APPENDIX ONE

The Miller's Tale (Lines 3547- 3600)

'Anon go gete us faste into this in   3547
A knedyng-trogh, or ellis a kymelyn
For ech of us, but looke that they be large,
In which we mowe swymme as in a barge,   3550
And han therinne vitaille suffisant
But for a day, − fy on the remenant!
The water shal aslake and goon away
Aboute pryme upon the nexte day.
But Robyn may nat wite of this, thy knave,   3555
Ne eek thy mayde Gille I may nat save;
Axe nat why, for though thou aske me,
I wol nat tellen Goddes pryvetee.
Suffiseth thee, but if thy wittes madde,
To han as greet a grace as Noe hadde.   3560
Thy wyf shal I wel saven, out of doute.
Go now thy wey, and speed thee heer-aboute.
But whan thou hast, for hire and thee and me,
Ygeten us thise knedyng-tubbes thre,
Thanne shaltow hange hem in the roof ful hye,   3565
That no man of oure purveiaunce espie.
And whan thou thus hast doon, as I have seyd,
And hast oure vitaille faire in hem yleyd,
And eek an ax, to smyte the corde atwo,
Whan that the water comth, that we may go,   3570
And breke an hole an heigh, upon the gable,
Unto the gardyn-ward, over the stable,
That we may frely passen forth oure weye,
Whan that the grete shoure is goon away,
Thanne shaltou swymme as myrie, I undertake,   3575
As dooth the white doke after hir drake.
Thanne wol I clepe, 'How, Alison! How, John!
Be myrie, for the flood wol passe anon.'

And thou wolt seyn, 'Hayl, maister Nicholay!
Good morwe, I se thee wel, for it is day.'   3580
And thanne shul we be lordes al oure lyf
Of al the world, as Noe and his wyf.
But of o thing I warne thee ful right:
Be wel avysed on that ilke nyght
That we been entred into shippes bord,   3585
That noon of us ne speke nat a word
Ne clepe, ne crie, but be in his preyere;
For it is Goddes owene heeste deere.
Thy wyf and thou moote hange fer atwynne;
For that betwixe yow shal be no synne,   3590
Namoore in lookyng than ther shal in deede.
This ordinance is seyd. Go, God thee speede!
Tomorwe at nyght, whan men ben al aslepe,
Into oure knedyng-tubbes wol we crepe,
And sitten there, abidyng Goddes grace.   3595
Go now thy wey. I have no lenger space
To make of this no lenger sermonyng.
Men seyn thus, "Sende the wise and sey no thing".
Thou art so wise, it needeth thee nat teche.
Go, save oure lyf, and that I the biseche.'   3600

See chapter 13. The full text of 'The Miller's Tale', line numbering identical
with references in this book, may be found in Robinson ed. (1933): 56-65;
Benson ed. (1988): 66-77; and Cawley ed. (1958): 83-103

APPENDIX TWO

EMPIRICAL SEMICS

An example of an analysis carried out in 1988 for the purpose of illustrating the relation between introspective semics and empirical semics. As an instantiated reader at the level of introspective semics, Trevor Eaton completed a questionnaire (see LS page 204) devised on the basis of the passage from *The Miller's Tale*, reproduced in Appendix One. No aesthetic or 'literary' talents are presupposed. The result below is nothing more than a record of responses provided by an ordinary reader on one occasion. The completed questionnaire provides material, along with other subjects' responses, for investigation at the level of empirical semics. See also Chapter 11 *passim*.

APPENDIX: FRAME PROFILES OF VERBS: *MILLER'S TALE* lines 3547-3600

	LINE	1	2	3	4	5	M	A	B	C	D	E	F	G	H	II	III	IV	V
go gete	3547	•					•									•	•	•	
looke			•				•									•	•	•	
be			•				•									•	•		
mowe swimme	3550			•												•			
han		•								•						•	•	•	
shal aslake				•	•											•			
(shal) goon				•	•											•			
may (nat) wite		•									•					•	•	•	
may (nat) save		•	•	•	•		•				•					•		•	
axe							•									•	•	•	
aske							•									•			
wol (nat) tellen							•									•	•	•	
suffiseth							•									•	•	•	
to han	3560				•											•			
hadde					•														
shal saven				•	•	•	•									•	•	•	
go		•					•									•	•	•	
speed		•					•									•	•	•	
hast ygeten		•						•								•	•	•	
shaltow hange		•							•							•	•	•	•
espie		•									•					•	•		•
hast doon		•						•	•		•					•	•	•	
have seyd							•	•	•		•						•	•	
hast yleyd		•										•				•	•	•	•
to smyte				•												•			•
comth	3570			•												•			?

APPENDIX: FRAME PROFILES OF VERBS: *MILLER'S TALE* lines 3547-3600

	LINE	1	2	3	4	5	M	A	B	C	D	E	F	G	H	II	III	IV	V
may go				●												●			?
breke				●												●			
may passen				●												●			
is goon				●												●			
shaltou swymme				●												●		●	?
undertake							●									●		●	
dooth				●			●									●	●		
wol clepe				●												●			
be				●												●		●	
wol passe					●											●		●	
wolt seyn				●												●		●	
se	3580			●												●			
is				●												●			
shul be					●											●		●	
warne							●									●	●	●	
be avysed							●									●	●	●	
ben entred			●										●			●	●		
speke			●												●	●	●		
clepe			●												●	●	●		
crie			●												●	●	●		
be			●												●	●			
is							●								●	●		●	
moote hange			●										●			●	●	●	
shal be	3590		●											●		●	●		
lookyng			●											●		●	●		
shal (be)			●											●		●	●		
is seyd							●									●	●	●	
speede		●					●									●	●	●	
ben			●													●	●		
wol crepe			●									●				●	●	●	
(wol) sitten	3595		●									●				●	●		
abidyng			●									●				●	●		
go		●					●				●					●	●	●	
have							●									●	●	●	
to make							●									●			
sermonyng							●									●		●	
seyn							●									●			
sende							●									●			
sey							●									●	●		
art							●									●			
needeth							●									●			
teche							●									●			
go	3600	●					●				●					●	●	●	
save		●	●				●				●					●		●	
biseche							●				●					●	●		

Frame Profiles of Verbs: Miller's Tale - *lines 3547-3600.*

APPENDIX THREE
INTROSPECTIVE SEMICS

An example of an analysis at the level of introspective semics. This was prepared for 'A' level pupils sitting the traditional 'literary' courses in English. Literary criticism is modally reduced within literary semantics to the level of introspective semics.

LEVELS OF MODALITY IN CHAUCER'S *MERCHANT'S TALE*

Cynical view of women and marital relations is reinforced at each level. (My comments here within literary semantics are at the level of theoretical/introspective semics.)

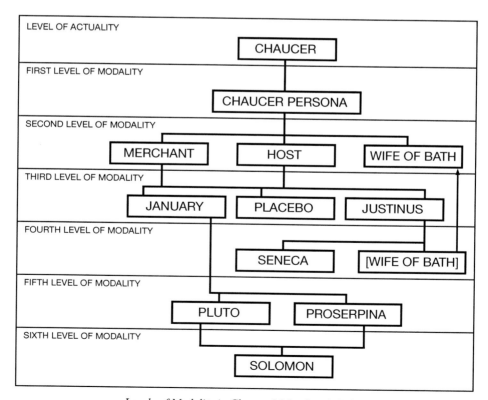

Levels of Modality in Chaucer's Merchant's Tale.

[Line references below are to Robinson ed., Benson ed. and Cawley ed., see APPENDIX ONE and Bibliography]

CHAUCER	Not involved except as the creator of the whole work
CHAUCER PERSONA	Not involved unless some early (ironic) lines (1267 onwards) are attributed to Chaucer the pilgrim.
MERCHANT	See, for instance, *Merchant's Prologue, passim*; lines 1267 onwards; and, as teller of the story, *passim*.
HOST	See Epilogue of the Tale.
JANUARY	See, for instance, 2364-2418.
PLACEBO	See, for instance, 1492-1505. (satire?: lords choose sycophantic advisers)
JUSTINUS	See, for instance, 1655-1682 (ironic use of painful warning in guise of apparent reassurance).
SENECA	See 1523 onwards, cited by Justinus.
[WIFE OF BATH]	Modality error (1685); really belongs to Second Level of Modality - she is a fictional 14th century pilgrim, not a character known to Justinus.
PLUTO	See 2254-2263 (mythological reinforcement of theme of marital strife).
PROSERPINA	See 2264-2310 (even mythical characters experience marital strife).
SOLOMON	See line 2242, where Pluto, a mythical deity (Fifth level), cites a biblical personage (Sixth level) to justify intervening in a marital dispute (Third Level).

The levels move from Chaucer, through six levels of modality, taking in on the way Seneca, a Stoic philosopher, Greek deities and the biblical character, Solomon, 10th century B.C. This complexity is compounded by Justinus' reference to the Wife of Bath: he is a character in the Tale, whereas she is on the pilgrimage. It is an ethical tangle encompassing classical, biblical, mythical and fictional societies. The coherent message which seems to emerge is that, unless you are very fortunate, marriage is a grim business - especially if there is a big age difference. The harshness is softened by a sinister humour. Pupils desiring a compassionate portrayal of marriage should read *The Friar's Tale* and *The Summoner's Tale*, where poor couples living devout, harmonious but poverty-stricken lives are assailed by rapacious ecclesiasts. To infer from *The Merchant's Tale* that Chaucer had a cynical view of marriage would be unwarranted. Indeed, few extrapolations from the text of *The Canterbury Tales* to Chaucer's own beliefs would stand up at the level of empirical semics, so little does he reveal of his inner thinking.

APPENDIX FOUR

A TEACHER-CENTRED MODEL FOR EDUCATION

John Passmore's Triadic Model

John Passmore's book, *The Philosophy of Teaching* (London, Duckworth, 1980), mainly comprising rewritten material drawn from earlier lectures, is in three parts: (1) Programmatic; (2) The Grammar of Pedagogy; (3) Some Applications. Professor of Philosophy at the Australian National University, he modestly avows that he has never been satisfied either by what he has written or by almost anything he has read about teaching. The purpose for this review is to suggest the reasons for his dissatisfaction, for I picked up this book as someone who, having had expectations raised by his earlier writing [LS:12; 42; 242], felt he had been deserted both by his acute philosophical perception and his lucid command of English.

Part I is the most purely philosophical. The rôle of philosophy in education, Passmore writes, has been a matter for controversy, some philosophers arguing that their concern is not directly with the processes of education but merely with the clarification and classification of educational theories propounded by others. Concentrating on the problems of teaching and learning, he takes the view that related concepts – observation, experience, understanding, imagination, appreciation, capacities, criticisms, rules, habits and methods *are* the domain of philosophy.

He goes on to analyse the process of teaching: it is a triadic relationship, involving a teacher, a person taught and a subject disseminated. The trainer of teachers should bear in mind that he is not only teaching a subject, but also instructing individuals (page 28). In rejecting the view that there is a single method of teaching, the author comes closest to the objections I shall make. He then considers the triad in more detail.

In Part II, he critically examines the various functions which teachers are, or might be, called upon to carry out. He makes a distinction between closed and open capacities. By demonstration, instruction, correction, praise, warning, the teacher can inculcate such closed capacities as the learning of tables. But open capacities such as writing creatively, by definition, raise the question: how can we teach that which may be recognised as adequate only after the pupil has produced it? An open capacity seems to involve the capability to go beyond what has been taught. Then there are 'broad' and 'narrow' capacities, where 'broad' means 'of wide application'. Chess is open, but narrow; counting is broad but closed. Teachers should, he concludes, concentrate upon the open and the broad. Many of the methods appropriate to teaching closed capacities are also useful in the furtherance of these preferred skills, but enthusiasm and encouragement from the teacher are of great importance.

Passmore proceeds to the question of teaching to acquire information. One of the refreshing aspects of this book is its emphasis upon the need for the transmission of information. The three chapters he devotes to this are aimed at correcting the view – a vestige from the 1960s (page 63) – that the imparting of facts by the teacher is to be regarded with suspicion. Whilst strongly critical of the Gradgrind extreme, he argues that there is a body of facts some large part of which all educated people need, and that facts are not to be divorced from our sense of the structure and significance of the universe – 'in acquiring information, we do not simply acquire *that* piece of information' (page 81).

The balance is redressed in the subsequent chapters devoted to the imaginative and critical capacities. These are no less important than the imparting of information; indeed the two are not really to be held separate: 'it is quite wrong to draw a sharp antithesis between imparting facts and fostering information' (page 149). Discipline is an important factor in the encouragement of imaginative capacity (p.152). It is also politically desirable in a free society that children be trained to be imaginative (Page 164). In the following chapter, Passmore develops this political point, arguing that authoritarian systems of education often produce pupils who are critical only of those other people who are deviant and imaginative (page 170). Criticism and imagination are antithetical qualities and from this contrast is drawn a solution which is so often the theme of the book: that in education, the guiding principle is to maintain an intelligent and vigilant balance between the extreme and opposite zeals. The remaining chapters in this section deal with teaching to care and to be careful, and teaching to understand.

Section III, entitled 'Some Applications', contains two chapters, one on the teaching of English, the other on sex education. I will now proceed to critical examination of the book.

The most striking deficiency of *The Philosophy of Teaching* is the author's failure to come to come to terms with the practising teacher. Not one of the thirteen chapters is devoted to this necessary member of the triad presented in the first part. This is not to say that the teacher is not mentioned: s/he crops up frequently in the nine chapters comprised by Part II. The teacher, we are told, for instance, is to arouse interest (page 39); to warn, correct and advise (page 47); to teach open capacities (page 48); to help the pupil to observe (page 63); to warn about the dangers of generalisation (page 69); to ensure that the child understands *information* (pages 84-85) and is actively involved (page 89); to cultivate the imagination (page 148); to place special emphasis upon problems to which the answer is not known (page 179); to *vary* his problems and exercises (page 203); to teach the child to love (page 195). There is a short passage of exhortation to those whose task it is to train teachers (pages 50-51). But the teacher is portrayed in this book as a shadowy projection for Passmore's own ethical and professional notions. There is no indication that the author remembers what it is like to be a secondary school teacher: no sign that he recalls the dreadful compulsion to decide amongst the infinite possibilities (and impossibilities) prescribed on the one hand by the teacher's own personality, talents, knowledge, commitments, and on the other by the volcanic proximity of a class of adolescents; the realisation, furthermore, that the choices made will set into being systems and sub-systems of relationships, which will extend in chained cause-effect to the end of his career.

Some years ago, I read John Passmore's early book *100 Years of Philosophy*: it seemed to me an interesting and well-handled treatment of a very turbulent period in the history of human thought. Given, then, Passmore's standing as a philosopher, Chapter 2, 'The Concept of Teaching', might have been expected to be the most illuminating. It is not. Parts of it read like a parody of an elementary text book on predicate calculus. Having discussed how far a definition of 'teaching' is possible, or useful, he presents his triadic relation: 'For all X, if X teaches, there must exist somebody who, and something that, is taught by X.' He compares 'teach' which he regards as a covert triad, with 'give' an overt triad. He then considers what can be substituted for 'X' in the above formulation.

Theoretical Semics Applied to the Theory of Education

Theoretical semics is primarily an analytical tool devised to operate within literary semantics. But, with modal extension, its range can be adapted to the theory of education. I reiterate that the entirety of this book, **Literary Semantics**, belongs to the level which I hope by now is firmly established: this is no more than a personal view, based upon what I believe I have observed and it deserves no wider empirical authority. The account is offered at whatever may be the equivalent level in education of **theoretical**, not **empirical semics**.

The following extracts are representative of the tenor of Passmore's chapter

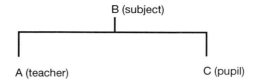

*Figure 16.   The Modal Structure of Educational Discourse.
Passmore's Model: A Triadic Relation.*

2: 'If "teaching" is being used in its occupational sense, as in "X teaches science to senior students", X can only be replaced by members of the teaching profession … Not only can anybody try to teach, but anybody can succeed in teaching something to somebody.' Then, further on, 'The falsity of the proposition that anybody can teach anything to anybody is what justifies teacher training.' Does this mean more than 'Teachers must be *trained*, because teaching is itself a skill which can be learned?' The jargon of philosophical analysis is here being put to perverse use: devised to clarify, it is here being employed by Passmore *in this chapter* to muddy the waters of the discourse of education (I emphasize 'in this chapter', because the rest of the book is free from such affectation). The author then resumes his argument, turning to the 'something' and 'somebody' in his triad, considering such questions as: Can everybody be taught? And does 'somebody' refer to an individual or to a class? On this latter question, he concludes, 'It will be perhaps best to say that what X teaches is *somebody-in-a-class* (his italics), treating the case where X is the sole person taught as a limiting case' (page 31).

What any practising teacher in a secondary school is going to make of this chapter is not difficult to anticipate. Faced with the Monday prospect of a succession of seven large and probably recalcitrant classes launched relentlessly into his presence, he will derive neither clarification nor comfort from Passmore's 'What X teaches is *somebody-in-a-class*', and he is likely to receive the situation where 'X is the sole person taught as a limiting case' with a snort of contumely. For most teachers, the size of the class is not a matter for abstruse disputation: it is a brute fact of daily life. One problem in education seems to be that the theorist in his cushioned institution brings forth notions and the overworked teacher is too exhausted to point out their fatuity. [The reader will perhaps allow me to interject a retrospective, personal comment. When I wrote this review article in 1980, I was myself teaching an eight-period day as an assistant teacher at the chalk face, in a state secondary school in Kent, where I spent over twenty years, teaching English, Logic, Philosophy and Psychology.]

It might be countered, returning to the review of Passmore, that this objection misses the drift of this chapter, whose purpose is philosophical analysis: the fact that classes are, contingently, large, does not preclude our speculating about what should be, or might be. Passmore, however, scarcely points out anything of moment and, in any case, the main fault of this section lies more deeply than such defence can mend.

Professor Passmore, in philosophically and painstakingly dissecting the teaching relationship, fails to make an observation fundamental to its analysis: when he, or any other theorist, writes about teaching, the relationship ceases to be triadic – it becomes at least pentadic. To adopt and extend his own jargon: 'There exists a Y, who communicates something to X, who teaches something to someone.' We have, in this particular case: **A** = Passmore himself; **B** = what Passmore tries to communicate; **C** = the teacher who reads his book; **D** = something the teacher teaches; **E** = someone the teacher teaches. This may be represented diagrammatically:

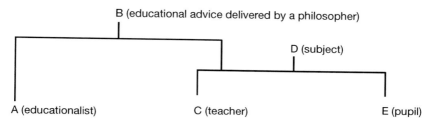

Figure 17.   The Modal Structure of Educational Discourse.
Inherently a Pentadic, not a Triadic, Relation.

This is not a mere metatheoretical quibble. Failure to observe the extension has led Passmore to perpetuate an unfortunate tradition in discourse about education. It is true that the author differentiates the philosophy of teaching from the philosophy of education (page 16), but the former surely presupposes, and must be consistent with the latter. Analysis in the light of communication theory suggests that the transmission-reception relation in which Passmore is immediately involved is **A-B-C**. Yet the book is written as if what were really under discussion is **A-B-[D-]E**. It exemplifies a common tendency on the part of the educational theorist: to regard his own relationship with the pupils as direct and, subtly telescoping **A-B-[C-D]-E**, to treat the teacher as a non-entity, necessary but mindless, who interposes himself between the theorist and his charges. I would have thought that the simple, modal, hierarchical structure above was salient enough to leap out at anyone writing a book on education, but the point seems to have passed this author by. Perhaps this distortion is the root of Passmore's dissatisfaction with his own and others' writings on education.

It is common for educationalists to appeal for a 'child-centred' theory. A more realistic approach would be to insist that it be teacher-centred, that is, to stress **C-D-E**, not **A-D-E**, in Figure 17. A theory which ignores the teacher and idealises the child almost inevitably becomes centred upon the educationalist himself. It is an exceptional child who devotes the long vacation to reading books on pedagogy. The teacher is, I would like it to be assumed – and if he is not, there is small remedy – a responsible, educated, committed individual, with his own patterns of belief, the only person in a position fully to judge the pupils in his care, to see what they need, what they are capable of, and to adapt what he knows and believes to what he believes they know and understand.

Passmore's profuse employment of half-formalised propositions, his repetition of existentials and his failure to go beyond, or even deal adequately with, the facile triad that every teacher is perforce only too aware of, render this chapter unreadable and uninformative.

The second criticism I wish to make of this volume concerns the part to be played in educational theory by levels of discourse. It was to be expected that the author of such a book would have made some attempt to untangle the complex skeins of modes of commitment that underlie the discourse of education. Certainly Passmore makes a large number of useful pedagogical distinctions: for instance, closed v. open and broad v. narrow capacities; his analysis of the sources of information (page 60); his differentiation among imaging, imagining and being imaginative (page 146). But these are low-level categories, applicable to teaching methodology. He raises, yet only inadequately discusses (pages 87-89), the much more fundamental question concerning validation of assertions made within the discourse of education as a whole. He is so much preoccupied with advising, without noticing, teachers that he omits to examine the intellectual instruments he himself employs. The most important of these omissions is the place of the empirical within the philosophy of education.

It has been objected that the natural sciences have managed quite well without an integrated theory of the discourse in which their findings are couched. This assumption is debatable, but one clear difference between the theory of, say, atomic physics and the philosophy of teaching is that the former concerns non-linguistic entities; the latter is mainly *discourse about discourse*. Secondly, the philosopher of education aspires to go beyond the atomic physicist's objective of describing and explaining occurrences in the 'real' world. He wishes, in addition, to transform the target-discourse – that is to say, the language of the classroom itself. That the language of education should come to grips with its own metatheory seems therefore essential.

'It is a purely empirical question, of course, whether and how much particular individuals can learn' (page 29). 'The question how that class is best constituted if the teaching is to be most effective, e.g. whether children can best be taught in a small or large class, in a class of intellectual equals or in a diversified class, is an empirical one' (page 31). The word 'empirical' is used in such asides by Professor Passmore throughout the book, but he does not explain what he understands by the term; what the rôle of the empirical *is* within the theory of education; whether its function is precisely analogous to the part it plays in the natural sciences; nor does he propound principles whereby a proposition in education may be empirically established. Furthermore, the reader is not informed what the alternative non-empirical categories are. It seems to be assumed, for example, that separating the logical from the empirical presents no philosophical difficulties: 'Being critical is not only logically but empirically dissociated from being in possession of certain facts about criticism' (page 166). This is precisely that kind of distinction which an undoubtedly eminent philosopher could usefully have explained. He lets it pass without further comment.

Then there are empirical statements presented without evidence to substantiate them: that a scientist's daily inspirations can result only from the reading of imaginative science (page 157); that confining a child's education to dogmatically presented facts and to habit formation destroys fancy (page 152); that authoritarian systems of education very commonly produce pupils who are critical only of those who are imaginative (page 170). We find 'emotive' statements: to read Churchill's wartime speeches is to be brought closer to life than one is brought by inspecting the panelling in the House of Commons (page 65); imaginativeness, or disciplined fancy, lies at the very heart of a free society (page 164). Other statements are anecdotal, concerning Passmore's own experience of being caned (page 128), and his learning of mathematics (page 144). Also there is the mood of the ethical and the moral which pervades the book.

This last element produces philosophical problems which Passmore does not touch upon, originating from his conflation of **B** and **D** with consequent virtual excision of **C**, in Figure 17. Moral and ethical viewpoints vary from person to person. If the teacher, and this is highly probable, has a different set of commitments from Passmore, then he will find himself continually manoeuvred into positions he does not accept. English teachers, for instance, who adopt general information as their central point of concern are unequivocally accused of doing so out of despair (page 216). To what category of propositions does this belong?

Reciprocal Perspective

This question returns me to the author's neglect of the teacher. What is needed philosophically is an appraisal of alternative possible and acceptable sets of teaching commitments whose implications are then followed through. The educational theorist, instead of issuing moral and ethical directives, would instruct the (prospective) teacher in the *range of possibilities* within the **syllabus**, as defined in the Glossary; he would then help the teacher to fulfil his, the teacher's own – not Passmore's – aims, when he had decided what sort of teacher he wanted to be. The ***unwritten and unuttered*** pact between the teacher and the pupil is,

'We, – that is to say: I, your teacher, as indeed you, my pupil – are going to die. Having lived longer than you, I have made a range of life-choices which you are free to consider; and then accept, select or reject.' That is why computers can never replace teachers. Computers are not mortal and they are not human. It is a warning to all educationalists to tread very carefully, so as not to disturb this relationship.

As I argued in chapter 5 of this book, the concern of the educational theorist is primarily with the theory of the **syllabus**: that system of obligations, both **jussive** and **hortative**, which will best enable the teacher to reconcile with the drive of his own personality the needs of the community on the one side, and the dynamics of the classroom situation on the other.

In these criticisms, I have confined myself to the purely philosophical short-comings, as I see them, of *The Philosophy of Teaching*. It nevertheless contains a great deal that I agree with. The disappointing aspects of Passmore's analysis are: so much of what seems to me to be common sense did not require a distin-guished philosopher to say it; and the modal structure of educational discourse is grotesquely distorted. There remains a great deal to be said on this subject. In the meantime, the diagram below presents a more realistic picture of the pentadic relation: the educationalist communicates *directly* with the teacher. His relation with the pupil and subject is oblique.

We are here back to Passmore's 'triad' **ABC,** except that in Figure 16 the educationalist remained concealed, exerting latent authority. Figure 17 revealed his presence. Figure 18, below, by **reciprocal perspective**, presents the reality. The practising teacher's direct relation with the pupil ABC is conveyed on the right of the diagram. The direct communication with the educationalist comes only if he happens to be talking what makes sense in chalk-face terms and the teacher perchance is listening. That is the actuality of the process. Only by talking *to* – rather than talking *at* – and accepting, teachers as persons with diverse individualities and feelings and ethical drives will the educationalist ever gain the respect of the teaching profession.

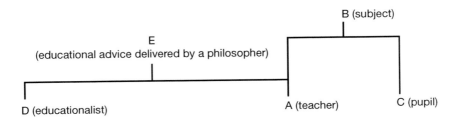

*Figure 18.   The Modal Structure of Educational Discourse.
The Educationalist in Reciprocal Perspective.*

BIBLIOGRAPHY

Alston, W. P. (1963). 'The Quest for Meaning'. *Mind*, January: 79-87.

Angeles, Peter A. (1981). *A Dictionary of Philosophy*. London: Harper and Row.

Armour, L. (1962). 'Value Data and Moral Rule'. *Philosophical Quarterly* 12:228-238.

Asimov, I. (1965). *The Human Brain: its Capabilities and Functions*. London.

Ayer, A.J. (1953). *Language, Truth and Logic*. London. First published 1936.

Ayer, A.J. (1956). *The Problem of Knowledge*. London.

Bailey, R.W., see Doležel, Lubomír.

Balter, Michael. (2002). 'BSE in Sheep? Humiliated Lab Fights to Save Face.' *Science* 295: 792-93.

Bateson, F.W. (1950). *English Poetry: A Critical Introduction*. London.

Bateson, F.W. (1966). 'Editorial Postscript' to a review by Helen Vendler of *Essays on Style and Language*, ed. Fowler. *Essays in Criticism*. 16/4:464-5.

Bateson, F.W. (1967). 'Argument II. Literature and Linguistics', Part II. *Essays in Criticism*. 17/3:335-47. See Fowler, Roger.

Bateson, F.W. (1968). 'Argument II (continued): 'Language and Literature'. Part II. *Essays in Criticism*. 18/2:176-82 . See Fowler, Roger.

Bateson, F.W. (1969). 'A reply to Cay Dollerup'. *Essays in Criticism*. 19/4:426-33. See also Dollerup, Cay.

Bateson, F.W. (1970). 'Stilus, "An Iron Implement".' *Essays in Criticism*. 20/2:264-8.

Bateson, F.W. 'Linguistics and Literary Criticism'. In *The Disciplines of Criticism*. Ed. Demetz, Peter. *et al*. New Haven, Connecticut.

Beardsley, Monroe, see Wimsatt, W.K. Jr.

Bennett, James R. (1976). 'A Stylistics Checklist'. *Style*. 10:350-401.

Benson, Larry D. ed. (1988). *The Riverside Chaucer*. Oxford: Oxford University Press. Based on Robinson, F.N. ed. *The Poetical Works of Geoffrey Chaucer*.

Black, Max. (1949). *Language and Philosophy: Studies in Method*. Ithaca,

New York.

Black, Max. (1962). *Models and Metaphors: Studies in Language and Philosophy*. Ithaca, New York.

Blackmur, R.P. (1954). *Language as Gesture*. London.

Bliss, A.J. (1958). *The Metre of Beowulf*. Oxford: Blackwell.

Blunt, Wilfred. (1971). *The Compleat Naturalist: A Life of Linnaeus*. Appendix by William T. Stearn. London: Collins.

Bradbury, Malcolm, ed. (1971). *Contemporary Criticism*. London.

Brennan, J.G. (1957). *A Handbook of Logic*. New York.

Bronzwaer, W.J.M. (1967). Review. *Journal of Aesthetics and Art Criticism*. Winter:262-4.

Brooks, Cleanth. (1949). *The Well Wrought Urn*. London.

Buneman, O.P., see Zeeman, E.C.

Campbell, Norman. (1952). *What is Science?* New York.

Carroll, John B. (1960). 'Vectors of Prose Style'. In *Style in Language,* ed. Sebeok:283-92. New York.

Catt, Ivor. (1969). 'Dinosaur Among the Data'. *The New Scientist*. 6.3: 501-2.

Cawley, A.C., ed. (1958). *Geoffrey Chaucer: Canterbury Tales*. London.

Chambers, R.W. (1955). *Man's Unconquerable Mind*. London. First published 1939.

Chatman, Seymour, and Levin, Samuel R. (1967). *Essays on the Language of Literature*. Boston, Massachusetts.

Chomsky, Noam. (1965). *Aspects of the Theory of Syntax*. Cambridge, Massachusetts.

Chomsky, Noam. (1966). *Cartesian Linguistics*. New York.

Chomsky, Noam. (1968). *Language and Mind*. New York: Harcourt, Brace and World.

Chomsky, Noam. (1969). John Locke Lecture, delivered at University College, London, on April 29th 1969. Excerpted in *The Times Literary Supplement*:15th May 1969:523-25.

Chomsky, Noam. (1968). 'Noam Chomsky and Stuart Hampshire discuss the Study of Language', a discussion on the BBC Third Programme. Printed in *The Listener*: 30th May, 1968:687-691.

Coghlan, Andy. (2001). 'BSE: The Chaos Continues'. *New Scientist* 27.10:14-16.

Cohen, L.J. (1962). *The Diversity of Meaning*. London.

Cohen, M.R., and E. Nagel. (1957). *An Introduction to Logic and the Scientific Method*. First published in England, 1934. London: Routledge.

Collinge, N.E. (1958). *Notes and Queries*. June:265-6.

Coulton, G.C. (1963). *Chaucer and his England*. London. First published 1908.

Crane, R.S. (1957). *The Languages of Criticism and the Structure of Poetry*. University of Toronto Press. Copyright 1953.

Cresswell, M.J., see Hughes, G.E.

Crystal, David, and Davy, Derek. (1969). *Investigating English Style*. London.

Curry, W.C. (1960). *Chaucer and the Medieval Sciences*. London. Copyright 1926.

Daiches, David. (1956). *Critical Approaches to Literature*. London.
Daiches, David. (1948). *A Study of Literature*. Ithaca NY.
Davie, Donald. (1955). *Articulate Energy*. London.
Davy, Derek, see Crystal, David.
Dawson, C.M. (1951). Article in the *Explicator*. February, 1951.
Demetz, Peter, *et al.*, (eds.) (1968). *The Disciplines of Criticism*. New Haven, Connecticut.
Dixon, R.M.W. (1963). *Linguistic Science and Logic*. The Hague.
Dixon, R.M.W. (1965). *What is Language?* London.
Doležel, Lubomír and Bailey, Richard W. eds. (1969). *Statistics and Style*. New York.
Dollerup, Cay. (1969). 'The Mode of Existence of the Criticism of Literature'. *Essays in Criticism*. 19/4:420-26.
Dry, Helen. (1983). 'The Movement of Narrative Time'. *Journal of Literary Semantics*. 12:19-53.

Eaton, Ruth. (1988). 'Children and Sarcasm: A Psycholinguistic Study'. *Journal of Literary Semantics*. 17:122-48.

(The present book *Literary Semantics*, comprises the following publications revised and reshaped.)
Eaton, Trevor. (1966). *The Semantics of Literature*. The Hague, Mouton. **[Chapters 1, 2, 3]**
Eaton, Trevor. (1970).'The Foundations of Literary Semantics'. *Linguistics*. October. 62:5-19. **[Chapter 4]**
Eaton, Trevor. (1972). *Theoretical Semics*. The Hague, Mouton. **[Chapters 4, 5, 6, 7, 8]**
Eaton, Trevor. (1978). 'Literary Semantics: Modality and "Style" '. *Journal of Literary Semantics*. 7.1:5-28. **[Chapters 9, 10]**
Eaton, Trevor. (1979). 'The Limits of Empirical Semics'. Review article. *Journal of Literary Semantics*.8.2:109-117. A review of Rien T. Segers. *The Evaluation of Literary Texts*. Lisse, The Netherlands. **[Chapter 11]**
Eaton, Trevor. (1982). Review of John Passmore's *The Philosophy of Teaching*. (1980). London. In *Educational Studies*. 8.1:82-5. **[Appendix Four]**
Eaton, Trevor. (1996). 'Literary Semantics as a Science'. *Journal of Literary Semantics*. 25.1:7-65. Includes an early version of the Glossary, 'A Discourse Structure for Literary Semantics'. **[Chapters 12, 13, 14]**
Eaton, Trevor. (1999). 'Literary Semantics – An Academic Discipline: A Document for Discussion'. *Journal of Literary Semantics*.28.2:133-36. **[Chapter 15]**
Eaton, Trevor. (2003). 'How Meta Can You Get?: A Model for the Human

Sciences'. *Journal of Literary Semantics*. 32.2:177-92. **[Chapter 15]**

Eaton, Trevor. (1980). Review of Iser (1978). *The Act of Reading: A Theory of Aesthetic Responses. Style*. 14/12:179-82.
Edgerton, Mills F. (1967). 'A Linguistic Definition of Literature'. Reprinted from *Foreign Language Annals*. December:119-130.
Eliot, T.S. (1953). *Selected Essays*. London. First published 1932.
Eliot, T.S., see also Pound, Ezra.
Empson, William. (1956). *Seven Types of Ambiguity*. London.
Empson, William. (1964). 'The Ancient Mariner'. *Critical Quarterly*. Winter.
Enkvist, Nils Erik, John Spencer and Michael J. Gregory. (1964). *Linguistics and Style*. Oxford.

Firth, J.R. (1957). *Papers in Linguistics, 1934-1951*. London.
Fisk, Dorothy. (1959). *Dr. Jenner of Berkeley*. London.
Flew, Antony. (1979). *A Dictionary of Philosophy*. London: Pan Books.
Foster, Richard. (1962). *The New Romantics: A Reappraisal of the New Criticism*. Indiana.
Foulkes, A.P. (1975). *The Search for Literary Meaning: A Semiotic Approach to the Problem of Interpretation in Education*. Frankfurt.
Fowler, Roger, ed. (1966). *Essays on Style and Language*. London.
Fowler, Roger. (1967). 'Argument II. Literature and Linguistics'. Part I. *Essays in Criticism*. 17.3:322- 35. See Bateson, F.W.
Fowler, Roger. (1968). 'Argument II (continued): Language and Literature'. Part I. *Essays in Criticism*. 18.2:164-176. See Bateson, F.W.
Fowler, Roger. (1966). 'Linguistics, Stylistics, Criticism?' *Lingua*. 16:153-65.
Fowler, Roger. (1970). 'Against Idealization: Some Speculations on the Theory of Linguistic Performance'. *Linguistics*. November.
Fraser, Colin. 'Discussion'. In *Psycholinguistics Papers*: 115-20. See Lyons, John.
Fraser, G.S. (1960). *Ezra Pound*. Edinburgh.
Fraser, Hugh and O'Donnell, W.R. eds. (1969). *Applied Linguistics and the Teaching of English*. London: Longmans. See Rodger, Alex.
Freundlieb, Dieter. (2000). 'What is Literary Semantics?' *Journal of Literary Semantics* 29.2:135-140.
Fries, C.C. (1957). *The Structure of English*. London.

Gardner, Helen. (1959). *The Business of Criticism*. Oxford.
Gellner, Ernest. (1969). 'On Chomsky'. *New Society*. 29.5:831-33.
Graves, Robert. (1949). *The Common Asphodel*. London.
Gray, Bennison. (1969). *Style: The Problem and its Solution*. The Hague: Mouton.
Gray, Bennison. (1975). *The Phenomenon of Literature*. The Hague.
Greenwood, E.B. (1970). 'The Sceptical Dane: A Note on Cay Dollerup's

Doubts about the Objectivity of Literary Criticism'. *Essays in Criticism.* 20.2:271-3.

Gregory, Michael, see Spencer, John.

Gribbin, John and Mary Gribbin. (1997*). Mendel (1822-1884) in 90 Minutes.* London: Constable.

Grossberg, Stephen. (1969). 'On the Serial Learning of Lists'. *Mathematical Biosciences.* 4:201-253.

Halliday, M.A.K. (1967). 'The Linguistic Study of Literary Texts'. In *Essays on the Language of Literature.* Ed. Seymour Chatman and Samuel R. Levin: 217-223. Boston. Reprinted from *Proceedings of the Ninth International Congress of Linguists* ed. H. Lunt.

Halliday, M.A.K., Angus McIntosh and Peter Strevens. (1964). *The Linguistics Sciences and Language Teaching.* London: Longmans.

Halliday, M.A.K., and Angus McIntosh. (1966). *Patterns of Language.* London.

Halliday, M.A.K. and Ruqaiya Hasan. (1976). *Cohesion in English.* London: Longmans.

Hanauer, David. (1995). 'Literary and Poetic Text Categorization Judgments.' *Journal of Literary Semantics.* 24:187-210.

Hardie, W.F.R. (1968). *Aristotle's Ethical Theory.* Oxford.

Harrison, J. (1963). 'Does Knowing Imply Believing?' *Philosophical Quarterly.* 13:322-32.

Hasan, Ruqaiya. (1968). 'Grammatical Cohesion in Spoken and Written English'. Part One. Paper No. 7. *Programme in Linguistics and English Teaching* (Communications Research Centre). London. See also Halliday, M.A.K.

Hempel, Carl G. (1966). *Philosophy of Natural Science.* Englewood Cliffs.

Hesse, Mary B. (1970). *Models and Analogies in Science.* Notre Dame, Indiana.

Hester, Marcus B.(1967). *The Meaning of Poetic Metaphor.* The Hague.

Hjelmslev, Louis. (1963). *Prolegomena to a Theory of Language.* Translated by Francis J. Whitfield. Madison, Wisconsin. The work first appeared in Danish in 1943.

Hockett, Charles. (1968). *The State of the Art.* The Hague.

Hogben, George L. (1977). 'Linguistic Style and Personality'. *Language and Style.* 10:270-84.

Holt, John. (1964). *How Children Fail.* New York.

Hospers, John. (1970). *An Introduction to Philosophical Analysis.* London.

Hough, Graham. (1966). *An Essay on Criticism.* London.

Hoyle, F. (1957). *The Nature of the Universe.* Oxford.

Huddleston, R. (1984). *Introduction to the Grammar of English.* Cambridge.

Hughes, G.E. and M.J.Cresswell. (1968). *An Introduction to Modal Logic.* London: Methuen.

Hungerland, Isabel. (1958). *Poetic Discourse.* Berkeley and Los Angeles.

Iser, Wolfgang. (1978). *The Act of Reading: A Theory of Aesthetic Response.*
    Baltimore and London: Johns Hopkins University Press.

Jeffrey, Richard. (1981). *Formal Logic: Its Scope and Limits.* New York.

Kane, George. (1965). *The Autobiographical Fallacy in Chaucer and Langland
    Studies.* London.
Katz, Jerrold J. (1966). *The Philosophy of Language.* New York.
Kenny, Anthony. (1978). *The Aristotelian Ethics.* Oxford.
Kintgen, Eugene R. (1977). 'Reader Response and Stylistics'. *Style.* 11:1-18.
Kittredge, G.L. (1960). *Chaucer and his Poetry.* Harvard University Press.
    First published 1915.
Klaeber, Fr. (1950). *Beowulf and the Fight at Finnsburg.* Boston D.C.
Koch Walter A. (1966). *Recurrence and a Three-Modal Approach to Poetry.*
    The Hague: Mouton.
Koestler, Arthur. (1967). *The Ghost in the Machine.* London.
Kuhn, T.S. (1959). *The Copernican Revolution.* New York. Copyright 1957.

Lacey, A.R. (1976). *A Dictionary of Philosophy.* London: Routledge.
Leavis, F.R. (1948). *The Great Tradition.* London.
Leavis, F.R. (1969). *English Literature in Our Time and the University.* London.
Leavis, F.R. (1937). 'Literary Criticism and Philosophy: A Reply'. Scrutiny.
    6:59-70.
Leavis, F.R. (1969). '"English" – Unrest and Continuity', an opening address at
    a Colloquium on "English" held by the University of Wales at Gregynog.
    Reprinted in *The Times Literary Supplement.* 29.5:569-72.
Leech, Geoffrey N. (1969). *A Linguistic Guide to English Poetry.* London.
Lemmon, E.J. (1965). *Beginning Logic.* London: Nelson.
Lemmon, E.J. (1968). *Introduction to Axiomatic Set Theory.* London.
Lewis, C.S. (1960). *Miracles.* London, 1960. First published 1947.
Lipski, John M. (1976). 'On the Metastructures of Literary Discourse'. *Journal
    of Literary Semantics.* 5.53-61.
Lodge, David. (1966). *Language of Fiction.* London.
Lowes, John Livingston. (1956). *Geoffrey Chaucer.* Oxford. First edition 1934.
Lowes, John Livingston. (1951). *The Road to Xanadu.* London. First English
    edition, 1927.
Lyons, John. (1968). *Introduction to Theoretical Linguistics.* Cambridge
    University Press.
Lyons, John. (1977). *Semantics.* Cambridge University Press.
Lyons, John., and R.J. Wales. (1966). *Psycholinguistics Papers.* Edinburgh.

McIntosh, Angus, see Halliday, M.A.K.
McNeill, D. 'Developmental Psycholinguistics'. In *The Genesis of
    Language*:15-82. See Smith, Frank.

Maslow, Alexander. (1961). *A Study in Wittgenstein's 'Tractatus'*. California.

Medawar, P.B. (1969). *Induction and Intuition in Scientific Thought*. Philadelphia.

Mellone, S.H. (1966). *Elements of Modern Logic*. London: University Tutorial Press. First published 1934.

Mendel, Gregor. (1965 [original publication in German 1866]). *Experiments in Plant Hybridisation*. Edited version of translation produced by the Royal Horticultural Society of London in 1901. Ed. J. Bennett. Translated by C.T. Druery and William Bateson. Edinburgh: Oliver and Boyd.

Metzing, D. ed. (1979). *Frame Conceptions and Text Understanding*. Berlin.

Miller, George A., see Smith, Frank, and Weir, Ruth.

Milner, G.B. (1969). 'Siamese Twins, Birds and the Double Helix'. *Man*. 4.1 March.

Minsky, M. (1979). 'A Framework for Representing Knowledge'. In Metzing, D. ed. above.

Mohrmann, C., Sommerfelt, A. and Whatmough, J., eds. (1962). *Trends in European and American Linguistics, 1930-1960*. Utrecht: Spectrum.

Morris, C.W. (1955). *Signs, Language and Behavior*. New York. Prentice-Hall Inc. Copyright 1946.

Muller, Charles 'Lexical Distribution Reconsidered: The Waring-Herdan Formula':42-56. In *Statistics and Style*, see Doležel, Lubomír.

Nagel, E., see Cohen M.R.

Nowottny, Winifred. (1962). *The Language Poets Use*. London.

O'Donnell, W.R., see Fraser, Hugh.

Ogden, C.K., and I.A. Richards. (1945). *The Meaning of Meaning*. London. First published 1923.

Osgood, C.E., Suci, G.J. and Tanenbaum P.H. (1957). *The Measurement of Meaning*. Urbana, Illinois: University of Illinois Press.

Osgood, C.E. (1962). 'Studies on the Generality of Affective Meaning Systems'. *American Psychologist*, January: 10-28.

Osgood, C.E. (1959). 'Semantic Space Revisited'. *Word*:192-201.

Palmer, F.R. (1974). *The English Verb*. London.

Palmer, F.R. (1979). *Modality and the English Modals*. London.

Palmer, F.R., (1986). *Mood and Modality*. Cambridge.

Passmore, John. (1957). *A Hundred Years of Philosophy*. London:Duckworth.

Passmore, John. (1980). *The Philosophy of Teaching*. London.

van Peer, W. (1983). 'Poetic Style and Reader Response: An Exercise in Empirical Semics'*Journal of Literary Semantics*. 12:3-18

Perkins, M.R. (1982). 'The Core Meanings of the English Modals'. *Journal of Linguistics*. 18:245-73.

Perkins, M.R. (1983). *Modal Expressions in English*. London
Pollard, Denis E.B. (2002). 'Literary Semantics as an Academic discipline: A
    Cautionary Catechism'. *Journal of Literary Semantics*. 31/1:77-82.
Pollock, Thomas Clark. (1942). *The Nature of Literature*. Princeton.
Pomorska, Krystyna. (1968). *Russian Formalist Theory and its Poetic
    Ambiance*.The Hague.
Pope, J.C. (1942). *The Rhythm of Beowulf*. New Haven, Connecticut.
Popper, Karl R. (1969). *Conjectures and Refutations: The Growth of Scientific
    Knowledge*. London: Routledge.
Pound, Ezra. (1954). *Literary Essays of Ezra Pound*. Introduction and edited
    by T.S. Eliot. London.
Premack, David, and Arthur Schwartz. 'Preparations for Discussing
    Behaviorism with Chimpanzee'. In *The Genesis of Language*: 295-335.
    See Smith, Frank.

Quine, Willard Van Orman. (1953). *From a Logical Point of View*. Cambridge,
    Mass.:Harvard University Press.
Quine, Willard Van Orman. (1967). *Word and Object*. Cambridge, Mass.: MIT
    Press. First published 1960.

Ransom, John Crowe. (1941). *The New Criticism*. Norfolk, Connecticut.
Reid, I. (1988). 'Genre and Framing: The Case of Epitaphs'. *Poetics* 17:25-35.
Rescher, N. (1968). *Topics in Philosophical Logic*. Dordrecht.
Richards, I.A. (1945). *The Meaning of Meaning* (with Ogden, C.K.). London.
    First published 1923.
Richards, I.A. (1959). *Principles of Literary Criticism*. London. First published
    1924.
Richards, I.A. (1954). *Practical Criticism*. London. First published 1929.
Richards, I.A. (1955). *Speculative Instruments*. London.
Riffaterre, Michael. 'Criteria for Style Analysis'. In *Essays on the Language of
    Literature*: 412-30, see Chatman, Seymour.
Righter, William. (1963). *Logic and Criticism*. London.
Robinson, F.N. ed. (1933). *The Poetical Works of Geoffrey Chaucer*. Cambridge,
    Massachusetts.
Robson, W.W. (1966). *Critical Essays*. London.
Rodger, Alex. 'Linguistics and the Teaching of Literature':88-98; and
    'Linguistic Form and Literary Meaning':176-216. In *Applied Linguistics
    and the Teaching of English*. See Fraser, Hugh.
Russell, Bertrand. (1956). *Human Knowledge: Its Scope and Limits*. London.
    First published 1948.
Russell, Bertrand. (1967). *The Autobiography of Bertrand Russell 1872-1914*.
    London.

Saporta, Sol. 'The Application of Linguistics to the Study of Poetic

Language':82-93. In *Style in Language*, see Sebeok T.

Schank, R.C. and Riesbeck, C.K. eds. (1981). *Inside Computer Understanding*. New Jersey.

Schneider, Elizabeth. (1966). *Coleridge, Opium and Kubla Khan*. New York.

Schwartz, Arthur, see Premack, David.

Searle, J.R. (1979). *Expression and Meaning: Studies in the Theory of Speech Acts*. Cambridge University Press.

Sebeok, Thomas A. ed. (1960). *Style in Language*. Cambridge Mass.: MIT Press.

Segers, Rien T. (1978). *The Evaluation of Literary Texts*. Lisse, The Netherlands.

Sinclair, John McH. (1968). 'A Technique of Stylistic Description'. *Language and Style*. Autumn: 215-42.

Sinclair, John McH. 'Taking a Poem to Pieces'. In *Essays on Style and Language*: 68-81, see Fowler, Roger, ed.

Smith, Frank and George A. Miller ed. (1966). *The Genesis of Language: A Psycholinguistic Approach*. Massachusetts.

Spencer, John and Michael Gregory. 'An Approach to the Study of Style':59-105. In *Linguistics and Style*, see Enkvist, Nils Erik.

Sperber, D. and Wilson, D. (1986). *Relevance: Communication and Cognition*. Oxford: Blackwell.

Spitzer, Leo. (1962). *Linguistics and Literary History: Essays in Stylistics*. New York. Copyright 1948.

Spitzer, Leo. '*Explication de Texte* Applied to Three Great Middle English Poems'. *Archivum Linguisticum*. 3:1-22; 137-65.

Spitzer, Leo. 'Answer to Mr. Bloomfield'. *Language*. 20:245-51.

Stebbing, L. Susan. (1943). *A Modern Elementary Logic*. London: Methuen.

Stevenson, C.L. (1948). 'Meaning: Descriptive and Emotive'. In 'A Symposium on Emotive Meaning'. *Philosophical Review*, March:127-43. The Symposium also includes papers by I.A. Richards and Max Black which are reprinted in *Speculative Instruments* and *Language and Philosophy* respectively.

Stevenson, C.L. (1950). *Ethics and Language*. New Haven, Conn.:Yale University Press. Copyright 1944.

Strevens, Peter, see Halliday, M.A.K.

Suci, G.J., see Osgood, C.E.

Sullivan, Nancy. (1968). *Perspective and the Poetic Process*. The Hague: Mouton.

Suther, Marshall. (1965). *Visions of Xanadu*. Columbia.

Tannen, Deborah ed. (1993). *Framing in Discourse*. Oxford.

Tannenbaum, P.H., see Osgood, C.E.

Teilhard de Chardin, Pierre. (1959). *The Phenomenon of Man*. London.

Thomas, Dylan. (1957). *Under Milk Wood*. London: Dent.

Thorburn, W.M. (1918). 'The Myth of Occam's Razor'. *Mind*. 27:345-53.

Tillyard, E.M.W. (1943). *The Elizabethan World Picture*. London.
Tillyard, E.M.W. (1958). *The Muse Unchained*. London.
Toulmin, S. (1953). *The Philosophy of Science: An Introduction*. London:Hutchinson University Library.
Trilling, Lionel. (1966). *Beyond Culture*. London.
Tudge, Colin. (2002). *In Mendel's Footnotes: An Introduction to the Science and Technologies of Genes and Genetics from the 19th Century to the 22nd*. London.

Ullmann, Stephen. (1957). *The Principles of Semantics*. Glasgow: Jackson. Oxford: Blackwell. First published 1951.
Ullmann, Stephen. (1962). *Semantics*: *An Introduction to the Science of Meaning*. Oxford.
Ullmann, Stephen. (1973). *Meaning and Style*. Oxford: Blackwell.
Urban, W.M. (1951). *Language and Reality*. London: Allen and Unwin. First published 1939.

Vendler, Helen H. (1966). Review of Roger Fowler, ed. *Essays on Style and Language*. *Essays in Criticism*. October:457-63. See Bateson F.W.

Wales, R.J., see Lyons, John.
Watson, George. (1969). *The Study of Literature*. London.
Weber, J.J. (1982). 'Frame Construction and Frame Accommodation in a Gricean Analysis of Narrative'. *Journal of Literary Semantics*. 11:90-94.
Weinreich, Uriel. (1958). 'Travels through Semantic Space'. *Word*: 346-366; see also a brief tailpiece in *Word*, 1959, at the end of Osgood's article 'Semantic Space Revisited'.
Weir, Ruth. (1962). *Language in the Crib*. Introduction by George A. Miller. The Hague.
Wellek, R. and A.Warren. (1961). *The Theory of Literature*. London. First published 1949.
Wellek, R. (1937). 'Literary Criticism and Philosophy'. *Scrutiny*. 5:375-83.
Werth, Paul. (1977). 'The Linguistics of Double Vision'. *Journal of Literary Semantics*. 6.3-28.
Wheelwright, Philip. (1959). *The Burning Fountain*. Bloomington, Indiana.
Wheelwright, Philip. (1962). *Metaphor and Reality*. Bloomington, Indiana.
Whitelock, Dorothy. (1951). *The Audience of Beowulf*. Oxford.
Whorf, B.L. (1956). *Language, Thought and Reality: Selected Writings of Benjamin Lee Whorf*. Ed. J. Carroll. New York: Wiley.
Wilson, D., see Sperber, D.
Wimsatt, W.K. Jr. (1958). *The Verbal Icon: Studies in the Meaning of Poetry*. Part written in collaboration with Monroe Beardsley. New York.
Winograd, T. (1972). *Understanding Natural Language*. New York.
Winograd, T. (1983). *Language as a Cognitive Process*. Reading, Massachusetts.

Wittgenstein, L. (1955). *Tractatus Logico-Philosophicus*. London. First published in England in 1922.

Woods, John. (1974). *The Logic of Fiction: A Philosophical Sounding of Deviant Logic*. The Hague.

Woozley, A.D. (1957). *Theory of Knowledge*. London. First published 1949.

von Wright, G.H. (1951). *An Essay in Modal Logic*. Amsterdam.

Zeeman, E.C.(1962). 'The Topology of the Brain and Visual Perception':240-56. In *Topology of the 3-Manifolds*, ed. M.K. Fort. New Jersey.

Zeeman, E.C. (1965) 'Topology of the Brain' (1965). *Mathematics and Computer Science in Biology and Medicine*:277-92. (Medical Research Council).

Zeeman, E.C., and O.P. Buneman. *Tolerance Spaces and the Brain*. (Mimeograph, no date).

304

SUBJECT INDEX

NAME INDEX

Trevor Eaton

LIST OF FIGURES

The book contains various diagrams to which cross reference is made by page number. Those diagrams most frequently referred to in explaining the theoretical structures outlined in the book are listed below.